Waivers & Releases Of Liability

9th edition

By

Doyice J. Cotten
&
Mary B. Cotten

***

Sport Risk Consulting
Statesboro, GA 30458

www.SportWaiver.com

Waivers & Releases of Liability 9th ed.

Available from

Sport Risk Consulting
403 Brannen Drive   Statesboro, GA 30458
912 764-4848
djcotten@gmail.com
or
www.sportwaiver.com

Disclaimer

The information in this book is intended as accurate and authoritative educational material relative to liability waivers and other related documents.   It is sold with the understanding that the authors and publishers are not engaged in rendering legal advice. Readers requiring legal advice should consult an attorney who is competent in this area.

Although every effort has been made to ensure that the information presented herein is timely and accurate, the authors and publishers do not guarantee the accuracy of the information in this book, nor do they guarantee the effectiveness of waivers, releases, or other documents developed based upon the information presented. The authors recommend that readers refer to the cases cited for more information.

Waivers & Releases of Liability
9th Edition

Table of Contents

Cover Photo

Thanks to Robert Arnold
Launch Franchising
Warwick, R.I.

Preface to the 9th Edition

The first edition of this book was published in 1996; it consisted of 64 5" x 7" inch pages. Much has happened in the world of liability waivers over the past 20 years, and consequently, the book has continued to grow with each edition. That first edition was based upon about 400 sport, recreation, and fitness waiver cases; this edition is based on approximately 1400 waiver cases, many of which are cited and listed in the List of Cases.

The goals of the first edition were (1) to summarize the waiver law in each state (though the law in most states was not as well-developed as it is today) and (2) to teach sport, recreation, and fitness professionals how to go about writing a waiver. Today, the goals are much the same – we try (1) to keep professionals up-to-date on waiver law; (2) to help them to understand what waivers can and cannot do; and (3) to provide information about what a waiver should say and how it should be said.

Today, in many states we have dozens of waiver cases from which to draw; in other states, however, there are sometimes only a handful of cases – as few as 1 or 2. As more cases become available, two things tend to happen. First, the state waiver law becomes clearer and we can be more confident of the law in those states. Second, as new rulings occur, they often bring about changes in the waiver law.

It is important that the reader remember that **none of the law regarding waivers is set in stone** and that all of the interpretations in this book are subjective and often a matter of opinion. The reader should keep this in mind and realize that about the only generalizations regarding waiver law that you can count on are (1) that, depending upon the state you are in, waiver law differs, and (2) WAIVER LAW CHANGES.

How do I use this book?

Professionals read and use this book for a number of reasons. Some want to learn more about waivers and their effectiveness (e.g., insurance professionals). Others read it to better evaluate the waiver they are currently using (e.g., sport, recreation, and fitness professionals). Many use it to help them develop their own waiver (e.g., sport, recreation, and fitness professionals) or to learn how to improve the waivers they write (e.g., practicing attorneys). The authors have spent many hours searching for sport, recreation, and fitness waiver cases in researching this book and have found most (currently around 1400 cases), but certainly not all such cases.

Regardless of the reason for using the book, the authors continue to caution the reader regarding liability waivers. Waiver law is not written in stone. It is an ever-changing process and varies greatly from state to state. And in three more years, there will probably be two to three hundred more cases and in many instances, the law will change. We have tried to present the material in a manner that would be useful to the reader. We have certainly missed some things and may have misinterpreted others. So the reader is encouraged to look up the cases cited and read the original documents; then draw your own conclusions.

The authors have a free website, **Sportwaiver.com**, on which they post regular articles on waivers, risk management, and related news items. It provides a good way to keep up-to-date on developments regarding waivers and risk management.

***

Once you have a waiver or participant agreement that you believe will help protect you from liability, you are not finished. Keep in mind that the participant agreement is just one small segment of what you can do to protect yourself and your business from liability. It is critical that you institute, if you do not have one, a comprehensive, **ongoing risk management program.** If you already have a risk management program, continue to maintain and improve that program. Your risk management program should include such protections as a comprehensive *insurance program*, a well-thought-out *documentation program*, vigilant staff *hiring practices*, effective *staff training*, establishment of a sound *emergency care plan*, regular *inspections*, careful *maintenance* of all equipment and facilities, and planned *supervision* of activities, facilities, and staff. **Learn all you can about risk management** through reading articles, risk management books, and attending risk management presentations at conferences. Additionally, it is very helpful to bring in risk management consultants who are familiar with recreation, fitness, and sport businesses for major inspections and for risk audits.

Chapter 1

The Waiver and its Function

Introduction

Service providers in recreation, fitness, and sport often use contracts and other documents to help protect themselves and their businesses from the financial effects of lawsuits that frequently result when injuries occur. Some of these documents include assumption of risk agreements, agreements to participate, liability waivers or releases, and indemnification agreements.

Injuries in recreation, fitness, and sport activities are common and unavoidable. **Injuries arise from three causes** – 1) the risks that are inherent to the activity, 2) the ordinary negligence of the provider, its employees, and its agents, and 3) extreme forms of negligence on the part of the provider, its employees, or its agents.

The first cause of injury is accidents resulting from the **inherent risks** of the activity. The inherent risks of an activity are those risks that are normal or natural to the activity and cannot be eliminated without changing the primary nature of the activity. Examples would include someone suffering a back injury while trying to lift a weight, an aerobics participant pulling a muscle while stretching, a hiker spraining an ankle on a rocky trail, and a kayaker striking a boulder in a stream. Assumption of risk agreements and agreements to participate can help to protect against liability for injuries resulting from these risks.

The second cause of injury is the **ordinary negligence** of the service provider (including its employees or agents) or fitness professional (such as an independent contractor). Ordinary negligence is the failure to act as a reasonably prudent professional would act under the circumstances; the failure to use the care that a prudent or careful person would use. Examples of injuries caused by negligence might include a person injured when a frayed cable on a weight machine snapped, a player struck with a racquet when the supervisor allowed eight players on one racquetball court, a whitewater rafting operator sending out a raft with a defective seat, or a riding stable renting a horse with defective tack. Liability waivers and indemnification agreements can help to protect against liability for injuries resulting from the ordinary negligence of the provider.

The third cause of injury arises when the service provider (including its employees or agents) or fitness professional (such as an independent contractor) is guilty of an **act far below the normal standard of care** (sometimes called **aggravated negligence**). Such acts include actions classified as **gross negligence, reckless conduct, willful and wanton conduct, or conduct constituting an intentional tort** (i.e., where a person's actions were done with the intent to injure or where injury is substantially certain to result). Which term is used depends on the nature of the act and in which state the act occurred. It is important to note that 1) not all of these concepts are recognized in every state and 2) their definitions may differ by state. In general, protective documents are not effective when the injury results from actions that go beyond ordinary negligence. Exceptions are discussed in Chapter 2.

Protection from Liability

With injuries come pain and expense – and pain and expense are often followed by lawsuits against the provider. When participants are hurt, regardless of the cause of the injury, many injured participants want others to shoulder the blame and to absorb the subsequent medical expenses.

It is obvious that if those in the industry are to be financially secure from liability, they, as business owners, employees, or independent contractors, must take steps to protect themselves financially. The best way to do this is with the implementation of a sound risk management program. **Risk management** is a process by which the risks of physical injury and the risk of fiscal threats are lessened or managed. Risk management is comprised of many components – an operational risk management plan, insurance, regular inspections of facility and equipment, sound employment practices, and much more. Another significant component of a successful risk management plan is the primary subject of this book – **liability waivers** and **other protective documents.** Some of those addressed in this book include the assumption of risk agreement, the waiver, the indemnification agreement, and the participant agreement – a combination of the preceding three. See Figure 1.1 for a summary of the effects of protective documents upon liability for injuries resulting from the three causes.

The Assumption of Risk Agreement

The **assumption of risk agreement** is one whereby the participant in an activity agrees prior to participation to assume the inherent risks of the activity. The agreement should inform the participant of the nature of the activity, the risks inherent in the activity, and the potential consequences of those risks. This agreement can be very similar to the agreement to participate (see Chapter 4) and should serve to strengthen the **primary assumption of risk** defense as well as the **secondary assumption of risk** defense (sometimes referred to as **contributory negligence**).

Providers are not generally liable for injuries resulting from the inherent risks of the activity because normally the participant assumes such inherent risks. However, many courts have ruled that providers can be liable for injuries resulting from inherent risks if 1) the participant did not know, understand, and appreciate the inherent risks of the activity or 2) if participation was not voluntary. Thus, it is important that the provider have appropriate defenses for such liability.

It is important to note that the assumption of risk agreement helps with liability protection for injuries resulting from inherent risks only. It provides no protection against claims alleging negligence on the part of the provider. *King v. University of Indianapolis* (2002) illustrates a case in which a good assumption of risk agreement offered no protection against a claim of negligence. On the other hand, the court in *Stowers v. Clinton Central School Corporation* (2006) admitted an acknowledgement and release form into evidence which neither contained the word "negligence" nor relieved the defendant of liability for negligence. The court said the form was relevant to the defense of incurred risk (assumption of risk) since it provided evidence that the plaintiff knew and appreciated the risks involved and voluntarily accepted those risks.

The Waiver

The term **"waiver"** is used to denote a pre-injury agreement between a participant and a service provider by which the participant agrees to release the service provider from liability for injuries resulting from the ordinary negligence of the service provider. This agreement is sometimes referred to as an **"express assumption of risk**," an "**exculpatory clause**," a "**covenant not to sue**," and frequently as a "**release**." There are some technical differences among these, but, in general, they all refer to the same type of agreement. "Release" and "waiver" are equally popular terms in the literature, but "release" is also often used to designate a settlement agreement signed by the two parties after the injury has occurred. For this reason, the authors will attempt to consistently use the term "waiver" in referring to pre-injury agreements and the term "release" when addressing post-injury or settlement agreements. (For more on terms, refer to Appendix A).

Figure 1.1
Three Causes of Injury and the Effect
Of a Protective Document in Each Case

	"Accident" or Inherent Risk	Negligent Act	Extreme Act
What Caused The Injury	**Example:** Participant injures his back while lifting weights on his own.	**Example:** Client trips over a loose wire running to a speaker placed in a hazardous location by aerobics instructor.	**Example:** Client slips on slippery floor in dressing room area following **several** reported falls & injuries in that area.
Fault of Provider	No fault. Neither the provider nor employees did anything that caused the injury *provided the participant was aware of, or was made aware of, the activity risks*. **No Negligence**	Employee was careless and created a dangerous condition. **Negligence**	Provider knew of a significant dangerous condition and failed to take corrective measures. **Gross Negligence (or other Extreme Action)**
Liability of Provider	Provider is NOT liable if client assumed risk. *To assume the risk, the client must be aware of the risk*, so provider should be able to show that participant was warned of the risks.	Provider is liable for injuries caused by the provider, its employees, or agents.	Provider is liable for extreme acts causing injury if provider had "notice of" or condoned the act.
Protection Afforded by Assumption of Risk Agreement	Assumption of risk section provides evidence of knowledge of inherent risks, voluntary participation, & assumption of inherent risks.	None	None
Waiver	Waiver section can include release of liability for inherent risks.	Waiver section can protect provider in most states.	None in most states.
Indemnity Agreement	Indemnity agreement may shift liability for inherent risks from provider to another party.	Indemnity agreement may protect provider from liability for provider's negligent acts by shifting the liability to another party.	Indemnity agreement will not shift liability from the provider for extreme acts in most states.

What does the waiver do? *The waiver relieves the service provider of liability for ordinary negligence* (i.e., mistakes, errors of commission or omission, or faults by the provider that caused the participant to suffer injury). In effect, it relieves the provider of the duty of ordinary care. For example, a health club patron (*Cox v. US Fitness, LLC,* 2013*)* fell and suffered a severe wrist injury while working with a personal trainer. She claimed the trainer negligently instructed her to perform a dangerous exercise and used equipment in an unsafe manner. US Fitness and the personal trainer may have been negligent and caused the client to suffer injury; however, by signing the waiver, the client released the health club and personal trainer from liability for injuries resulting from health club negligence. Subsequently, the appellate court upheld the **summary judgment**[1] ruling by the lower court. So the case was dismissed; the waiver protected the health club and the trainer from liability for their any negligence.

Do waivers work? Most activity injury claims allege negligence and, under tort law, providers are usually liable for such injuries. The primary function of the waiver is to protect the provider from liability for ordinary negligence and, when used in the correct circumstances, waivers can provide liability protection in almost all states. In fact, *a well-written waiver that is voluntarily signed by an adult can, under many circumstances, protect a service provider from liability for injuries resulting from provider negligence in 45 or more states* (see Chapter 8 for detailed information on each state).

The Indemnification Agreement

An **indemnification agreement** is an agreement signed prior to participation by which the participant or another party agrees to reimburse the provider for any monetary loss resulting from 1) an injury or loss to the participant or 2) an injury or loss in some way caused by the participant. The indemnification agreement can provide for attorney's fees and other legal expenses in some jurisdictions and under certain circumstances.

Such agreements can provide protection against liability for both inherent risks and risks of ordinary negligence by the provider. Like waivers, however, they generally do not protect when the conduct was grossly negligent, reckless, willful or wanton, or intentional.

In general, indemnification agreements are most likely to be enforced when the two parties are both business entities. A Connecticut court (*Roman v. City of Bristol*, 2007) indicated that the enforceability of an indemnity agreement is, in part, dependent upon whether the parties are "sophisticated business entities." Courts in some states are reluctant to enforce an agreement between a provider and a client in which the client is expected to indemnify a provider for the negligence of the provider. Also, parents are sometimes called upon to indemnify a provider so that a minor child can participate in an activity. Parental indemnification has been enforced in very few states (see Chapter 3).

The indemnification agreement does not eliminate the liability of the provider. The provider can still be sued; however the indemnifier has contracted to repay the provider for losses incurred. A major limitation of an indemnity agreement is that the indemnifier may not be financially able to meet the obligation should the need arise. The indemnifier is often not the plaintiff or recipient of the award given, plus the award might be insufficient to cover all of the defendant's loss (e.g., court expenses, legal fees).

---

[1] **Summary judgment** is a procedural device by which the judge can decide a case, eliminating the need for a trial. Summary judgment is appropriate when, after considering evidence in the light most favorable to the non-moving party, the judge finds "the movant shows that there is no genuine dispute as to any material fact and the movant is entitled to judgment as a matter of law" (**Fed. R. Civ. P. 56(a)).** A *genuine issue* is one that could be resolved in favor of either party; a *material fact* is one which could potentially affect the outcome of the case.

For instance in the *Cox* case discussed above, the judge saw that under Illinois law, the waiver was enforceable to protect US Fitness from liability for injuries due to negligence; so even if all of Cox's claims of US Fitness negligence are true, US Fitness is not liable. Therefore, the case was dismissed and summary judgment was granted, thereby saving court time and both parties money.

The Participant Agreement

The **participant agreement** is a comprehensive protective document that includes an **assumption of risk agreement**, a **waiver of liability for negligence**, an **indemnification agreement**, and other protective language designed to provide maximum protection. The participant agreement does more than just protect the provider from potential liability – it also serves as **tool for information exchange** and a means of **building a greater rapport** between the provider and the client (Gregg and Hansen-Stamp, 2003). This document is intended to widen the protection to include both the inherent risks of the activity and the ordinary negligence of the provider, its employees, and its agents. This agreement will be discussed in detail in Chapter 5. Please note that in this book, the term "waiver" will often be used in interchangeably with the term "participant agreement." Also note that a "participant agreement" is not the same as an "agreement to participate" which only protects against liability for inherent risks. The agreement to participate will be addressed in detail in Chapter 4.

How Liability Agreements Are Used

Prior to Participation in Activities. The most common use of participant agreements, assumption of risk agreements, waivers, and indemnification agreements is to gain release from liability prior to participation in a sport or recreational activity.

When Renting or Loaning Equipment. Another common use of waivers is when renting or loaning equipment to participants. Generally, the exculpatory language is included in the rental agreement. In general, these waivers are effective; however, they may not protect the provider from liability if the equipment is defective. (*Braun v. Mount Brighton, Inc.*, 1989) In addition to the assumption of risk, the exculpatory language, and the indemnity language, rental agreements may contain other provisions. For example, a bicycle rental agreement might 1) require that the renter assume responsibility for the bicycle, 2) have the renter acknowledge the limits and availability of a helmet, and 3) limit the use of the bicycle to bicycle trails.

In Facility Rentals or Leases. Third, providers often rent or lease a facility to individuals, groups, or organizations. A waiver and an indemnity agreement are often included within the rental or lease contract; however, the provider might require that a stand-alone waiver and indemnity agreement be completed. The waiver is to protect against liability for the negligence of the facility provider and the indemnity agreement is to reduce the financial risk of the facility provider for incidents that are the fault of the party leasing the facility or others during the duration of the lease.

Special Events and Instructional Activities. Fourth, waivers are utilized for special events (e.g., 5K run, aerobics marathon) and for certain instructional activities. The waiver language is generally included within the event contract. Ski schools, motorcycle schools, instructional camps, and any number of other types of instruction providers generally require that a waiver be signed.

Disclaimers on Tickets or Signs. And finally, a disclaimer or exculpatory language is frequently included on tickets or is posted on signs. Such disclaimers on tickets are rarely upheld because they usually fail to meet the requirement of clarity or show a meeting of the minds. There is no harm in including the language on a ticket or posting it, but the provider should operate under the assumption that it will not protect against liability. See Chapter 6 for more information.

Conclusion

In summary, the provider can usually gain significant protection from liability by using assumption of risk language, exculpatory waiver language, and indemnification language. Conveniently, the provider can combine all of these into one comprehensive document – the participant agreement.

Since no document will usually afford liability protection to the provider for gross negligence or aggravated negligence, the provider should always seek additional protection through risk management techniques, which includes liability insurance, regular inspections, employee training, and sound record-keeping as well as other risk management procedures. Figure 1.1 shows the relationship between the cause of the injury, the source of liability, and the major components of the participant agreement.

The reader is also directed to Appendix A for a comparison of various participant forms used to limit the liability of service providers for injuries. The Appendix will be a valuable resource for reference in understanding the terms used throughout the book and in interpreting any document that purports to limit liability.

Chapter 2

Why Waivers Sometimes Fail

In most states a well-written waiver can protect a recreation, fitness, or sport provider, its employees, and its agents from liability for injuries resulting from ordinary negligence. However, those relying upon waivers for liability protection should keep in mind that waivers are not foolproof and have some serious limitations.

The first, and most important, limitation is that waivers are not enforceable if they violate the established **public policy** of the state. Public policy differs from state to state – therefore, waiver law differs from state to state. Public policy related limitations will be discussed in the first half of this chapter. Waivers also have other **limitations unrelated to public policy**, which also vary by state and will be discussed later in this chapter.

WAIVER LIMITATIONS RELATED TO PUBLIC POLICY

While the courts in most states disfavor waivers and strictly construe them against the relying party, in most states waivers are deemed valid and enforceable as long as they are not against public policy. **Public policy** has been defined many ways. The court in *Merten v. Nathan* (1982) described public policy as "that principle of law under which freedom of contract or private dealings is restricted for the good of the community." **Black's Law Dictionary** (1990) said public policy refers to man's duty to his fellow men; being against public policy means that the act is not in the best interest of the public as a whole. As an example, a school system policy requiring all students to sign waivers releasing the school system from liability for injuries caused by negligence might not be in the best interest of the public as a whole.

Rulings that a waiver violates public policy have been based upon many factors. A waiver can be deemed to be against public policy based on any one of these factors or based upon a combination of more than one. The following are five general factors which are used to determine public policy; if the waiver is found to violate one or more of these factors, the waiver will likely be held unenforceable as against public policy. Keep in mind, however, that the legislature and/or courts in each state determine and define what constitutes public policy in that particular state – and often, a factor that violates public policy in one state may not violate public policy in a neighboring state.

Involves an Essential Service or a Public Interest

A service is an **essential service** when it is a necessary service depended upon by a large number of citizens (e.g., water, electricity, medical). A matter is of **public interest** when the general public has a pecuniary interest that affects the public's legal rights or liabilities. Generally something is an essential service or of public interest if it affects the public as a whole (or at least a large portion of the public) rather than a small segment.

The California Supreme Court listed characteristics that identify a contract (or waiver) to be of public interest (*Tunkl v. Regents of University of California*, 1963). The *Tunkl* court indicated that a contract to which *some* of these factors (giving no required number) applied would be a matter of public interest.

- It concerns a business of a type generally thought suitable for public regulation.
- The party seeking exculpation is engaged in performing a service of great importance to the public, which is often a matter of practical necessity for some members of the public.
- The party holds himself out as willing to perform this service for any member of the public who seeks it, or at least for any member coming within certain established standards.
- As a result of the essential nature of the service, in the economic setting of the transaction, the party invoking exculpation possesses a decisive advantage of bargaining strength against any member of the public who seeks his services.
- In exercising a superior bargaining power the party confronts the public with a standardized adhesion contract of exculpation, and makes no provision whereby a purchaser may pay additional reasonable fees and obtain protection against negligence.
- Finally, as a result of the transaction, the person or property of the purchaser is placed under the control of the seller, subject to the risk of carelessness by the seller or his agents.

Using these criteria, waivers regarding the municipal water supply involve an essential service and would not be enforceable; on the other hand, health and fitness activities associated with a health club are not considered essential and a waiver would be enforceable because the services can be obtained through other means or sources (*DeAsis v. Young Men's Christian Association of Yakima (YMCA)*, 2014). Also, recreation, fitness, and sport activities such as sky diving, skiing, horseback riding, and bike racing do not generally involve a large percentage of the public and are seldom considered of public interest. An exception to this is in Vermont where the Supreme Court found certain waivers required of skiers to be against public policy because they affected a large number of the public. (*Dalury v. S-K-I, Ltd.,*1995; *Spencer v. Killington, Ltd.*, 1997; *Umali v. Mount Snow Ltd.*, 2003).

While the courts in many states have adopted the *Tunkl* criteria for determining if a matter is of public interest, not all agree. For example, the highest court of Maryland declined to do so stating "the ultimate determination of what constitutes the public interest must be made considering the totality of the circumstances of any given case against the backdrop of societal expectations" (*B.J.'s Wholesale Club, Inc. v. Rosen*, 2013). It went on to say that the concept is amorphous and not easily defined; that, in defining societal expectations, courts should look to relevant statutory and common law.

Generally, when a waiver involves an essential service or affects public interest, the waiver is void as against public policy. Occasionally, however, a waiver will be enforced because it is in the public interest. For instance, in *Marcinczyk v. State of New Jersey Police Training Commission* (2009), a waiver challenged by an injured trainee was enforced, partly because the training program benefitted the public interest by providing an important service.

Special Populations

There are times when it is of public interest to protect special populations from the effects of waivers. One population to which this applies is **minors.** This topic is discussed in detail in the next chapter. A second group that often has special protection is **minors in childcare programs**. Since childcare is an essential activity for working families, courts have found that the enforcement of liability waivers protecting such providers would be against public policy. A waiver was at issue in a case involving a childcare program (*Gavin v. YMCA of Metropolitan Los Angeles,* 2003). The court ruled that waivers signed by parents in the YMCA *childcare* program were unenforceable as against public policy. The court stated that permitting a childcare provider to contract away its duty of ordinary care is antithetical to the very nature of such services. In a more recent California case (*Lotz v. The Claremont Club,* 2013), the appellate court failed to enforce a parental waiver relating to a child in a childcare program. The father had purchased a family membership to a sports club. Ten-year-old Nicholas was left in the club's childcare department and suffered injury during a dodge ball game. The court cited *Gavin,* found the waiver void as against public policy, and remanded the case for trial.

Another special population is seniors with disabilities participating in **senior daycare programs** that provide health support and therapeutic services. Two California cases shed some light on this issue. In *Shawa v. City of Fairfield* (2013), Ragda Shawa, age 56 and disabled as a result of the removal of a brain tumor, was admitted to the program which provided social and recreational activities to participants using walkers or wheelchairs. She fell in the bathroom while under supervision and was injured. The California trial court granted summary judgment in favor of the city. The appellate court reversed the lower court decision, ruling the waiver to be unenforceable as against public policy. In fact, the circumstances met each of Tunkl's six criteria for public interest.

In contrast, another California case involving the injury of a 73 year-old senior in a senior program ruled the required waiver enforceable (*YMCA of Metropolitan Los Angeles v. Superior Court,* 1997). The woman fell while walking near tables with a jewelry display. The YMCA provided a senior program with limited recreational activities, socializing, and an inexpensive lunch. The program did not include supervision, care, or therapeutic services to disabled adults. The court found that while the program was important, it provided recreational activities, not activities for special needs individuals; the court enforced the waiver.

NOTE: Readers and writers often confuse the terms "public policy" and "public interest." In fact, many writers erroneously use the terms interchangeably. Public interest, however, is simply one factor in determining if something violates public policy.

Common Carriers

Legaldictionary.thefreedictionary.com defines a **common carrier** as "An individual or business that advertises to the public that it is available for hire to transport people or property in exchange for a fee." In a 2015 Illinois case (*Dodge v. Grafton Zipline Adventures, LLC*), the plaintiff claimed that the waiver was unenforceable because "zipline courses are common carriers under Illinois law, and as such, they cannot exempt themselves from liability for their own negligence."

The court stated that while courts disfavor waivers, contracting parties are free to agree to allocate risk of negligence as they please so long as they do not violate public policy. It went on to say that waivers between "the public and those charged with a duty of public service, such as those involving a common carrier, an innkeeper, a public warehouseman, or a public utility, have been held to be unenforceable as contrary to public policy." It pointed out that courts have ruled that "exculpatory agreements between common carriers and passengers are unenforceable because of the special social relationship of a semipublic nature that permeates the transaction between the parties." Hence, the court declared that it is well-settled that waivers relieving common carriers of liability for their negligence is void as against public policy.

The court noted that Illinois courts have ruled elevators, a scenic railway at an amusement resort, a merry-go-round, a taxicab, and a Ferris wheel to be common carriers. The court made the distinction that escalators and segway scooters were not common carriers because the user has an active role in his or her own safety. It became necessary to determine if *Grafton* was a "common carrier" or a "private carrier." A common carrier must accept as a passenger any person offering himself or herself for passage; whereas a private carrier contracts to deliver goods or passengers in a particular case for hire or reward.

The court determined that whether *Grafton* was a common carrier is a question of fact dependent upon the nature of the business in which it is engaged. Questions needing to be answered were: 1) whether Grafton Zipline had control and regulation of the passengers' conduct and of the operation of the carriage; 2) whether the plaintiff actively participated in the transportation and contributed to her own safety; 3) whether there was a disparity of bargaining power between the parties; and 4) whether Grafton Zipline made a profession to carry all who applied for carriage. For that reason, the court remanded the case to trial court for determination.

Of course, law regarding common carriers is state law and will vary somewhat by state. For instance, in California, ski lifts, elevators, and escalators are considered to be common carriers (*Justia*). It is safe to say, however, if state law determines that the actions of an activity provider achieves common carrier status, waivers by the provider will not be valid and enforceable.

Conflicts with a Statutory Duty

Courts are consistent in holding that it is against public policy to waive a statutory duty. The following cases illustrate instances in which waivers failed because they conflicted with health or safety statutes. In the **Florida** case, *Tassinari v. Key West Water Tours* (2007), a U.S. District Court held that a waiver used by a boat rental company was not enforceable because the company had violated Florida boater safety statutes. Another example may be found in *McCarthy v. National Association for Stock Car Auto Racing Inc* (1967). in which the **New Jersey** court held that a provider contracting away safety requirements prescribed by state safety statutes is contrary to public policy. In *Capri v. L.A. Fitness International* (2006) a **California** club patron sued L.A. Fitness for negligence and **negligence** *per se* (a violation of a statute leading directly to injury). The club was attempting to waive liability for a violation of a provision of the Los Angeles County Code and the Health and Safety Code. The court enforced the waiver against the negligence claim, but did not enforce it against the *negligence per se* claim because a party cannot contract away liability for negligent violations of statutory law. The court in a Florida jet ski case (*Straw v. Aquatic Adventures*, 2011) had a similar result in that the waiver was not enforced against the negligence *per se* claim. In a **Utah** ski case (*Jozewicz v. GGT Enterprises, LLC*, 2010), the plaintiff rented skis for which a safety recall notice was in effect. Since the operator was in violation of the Consumer Product Safety Act, the waiver was not enforceable. Likewise, a **Delaware** court (*Slowe v. Pike Creek Court Club, Inc.*, 2008) stated that waivers for actions violating public health and safety regulations contravene public policy.

Sport Safety Statutes

Most states have enacted at least one of what are sometimes called **sport safety acts** or **shared responsibility statutes** (e.g., equine, ski, whitewater rafting) intended to define or limit the liability exposure of operators of selected activities. Some of these statutes hold the operator to a duty of ordinary care. When they do, a waiver cannot protect the operator in the event of ordinary negligence. Other statutes prescribe a list of specific duties of the operator. If the injury is caused by failure to meet one of those duties, the waiver will not protect. Other sport safety statutes do not require ordinary care or list mandatory duties of the provider. In these cases, the statute does not directly affect the use or validity of waivers.

Sport safety statutes that require a **duty of ordinary care** include Alaska's **AS 05.45.010-.210** which prohibits the enforcement of waivers by ski area operators. A North Carolina statute **(NC Gen Stat §99C-2(c)(7))** requires ski area operators to engage in non-negligent conduct; consequently, a federal court failed to enforce a North Carolina ski waiver (*Strawbridge v. Sugar Mountain Resort* (2004). The court stated that the enforcement of a ski waiver would violate the statute and would be unenforceable since it runs counter to the public interest. The New Mexico legislature passed an Equine Liability Act **(NMSA 1978, sec. 42-13-4 [1993])** that mandates that equine providers have a duty to not be negligent. Based on this statute, the New Mexico Supreme Court held that providers could not avoid this statutory duty by the use of liability waivers (*Berlangieri v. Running Elk Corporation*, 2003). Waivers were not upheld in two West Virginia whitewater rafting cases because **WVa Code Sec. 20-3B-3(b)** imposes a standard of care upon commercial whitewater guides (*Murphy v. North American River Runners, Inc.*, 1991; *Johnson v. New River Scenic Whitewater Tours, Inc.*, 2004).

Statutes in some states state that the operator has a duty to **follow the specified duties** prescribed in the statute. The Colorado statute (**Colo Rev Stat § 33-44-104(1)**) prohibits protection by the waiver if the operator violated any of the specified duties. Other states following this strategy include Idaho (**Idaho Code 6-11-1107**); New Mexico (**NM Stat Ann §24-15-11**); West Virginia (**WVa §20-3A-6**); and Utah (**Utah Code Ann §78B-4-401**). The court in a Tennessee case (*Teles v. Big Rock Stables*, 2006), referenced the state equine statute (**T.C.A. 44-20-104**). The waiver protected the stables from liability for ordinary negligence, but did not release the statutory liability for injuries resulting from faulty tack. Other related cases include *Anderson v. Vail Corp.*, CO, 2010; *Rothstein v. Snowbird Corp.*, UT, 2007.

In contrast, in many cases the state **does not require** a duty of ordinary care or include specified duties that must be met to avoid negligence. The following are examples of instances where the statute does not require a duty of ordinary care. In *Penunuri v. Sundance Partners, Ltd.* (2011), the court ruled that the Utah Equine Act (**Utah Code Ann. 78B-4-201 to-203**), while protecting providers from liability for inherent risks, presupposed the continued use of waivers between equine activity sponsors and participants as protection from liability for ordinary negligence. (It is interesting to note that the Utah Equine Act does not require a duty of ordinary care while the Utah Skier Safety Act in the previous paragraph does require a duty of ordinary care.) Michigan statute **MCLA 691.1664-4(2)** provides that "Two persons may agree in writing to a waiver of liability beyond the provisions of this act and such waiver shall be valid and binding by its terms." A Michigan court (*Terrill v. Stacy*, 2006) found that a waiver barred a negligence claim. In *Raveson v. Walt Disney World*, (2001) the court declared there was nothing in the Florida statute (**Fla. Stat. ch. 773.03(2)(b)**) that would prevent waivers.

Considerations Regarding the Nature of the Waiver

Certain considerations involving the nature of the waiver can result in the waiver violating the public policy of the state. Three of these considerations are: 1) when the waiver is an adhesion contract; 2) when the waiver is unconscionable; and 3) when the parties were not equal in bargaining power.

Adhesion Contracts

Waivers used by providers of recreation, fitness, and sport activities are generally considered adhesionary. An **adhesion contract** is a "standardized contract which is imposed and drafted by the party with superior bargaining power and which relegates the subscribing party only the option of signing the contract or rejecting it" (i.e., allowing no opportunity to bargain) (*Westlye v. Look Sports, Inc.*, 1993).

A common misconception is that adhesion contracts are not enforceable; the fact is, however, that *an adhesion contract is usually fully enforceable absent the presence of two judicially imposed limitations*. The first is that the contract must fall within the reasonable expectations of the weaker or adhering party and the second is that the contract must not be unduly oppressive or unconscionable under the applicable principles of equity (*Heilig v. Touchstone Climbing, Inc.*, 2007). In a Massachusetts case (*Brush v. Jiminy Peak Mountain Resort*, 2009), the court indicated that in Massachusetts recreation-related waivers are not adhesionary because the activity is not an essential service. Contracts of adhesion are sometimes against public policy, *but generally those involving recreation, fitness, and sport are not ruled contrary to public policy since clients are under no compulsion to sign and may seek such services elsewhere.* A Colorado court held that because a waiver is on a printed form and offered on a take-it-or-leave-it basis does not make it unfair – particularly when similar services may be obtained elsewhere (*Espinosa v. Arkansas Valley Adventures, LLC*, 2014).

In a California case (*Schoeps v. Whitewater Adventures LLC*, 2005) regarding a woman who had signed a whitewater rafting waiver, the court stated that the most oppressive aspect of the situation was that, had she not signed, she might have been left without transportation in an isolated area. The court recognized that she had only a few minutes to decide whether to sign the waiver and would have lost her pre-paid ticket price had she refused to sign. However, they felt that this is not sufficient to constitute oppression or lack of a meaningful choice, particularly since the brochure had stated that a waiver was required. The exceptions are when the service offered is deemed to be essential in nature, and thereby creates a decisive bargaining advantage (Se*igneur v. National Fitness Institute, Inc.*, 2000) or when the contract is unconscionable.

Unconscionable Contracts

Black (1990) defined an **unconscionable contract** as a contract that is so grossly unfair to one of the parties, because of stronger bargaining power of the other party, which no man in his senses would make. A waiver may be found to be unenforceable if it is deemed unconscionable. Both procedural and substantive unconsionability must be present in order for an agreement to be deemed unconscionable. **Procedural unconsionability** exists when a party lacks a meaningful opportunity to agree to the clause terms because of 1) unequal bargaining power, 2) an adhesion contract, and 3) its effects are not readily discernible. **Substantive unconsionability** focuses on the one-sidedness of the contract terms (*Burnett v. Tufguy Productions, Inc.*, 2010).

Courts generally rule that recreation and sport waivers are not unconscionable. The New Jersey Supreme Court in *Stelluti v. Casapenn Enterprises, Inc.* (2010) stated that the court uses a sliding scale involving how the contract was formed and whether public interest is involved. A Pennsylvania court, involved in determining the document was not unconscionable, considered if the contract 1) was voluntary, 2) involved the economic well-being of the signer, and 3) involved a recreational activity (*Martin v. Montage Mountain*, 2000). A Tennessee appellate court upheld a waiver signed by an adult student who was injured in a motorcycle riding class. The fact that she had paid a non-refundable $200 tuition before she was informed that a waiver would be required did not make the waiver unconscionable (*Maxwell v. Motorcycle Safety Foundation, Inc.*, 2013). Maxwell had read and understood the waiver – and had not objected to the waiver when she signed it.

Special Relationships that Affect Waivers

Four types of social or special relationships can make exculpatory agreements unenforceable (*Hamer v. City Segway Tours of Chicago, LLC*, 2010). They are 1) when there is a duty of public service, 2) when there is a great disparity in bargaining power, 3) when the waiver is required of an employee by an employer, and 4) when a duty is owed to an invitee in one's place of business.

Duty of Public Service

One such relationship is between the public and those charged with a **duty of public service**. *Generally, waivers used when there is such a duty are not enforceable.* This would include common carriers, innkeepers, hospitals, physicians, and public utilities. **Physicians** may use informed consent agreements to protect them from liability for inherent or informed risks; however, physicians are usually unable to gain protection from their own negligence through the use of waivers.

This does not seem to be case for **athletic trainers**. A women's golf team member was injured and later claimed the team athletic trainer improperly diagnosed her injury and failed to refer her to a qualified specialist. The **Ohio** court said the golfer was not entitled to relief because she had signed a waiver that specifically released the trainer from liability (*Bader v. Ferri*, 2013). In a similar case involving a university varsity athlete who was injured while weight training or practicing field hockey (*Roe v. Saint Louis University*, 2012), the athlete alleged negligent treatment by the athletic trainer. The Sports Medicine Authorization and Acknowledgment of Risk Form, previously signed by the athlete, contained a waiver releasing the university and its employees from liability for negligence. The **Missouri** court held that the waiver released the defendants from all liability for negligence.

Unequal Bargaining Power

A waiver will generally not be enforced if one of the parties has a clearly dominant bargaining position over the other; courts, however, generally consider sport, recreation, and fitness activity providers and their clients to have equal bargaining power because the service is not essential and the client has other options. Some courts specify that the agreement must be signed knowingly (implying that the signer understood the meaning of the contract) and willingly (suggesting that the signer was under no economic or other duress) (*Clanton v. United Skates of America*, 1997). A Minnesota court (*Schlobohm v. Spa Petite, Inc.*, 1982) stated that there is no disparity of bargaining power if the service is not necessary or if it could be obtained elsewhere. An Oklahoma court (*Manning v. Brannon*, 1997) stated that the equality of bargaining power is determined by assessing 1) the importance of the subject matter to the physical or economic well-being of the party agreeing to the waiver and 2) the amount of free choice that the party could have exercised when seeking alternate services.

Examples of parties that are generally considered unequal include teacher-student, doctor-patient, and employer-employee. Service providers such as health and fitness clubs, ski resorts, and rafting companies are not generally considered to have a superior bargaining position over clients since the client is free to go to another club or to acquire the same health and fitness benefits through other avenues. The inequity must generally be such that the signer did not willingly sign the waiver. Courts have been very consistent in ruling that parties that sign waivers in order to participate in recreation, fitness, or sport activities are not at such a disadvantage because they are under no compulsion to participate in the activity.

In *Moore v. Waller* (2007), a health club patron who suffered injury during a kickboxing demonstration claimed the waiver was invalid because of unequal bargaining power. The court responded that it did not suppose Moore had equal bargaining power, but said that he did not meet the criteria needed to invalidate the contract. He showed no evidence 1) that he objected to the waiver provision at the time, 2) that he attempted to bargain for different terms, or 3) that the contract involved a necessary service.

The issue of whether the signer has an opportunity to bargain has been addressed in some states. A few waivers have failed as a result of Supreme Court rulings in Wisconsin, Connecticut, and more recently, Oregon due, at least in part, to the failure of the signer to have an opportunity to bargain over the terms of the contract (*Atkins v. Swimwest Family Fitness*, 2005; *Hanks v. Powder Ridge Restaurant Corporation*, 2005; *Reardon v. Windswept Farms, LLC*, 2006; *Bagley v. Mt. Bachelor, Inc.*, 2014).

Several tactics have been suggested to prevent a waiver from being adhesionary or unconscionable due to the lack of **opportunity to bargain**.

Tunkl (1963) implied that standardized adhesion contracts would be more acceptable if the signer were able to **pay an additional reasonable fee and avoid signing the waiver**. A Connecticut court (*Reilly v. Michelle Leasure*, 2010) reiterated that giving the participant the option of paying a higher fee in lieu of signing the waiver might help. In a Wisconsin Case (*Hickey v. T.H.E. Insurance Company*, 2013), the waiver was enforced, in part, because the plaintiff was given the option of paying an additional $15 fee per day in lieu of signing the waiver. The judge in a California case *(Shawa v. City of Fairfield*, 2013), when discussing bargaining strength, pointed out that the waiver at issue contained no provision whereby a participant could pay an additional fee to avoid the waiver. The option of an additional fee would provide the participant with a bargaining opportunity and might make waivers more acceptable in states like Wisconsin, Connecticut, and Oregon. The *Hickey* court also indicated that **publicizing the waiver requirement in advance** would leave the patron in less of a "dilemma" on the day of recreation. These options might make a waiver less adhesive and more likely to be enforced.

Wisconsin attorney Alexander "Sandie" Pendleton presented several options that provide an opportunity to bargain[2]. He suggested three possible approaches:

- The option of a reasonable additional fee to avoid the waiver (see Figure 2.1),

---

[2] Alexander Pendleton, *Enforceable Exculpatory Agreements: Do They Still Exist?* 78 Wis. Law. 10 (Aug. 2005) (article available on-line).

- The use of a partial waiver (i.e., offering a choice between the full waiver and a partial waiver at an increased price (an example of the partial waiver would be to waive all claims except those for catastrophic injuries totaling more than $500,000), and
- With on-line waivers, the provider, as part of the registration process, might provide an opportunity for the participant to purchase an inexpensive event insurance policy.

Figure 2.1
Example of an Additional Fee Non-Waiver Option

"Participant's Option" Section
(Place Immediately before Waiver)

Participant's Option
I have read the below Waiver Agreement in its entirety. I realize I do not have to sign it. I freely choose either Option A or Option B:
Option A: PAY AN EXTRA $500, and not sign the below Waiver Agreement   _____
Option B: PAY NOTHING EXTRA, and sign the below Waiver Agreement of my own free will   _____
(Check only A or B)

Date: _____   Participant's Signature: _____

A fourth option might involve a "reasonable" additional fee for a waiver that waived liability for all injuries except catastrophic injuries. The service provider would need to purchase a policy that would cover only catastrophic injuries.

In the case of extra fees, the term "reasonable" is open to interpretation by the court. A court might be willing to consider an extra fee that is 25 to 50% of the original fee constituted an opportunity to bargain, whereas a fee that is 100% of the original fee (or more) might not be considered "reasonable" by the court.

Employer-Employee Relationships

The relationship between **employers and employees** (sometimes referred to as the **master-servant relationship)** is the third type relationship that limits liability waivers. Waivers involving employer/employee relationships are generally considered to be against public policy (*Landren v. Hood River Sports Club, Inc.*, Ore., 2001; *Trumbower v. Sports Car Club of America, Inc.*, Okla., 1976; *Maggart v. Almany Realtors, Inc.*, Tenn., 2007). In fact, the Wyoming Constitution (**Wyo.Con., Art. 19, sec. 7**) forbids the enforcement of release agreements when an employment relationship exists between the parties.

In most cases, waivers signed by employees are not enforceable because of the economic hold that the employer has over the employee (*Maggert v. Almany Realtors, Inc.*, 2007; *Valley National Bank v. National Association for Stock Car Auto Racing, Inc.*, 1987). In *Brown v. Soh* (2004), a racing school instructor was struck by a car manned by a student and another instructor. The plaintiff filed suit against the driver, the instructor, and the Skip Barber Racing School. The appellate court upheld the waiver against the employer; however, the Connecticut Supreme Court reversed the ruling (*Brown v. Soh*, 2006) and remanded the case for trial instructing that the motion for summary judgment be denied. The Connecticut Supreme Court stated that exculpatory agreements in the employment context violate public policy. Similarly, Washington courts hold that an employer cannot require an employee to sign a waiver releasing the employer from liability for job-related injuries caused by employer negligence because there is a disparity of bargaining positions (*Wagenblast v. Odessa School No. 105-157-166J*, 1988). In a South Carolina case (*Fisher v. Stevens*, 2003), summary judgment in favor of the defendant was denied because there was a genuine issue of fact regarding whether a master/servant relationship existed between Fisher and the speedway.

The long-held public policy prohibiting enforcement of waivers required of employees by employers because of bargaining position is not without exception. In a 2012 Idaho climbing wall case

(*Morrison v. Northwest Nazarene University*), the university required employees to experience a "team building exercise" and to sign a waiver, indemnity agreement, and assumption of risk prior to doing so. Morrison fell from the climbing wall and was seriously injured; he sued contending the waiver was unenforceable because he was in an obvious disadvantage in bargaining power. The court said that since he did not tell the employer that he did not want to climb the wall and was not ordered to do so anyway, there was insufficient evidence to show that there was an obvious disadvantage in bargaining power. The court upheld the waiver. An employee was injured while teaching horseback riding (*Young v. Prancing Horse, Inc.*, 2005). She filed suit against her employer but the court upheld the waiver she had signed.

Courts have also enforced waivers when the employee works only **part-time** or does not perform the job as a livelihood. A man working as a race track starter was struck by a car and sued the employer (*Finch v. Andrews*, 1993). The court held that it need not address the public policy because the employee was not subject to economic coercion because he was part-time and his livelihood was not at risk. In *Brown v. Robbins* (2007), a waiver signed by a race official working for $50 per night was enforced because the plaintiff worked because he wanted to be near races. There was no unequal bargaining power and both parties mutually accepted what the other was offering.

Independent Contractors. What might be called **quasi employer-employee** relationships would include independent contractors, volunteers, and interns. While they may not technically be employees, they do have distinctive relationships that might need to be considered.

Waivers signed by **independent contractors,** as with employees, have been found to be against public policy. In a 2006 Connecticut case (*Colagiovanni v. New Haven Acquisition Corp.*, 2006), the court held that the waiver signed by the independent contractor (a newspaper carrier) releasing the party with whom he contracted (the newspaper company) from liability was void as against public policy. The court felt that the circumstances were the same as those when an employer requires an employee to sign a waiver and was characterized by an inequality in bargaining positions. Likewise, in *Speedway SuperAmerica v. Erwin* (2008), the court held that a waiver/indemnification agreement signed by an independent contractor was against public policy because of the unreasonable terms of the agreement and the inferior bargaining position of the contractor.

Volunteers. Waivers between an employer and a **volunteer** are generally enforced. Two Michigan courts have ruled for the defendants (*Brown v. Northwoods Animal Shelter*, 2011; *Theodore v. Horenstein*, 2009) when a volunteer filed suit for an injury after having previously signed a waiver. The *Brown* court enforced the waiver stating that requiring volunteers to sign a hold harmless release does not violate public policy. In a similar case in South Dakota (*Holzer v. Dakota Speedway, Inc.*, 2000), the court commented that the plaintiff worked at the track as a non-paid volunteer and not as a livelihood. The court added that no public interest was involved because the waiver was an agreement between individuals and would have little, if any, impact on the general population.

Interns. Sometimes an **intern** is required to sign a waiver in order to participate in a college internship with a business. A 2012 Oregon case involved an employer-intern relationship in which the young lady was attacked by a chimpanzee at a chimpanzee sanctuary. Miss Howard had signed a waiver which was enforced by the court (*Howard v. Chimps, Inc.*, 2012). Two factors that might have influenced the decision were 1) the waiver appeared in the internship manual and 2) a disclaimer was at the bottom of each page of the manual stating: "I know that the [defendant's] company policies and other related documents do not form a contract of employment …."

Agency. Waiver cases sometime turn on the issue of **agency.** An **agent** is one having express or implied authority to represent or act on behalf of another (the **principal**).(*Oran v. Fair Wind Sailing, Inc.*, 2009) The court held that the waiver protected not only the named party, Fair Wind Sailing, Inc., but also the principal (BFM) even though BFM was not named on the waiver.

In contrast, a Florida court found that Carnival was not liable for the actions of a tour company (*Young v. Carnival Corp.*, 2011) because there was no principal-agent relationship. In another Florida case (*Johnson v. Unique Vacations, Inc.*, 2012), a tourist purchased a horseback riding excursion at a desk in a resort, was injured during the ride provided by an independent contractor, and filed suit against the resort. Agency status was not established, in part, because the plaintiff had signed a disclaimer clearly stating that the provider was not an agent of the resort.

Invitee in a Place of Business

It is well-established that the common law imposes a duty of care on business owners to maintain safe premises for their business invitees (clients or potential clients). Justification of this is that the law recognizes that an owner is in a better position to prevent harm than is the invitee. Courts recognize, however, that participation in sports will result in injuries and grant businesses providing sports opportunities permission to utilize liability waivers to protect themselves financially.

The **New Jersey** Supreme Court, in *Stelluti v. Casapenn Enterprises, LLC* (2010), applied a standard that balances the public policy interest in freedom to contract with the standard of conduct of maintaining safe premises for business invitees that is commensurate with the risk of the activity. Since the case involved an injury on a treadmill in a health club, the court did not determine or discuss the validity of other aspects of the agreement (i.e., whether the waiver would be enforceable had the injury occurred on the club's sidewalks or parking lot).

In 2014, a **New Jersey** appellate court examined a health club case in which the plaintiff was injured on stairs leading away from the pool area; the slip-resistant surface on the bottom step was worn away (*Walters v. YMCA*). Walters had signed a waiver protecting the health club from personal injuries while on any YMCA premises or "as a result of a YMCA sported activities [sic]." The injury did not occur while in the pool or while entering or exiting the pool. Since the incident could have occurred in any business setting, the plaintiff argued the defendant should be held liable pursuant to the common law duty all business owners owe to invitees. Thus the court was called on to answer the question left unanswered by the *Stelluti* court. The appellate court stated that enforcing "the expansive scope of the waiver would eviscerate the common law duty of care owed" to invitees; it ruled the waiver was unenforceable as against public policy.

In an earlier case (*Sweat v. Big Time Auto Racing, Inc.*, 2004), the **California** court went beyond a literal reading of the language in the waiver which suggested that the release was intended to cover negligent acts anywhere on the speedway premises, not just in the pit area. The court felt this clouded the purpose of the release and used extrinsic evidence to interpret the scope of the waiver. The court found the purpose of the waiver was to require a fan to expressly assume the risk of injury associated with being in close proximity to the dangerous activity of automobile racing; it ruled that a collapsing bleacher bore no relationship to the purpose of the agreement – thus the waiver failed to protect Big Time.

Illinois courts (*Simpson v. Byron Dragway, Inc.*, 1991; *Hawkins v. Capital Fitness, Inc.*, 2015) have stated that even broad waivers do not encompass all accidents without limit. In *Simpson*, the court concluded that the danger of a deer running onto a racetrack was not the type of risk that is intended by racetrack waivers. In the *Hawkins* case, a mirror fell from the wall injuring a patron in a health club. In the waiver, Hawkins released Capital Fitness from "any and all claims or causes of action" and waived his rights to "bring legal action or assert a claim. . . ." The court held that reasonable minds could differ as to whether this constituted an ordinary risk of health club participation and did not grant summary judgment to Capital Fitness.

The *Walters* and *Sweat* cases involved broadly worded waivers; the following cases involved more narrowly-worded waivers. In an *Arkansas* case (*ver Weire v. Styles*, 2013), a woman went to a raceway and signed a waiver permitting entrance to restricted areas. Later, ver Weire was injured in the bleachers where a loose plank caused her to fall and suffer injury. The plaintiff argued that the injury was completely unrelated to the unique and obvious dangers associated with automobile racing; that ver Weire was a business invitee and was owed the duty to maintain the premises in a reasonably safe condition. The court ruled that under these circumstances, the waiver was inapplicable and did not protect the defendant. It was of interest that the court failed to note that the waiver language specified protection for the defendant "… while in or upon the restricted area and/or while competing, officiating, observing, or working for or for any purpose participating in the event." This was not a broad waiver as was the case in *Walters*.

Likewise, in a **New York** auto racing case (*Stevens v. Payne*, 2015), the waiver was specific to the "risks rationally associated with the dangerous nature of automobile racing;" therefore, the waiver did not apply to faulty bleachers.

Most waivers contain broad language that intends coverage of non-sport related premises such as restrooms, sidewalks, and parking lots. Jurisdictions that limit waiver protections to the risks that normally accompany a sport afford activity providers less protection.

Signer Lacked Understanding and/or Unwittingly Signed

A number of factors can result in the signer lacking understanding of the waiver and signing when there was no intent to release. The waiver should be clear that the signer intended to relieve the provider of liability for injuries resulting from the negligence of the provider, its employees, or agents. Often, courts will not enforce a waiver that seems to have been **unwittingly signed.** One may sign a waiver unwittingly in a number of circumstances: 1) if the client is rushed and not given an opportunity to read the waiver; 2) in a case of fraud and misrepresentation; 3) when the waiver is inconspicuous; and 4) when the signer fails to read the waiver. *The first three can result in a waiver being signed unknowingly – and can sometimes cause the waiver to fail.*

Ambiguity

Courts in all states require that to be enforceable, a waiver must clearly and unambiguously express the intent of the client to relieve the provider from liability for its negligence. **Ambiguity** is defined as doubtfulness, or doubleness of meaning and is said to exist when reasonable persons can find different meanings in the language (Black, 1990, p. 79). One court stated it does not seem unfair to place the burden of producing a clear waiver on the service provider (*LaFate v. New Castle County*, 1999). Note, however, that a waiver is not ambiguous simply because the parties do not agree as to its meaning (*Platt v. Gateway International Motor Sports Corporation*, 2004). Further, when ambiguity exists, courts interpret the ambiguity in favor of the non-drafting party (*Zipusch v. LA Workout*, 2007).

A California court (*Solis v. Kirkwood Resort* Co., 2001) said that an ambiguity exists "when a party can identify an alternative, semantically reasonable, candidate of meaning of a writing." Most waivers that fail to protect the provider do so because the waiver is ambiguous in some way. Some of the factors that the courts examine in determining ambiguity follow.

Lack of Clarity. The first major source of ambiguity is the **lack of clarity** of the language. The following excerpts from three waivers help to illustrate three types of ambiguity found in waivers.

> I, the undersigned, assume all responsibility for horse and equipment, and all liability. It is understood that the management is not liable in case of accident. I also agree to pay for the damage to horse or equipment and special charge for overridden horse. (*Mizushima v. Sunset Ranch, Inc.*, 1987).

This example illustrates the ambiguity that can be created by the failure to use the word "negligence" within the waiver. The language does not make it clear that the signer is releasing Sunset Ranch from liability for injury resulting from the negligence of Sunset Ranch. The waiver was not upheld due to this ambiguity. Many other jurisdictions, however, would interpret "all liability" to include negligence and would enforce waivers with this type of language (*Jones v. Loews Santa Monica Hotel*, 2007). Another interpretation is that "all liability" includes liability for inherent acts, negligence, and even gross negligence. This interpretation can invalidate a waiver in some jurisdictions because waiving gross negligence is against public policy.

In *Schlumbrecht-Muniz v. Steamboat Ski and Resort Corporation* (2015), the plaintiff was present to participate in NASTAR ski races. She signed a waiver reproduced in part here.

In exchange for being permitted to participate in NASTAR events (the "**Event**"), I agree to the following:

I acknowledge that participating in the Event poses a RISK OF PERSONAL INJURY . . . and I knowingly and voluntarily ASSUME ALL **RISKS associated with my involvement in the Event** and the risk of injury caused by the condition of any property, facilities, or equipment used during the Event . . . . **I hereby release** . . . the applicable sponsoring ski area where the Event is held, and the Event sponsors . . . for any injuries, losses, damages . . . caused . . . by the Releasees, . . . **that are normally associated with participating in the Event**, or the condition of the property . . . used for the Event.[Bold emphasis added.]

This example illustrates ambiguity related to the interpretation of the scope of the waiver. After finishing her second race and exiting the race course, she skied down a trail headed toward the lift. She intended to meet some other racers at a picnic area but was injured when she collided with a snowmobile parked near the lift. One of the issues was whether the waiver was ambiguous. The court found the language "normally associated with participating in the event" could be interpreted in two ways. It might be understood to mean to bar all claims for injuries occurring anywhere at the sponsoring ski area before, during, or after the time of the race; alternatively, others could interpret it to mean it was limited to injuries that occur only on the race course during a race. Having alternate meanings or interpretations is the meaning of ambiguity.

In *Vahedy v. Remigio* (2013), a father signed a waiver to allow his daughter to participate in an adventure camp. The California court found ambiguity as to intent relating to several issues. A pertinent part of the waiver follows:

[I]n consideration of the permission granted [by] Jews for Jesus for my child to participate in this adventure trip[,] I voluntary [sic] agree for myself and my representatives [,] successors and assigns . . . to release, discharge and waive any and all claims or causes of action against Jews for Jesus and their respective successors and assigns from and for any and all liability including without limitation any personal injury, property damage or wrongful death, arising out of or relating to my child's participation in this adventure trip.

The court found that the waiver was unclear as to whose claims were being waived; it could be interpreted to apply only to the father's claims arising from the child's participation or, alternatively, it could be understood to waive any claims of the child. Several other ambiguity issues existed in the complete waiver.

Failure to Specifically Refer to "Negligence." Another major source of ambiguity in a waiver is the failure to make it clear that the waiver is intended to relieve the provider of liability for the ordinary "negligence of the provider, its employees, or its agents." There are many ways in which preparers of waivers attempt to do this; among them is language indicating relief from "any and all claims," "all liability," "all causes of action whatsoever," "any claim or lawsuit by me," and "from any fault of the provider." While these examples all seem inclusive of negligence, many courts have ruled that such expressions are ambiguous in that they do not make it clear that liability for injuries due to negligence and those due to the inherent risks of the activity are both being waived. Courts in some states require that the term "negligence" be included; generally, language such as "negligence," "negligent acts," or "ordinary negligence" is required in those states.

Failure to include the term "**negligence**" or its equivalent can be fatal to the waiver in a number of states. The authors have attempted in Figure 2.2 to categorize all states in terms of the word "negligence." It is important to note, however, that it is not always perfectly clear as to what language is required by the courts in a state. Courts in a large number of states stated that the use of the word "negligence" is not mandatory, but have indicated in one way or another that one would be wise to include the word "negligence." Figure 2.2 lists a large number of states falling into this category. The courts in some states have:

- had some courts requiring the term; others within the state do not require the term;
- strongly recommended the use of the term;
- stated that it would be very helpful for such contracts to set forth in clear and express terms that the signer is releasing others for their negligent acts.
- stated that a waiver containing the term is more likely to be upheld;
- stated the term is not required, but that the intent to release liability for negligence must be clearly, unequivocally, and unambiguously expressed;
- stated that the waiver must express intentions with "the greatest particularity" and expressly show the intent to release liability for negligence;
- held that the waiver can be enforced if the waiver as a whole is such that the intent of the parties is clear with regard to exactly what kind of liability is being released.

Figure 2.2
**State Law Regarding the Use of the Word
"Negligence" Requirement**

Insufficient Information or Waivers Not Enforced[3]	Do Not Require "Negligence"[4] And Allow Terminology Such as "any and all"		Do Not Require "Negligence" But Use or Have Very Strict Language Requirements[5]		Require the Term "Negligence"[6]
LA	Admiralty	MN	AZ	ND	AK
VA	AL	NM	DE	PA	CA
MS	AR	OH	DC	OR	CT
NE	CO	OK	FL	PR	HI
NC	GA	TN	IN	SC	ME
RI	ID	UT	KY	TX	MO
SD	IL	VI	MA	VT	MT
	IA	WA	NH	WI	NV
	KS	WV	NJ		NY
	MD	WY			
	MI				

A 2005 California court (*Mower v. City of Rialto*) stated that the general rule is that express, unequivocal language must be used to preclude liability for **active or affirmative negligence**. The court continued by saying that a waiver using general language which fails to mention negligence is construed to protect only against **passive negligence**. Some courts that have urged the use of the word "negligence" include *Sweeney v. City of Bettendorf* (2009); *Swartzentruber v. Wee-K Corp.* (1997); and *Dobratz v. Thomson* (1991). The *Swartzentruber* court noted that the "better practice" would be to expressly include the word "negligence" and the *Dobratz* court stated the use of the term would be "very helpful." Additionally, commentators have stated that the "word 'negligence' should increase the likelihood of the waiver being enforced" (Lesser, J.B., 2001) and "a risk adverse drafter should use the word 'negligence' in all exculpatory clauses" (K.G. Hroblak, 1998).

---

[3] Louisiana and Virginia (except for equine waivers) do not enforce personal injury waivers. No case law regarding the subject was found for the others.

[4] Courts in these states do not require use of the term "negligence" and do not express strong language requirements regarding intent of the waiver.

[5] These states do not require use of the term "negligence;" they do, however, have strict requirements for exculpatory language and generally recommend use of the term. One or more of the bullet points presented above apply to each of the states.

[6] At least some courts in these states require the term "negligence" or its equivalent.

It is good practice to refer to the "ordinary negligence of the provider, its employees, and its agents" in waivers in all states – regardless of the stand taken by the courts in that state. This language helps to make the purpose of the waiver crystal clear. The question one should ask is "If ambiguity is one of the major causes of waiver failure, shouldn't one include reference to "negligence" since that is the most effective way to reduce ambiguity in a waiver?" For more information, refer to the guidelines in Step 4 in Chapter 5.

Not Within the Contemplation. A third source of ambiguity is the lack of language that clearly indicates that both parties intended that the waiver relieve the provider of liability for the particular hazard or action causing the injury. This is referred to as **within the contemplation** of the signer or **within the scope** of the waiver.

A Navy SEAL was killed in a live fire drill when a bullet penetrated a "bulletproof" wall and struck him (*Ghane v. Mid-South Institute of Self Defense Shooting, Inc.*, 2014). The court stated that

> . . . it is not reasonable that SO2 Ghane, an experienced Navy SEAL, intended to release the defendants from following even basic safety standards in the design of the ballistic wall or the failure of the wall to perform as advertised.

Faulty supervision, a frayed cable on the weight machine, and a slippery floor in the shower area might be considered hazards that are normally included in the "negligence of the club." A California court (*Mower v. City of Realto*, 2005) held that "any activities incidental" to "the use of or participation at the … center…." applied to such acts as slipping in the shower or tripping on an object on the pool deck. On the other hand a club member who was injured by a jet of chlorine while swimming in the pool might not have contemplated such an event.

In a 2010 New Jersey case (*Semeniken v. Town Sports International, Inc.*), plaintiff was badly burned when flammable oil was sprayed inside the sauna. The court held that such a risk was not one normally associated with health clubs and ruled in favor of the plaintiff.

The manufacturer of a racecar failed to design or install a protective shield over the drive train; the driver was severely injured when the drive train flew upward into the driving compartment while she was competing (*Nesbitt v. National Muscle Car Association*, 2014). She sued, alleging among other things, that this type of incident was beyond the scope of the waiver and not within the contemplation of the signer. The Illinois court agreed with the trial court ruling that the failure was within the scope of the waiver and that plaintiff was given notice of the range of dangers assumed.

Interestingly, court rulings can sometimes yield surprising results (*Hawkins v. Capital Fitness, Inc.*, 2015). The Illinois court stated that a defendant must put the plaintiff on notice of the range of dangers for which the plaintiff assumes the risk of injury, but that the precise risk need not be contemplated. It further emphasized that even a broad waiver was not without limit; the court ruled that a genuine issue of fact arises as to whether the waiver includes the potential injury caused by a mirror falling off a health club wall. It reversed a lower court ruling enforcing the waiver and remanded the case.

Conflicting Statements in the Waiver or Use of Two Different Waivers. A fourth source of ambiguity is when conflicting statements appear in the waiver. It is important that language be consistent throughout the document. For instance, in a Florida case, the waiver was not upheld because actions protected against were given as any actions except "willful gross negligence" in one paragraph and as "any act or neglect" in another (*Sunny Isles Marina v. Adulami*, 1998). The Alaska Supreme Court found inconsistent language within a waiver and deemed it unenforceable because of ambiguity. The waiver promised to try to keep facilities safe and equipment in good condition; in contrast, it disclaimed liability for actions that failed to meet those standards (*Kissick v. Schmierer*, 2004).

Ambiguity can also arise when more than one waiver is required and there are differences between the waivers. Differences between waivers are particularly likely when the waivers are from two parties. See Chapter 5, Step 1 for a more discussion on this issue.

Lack of Specific Language. A fifth source of ambiguity can be a **lack of specificity of the waiver** or use of an **inapplicable waiver.** In a California case, a resort employee was injured while snowboarding. (*Vine v. Bear Valley Ski Company*, 2004) The resort produced a waiver the employee signed to obtain an employee season ski pass in which she released the resort from liability for injuries incurred while skiing. The court found the waiver ambiguous in that skiing does not necessarily include snowboarding.

In a Colorado case (*Messer v. Hi Country Stables Corporation*, 2012), the defendant owned two stables and used the same waiver (except for the name of the stables) at each. The plaintiff signed a waiver that contained the name of the other stables. The court found that the plaintiff had intended to waive liability, deemed it a **mutual mistake,** ordered a **reformation of contract,** and enforced the waiver.

Similarly, an Illinois plaintiff in *Cox v. US Fitness, LLC* (2013), argued that errors in a contract agreement regarding her sex and amount of her dues voided the agreement because it constituted fraudulent or misleading information. The court rejected the claim because typos or mistakes within the contract do not amount to fraud.

The plaintiff in a Missouri case (*Holmes v. Multimedia KSDK, Inc.*, 2013) alleged a waiver was ambiguous because the names of the sponsors of the event were not named in the waiver and the defendant sponsor was not a sponsor at the time she signed. The court rejected this idea saying that referring to "any event sponsors" releases all event sponsors, even those who are not yet sponsors when the waiver is signed.

"Negligence or Otherwise." The use of the phrase **"negligence or otherwise"** has been at issue on occasion. Plaintiffs have claimed that the phrase creates an ambiguity of scope. The Ball court (*Ball v. Waldoch Sports, Inc.*, 2003) examined the issue and held that the phrase created no ambiguity. The court referred to the fact that courts in 45 cases had failed to find the phrase to be ambiguous. The Ball court went on to say that even if it created an ambiguity of scope in the instant case, it would not mean the entire document was unenforceable. Ball might have gotten a different ruling had the court interpreted "otherwise" to included gross negligence or reckless misconduct.

Conspicuousness of the Waiver

Conspicuousness is a particular issue when a waiver is included within another document such as a membership contract; however, it is equally important that the exculpatory language be obvious in a stand-alone waiver. Courts frequently elect to not enforce a waiver when the signer failed to understand the meaning of the document because the waiver language did not attract the attention of the signer.

Courts in many states emphasize that the exculpatory language in a waiver must be conspicuous and stand out from the remainder of the document. Some courts require that the waiver section of membership and other multi-function agreements stand out in such a way that it is difficult for the signer to miss. One Texas court (*Charbonnet v. Shami*, 2013) stated that a waiver "is conspicuous when it draws the attention of a reasonable person looking at the face of the document such that the person ought to notice it." Texas provides that waivers satisfy two major requirements in order to be enforceable: 1) the conspicuousness requirement and 2) the express negligence doctrine.

For detail regarding how to make a waiver more conspicuous, see Chapter 5, Step 9; also, Chapter 6 under "Waivers within another Document," and under "Group Waivers."

Fraudulent Language

Fraud is any intentional perversion of truth for the purpose of inducing one to rely upon it, thereby surrendering some legal right. A California court (*Dieu v. McGraw*, 2011) stated that a release from liability for fraud and intentional acts violates the public policy of the State. Contracts which intend to exempt one from responsibility for his own fraud, whether willful or negligent, are against public policy (Civil Code sec. 1668). Fraud regarding a waiver might include false statements within a waiver or inducing a person to unknowingly sign a waiver.

A plaintiff in a California court alleged "fraud in the execution."(*Rosencrans v. Dover Images*, 2011). "**Fraud in the execution**" means that the signer was deceived so that he does not actually know what he is signing or does not intend to enter into a contract at all. Fraud in the execution does not apply if the plaintiff had a reasonable opportunity to discover the terms of the contract. Rosencrans had an opportunity to read and his failure to do so was due to his own negligence. In a subsequent California case (*Jones v. City of Ukiah*, 2013), a softball player signed a group waiver which was labeled in upper case letters that it was a roster and that all players must sign before playing. Below the heading in smaller typeface was the statement "A player signing his name on this Softball Roster form acknowledges that they have read and understand all of the provisions of the waiver and release form on the reverse side of the form." Below this language were spaces for roster signatures and the waiver was on the back of the page. The player alleged he arrived late, hurriedly signed the form without reading, the form was on a clipboard so the waiver was not visible, and he saw nothing called "waiver." The court said he was not prevented from reading the waiver; further, language on the front page did instruct him to "Read Waiver Before Signing." Consequently, the court affirmed the trial court ruling that Jones was bound by the waiver.

In another California case (*Jimenez v. 24 Hour Fitness USA, Inc.*, 2015), the employee knew Jimenez could not speak or read English and made gestures toward the computer showing the price and gestures indicating exercise – seeming to indicate for that price, the plaintiff could use the facility. Additionally, the employee did not call for a Spanish-speaking employee to help – which was his customary procedure. The defendant argued that non-verbal communications cannot, as a matter of law, amount to affirmative misrepresentation. The court's response was that while it not reasonable to rely on non-verbal communication when both parties speak the same language, in this case non-verbal communication was the only communication they had. The court felt that reasonable persons could find that the employee's actions constituted fraud and misrepresentation; thus this created a fact issue and should be determined by the jury. The court reversed the trial court summary judgment ruling and remanded it for trial.

Some acts that have resulted in claims of fraud include: 1) covering the waiver at the top of the sign-in sheet (*Shultz v. Paradise Cruises, Ltd.*, 1994); 2) misleading the client as to the purpose of the signature, such as using document titles like "waiting list" (*Del Raso v. United States of America*, 2001); 3) inclusion of untrue statements within the waiver, (*Merten v. Nathan*, 1982); and 4) failure to allow time to read the document.

When the issue is **fraudulent nondisclosure** of the contents of a contract, four elements are critical: 1) a party conceals a fact material to the transaction; 2) the fact is peculiarly within the concealing party's knowledge; 3) the concealing party knows the other party will act on the presumption that no such fact exists; and 4) the concealing party has a legal or equitable duty to communicate the fact. In *Chavez v. City of Santa Fe Springs* (2012), the plaintiff alleged **fraudulent inducement** after her son died in an accident on a camping trip. The city had promised that there would be supervision "at all times." However, the trip itinerary specified the campers would have unsupervised free time in which to explore. The appellate court held that there was sufficient evidence to raise triable issues and returned the case for trial. (See Avoiding Allegations of Fraud in Chapter 7 for more information).

Failure to Read

Some signers of waivers claim they signed unwittingly because they did not read the contract. Failure to read the document is an ineffective defense for a plaintiff since courts are consistent in holding that one is responsible for what one signs (*Brozyna v. Niagara Gorge Jetboating, LTD*, 2011). (See also Chapter 5, Step 8.)

Scope of the Waiver

Courts in most, or perhaps all, states hold that the scope of waivers is not unlimited. Most find that it is against public policy to enforce waivers for actions that go beyond the limits of ordinary negligence. These actions include reckless misconduct, willful/wanton acts, and, of course, intentional acts. In addition, courts in some states are reluctant to enforce waivers that they feel are extremely broad and seemingly all-encompassing. A third concern relating to the scope of the waiver is whether or not activity waivers should encompass incidents on the premises unrelated to the activity.

Aggravated Negligence[7]

While courts in most states enforce waivers protecting against liability for **ordinary negligence** (the failure to act as a reasonably prudent professional would act under the circumstances; the failure to use the care that a prudent or careful person would use), courts in most states generally hold that waivers intended to protect against **aggravated negligence** (i.e., **gross negligence, reckless conduct, willful or wanton conduct**, and **intentional acts**[8]) are against public policy. Consequently, courts in almost all states refuse to enforce waivers attempting to protect a provider from such extreme acts.

There are exceptions to this rule as some states do seem to enforce such waivers so long as the waiver language specifies intent to protect against gross negligence (or reckless conduct) (see Figure 2.3). Four states seem to enforce waivers for gross negligence and two enforce them for reckless or intentional acts as well (*Barber v. Eastern Karting Co.*, 1996). North Carolina and Pennsylvania courts have not settled the issue of waivers for gross negligence (*Bertotti v. Charlotte Motor Speedway, Inc.*, 1995; *Tayar v. Camelback Ski Corporation, Inc.*, 2012).

Figure 2.3
States that Have Enforced Waivers for Acts
Exceeding Ordinary Negligence[9]

States Enforcing Waivers in at Least One Case For Gross Negligence	States that have Enforced Waivers For Reckless or Intentional Acts
Florida Illinois Kentucky Pennsylvania[10] Virgin Islands	Florida West Virginia

---

[7] **Aggravated negligence** is a term used in Prosser and Keeton on Torts (5th edition) to describe the concepts of gross negligence, recklessness, and willful/wanton conduct.

[8] Terminology varies from state to state and most states do not recognize all of these terms. Generally, **gross negligence** is an extreme form of negligence in which one fails to use the care that even a careless person would use and generally constitutes a separate cause of action. It differs from ordinary negligence "in that a grossly negligent defendant must be consciously indifferent and his or her conduct must create an extreme degree of risk." **Reckless conduct,** sometimes grouped with gross negligence, usually denotes more serious conduct than gross negligence. More often, states generally use either **reckless conduct** or **willful and wanton conduct**, but seldom both. Their definitions are generally similar. Such conduct shows "a reckless disregard for the safety of others such as a failure, after knowledge of an impending danger, to exercise ordinary care to prevent it or a failure to discover the dangers through recklessness or carelessness when it could have been discovered by the exercise of ordinary care." **Intentional acts** do not fall in the category of negligence because they are done purposefully and not accidentally. A "person acts 'intentionally' if he desires to cause consequences of his act or he believes consequences are substantially certain to result." (Black, 1990, p. 810)

[9] *Theis v. J & J racing Promotions*, (Fla. 1990); *L. Luria & Son, Inc. v. Honeywell, Inc.* (Fla.,1984); *Borden v. Phillips*, (Fla. 2000); *Maness v. Santa Fe Park Enterprises, Inc.*, (Ill. 1998); *Donegan v. Beech Bend Raceway Park, Inc.*, (Ky., 1990); *Coughlin v. T.M.H. International Attractions, Inc.*, (Ky.,1995); *Valeo v. Pocono International Raceway*, (Pa., 1985); *Nicholson v. Mount Airy Lodge, Inc.*, (Pa.,1997); *Mandell v. Ski Shawnee*, Pa., 2007); *Barber v. Eastern Karting Co.*, (W.Va. law, 1996); *Murphy v. North American River Runners, Inc.* (W.Va., 1991); *Brown v. Robbins*, (N.C., 2007).

[10] The Pennsylvania Supreme Court in *Tayar v. Camelback Ski Corporation, Inc.* (2012) ruled that enforcement of waivers protecting against reckless acts is against public policy, but failed to rule regarding waivers for gross negligence. Some appellate courts have upheld waivers for gross negligence. For more information, see Pennsylvania section in Chapter 8.

For those in the recreation, fitness, or sport industries, it is often **difficult to distinguish between ordinary negligence and gross negligence**.[11] Common definitions of gross negligence are usually of little practical help (e.g., very great negligence, the absence of slight diligence, or the want of even scant care).

The two following cases provide good **examples of gross negligence**. Providers were found grossly negligent in a Massachusetts triathlon case (*Lautieri v. Bae*, 2003). In the bicycling leg of a triathlon, the race director failed to heed a number of industry safety standards regarding intersections – leaving the intersection at which the incident occurred 1) open to automobile traffic; 2) uncontrolled by police or volunteers; 3) with no warning signage for contestants or drivers; and 4) unmonitored. In a California case *(Martinez v. Swartzbaugh*, 2002), a lady was a successful bidder in a silent auction for a "ride around" as a passenger in a McLaren racecar. The "ride around" was to consist of a few leisurely laps around the track. Without warning, the driver suddenly accelerated to 140 mph while neither the driver nor the passenger had a helmet, seat belt, or other safety device. On the second lap, the driver lost control of the car and crashed, causing serious injuries to the passenger. There was sufficient evidence to give rise to a triable issue of fact as to whether the action was grossly negligent.

The reader can easily see that these acts far exceed the common acts of ordinary negligence such as failure to inspect a piece of equipment, failing to properly match a rider to an appropriate horse, or improperly adjusting ski bindings.

A recent Alabama case clearly illustrates the unenforceability of a waiver for an **intentional act**. A woman who got a tattoo on her breast sued for invasion of privacy when the artist published a photograph in a magazine (*Minnifield v. Ashcraft*, 2004). The plaintiff had signed a waiver, however, the court held that it was against public policy to enforce a waiver for an intentional act.

Waiver Language that is Too Narrow or Overly Broad Language

Waivers may fail because the language is not broad enough to provide the needed protections (e.g., failing to name the parties; failing to specify equipment-related injuries). Waivers also fail because the waiver is so broad as to violate public policy (e.g., so broad it is interpreted to include injuries caused by recklessness; to release any persons in any restricted areas from any liability). A good waiver encompasses reference to the major risks for which protection is needed, but does not try to encompass every risk of any kind, under any circumstance. This topic will be addressed in detail in Chapter 5 Step 4.

Whether an Activity Waiver Encompasses Incidents Unrelated to the Activity

There is a question regarding whether a broadly worded waiver (e.g., … release from liability for any and all injuries while participating or while on the premises.) should be enforceable in the event the incident resulting in injury was totally unrelated to the activity (e.g., an invitee slips and falls because of a worn non-skid pad on a stair step in the facility. Since the incident could have occurred in any business setting, should the defendant be protected by the waiver, or should the provider be held liable pursuant to the common law duty all business owners owe to invitees? This issue was discussed in more detail previously in Invitee in a Place of Business.

---

[11] In *Chavez v. City of Santa Fe Springs* (2011), a California appellate court provides a good example of how courts distinguish among the levels of aggravated negligence.

WAIVER LIMITATIONS NOT RELATED TO PUBLIC POLICY

Public policy is not the only serious threat to the enforcement of waivers intended to protect service providers from liability for their own negligence. Some other limitations relate to such subjects as: 1) non-signing parties; 2) strict liability; 3) faulty equipment rental; 4) diversity of citizenship; and 5) lack of capacity to contract.

Non-signing Parties

There are times when a question arises as to whether or not a party who did not sign a waiver is bound by the waiver. This commonly occurs in situations where one spouse signed a waiver and subsequently suffers injury or death and litigation is filed by the other spouse. Another situation in which this question arises is when one individual signs a waiver on behalf of other family members (e.g., a family health club contract or family ski pass); similarly, the question arises when one member of a party signs a waiver on behalf of other adult members of the party (e.g., two or three couples renting a houseboat). Subsequently, when the non-signing spouse, child, or adult suffers injury, the effect of the waiver on the non-signer is challenged.

Loss of Consortium

Loss of consortium refers to the loss of conjugal fellowship of a husband or wife and the right of each to the company, society, co-operation, affection and aid of the other. (Black, 1990, p. 309)

A loss of consortium claim may be made when the signer of the waiver is injured and the spouse or family files suit claiming loss of consortium. For example, a man joins a health and fitness club or enters a race and signs a waiver releasing the provider from liability for negligence. The man is then permanently paralyzed due to the negligence of the provider. The waiver is upheld and bars the man's claim. The non-signing wife, however, has also suffered as a result of the negligence of the provider and often sues claiming, among other things, loss of consortium. She has lost his income (which may place her in a financial bind), suffered expenses, and she has lost companionship and sexual relations from the husband.

In a number of states she has the right to file suit for her losses, independent of her husband's claim – an **independent cause of action**. If she shows legitimate damage, she is eligible to collect damages – in spite of the fact that her husband signed a valid waiver. *In these states, one can easily see that the waiver signed by the injured spouse might not provide complete protection for the provider.*

In other states, her right to a claim is dependent upon a valid claim by her husband, which was extinguished when the court upheld the waiver for his claim – a **derivative cause of action**. If this is the case, the waiver protects the provider against both the claims of the husband and those of the non-signing spouse. One can easily see that waivers in derivative states offer greater protection for the provider.

In *Zivich v. Mentor Soccer Club, Inc.* (1998), the mother of a young boy signed a waiver releasing the club from liability for injury to her son. The court upheld the parental waiver regarding the claims of the child and the signing parent; the court also enforced the waiver against the loss of consortium claims of the non-signing father. The court stated that although Mr. Zivich did not sign the release agreement, he was bound by the agreement because he accepted and enjoyed the benefits of the contract.

31

Wrongful Death

Wrongful death is an action brought on behalf of a deceased person's beneficiaries that alleges the cause of the death was the negligent or willful act of another. The law regarding wrongful death is similar to that of loss of consortium.

In some states the claim is **derivative** of a valid claim of the deceased. Colorado's wrongful death statute limits claims to those that could have been brought by the decedent if he or she had survived. In *Salazar v. On the Trail Rentals, Inc.* (2012), Salazar was killed in a snowmobile crash. The claim was not allowed because Salazar's waiver would have prevented a successful claim by Salazar had he survived.

In other states, a wrongful death claim constitutes an **independent cause of action** and is not prohibited by the waiver signed by the deceased. In a New Jersey Case (*Gershon v. Regency Diving Center*, Inc., 2004), the facts were strikingly similar to the facts in the *Madison* case. Each decedent, in order to participate in scuba classes, had signed a waiver intended to waive, for himself, his heirs, executors and assigns all causes of action for injury or wrongful death. The court stated that in New Jersey, wrongful death damages are intended to compensate the statutorily defined heirs for the pecuniary losses caused by the death of the decedent as a result of the tortious conduct of others. The court went on to state that

> Even if a decedent has the legal authority to bargain away the statutory right of his potential heirs, society's interest in assuring that a decedent's dependents may seek economic compensation in a wrongful death action outweighs the decedent's freedom to contract.

In states in which the cause of action is independent, as in the *Gershon* case cited above, the waiver probably will not provide complete protection for the provider.

But in a wrongful death claim, things are not always as simple as they seem – at least in California. In a California scuba diving case (*Madison v. Superior Court*, 1988), the court stated that the decedent had no power or right to waive his heirs' wrongful death claim. Paradoxically, it then held that a wrongful death plaintiff is subject to any defenses that could have been used against the decedent; the court then ruled against the plaintiff and enforced the waiver. A more recent California appellate court case involving an equestrian participant who was killed yielded a similar ruling (*Eriksson v. Nunnink*, 2015). The parents of the girl filed suit on a wrongful death claim. Even though in California heirs have an independent cause of action, courts have held that an express waiver of negligence by a decedent provides the defendant with a complete defense. The *Eriksson* court stated "although an individual involved in a dangerous activity cannot by signing a release extinguish his heirs' wrongful death claim, the heirs will be bound by the decedent's agreement to waive a defendant's negligence and assume all risk." Consequently, since Mia expressly assumed the risk, the defendant owed no duty of care, there was no breach of duty, and there was no premise for a wrongful death action.

Whether the provider is protected against both loss of consortium and wrongful death claims will vary from state to state and with the situation. Providers should consult a competent attorney to determine the extent of protection offered by waivers in their state.

Non-signing Party is Injured or Killed

In this situation one person signs for himself or herself and for others, but the person injured or killed is a non-signing party. For instance, many health and fitness clubs utilize a waiver that is located within a membership contract and have the head of the household sign the contract. In doing so, the club is seeking to immunize itself from litigation in the event of injury to the signer, the spouse, and all of the children.

A number of cases illustrate that the effectiveness of a waiver in this situation varies with both the state and the circumstances. In a **Georgia** case (*Hembree v. Johnson*, 1997), the wife signed a joint health club agreement including a waiver. Months later the husband signed an addendum making it an individual membership, but signed no waiver. The original waiver by the wife was upheld against the husband. In a

Kansas case (*Ko v. Bally Total Fitness Corporation*, 2003), a man took over another's health club membership contract, signed no waiver, and was held to the waiver signed by the original owner. A **Wisconsin** plaintiff had signed a ski waiver on behalf of his entire family (*Yauger v. Skiing Enterprises, Inc.*, 1996). When a family member was injured, the court enforced the waiver saying that the waiver was signed on behalf of and for the benefit of the non-signing party.

Similarly, in *Bergin v. Wild Mountain, Inc.* (2014), Bergin purchased season passes online for himself and his friend Knight. Bergin signed the waiver to complete the transaction. Months later, Knight was injured while skiing and filed suit. Bergin had not asked Knight about the waiver prior to agreeing to it; however, Knight admitted he had signed the waiver for previous seasons and would have authorized the signing had he been asked. The **Minnesota** court enforced the waiver.

In contrast, none of the waivers were upheld in the following cases: an **Idaho** husband signed a snowmobile rental agreement for himself and his wife (*Hanks v. Sawtelle Rentals, Inc.*, 1999); in **Wyoming** another husband signed a waiver and indemnification rafting agreement (*Madsen v. Wyoming River Trips, Inc.*, 1999); and in a **California** case, a man who had rented a houseboat had signed a waiver prior to an injury of a passenger (*Shrayber v. Holiday Harbor, Inc.*, 2003). The *Shrayber* court stated that the waiver cannot diminish the rights of a non-signing passenger while the *Hanks* court said that the waiver signed by the husband did not obligate the non-signing spouse. Likewise, in a **Texas** case (*Tabrizi v. L.A. Fitness International, LLC.*, 2011), a club member brought a guest to the health club. The guest, contrary to normal procedure, did not sign a waiver and subsequently slipped and fell while exiting the swimming pool. LA Fitness claimed the waiver defense premised on the member host's waiver. The court ruled in favor of Tabrizi and did not enforce the waiver.

Likewise, in *In re Aramark Sports and Entertainment Services, LLC* (2012), one man (Prescott) rented a powerboat for a daytrip to Rainbow Bridge for himself, his wife, and two other couples. Only Mr. Prescott signed the waiver and indemnification agreement. At some point the boat sank for an undetermined reason and both the Prescotts and one other couple drowned; one couple survived. The court, using **Admiralty Law** since the incident occurred on a navigable waterway, ruled that the waiver and indemnity agreement were enforceable only against Mr. Prescott's estate. The other parties (or their estates) were not bound by the waiver or indemnity agreement and could sue Aramark; however, after any loss, Aramark would be able to seek reimbursement for any loss from the indemnifier, Mr. Prescott's estate.

A good rule to follow is that when an agreement affects more than one person, it is best to have all affected parties sign the agreement. Again it would be wise to consult a knowledgeable local attorney regarding the pertinent law in your state.

Strict Liability

Strict liability is called liability without fault, because one does not have to prove fault for liability. Strict liability law generally applies in situations where one keeps wild animals, where one conducts ultra-hazardous activities such as fireworks displays, and where one manufactures a product that produces injuries. Under the theory of strict liability, one does not have to prove that the defendant was negligent; rather, people or corporations are held responsible for any harm caused by their actions or products, *regardless of whether they are at fault or not.* ***Generally, liability waivers do not protect one against strict liability.***

Strict Products Liability

Strict liability is one of the causes of action that can be pursued in products liability cases where an injury is caused by defective or hazardous products regardless of the care taken in designing or manufacturing the product. *Strict products liability originally applied only to manufacturers of defective products; the concept has been expanded to include others in the distribution supply chain.*

The concept is based on the idea that a manufacturer should be absolutely liable if, in placing a product on the market, it knew the product was to be used without inspection, and it proved to have a defect that caused injury (*Escola v. Coca Cola Bottling Co.*, 1944). A California court in *Westlye v. Look Sports, Inc.* (1993) stated that strict products liability applies to manufacturers, lessors, and retailers. The court perceived no substantial difference; each places an article on the market knowing that it is to be used without inspection for defect. The court went on to state that "Contractual disclaimers do not defeat strict products liability in tort."

Manufacturer Liability. *It is well established that neither product disclaimers nor express assumptions of risk (waivers) will protect the manufacturer of equipment in cases of strict liability.* The Colorado Supreme Court (*Boles v. Sun Ergoline, Inc.*, 2010), voided a waiver of the manufacturer of a tanning booth. Rather than resting on negligence principles, the court stated it "is premised on the concept of enterprise liability for casting a defective product into the stream of commerce." In strict products liability, the focus is on the nature of the product rather than the conduct of either the manufacturer or the person injured. The court referred to the Third Restatement which prohibits "contractual exculpations" from barring or reducing otherwise valid products liability claims for personal injuries by ordinary consumers against sellers or distributors of new products (*Restatement (Third) of Torts: Products Liability § 18 & cmt. d*). The court went on to say that "there appears to be virtually universal agreement on this point among the other jurisdictions considering the question. "

In *Sipari v. Villa Olivia Country Club* (1978), an injury resulted from the use of a 3-wheeled golf cart. Defendants were the country club and the cart manufacturer. The court stated that strict liability extends not only to manufacturers, but also to distributors and retailers. The Illinois court held that as a matter of public policy, one is liable and cannot contract away his own responsibility for having placed a defective product on the market for public use.

The *Simeone v. Bombardier-Rotax* (2005) court stated that Pennsylvania law permits waivers between businesses of equal bargaining power, but that a form release cannot shield a defendant business from liability when a consumer is injured by a defective product. The waiver specifying protection for suppliers did not protect the manufacturer because it was three parties away and was not a party to the transaction.

Lessors of Equipment. In a 2013 trail ride case (*Messer v. Hi Country Stables Corporation*, 2013), the plaintiff was injured when, after several adjustments, the saddle slipped causing a fall and injury. The United States District Court for the District of Colorado cited *Boles* in ruling that a waiver releasing "a manufacturer from strict products liability for personal injury, in exchange for nothing more than an individual consumer's right to have or use the product, necessarily violates the public policy of this jurisdiction and is void." The court ruled that the agreement did not protect Hi Country against the strict liability claim. Interestingly, the court also ruled that the strict liability claim failed, not because of the waiver, but because horseback riding constituted a service and not a product.

In *Sipari*, discussed under manufacturer liability, the court found that the strict liability applied to the country club renting the golf cart; the waiver did not protect.

Distributors and Retailers. In *Westlye*, discussed under manufacturer liability, the court held that a waiver did not protect the distributor of ski equipment from strict products liability; the court pointed to a strong policy against allowing product suppliers to disclaim liability for injuries caused by defect in products they place on the market.

Health Clubs & Other End Users of Equipment. Providers of sport and recreation services that utilize manufactured products are generally not considered to be liable when injuries result from an equipment defect. Courts generally look at three factors in determining strict products liability: 1) Was the company an end user of the product? 2) Was the company in the commercial manufacturing/distribution chain for the product? and 3) Was the purpose of the transaction to provide a service or a product?

In *Fisher v. Olde Towne Tours, LLC* (2011), Fisher signed up for a tour that included some snorkeling. She was provided a dingy; the dingy had no grab holds for support. When a large wave hit, she fell backward striking her back on the bench. The court ruled that strict product liability did not apply because Olde Town was the end user and was not in the supply chain. In a similar case (*Ferrari v. Grand*

Canyon Dories, 1995), the court did not hold a rafting operator strictly liable for a defective raft because use of the raft was incidental to the service provided. A third case involved a bungee/trampoline activity (*Wallace v. Busch Entertainment Corporation*, 2011). The defendant claimed the dominant purpose of the transaction was to participate in a "guided experience – not to use a product. The court agreed and enforced the waiver.

Five California health club cases illustrate that health club waivers are generally enforced in cases involving an equipment defect. The court in *Grebing v. 24 Hour Fitness USA, Inc.* (2015) stated that a defendant cannot be liable for products liability if the dominant purpose of the defendant's transaction was to provide a service rather than supplying a product. In *Ontiveros v. 24 Hour Fitness USA, Inc.* (2008), the court ruled that the club's primary role was as a supplier of a service, not products, and upheld the waiver. In yet another California case (*La Fata v. LA Fitness International, LLC*, 2008), the court ruled that strict liability does not apply when the transaction from which the injury arises involves a service and not the sale of a product. In *Kim v. L.A. Fitness International, LLC* (2011), a pulley became loose and caused an injury. The court stated that a waiver in a health club agreement may relieve the club of due care and release the club from liability for negligence. The release Kim signed waived all claims for personal injuries suffered while using LA Fitness facilities or equipment. In *Bhardwaj v. 24 Hour Fitness., Inc.* (2002), the plaintiff was injured when a large free weight machine broke. The court ruled "the doctrine of strict liability cannot be imposed against 24 Hour Fitness because its primary objective is to provide a service." The court added that the doctrine does not apply unless the defendant is involved in the commercial chain of distribution of the offending product.

Faulty Rental Equipment

Whether waivers will protect providers from liability for negligently maintained or faulty rental equipment is frequently at issue. In some states, courts have ruled that the waiver adequately protected against liability for negligent maintenance, adjustments, or defective equipment as long as the act of negligence was reasonably related to the purpose for which the release was given. A court in a California case said the waiver barred claims of negligence related to equipment (*Blau v. Mammoth Mountain Ski Area*, 2001). The case involved calibration of ski bindings. In a Pennsylvania case, the court said the waiver covered defective brakes on a rental bike (*Gimpel v. Host Enterprises, Inc.*, 1986).

In contrast, in a Michigan case, the court said waivers couldn't exonerate when the liability is based on negligently maintained or defective rental equipment (*Braun v. Mount Brighton, Inc.*, 1989).

Choice-of-Law and Forum Selection

Another limitation of waivers occurs when an issue exists regarding which state's law will be applied and where the case will be tried. If the choice-of-law and the forum selection (venue) of any subsequent litigation are not contractually agreed upon in the waiver, it is possible that a case might be tried in another state using the law of that state; consequently, the provider might not have the protection it expects to have.

Failure to include a choice-of-law clause and a forum selection clause leaves the provider vulnerable to being sued in a far away state under the law of that state. Choice-of-law and forum selection clauses within the waiver can generally help avoid this problem. For this reason, one should include both clauses within the waiver; that way, both parties contractually agree as to what state's substantive law shall apply (choice-of-law) and where any future legal action will be adjudicated (forum selection).

In the past, courts traditionally declined to enforce forum selection clauses. The United States Supreme Court ruling in *Bremen v. Zapata Off-Shore Co* (1972) marked a change in thinking in ruling that forum selection clauses should control if there is no strong showing that the clause should be set aside. Now both state and federal courts generally hold choice-of-law provisions and forum selection clauses to be presumptively enforceable providing there is a reasonable relationship between the transaction and the stipulated jurisdiction. Exceptions would be if there is some public policy against the provision or if there is some conflicting statutory provision.

Choice-of-Law

As a general rule, courts will enforce the choice-of-law agreed to by the parties in their contract. Section 187 of the Restatement (Second) of the Conflicts of Laws states that a court will follow the law of the state contractually chosen by the parties unless

". . . either (a) the chosen <u>state has no substantial relationship to the parties or to the transaction</u> or there is <u>no other reasonable basis for the parties' choice</u>; or (b) application of the law of the chosen state would be <u>contrary to fundamental policy of a state which has a materially greater interest</u> than the chosen state in the determination of a particular issue and which . . . would be the state of applicable law in the absence of an effective choice of law by the parties."[Underline added.]

In *McDonald v. Whitewater Challengers, Inc.* (2015), the injured party was a New York resident who was injured while rafting in Pennsylvania. She argued that because she signed the waiver in New York and is a New York resident, she was entitled to the benefit of New York law. The waiver provided that the venue was in Pennsylvania, but failed to specify that Pennsylvania law applied. Pennsylvania law states that when no law is specified in the contract, the court is to first determine if there is a conflict in the two laws (In this case it was important; the waiver would be enforceable under Pennsylvania law and unenforceable under New York law.) If a true conflict is found, the court then ascertains which state has the greater interest in the application of its law. The court determined that Pennsylvania had the greater interest because the business was located in Pennsylvania, the waiver was intended to protect Whitewater, and Whitewater has a right to expect the use of Pennsylvania law to be applied. Although the waiver was ultimately enforced, the solution would have been much simpler if the applicable state law had been specified in the contract.

In *Rutherford v. Talisker Canyons Finance Co., LLC* (2014), a minor was injured while training for a ski race in **Utah** sponsored by the United States Ski and Snowboard Association (USSA). Rutherford had signed a USSA liability waiver which contained a Colorado choice-of-law and forum selection clause. The Utah court held that Colorado did not have a substantial relationship or interest in the parties or transaction since the incident occurred in Utah and the parties were not from Colorado. The court did not enforce the clauses because Utah was the only state with an interest at stake.

Forum Selection

Similarly, courts generally enforce forum selections clauses agreed upon in advance;[12] however, there are times when the court chooses not to do so. Most state laws provide that such clauses should be enforced unless the party can make a strong showing that at least one of the following criteria (or similar) is met:
1) enforcement would be unreasonable or unjust;
2) the clause was fraudulent or overreaching;
3) enforcement would violate the public policy of the forum in which the suit is brought; or
4) trial in the specified court would create such a handicap to the plaintiff that, for practical purposes, the plaintiff would be deprived of his day in court.

The importance of a forum selection clause is illustrated by this case which featured a waiver without such a clause (*Bonne v. Premier Athletics, LLC,* 2006). The case involved a wrongful death action taken by the parents of a minor, competitive trampolinist. The boy and his parents lived in Ohio, the waiver was signed in Kentucky, one of the defendants was located in Kentucky, the sanctioning organizations were located in Indiana, the principal place of business of one defendant is in Tennessee, and the incident occurred in Tennessee. The court held that **Tennessee** was the state with the "most significant relationship" and that Tennessee law would apply. This was very important because the

---

[12] e.g., Exceptions are Idaho and Montana which do not enforce forum selection clauses.

Supreme Court of Tennessee has held that parental waivers are not enforceable while the Ohio Supreme Court has ruled that parental waivers are valid.

Gloria Barilotti was injured in a slip and fall incident at Atlantis Resort in the Bahamas (*Barilotti v. Island Hotel Company Limited*, 2014). Barilotti challenged the forum selection clause based on the lack of reasonable notice or communication of the clause. Plaintiff stated that 1) the clause was not presented prior to the check-in at the hotel and 2) rejection of the clause would subject the client to an onerous and significant financial penalty due to the cancellation policy. The court cited case law showing that forum selection clauses are presumptively valid and enforceable; a valid waiver is to be enforced in all but exceptional cases in which plaintiff makes a strong showing of unfairness. The court cited law that when a travel agent is notified of a requirement, the client is deemed to have constructive knowledge of said requirements. For this reason, the court ruled the clause enforceable.

In a case before the U.S. District Court for the District of New Jersey (*Kierstein v. Ostlund and Killington Resort*, 2014), the plaintiff signed a waiver that included the following forum selection clause:

> I consent to this agreement legally binding me, my heirs and assigns. I agree that any claim I may bring against Killington/Pico at any time for any reason shall be filed in Vermont State or Federal Court and tried under Vermont Law.

Kierstein lived in Connecticut, was injured at Killington Resort in Vermont, and filed suit in New Jersey. Killington moved to have the forum selection clause enforced and move the trial to Vermont. The court cited the U.S. Supreme Court (*Atl. Marine Const. Co. v. U.S. Dist. Court for W. Dist. Of Texas*, 2013) which ruled that when parties have signed a contract containing a valid forum selection clause, a district court may consider only public interest factors (which will rarely defeat a forum selection clause); as such, the practical result is that the clause should control in all except unusual cases.

In a New York case, plaintiff was injured in a motorcycle mishap in Florida; suit was filed in a New York court even though the waiver signed by the plaintiff specified Florida as the venue. Plaintiff's sole challenge to the clause was based on convenience and the hardship of paying for witnesses to travel to Florida for the action. The court ruled none of the criteria were met and enforced the clause (*Chiarizia v. Xtreme Rydz Custom Cycles*, 2007).

While forum selection clauses are usually enforced, the *Rutherford* case discussed in the choice-of-law section, illustrates an instance where the clause was not enforced. In that case, the United States Ski and Snowboard Association (USSA) waiver specified Colorado as the proper venue for any legal action. The Utah court explained that Colorado had no substantial relationship or interest in the parties or transaction and held that Utah was the proper venue. This was important because in Utah neither parental waivers nor ski waivers are enforceable; in Colorado, both are enforceable.

The general rule is that only the parties to the contract can enforce its terms of a forum selection clause, however, on occasion a party not named in the waiver wishes to invoke the forum selection clause. In a **New York** case (*Hluch v. Ski Windham Operating Corp.*, 2011), Ski Windham was not named as a protected party in the waiver. The court named three circumstances under which a non-party could invoke a forum selection clause: 1) third party beneficiary, 2) party to a global transaction, and 3) if non-party is "closely related" to one of the signatories. Ski Windham failed to establish a sufficiently close relationship with USSA (the signatory) for the enforcement of the forum selection clause.

Parental Forum Selection Clauses. Cases in a number of states have upheld parental forum selection clauses; in fact, even some states in which parental waivers are not enforced will enforce forum selection clauses signed by a parent on behalf of a child (*Burns v. Wilderness Ventures*, 2012, IL; *Morrow v. Norwegian Cruise Line LTD.*, 2002, PA; *Igneri v. Carnival Corp.*, 1996, NY). No cases have been found in which a court has refused to enforce a forum selection clause solely because the plaintiff was a minor (*Morrow v. Norwegian Cruise Line LTD.*, 2002; *Igneri v. Carnival Corp.*, 1996). The reasoning is that the forum selection clause does not deprive the minor of his or her right of redress for a wrong; it simply specifies the venue of the legal proceedings.

For more information on choice of law and forum selection clauses, see Chapter 5 Step 6. Also for more on cruise line contract choice of law and forum selection clauses, see Appendix B

Lack of Capacity to Contract

Capacity to contract refers to the legal qualification of an individual. Factors that can affect one's capacity in legal affairs include: 1) lack of mental ability; 2) incapacity due to the effects of drugs or alcohol; and 3) lack of legal age. The important point for the service provider is that courts will generally not uphold a waiver signed by one who lacks capacity – thus the waiver would fail to provide the sought-after protection.

Lack of Mental Ability

Persons lacking sufficient intelligence or mental functionality to be deemed competent or persons affected by illnesses such as Alzheimer's are not usually able to execute a contract. In *Holzer v. Dakota Speedway, Inc.* (2000), the plaintiff claimed to be of sub-normal intelligence (poor student, low reading comprehension, passed through school), thus was not capable of understanding the document. Court said he knew there were dangers and enforced the waiver. Likewise, in *Haines v. St. Charles Speedway, Inc,* (1989), a racecar driver tried to avoid a waiver because he had only third grade reading ability. The Missouri court said it was his duty to procure someone to read and explain it to him prior to signing. In a Tennessee case, the court ruled that a parent could not indemnify a business on behalf of a mentally retarded son (*Childress v. Madison County*, 1989).

Incapacity Due to the Effects of Drugs or Alcohol

Courts have ruled that persons who are incapacitated to the extent they don't understand the consequences of their actions may not be held to a contract. In *Ervin v. Hosanna Ministry* (1995), a woman signed a waiver when admitted to a rehabilitation center after an injury. She claimed she could not remember signing the waiver. The court ruled the waiver invalid because of diminished mental capacity resulting from drug and alcohol abuse. In *Johnson v. Robert Dunlap and Racing, Inc.* (1981), plaintiff signed a post-injury release while in the hospital. The release was not upheld when the physician testified that at the time he lacked capacity to understand the waiver because of drugs administered. In *Shultz v. Paradise Cruises, Ltd* (1994), summary judgment was denied because the plaintiff was under the effects of medication when the release was signed. A Michigan court has ruled that a waiver is not enforceable if the releasor is dazed, in shock, or under the influence of drugs (*Duncan v. Ryba Company*, 1999).

Below Legal Age

Legal age to contract is 18 in most states (19 in Nebraska and Alabama). Contractual waivers such as those relating to recreation, fitness, and sport made by minors are voidable by the minor. Courts have also traditionally held that such contracts made on behalf of minors by the parents are also voidable. This has changed in many states and seems to be in the process of changing in other states. The question of minors and waivers will be addressed on a state-by-state basis in Chapter 3.

Chapter 3

Waiver Law and Minor Participants

Recreation, fitness, and sport service providers often offer services and programs for minor participants or clients. Most professionals now realize that in almost every state, a well-written, properly administered waiver signed voluntarily by an adult can protect the relying service provider or professional from liability for injury resulting from the ordinary negligence of the provider or professional. Nevertheless, providers still should have at least three questions regarding waivers for minor participants: "Will waivers protect me when the participant is a minor?" "Will a waiver protect me if a parent signs on behalf of a minor participant?" and "If waivers cannot provide the liability protection needed, what can I do to protect myself and my business?"

Waivers Signed only by a Minor

For the answer to the first question, one must turn to contract law, which says that three elements of a valid contract are competency of the parties, consideration, and legality. Under contract law, it is well established that *a waiver signed only by a minor is voidable* because a minor (below age 18 in most states, 19 in Nebraska and Alabama) lacks capacity and is not competent to contract. This means that the minor has the option of voiding the contract in the event of injury. Except for contracts for necessities such as food, clothing, and medical care, contracts signed only by a minor are voidable by the minor. In some states, however, one or more of the following exceptions might be found: 1) when the minor contracts to support an illegitimate child; 2) when signing bail bonds; 3) when approved by the court; and 4) in some jurisdictions, if the minor received benefits under the contract (*Calamari and Perillo*, 1977). Since none of these really apply to recreational activities, a waiver signed only by a minor would be very unlikely to provide the liability protection sought by the provider of recreational activities.

An older Florida court *(Lee v. Thompson*, 1936) explained the reasoning as:

Except as to a very limited class of contracts considered binding, as for necessities, etc., the modern rule is that the contract of an infant is voidable rather than void ... To say that the executed contract of an infant is voidable means that it is binding until it is avoided by some act indicating that the party refuses longer to be bound by it.

A more recent Florida appellate court (*Dilallo v. Riding Safely, Inc.*, 1997) maintained the state's policy of protecting minors, ruling that a minor child injured because of a defendant's negligence is not bound by a contractual waiver of his or her right to file a lawsuit.

Misrepresentation of Age

Providers often ask if a waiver is enforceable if a minor misrepresents his age and signs a waiver claiming to be of majority age. A 2004 Pennsylvania court (*Emerick v. Fox Raceway*, 2004) did not enforce such a waiver when a 16-year-old claimed to be 18 in order to participate in a motocross race. The court held that since it is foreseeable that minors will misrepresent their age in order to engage in motorcycle racing, a raceway has a duty to create and follow age-verification procedures to screen out minors. They went on to say that since the activity involved "a high degree of danger, a high degree of care was required." The court stated that since the minor also bore some responsibility for his actions, that it was appropriate to submit the issue of comparative negligence to the jury.

Parental Waivers (Signed by a Parent or Legal Guardian)

Whether a waiver signed by a parent or legal guardian on behalf of a minor (a **parental waiver**) is enforceable depends largely on the state. Just a few years ago, parental waivers were enforceable in only a handful of states; now, that number is in the teens (See Figure 3.1. Additional strategies involve the inclusion of **parental indemnity agreements** and **parental agreements to arbitrate** a claim.

Parental Waivers

Providers frequently require that parents or guardians sign a waiver on behalf of a minor participant. For years the conventional wisdom was that the parent could not sign away the rights of the minor – thus waivers signed by parents on behalf of minor participants were thought to be invalid and courts in many states ruled such a waiver to be voidable by the minor participant.

The common rationale was that, absent court appointment, parents have no authority to release or compromise claims or causes of action belonging to minors. The Washington Supreme Court (*Scott v. Pacific West Mountain Resort,* 1992) reasoned that since a parent cannot release a child's cause of action after an injury, the parent has no authority to release the cause of action prior to the injury. More recently, the Utah Supreme Court (*Hawkins v. Peart,* 2001) agreed with this rationale stating, "…if anything, the policies relating to restrictions on a parent's right to compromise an existing claim apply with even greater force in the pre-injury exculpatory clause scenario."

However in recent years, courts in a number of states have elected to enforce parental waivers signed on behalf of a minor. In addition, the Colorado, Alaska, and Minnesota legislatures have each passed a statute **(S.B. 03-253 [2003]; A.S. 09.65-202; MN ST 604.055)** allowing enforcement of waivers signed by the parent. Consequently, whether a waiver signed by a parent on behalf of a minor participant is enforceable depends, in part, upon the state in which the case is tried.

The rationale for enforcing parental waivers was expressed by the Ohio Court of Appeals:

> Permitting organizations that sponsor recreational activities to protect themselves from liability, by requiring parents to sign dual exculpatory and indemnification agreements, furthers that interest. The "release" in the instant case provides an excellent example of the relationship between such agreements and the Supreme Court's extension of the General Assembly's desire to promote recreational activities on public lands . . . (*Zivich v. Mentor Soccer Club, Inc.*, 1997 p.33)

The Ohio Supreme Court went on to expand the rationale with the following:

> Another related concern is the importance of parental authority ... Judge Ford found that the right of a parent to raise his or her child is a natural right subject to the protections of due process. Additionally, parents have a fundamental liberty interest in the care, custody and management of their offspring. Further the existence of a fundamental, privacy–oriented right of personal choice in family matters has been recognized under the Due Process Clause by the United States Supreme Court ....
>
> Based upon these protections, Judge Ford believes that many decisions made by parents "fall within the penumbra of parental authority, e.g., the school that the child will attend, the religion that the child will practice, the medical care that the child will receive, and the manner in which the child will be disciplined." (*Zivich v. Mentor Soccer Club, Inc.*, 1998)

Figure 3.1 is a table summarizing the estimated likelihood of parental waivers being enforced in each state. Courts in 24 states have ruled that parental waivers are not enforceable. In one, Florida, the Supreme Court has ruled prohibiting enforcement of parental waivers used by commercial entities. In 18 states, no case law was found that clearly indicates whether the courts would enforce a parental waiver; discussion within the rulings in some of the states hint that parental waivers would be enforceable. For clarity, the final category is divided into three groups. The first group includes ten states in which statutes allow the enforcement of parental waivers for a named activity. The second group includes five states in which the courts will (or have in the past) enforce waivers for non-profit school and/or community recreation programs. The third group consists of ten states in which courts either 1)have enforced waivers used by commercial sport and recreation providers, but have not ruled on non-commercial school and/or

Figure 3.1
Parental Waiver Law by State

Courts Do Not Enforce Parental Waivers	Insufficient Information to Predict Enforcement Of Parental Waivers	Courts Enforce Parental Waivers Under Some or All Circumstances		
		Specific Activity Named by Statute	Non-Profit School-Community Recreation	Enforces Waivers by Either Commercial Entities or by Both Commercial and Non-Profit School-Community Recreation Entities
AL AR CT FL[13] HI IA IL LA ME MI MS NJ NY OK OR PA RI TN TX UT VA WA WV WI	AZ[14] DC GA ID KS KY MO MT NE NV NH NM PR SC SD VT VI WY	AZ[15] GA[17] FL[19] HI[20] IL[22] IN[24] KY[25] MN[26] UT[27] VA[28]	CT[16] FL[18] ND NY[21] NC	AK DE CA CO IN MD MA MN OH WI[23]

[13] **Florida** Supreme Court has ruled that parental waivers used by commercial recreation entities are unenforceable.

[14] The Arizona Supreme Court has interpreted the **Arizona** Constitution to mean that all assumption of risk questions are a matter for the jury and not to be decided by summary judgment. (See the Arizona section in Chapter 8.)

[15] **A.R.S 12 – 553 A.2** equine statute allows owners to use parental waivers for liability protection.

[16] Supreme Court rulings in **Connecticut** and **Wisconsin** seem to indicate that any sport- or recreation-related waivers are unenforceable in those states. (See the appropriate state sections in Chapter 8 for more information.)

[17] **OCGA § 4-12-4** equine statute allows parental waivers.

[18] Parental waivers for school- or community-based activities are still enforced by appellate courts in some **Florida** jurisdictions.

[19] The Motorsport Non-Spectator Liability Release statute **(F.S. 549.09)** provides that parental waivers are enforceable for minor competitors in certain motorsport events in **Florida**.

[20] **Hawaii** statute **§663-10.95** allows the enforcement of parental waivers for motorsports participants (with a witness).

[21] A federal court enforced a parental waiver, but similar rulings by **New York** courts are questionable.

[22] Equine Statute **745 ILCS 47/1-25** allows the enforcement of parental waivers for equine activities.

[23] See the **Connecticut** footnote above.

[24] **I.C. 34-28-3** Partial Emancipation for Minors to Participate in Automobile and Motorcycle Racing Act allows waivers and indemnity agreements by certain minors and their parents for participation in professional racing events in **Indiana.**

[25] **Kentucky** statute **(KRS 247.4027(2)a)** provides that parental waivers with a required warning can protect equine providers from liability for inherent risks, but not for negligence.

[26] Minnesota statute **MN ST § 604.055** allow enforcement of parental equine waivers.

[27] The Limitations on Liability for Equine and Livestock Activities Act **(Utah Code Ann. 78B-4-203(2)b)** specifies that a release for a minor participant signed by the minor's legal guardian shall be sufficient if it includes the definition of inherent risk in Section **78B-4-201** and states that the sponsor is not liable for those inherent risks.

[28] Virginia Statute **VCA §3.2-6202** allows enforcement of parental equine waivers.

recreation waivers, or 2) have enforced waivers used by both commercial sport and recreation providers and waivers used by non-profit school and/or community recreation programs. These two are listed together because logic would have it that courts enforcing commercial waivers would almost certainly enforce waivers used by non-profit entities.

Ratification of Waivers. "Ratification" in contract law is "the act of adopting or confirming a previous act which without ratification would not be an enforceable contractual obligation."[29] Black goes on to say that ratification is manifested by written word, spoken word, or by conduct.

Ratification was at issue in an Oregon snowboarding case in which the parent signed a parental waiver in order to purchase a season pass on behalf of his 17-year-old son. The young man soon turned 18 and shortly after that proceeded to use the pass on the ski lift at least 119 times over a 26 day period. He suffered injury and sued Mt. Bachelor for negligence (*Bagley v. Mt. Bachelor, Inc.* 2013).

In Oregon, as in many states, a former minor can disaffirm a contract within a reasonable time after reaching the age of majority or may ratify a contract after reaching that age by manifesting intent to let the contract stand. Mt. Bachelor invoked the affirmative defense of waiver saying that by failing to disaffirm the waiver agreement within a reasonable time after reaching the age of majority, by accepting the benefits of the agreement, and by "objectively manifest[ing] his intent to affirm" it through riding the lift 119 times, Bagley had ratified the waiver and was bound by it. The court cited **Williston on Contracts** 9:17 @170 "[I]f the infant after attaining majority voluntarily receives performance in whole or in part from the other party to the contract, this will amount to a ratification" in ruling that the waiver was enforceable because Bagley had ratified the contract.

Parental Waiver Law by State

The parental waiver law in each state is summarized below (no case law addressing minor participants was found for states that are not listed). The summary is kept brief for the sake of space; readers requiring more detail are referred to the listed citations. Parental waiver cases and applicable statutes found for each state are presented either in the summary or in the footnotes to enable the reader to read the case law and statutes and draw his or her own conclusions.

Parental indemnity agreements (discussed later in this chapter) are highlighted in bold. The authors feel that if the courts in a state uphold parental indemnification agreements by which the parent has agreed to indemnify or repay the provider for loss resulting from an injury to the minor, the claim of the minor is, in effect, neutralized because the parent would have to repay the provider for any award going to the minor. Thus, the waiver and the indemnification agreement are considered together since the effect of the two agreements is much the same. Both protect the provider from financial loss.

Alabama[30]
Does Not Enforce – Commercial or Non-Profit
Enforces – Forum Selection Clauses

In *J.T., Jr. v. Monster Mountain, LLC* (2010), the court determined that a waiver signed by J.T. and his coach (with a notarized document signed by the parent authorizing the coach to "act as our son's legal guardian in our absence for the purpose of signing all release of liability and registration forms and to give consent for medical treatment") was not enforceable. Alabama applies the longstanding common law rule that, except for a contract for necessaries, "a minor is not liable on any contract he makes and that he may disaffirm the same." The court stated this rule is firmly entrenched in common law and exists to protect minors from being taken advantage of by others due to minors' "improvidence and incapacity."

---

[29] Black's Law Dictionary, 1990, p.1261.
[30] *J.T., Jr. v. Monster Mountain, LLC*, 2010.

Alabama has also restricted the right of a parent or guardian to make a post-injury settlement of a minor's claim without court approval.

Another court has ruled **forum selection clauses** to be enforceable if the minor benefits under the contract.

Alaska
Enforces – Commercial & Non-Profit

Statute (**A.S. 09.65-202**) provides that a parent may release or waive the child's prospective claim for negligence against a provider of a sports or recreational activity.

Arkansas
Does Not Enforce – Commercial or Non-Profit

In the only case (*Williams v. U.S.*, 1987), a boy drowned in an air force base swimming pool. Even if language had been adequate to absolve government of liability, the waiver would be against public policy because to grant the government care without encouraging reasonable care violates tenets of fairness.

Arizona[31]
Status Unclear
Enforces for Equine - Both Commercial & Non-Profit

In *Bothel v. Two Point Acres, Inc.* (1998), the court did not enforce a waiver signed by the minor and father because it did not cover the type of incident that was involved. Minor status was not addressed which might indicate that the waiver would have been enforced if applicable.

Arizona statute (**A.R.S 12 – 553 A.2**) provides that an equine owner is not liable for an injury if the parent or legal guardian of the minor has signed a release before taking control of the equine.

California[32]
Enforces – Commercial & Non-Profit

It is well established that a parent may contract on behalf of his or her children for both school/community recreation programs and for-profit providers. Since *Hohe v. San Diego Sch. Dist.* (1990), California courts have enforced many parental waivers. No public policy forbids shifting the burden of risk by contract. Courts have stated that permitting contracts with parents to limit litigation holds costs down and encourages participation opportunities. Waiver use by **childcare providers** is against public policy (*Gavin v. YMCA of Metropolitan Los Angeles*, 2003).

---

[31] *Gomez v. Maricopo*, 1993.
[32] *Celli v. Sports Car Club of America, Inc.*, 1972; *Wattenbarger v. Cincinnati Reds, Inc.*, 1994; *Aaris v. Las Virgenes Unified Sch. District*, 1998; *Pastor v. Putney Student Travel, Inc.*, 1999; *Lashley v. East County Gymnastics*, 2001; *Jorst v. D'Ambrosio*, 2001; *West v. Sundown Little League of Stockton*, 2002; *El-Halees v. Chauser*, 2002; *McGowan v. West End* YMCA, 2002; *Platzer v. Mammoth Mountain Ski Area*, 2002; *Gavin v. YMCA of Metropolitan Los Angeles*, 2003; *Cortez v. Ceres Unified School District*, 2003; *City of Santa Barbara v. Superior Court of Santa Barbara County*, 2006; *Pulford v. County of Los Angeles* 2004; *Eriksson v. Munnink*, 2011; *Patel v. ABC Unified School District*, 2011; *Rosencrans v. Dover Images*, 201; *Cooper v. Aspen Skiing*, 2002; *Ormiston v. California Youth Soccer Association*, 2011; *Chavez v. City of Santa Fe Springs*, 2011; *Lotz v. The Claremont Club*, 2013; Eriksson v. Nunnink, 2015.

Colorado [33]
Enforces – Commercial & Non-Profit

The Colorado legislature passed a statute (**C.R.S. 13-22-107 [2003]**) that allows a parent to sign a waiver on behalf of a child releasing the provider from liability for ordinary negligence. An appellate court (*Wycoff v. Grace Community Church,* 2010), has since ruled that a parental waiver must clearly inform the parent of the risks of the activity. In more recent cases (*Squires v. Breckenridge Outdoor Education Center,* 2013; Hamill v. Cheley Colorado Camps, Inc., 2011), the courts found that the waiver adequately informed the parents of the risks and enforced the waivers.

Connecticut
Enforcement Doubtful – Commercial or Non-Profit
May Enforce Parental Indemnity Agreement

The *Fisher v. Rivest* (2002) court ruled that public policy supports the enforcement of waivers so that organizations such as Little League can continue to provide activities for youngsters. Since that time, two Supreme Court rulings may indicate that no sport- and recreation-waivers are enforceable (See Chap. 8). In similar cases involving parental indemnity, two courts have yielded conflicting rulings.

The *Saccente v. LaFlamme* (2002) and the *Keeney* v. *Mystic Valley Hunt Club, Inc.,* (2003) courts yielded conflicting rulings in two near-identical cases. *Saccente* enforced the **parental indemnity agreement** and held that parental immunity did not apply. The *Keeney* court did not enforce the contract saying that it was prevented by parental immunity.

A school girl was injured in a school trip to China (*Munn v. Hotchkiss School,* 2013). The U.S. District Court for the District of Connecticut relied on *Reardon* and *Hanks* in deeming the waiver against public policy; interestingly, the court did not address the fact that it was a parental waiver.

Delaware
Enforces – Commercial

A health club provided an indoor playground for the young children of clients; a 3-year-old fell and was injured. The Superior Court (a trial court; Delaware has no intermediate court) ruled that the waiver barred the mother's claims and protected the health club (*Hong v. Hockessian Athletic Club,* 2012).

---

[33] *Jones v. Dressel,* 1978; *Del Bosco v. United States Ski Assn.,* 1993; *Brooks v. Timberline Tours, Inc.,* 1996; *Cooper v. The U.S. Ski Asso.,* 2000; *Cooper v. Aspen Skiing Company,* 2002; *Pollock v. Highlands Ranch Community Association, Inc.,* 2006; **Squires v. Breckenridge Outdoor Education Center, 2013.**

Florida[34]
Does Not Enforce - Commercial
Enforces – Non-Profit
Enforces for Motor Sports – Commercial
Enforces – Arbitration Agreements

The Florida Supreme Court (*Kirton v. Fields*, 2008) has declared that parental waivers designed to protect commercial entities from liability for negligence are unenforceable. Parental waivers allowing a minor to participate in commonplace child-oriented community- or school-supported activities are enforceable as of now.

The Motorsport Non-Spectator Liability Release statute **(F.S. 549.09)** provides that parental waivers are enforceable for minor competitors in certain motorsport events.

F.S. 744.301 provides that the natural guardian, on behalf of the minor, may waive in advance any claim against a commercial activity provider resulting from the *inherent risks* of the activity. It defines inherent risks to include the failure of the provider to warn of the risks, negligent acts by other participants, and negligent acts by the minor child.

Georgia[35]
Possibly Enforces – Commercial & Non-Profit

In *Mays v. Valley View Ranch, Inc.* (2012), the court did not address the waiver in any detail, but ruled that the equine waiver was effective because it contained the warning required by the equine statute **(OCGA § 4-12-4)**. In two more recent cases involving minors, neither the minor status of the parties nor the validity of the waiver was not addressed and the ruling was based on assumption of risk in one case (*Christian v. Eagles Landing Christian Academy*, 2010) and Recreation Property Act immunity in the other (*Cooley v. City of Carrollton*, 2001). The first case involved a cheerleader injured while performing a stunt and the second involved a disabled minor in an afterschool recreational and swimming therapy program.

Three cases have indicated that Georgia courts might enforce pre-injury parental waivers. A parental waiver of varsity eligibility (*DeKalb County School System v. White*, 1979) and an indemnification agreement (*Geo. R. Lane & Associates v. Thomasson*, 1980) at an apartment complex were enforced. Also, in a pre-injury case where the waiver was signed by the minor only, the court (*Smokey, Inc. v. McCray*, 1990) stated it was significant that the waiver was signed only by a minor. While none of these is definitive, there seems to be a good chance that the court would support a pre-injury parental waiver.

---

[34] *Goyings v. Jack and Ruth Eckerd Foundation*, 1981; *O'Connell v. Walt Disney World Co.*, 1982; *Carlisle v. Ulysses Line Ltd.*, 1985; *Global Travel Marketing, Inc, v. Shea*, 2005; *Gonzalez v. City of Coral Gables*, 2004; *Lantz v. Iron Horse Saloon, Inc.*, 1998; *Fields v. Kirton*, 2007; *Krathen v. School Board of Monroe County, Fla.*, 2007; *In Re the Complaint of Royal Carribean Cruises LTD*, 2005; *In re: The Complaint of Royal Caribbean Cruises*, 2006; *Applegate v. Cable Water Ski, LC*, 2008.
[35] *DeKalb County School System v. White*, 1979; *Smokey, Inc. v. McCray*, 1990; *Geo. R. Lane & Associates v. Thomasson*, 1980; *Cooley v. City of Carrollton*, 2001; *Meredith and Durhamtown Plantation v. Meredith*, 2011; *Christian v. Eagles Landing Christian Academy*, 2010.

Hawaii
Does Not Enforce – Commercial or Non-Profit

Two statutes are applicable. The first **(HRS 663-10.95)** reads that a motorsport facility waiver attempting to protect the facility from liability for negligence against a minor is unenforceable against the minor or his/her representative. The statute also prohibits the enforcement of motorsport indemnity agreements against minors. The second statute **(HRS 663-1.54)** seems to say that waivers will protect only against the inherent risks of recreational activity – not negligence.

Idaho
Status Unclear - Commercial

A minor (*Davis v. Sun Valley Ski Education Foundation, Inc.*, 1997) was injured when she went off the course training for a ski race. She and a parent had signed a waiver, but it was not upheld due to the wording of the waiver. Minor status was not addressed which would seem to indicate that the waiver might have been enforced if wording had been acceptable.

Illinois[36]
Does Not Enforce – Commercial or Non-Profit
Enforces – Parental Equine Waivers

Neither a parent nor guardian has authority to release, waive, or compromise a child's legal right of action (*Meyer v. Naperville Manner, Inc.*, 1994) Even if parent is appointed guardian, the court must approve any agreement. The *Wreglesworth* Court held that the same is true for indemnity agreements. **745 ILCS 47/1-15** allows parental equine waivers.

Indiana[37]
Enforces – Commercial &Non-Profit
Enforces – Motorsport Waiver for Emancipated Minor

In a 2012 parental waiver case (*Wabash County Young Men's Christian Association v. Thompson*, 2012), a mother signed a waiver so that her daughter could play softball. The appellate court stated that **Ind. Code 29-3-9-7(b)** requiring court approval for post-injury settlements does not apply to pre-injury waivers; the court subsequently held that pre-injury parental waivers are valid. Interestingly, the waiver was not upheld because the waiver did not clearly specify that it protected against negligence by the provider.

In a 2014 skiing case (*Sauter v. Perfect North Slopes*, 2014), a U.S. District Court ruled a parental waiver to be unenforceable because of ambiguity in its wording. From the approach and discussion by the court, it appears that if the waiver had been unambiguous, it would have been enforced in favor of the commercial entity, Perfect North Slopes.

---

[36] *Wreglesworth v. ARCTO, Inc.* 2000.
[37] *Huffman v. Monroe County Community School*, 1991; Stowers v. Clinton Central School Corporation, 2006).

An Indiana Statute **(I.C. 34-28-3)** provides that minors who have been emancipated in order to participate in automobile or motorcycle racing may not avoid a contract, a liability release, or an indemnity agreement by reason of the minor's age.

Iowa[38]
Does Not Enforce – Commercial or Non-Profit

A mother signed a waiver for an **educational field trip**. The court (*Galloway v. State of Iowa*, 2010) ruled that pre-injury parental waivers are unenforceable because of public policy.

Kentucky
Status Unclear – Commercial & Non-Profit

Parental waivers for equine activities that contain the warning specified in the equine statute and signed by the parent/guardian are enforceable for inherent risks, but not for negligence **(KRS 247.4027(2)a).** No cases have been found indicating how courts will react to parental waivers in other activities.

Louisiana
Does Not Enforce – Commercial or Non-Profit

The limitation of liability for causing physical harm to another party is null by statute **(La. Civ. Code art. 2004)** for both adults and minors.

Maine[39]
Does Not Enforce – Commercial or Non-Profit
Enforces Parental Indemnity Agreement

The court in *Rice v. American Skiing Company* (2000) held that the right of the infant to his negligence claim was paramount, thus the parental waiver was unenforceable.

Courts may uphold an **indemnification agreement** that expressly indemnifies the indemnitee against its own negligence in a manner that clearly reflects the mutual intent of the parties. "A clear reflection of mutual intent requires language from the face of which the parties unambiguously agree to indemnification for indemnitee negligence" (*Rice*).

Maryland
Enforces – Commercial & Non-Profit

The Court of Appeals of Maryland, Maryland's highest court, has stated that the General Assembly has passed statutes that empower parents to exercise authority on behalf of their minor children on the most important aspects of a child's life, including education, medical treatment, immunizations, and religion. The court continued by saying that the Court will defer to a parent's determination that the potential risks

[38] *Lathrop v. Century Inc.*, 2002
[39] *Doyle v. College*, 1979.

of a recreational activity are outweighed by the possible benefit to the child. The court said that such a waiver was not a "transaction affecting the public interest." On that basis, the Court elected to enforce liability waivers signed by parents on behalf of minor children (*BJ's Wholesale Club, Inc. v. Rosen, 2013*). The Court also stated that the distinction between commercial and non-commercial entities (a distinction held in many jurisdictions) is without support in Maryland.

Massachusetts[40]
Enforces – Commercial & Non-Profit
Enforces – Parental Indemnity Agreement

Massachusetts courts (*Sharon v. City of Newton*, 2002; *Vokes v. Ski Ward, Inc.*, 2005) uphold parental waivers. The court said state law presumes that fit parents act in furtherance of the welfare and best interest of their children. Parents make decisions regarding care, custody, & upbringing of their children. Decisions regarding risk comports with the fundamental liberty interest of parents in rearing their children. The court in *Quirk v. Walker's Gymnastics and Dance* (2003) held "such waivers are clearly enforceable even when signed by a parent . . .," but noted that a waiver with the minor's signature alone would not be enforced.

The *Eastman* court ruled that an **indemnity agreement** was enforceable saying such clauses are to be fairly and reasonably construed to determine the intent. The clause was deemed enforceable provided defendant violated no statutory duty.

Michigan[41]
Does Not Enforce – Commercial or Non-Profit
May Enforce – Indemnification Clause

The Michigan Supreme Court (*Woodman v. Kera, LLC d/b/a Bounce Party*, 2010) ruled that parental waivers are not enforceable because a parent has no authority to waive the rights of to the child. Note: One Justice, in a footnote, stated that a parent can contract to **indemnify** the defendant for losses arising from injuries to the child.

Minnesota[42]
Enforces– Commercial

The appellate court in *Moore v. Minnesota Baseball Instructional School* (2009) enforced a waiver signed by the parent of the injured minor. The issue of minor status was not raised. In a more recent case (*Salinger v. Leatherdale*, 2012), an appellate court upheld a waiver signed by a parent on behalf of a 12-year-old daughter. The waiver successfully protected against ordinary negligence, but not against gross negligence. Furthermore, Subdivision 2 of **MN ST 604.055** defines "party" to include "a minor or another who is authorized to sign or accept the agreement on behalf of the minor." Thus, the statute provides for the enforcement of parental waivers.

---

[40] *Eastman v. Yutzy*, 2001; *Quirk v. Walker's Gymnastics and Dance*, 2003; *Vokes v. Ski Ward, Inc.*, 2005.
[41] *Smith v. YMCA of Benton Harbor/St. Joseph*, 1996.
[42] *Wu v. Shattuck-St. Mary's School*, 2005; *Scoles v. Franzin*, 1991.

Mississippi[43]
Probably Does Not Enforce – Commercial or Non-Profit

In a 1948 case, the Mississippi Supreme Court held that neither minors nor their representatives can waive anything for them (*Koury v. Salk*). In a 1998 case (*Quinn v. Mississippi State University*, 1998), a baseball coach accidentally struck a boy with a bat while instructing on hitting. The father and son had signed a waiver that was not enforced because it was not clear as to what acts were contemplated by the parties. Minor status was not addressed which would seem to indicate that the waiver might have been enforced if the wording had been appropriate. However, in *Quinn*, a dissenting judge pointed out that a 12 year old cannot be bound by his signature and that a minor's representatives can waive nothing on behalf of the minor. He stated that for more than a century, the court has zealously protected the rights of minors.

Missouri
Status Unclear – Commercial & Non-Profit
Probably Does Not Enforce – Parental Indemnity Agreement

A minor was injured while jet skiing after his father signed an **indemnity agreement** (*Salts v. Bridgeport Marina, Inc.*, 1982). Missouri law does not favor indemnity contracts where parties are of unequal bargaining power. Despite the seemingly all-inclusive language of the agreement signed by the father, the court did not enforce the agreement since it felt the agreement did not show a "clear and unequivocal intent" of the father to act as the insurer of negligent acts of the marina.

Montana
Insufficient Information – Commercial or Non-Profit

Revised statutes **MCA Section 1. Section 27-1-753** and **MCA Section 2. Section 28-2-702** remove the previous prohibition on enforcement of waivers for sport and recreational activities. The statute does not address the enforceability of parental waivers but states "This section does not prohibit a written waiver or release entered into prior to engaging in a sport or recreational opportunity ...." It is possible that the statute could be read to apply to any participant, including minors.

Nebraska [44]
Status Unclear – Commercial & Non-Profit
Unclear – Parental Indemnity Agreement

Parental waiver and **indemnity agreement** was not ambiguous, but the indemnity depended upon who was negligent; thus the court could not rule. It seems to indicate that the indemnification part of the parental waiver would be enforceable.

---

[43] *Koury v. Salk*, 1948.
[44] *Poole v. South Plainfield Bd. of Ed.*, 1980; *Colfer v. Royal Globe Insurance*, 1986; *Fitzgerald v. Newark Morning Ledger Company*, 1970.

New Jersey[45]
Does Not Enforce – Commercial or Non-Profit
Enforces – Parental Arbitration Agreements

The New Jersey Supreme Court (*Hojnowski v. Vans Skate Park*, 2006) affirmed that parents have no authority to waive the rights of a minor child. The court did, however, enforce an arbitration agreement, ruling that there was no public policy prohibiting a change in forum.

New York[46]
Probably Does Not Enforce – Non-Profit
Does Not Enforce – Commercial
Does Not Enforce – Parental Indemnity Agreement

Although there have been several cases in which New York courts have ruled parental waivers unenforceable, a 2012 ruling by a U.S. District court allowed the enforcement of a waiver signed by a parent. In a complicated and confusing summer camp case (*Walker v. Young Life Saranac Village*, 2012), the court seems to have upheld a parental waiver in a questionable decision. The waiver did not include a specific mention of "negligence" or indicate protection against negligence was intended – a requirement, heretofore, mandated in New York. Additionally, there was confusion as to whether the waiver was prohibited by G.O.L. 5-326.

There have also been three significant decisions regarding the matter. The *Kaufman v. American Youth Hostels* court held that an infant does not have the capacity to bind himself and that agreement not to sue signed by parent and infant was voidable and not binding upon the minor. However, when the contract is to the infant's benefit, it is binding on the other party. In V*aldimer v. Mount Vernon Hebrew Camps*, the court held the **indemnification agreement** by the parent is unenforceable because the child can be penalized for the parent's indiscretion. Only a court can bind an infant to a contract settling an injury claim. The *Igneri* v. *Carnival Corporation* (1996) and *Smith v. West Rochelle Travel Agency* (1997) courts enforced contracts on cruise ship tickets for forum selection and a disclaimer of liability, respectively.

North Carolina
Enforces – Non-Profit
Probably Would Not Enforce – Commercial

A U.S. District Court enforced a parental waiver signed by the parent of a 15-year-old girl to participate in an obstacle course at a JROTC orientation program (*Kelly v. United States of America*, 2014). Since no previous North Carolina courts had ruled on the enforceability of a parental waiver, the federal court

---

[45] *Dinenno v. Lucky Fin Water Sports, LLC*, 2011; *Hojnowski v. Vans Skate Park*, 2005.

[46] *Applbaum v. Golden Acres Farm and Ranch*, 2004; *Cunningham v. State*, 1942; *Moore v. American Santic Line, Inc.*, 1941; *Valdimer v. Mount Vernon Hebrew Camps, Inc.*, 1961; *Kotary v. Spencer Speedway*, 1975; *Santangelo v. City of New York*, 1978; *Tepper v. City of New Rochelle School Dist.*, 1988; *Fugaro v. Royal Caribbean Cruises, LTD.*, 1994; *Rogowicki v. Troser Management, Inc.*, 1995; *Alexander v. Kendall Central School District*, 1995; *Igneri v. Carnival Corporation*, 1996; *Smith v. West Rochelle Travel Agency, Inc.*, 1997; *Kaufman v. American Youth Hostels, Inc.*, 1957; *Viteritti v. Baseball Heaven, LLC*, 2013; *Walker v. Young Life Saranac Village*, 2012.

considered the public interest in protecting the safety of minor children in programs like JROTC and the countervailing public interest in facilitating JROTC's ability to provide non-commercial services to children without the risks of overwhelming litigation costs. After studying arguments for each, the court felt the arguments for enforcement of parental waivers were more persuasive.

North Dakota
Enforces – Non-Profit
Probably Enforces – Commercial

The court in *Kondrad v. Bismarck Park Dist.* (2003) held that the clear and unambiguous waiver signed by the parent exonerates the Park District for injuries suffered during an after-school program. This ruling, made by a U.S. District court, seems to run counter to indications in state courts. In a subsequent case involving a minor, the court did not enforce the waiver because it was ambiguous (*Hillerson v. Bismarck Public Schools*, 2013). The court made no indication that minor status mattered.

Ohio[47]
Enforces – Commercial & Non-Profit

The Ohio Supreme Court (*Zivich v. Mentor Soccer Club,* 1998), stating that parents have a fundamental liberty interest in the custody and management of their children (e.g., religion, school, medical care, and discipline), ruled to enforce the waiver signed by the parent. The court endorsed the right of a parent to raise his or her child and held that parents have the authority to bind their minor children to agreements in favor of volunteers and sponsors of nonprofit sport activities involving ordinary negligence.

In addition, parental waivers signed in accordance with the state equine statute (**ORC 2305.321(2)(a)**) are enforceable.

Oregon
Does Not Enforce – Commercial or Non-Profit

In *Bagley v. Mt. Bachelor, Inc.* (2013), the focus was on the ratification of a waiver by a recently turned non-minor. The court made it clear that a minor has the option of disaffirming a parental waiver within a reasonable time after reaching the age of majority. It added that if the infant after attaining majority voluntarily receives performance in whole or in part from the other party to the contract, this will amount to ratification, thereby resulting in an enforceable waiver.

---

[47] *Zivich v. Mentor Soccer Club,* 1997; *Mohney v. USA Hockey, Inc.,* 1999; *Summers v. Slivinsky,* 2001; *Mohney V. USA Hockey, Inc.,* 2005; *Markowitz v. Bainbridge Equestrian Center,* 2007; *Walker v. Mahoning County,* 2009; *Wolfe v. AmeriCheer,* 2012.

Oklahoma
Does Not Enforce – Commercial or Non-Profit

The U.S. District Court for the Western District of Oklahoma addressed the question of the enforceability of parental waivers (*Wethington v. Swainson*, 2015). Since there was no relevant Oklahoma case law, the court had to predict how the Oklahoma Supreme Court would rule on the issue; the federal court held that the Oklahoma Supreme Court, recognizing its duty to protect minor children, would find the parental waiver unenforceable.

Pennsylvania [48]
Does Not Enforce – Commercial or Non-Profit

Parents do not have the authority to release the claims or potential claims of a minor and the minor can disavow waiver signed by the parent. In a case in which the mother signed a waiver for both minor's and mother's potential claim (*Simmons v. Parkette National Gymnastic Training Center*, 1987), the court ruled that the waiver was not enforceable against the claims of the minor. The waiver, however, did bar the mother's claim. For more information, see the Pennsylvania section in Chapter 9.

Rhode Island[49]
Probably Does Not Enforce – Commercial or Non-Profit

The Supreme Court of Rhode Island, in a non-sport post-injury case involving a five-year-old who was struck by a car while on his tricycle, stated that the rights of a minor are subject to the supervision of the court and must be protected by it (*Julian v. Zayre Corporation*, 1978). The court made clear that a parent cannot compromise or release a minor child's cause of action absent statutory authority. While this case involved a post-injury settlement release, the language of the court seems to indicate that the same ruling would hold for pre-injury releases or waivers. The Rhode Island statute **R.I. Gen. Laws §33-15.1-1** gives parents authority to make post-injury settlements for amounts of $10,000 or less.

Tennessee[50]
Does Not Enforce – Commercial or Non-Profit
Does Not Enforce – Parental Indemnification Agreements

A Tennessee court (*Childress v. Madison County*, 1989) has ruled that a parent or guardian of an infant or incompetent person cannot waive the rights of the infant or incompetent. The court in a case in which a 20-year-old mentally retarded student almost drowned while training ruled that **indemnity agreements** signed by a parent or guardian are invalid as they place the interests of the child or incompetent against those of the parent or guardian.

---

[48] *Apicella v. Valley Forge Military Academy*, 1985; *Shaner v. State System of Higher Education, No.1541 S 1989*, 1998; *Morrow v. Norwegian Cruise Lines Limited*, 2002; *Emerick v. Fox Raceway*, 2004; *Mavreshko v. Resorts USA, Inc.*, 2008.
[49] *Childress v. Madison County*, 1989
[50] *Rogers v. Donaldson- Hermitage Chamber of Commerce*, 1990; *Cave v. Davey Crockett Stables*, 1995.

Texas[51]
Does Not Enforce – Commercial or Non-Profit

In *Paz v. Life Time Fitness* (2010), the court held that a parental waiver is not enforceable in Texas. The child was injured in a summer day camp at a health club. The court in *Munoz* said that **Family Code 12.04 (7)** giving the parents the right to make decisions of substantial legal significance does not extend to the authority to waive the rights of the child. Such would be against the public policy to protect children.

Utah[52]
Does Not Enforce – Commercial or Non-Profit
Does Not Enforce – Parental Indemnity Agreements
Enforces for Equine Waivers – Both Commercial & Non-Profit

In a case in which the rider was injured when the horse was spooked, the Supreme Court (*Hawkins v. Peart*, 2001) ruled that a parent may not release a minor's prospective claim of negligence prior to or after injury. It also held that **indemnification** by a parent violates public policy. The court noted: we cannot uphold an agreement that shifts the source of compensation from the negligent party to the parent.

The **Utah Equine Act (UCA § 78B-4-201-203 (2)(b)** has been amended to permit a parent to sign a waiver on behalf of a minor. (See also *Penunuri v. Sundance Partners*, 2013.)

Vermont
Status Unclear – Commercial & Non-Profit
Probably Does Not Enforce – Parental Waivers for Ski Resorts

With no applicable statutes or case law, there is no indication as to how the courts would rule on pre-injury waivers. While waivers are generally upheld, the Supreme Court (*Dalury v. S-K-I, Ltd*, 1995) held that waivers affecting large numbers of citizens (e.g., skiing) are not enforceable in some cases. Subsequently, a ski waiver for a minor would probably not be enforceable.

Virginia
Does Not Enforce – Commercial or Non-Profit
Enforces - Parental Waivers for Equine

The Supreme Court (*Hiett v. Lake Barcroft Community Asso.*, 1992) ruled that public policy forbids the use of pre-injury waivers of liability for personal injury due to future acts of negligence — whether for minors or adults.

As with waivers for adults, parental waivers are against public policy. However, the Virginia Equine Activity Statute **VCA § 3.1-796.132(B)** provides for an exception allowing enforcement of parental waivers used in equine recreational activities.

---

[51] *Lowery v. Berry*, 1954; *Munoz v. II Jaz Inc.*, 1993; *McClure v. Life Time Fitness, Inc.*, 2014.
[52] *Rutherford v.Talisker Canyons Finance Co., LLC*, 2014.

Virgin Islands
Probably Enforces – Commercial & Non-Profit

No case offering a definitive ruling on parental waivers was found. In *Joseph v. Church of God (Holiness) Academy* (2006), the waiver failed due to ambiguity; however, the court provided two statements that indicated that parental waivers might be enforceable. The court stated 1) once the school allowed the child to stay after school, they were obligated, absent a waiver, to provide supervision; and 2) that even if the waiver did not waive the rights of the child, it could be effective against the claims of the mother.

Washington[53]
Does Not Enforce – Commercial or Non-Profit

In *Scott v. Pacific West Mountain Resort* (1992), the court ruled that a waiver signed by a parent releasing a provider from liability for negligence was not enforceable against future claims of the minor, however, it could protect against any future claims of the parent. The *Wagenblast* court had earlier held that waivers requiring parents to release the school district from liability for future negligence are invalid because they violate public policy. The *Barber* court ruled that a mother's release did not extinguish the child's loss of consortium claim.

West Virginia
Does Not Enforce – Commercial or Non-Profit
Does Not Enforce – Parental Indemnity Agreement
Enforces – Indemnity Agreement (By Non-Parent/Guardian)

The court in *Johnson v. New River Scenic Whitewater Tours, Inc.* (2004) ruled that a waiver signed by a parent or another person (representing the parent) on behalf of a minor is voidable. Likewise, the court ruled that an **indemnification contract** by a parent would not be enforceable.

Wisconsin[54]
Enforces – Commercial

In the *Osborn v. Cascade Mountain, Inc.* (2002) ski-binding case, the court upheld the waiver stating that it is recognized that a parent may waive a child's claim. In both the *Yauger* and the *Fire Insurance Exchange* cases, the courts have said that parents can waive the claims of the child on some occasions. A caution, however, recent Supreme Court rulings have raised the bar for enforcement of any waiver.

Wyoming
Status Unclear – Commercial & Non-Profit

---

[53] *Wagenblast v. Odsessa Sch. Dist.*, 1989; *Barber v. Cincinnati Bengals, Inc.*, 1994.
[54] *Yauger v. Skiing Enterprises, Inc.*, 1996; *Fire Insurance Exchange v. Cincinnati Insurance Company*, 2000.

In an equestrian case (*Sapone v. Grand Targhee, Inc.*, 2002), a rider was injured when her horse bolted. Neither the waiver nor minor status was addressed, however, the waiver was apparently not upheld since the case was remanded.

Parental Indemnity Agreements

A second strategy employed to avoid provider liability has been the use of parental indemnity agreements – an agreement by which the parent agrees to repay provider expenses resulting from the participation of the minor. The Utah Supreme Court in *Hawkins v. Peart* (2001) examined the issue of whether the indemnity agreement between the parent and the provider was against public policy. The court concluded that such an agreement creates an unacceptable conflict of interest between the parent and the minor stating:

> We are extremely wary of a transaction that puts parent and child at cross-purposes and tends to quiet the legitimate complaint of the minor child. Generally, we may regard the parent's contract of indemnity ... as an instrument that motivates him to discourage the proper prosecution of the infant's claim.... The end result is either the outright thwarting of our protective policy, or, should the infant ultimately elect to ignore the settlement and to press his claim, disharmony within the family unit. Whatever the outcome, the policy of the State suffers (p. 17).

Courts in **Illinois**, **New York**, **New Jersey**, **Tennessee**, and **West Virginia** have also indicated that such agreements were unenforceable.

On the other hand, courts in at least four states seem to enforce parental indemnity agreements. In 2001, the *Eastman v. Yutzy* Court held that, in **Massachusetts**, an agreement was enforceable saying such clauses are to be fairly and reasonably construed to determine the intent. Shortly thereafter, a **Connecticut** court (*Saccente v. LaFlamme*, 2002) upheld a parental indemnity agreement. Since the *Saccente* case, however, the Connecticut Supreme Court has made two rulings that may well mean that no recreation- or sport-related waivers are enforceable in the state. (See the Connecticut section in Chapter 8 for more information on this development.) In addition, a **Maine** court stated that parental indemnity agreements are enforceable if the agreement is clear and well-written (*Rice v. American Skiing Company*, 2000). Likewise, a **Missouri** court has enforced a parental indemnity agreement (*Salts v. Bridgeport Marina, Inc.*, 1982).

Parental Arbitration Agreements

Cases in recent years have revealed a third tactic available to help service providers protect themselves against liability. The approach is to include within the participant agreement a **clause calling for mediation or binding arbitration** in the event of a claim. **Mediation** is a process in which a neutral mediator works collaboratively with the opposing parties to identify the areas of conflict and to assist them in reaching a settlement or agreement that is mutually satisfactory. It is a consensual, non-binding process. **Arbitration** is a process by which the parties to a dispute submit their differences to the judgment of an impartial person or group appointed by mutual consent or statutory provision. It can be binding or non-binding. One approach is to call for mediation to be followed by binding arbitration should an agreement not be reached. Arbitration does not relieve the provider of liability, but may result in the claim being addressed in an environment that is more favorable for the provider (see Figure 3.2).

The Federal Arbitration Act (9 U.S.C. Sec. 2 [2000]), which applies to both federal and state court proceedings, states a strong federal policy that favors the enforcement of agreements to arbitrate. It provides, however, that the Act may be unenforceable "upon such grounds as exist at law or in equity for the revocation of any contract." The Supreme Court (*Perry v. Thomas*) has held that state law is applicable if that law arose to govern issues concerning the validity, revocability, and enforceability of contracts.

For the service provider, mediation and arbitration have several advantages over going to trial. Some of them are: 1) each process is generally much less expensive; 2) less time is required for mediation or arbitration; 3) the service provider is more likely to avoid damaging publicity that will hurt the business; and 4) either process is usually friendlier and less formal than a trial.

An Ohio court (*Cross v. Carnes*, 1998) followed the lead of the *Zivich* court in holding that an arbitration agreement required prior to an appearance on the Sally Jessy Raphael television show was binding on the minor. The Florida District Court of Appeals (*Shea v. Global Travel Marketing, Inc.*, 2003), held that a tour contract signed by the mother waiving her son's right to sue a safari operator and agreeing to subject the son's claim to arbitration was against Florida public policy and unenforceable; however the Florida Supreme Court (*Global Travel Marketing, Inc. v. Shea*, 2005) subsequently reversed the decision holding that a parent has the authority to agree, on behalf of the minor, to arbitrate claims that might arise. The court went on to say that with no prohibiting legislation, such agreements in commercial travel contracts are not against public policy.

A 2006 New Jersey court held that "it has long been the law of New Jersey that without statutory authority or judicial authorization, a parent has no ability to release a claim properly belonging to a child."(*Hojnowski v. Vans Skate Park*, 2006) It went on to say that there is no New Jersey statute, rule, or decision that authorizes a parent "to sign a pre-tort agreement limiting the liability of a tortfeasor...." (p.22) However, the court did uphold the portion of the agreement whereby the parent agreed that any claim would be subject to arbitration. The court reasoned that the substitution of one forum for another has not been deemed to be against public policy.

All parental arbitration cases found (including several that are not sport- or recreation-related) are presented in Figure 3.2. Examination of the table shows that, thus far, the majority of states addressing

Figure 3.2
Arbitration Cases Involving Rights of Minors[55]

Minor Bound by Agreement		
Doyle v. Giuliucci	CA	1965
Leong v. Kaiser Fnd. Hosp.	HI	1990
Douglas v. Pflueger Hawaii, Inc.	HI	2006
Cross v. Carnes	OH	1998
Costanza v. Allstate Ins.	LA	2002
Hojnowski v. Vans Skate Pk.	NJ	2006
Global Travel Marketing, Inc. v. Shea	FL	2005
Minor Not Bound by Agreement		
Troshak v. Terminix	PA	1998
Accomazzo v CEDU	ID	2000
Lewis v. CEDU	ID	2000
Fleetwood v. Gaskamp	TX	2002

the issue tend to enforce parental arbitration agreements. Providers in California, Florida, Hawaii, Louisiana, New Jersey, and Ohio might expect such agreements to be enforced. Interested readers should

---

[55] *Doyle v. Giuliucci*, 1965; *Leong v. Kaiser Foundation Hospitals*, 1990; *Douglass v. Pflueger Hawaii, Inc.*, 2006; *Cross v. Carnes*, 1998; *Costanza v. Allstate Insurance Co.*, 2002; *Hojnowski v. Van's Skate Park*, 2006; *Troshak v. Terminix International Co.*, 1998; *Lewis v. CEDU Educational Services, Inc.*, 2000; *Accomazzo v. CEDU Educational Services, Inc.*, 2000); *Fleetwood Enterprises, Inc. v. Gaskamp*, 2002); *Global Travel Marketing, Inc. v. Shea*, 2005.

examine the advantages and disadvantages of arbitration to determine if it is right for their situation. Much information is available on the Internet.

Recommended Approach with Minors

The third question presented at the beginning of this chapter was "If waivers may not provide the liability protection needed, what can I do to protect myself and my business?" The answer is that there is no foolproof protection, even when waivers are allowed. The authors suggest a two-pronged approach toward liability protection when dealing with minor participants.

Institute a Risk Management Program

The first recommendation is that the service provider establishes and implements an ongoing, comprehensive risk management program. Explanation of a comprehensive risk management program is beyond the scope of this publication, but such a program includes such concepts as adequate insurance protection, risk reduction procedures, regular inspections and follow-up, development of emergency procedures, selection and training of staff, and much more. A knowledgeable consultant in sport risk management should be hired to help the provider establish a comprehensive program. A sound risk management program helps to reduce risks by reducing injuries and by having the provider prepared to deal properly with injuries that may occur. It manages risk relating to all clients – not just minors.

Utilize a Participant Agreement

The second recommendation is that the service provider requires that the parents or legal guardians of the minor sign a participant agreement – containing an assumption of risk, a waiver of liability, and an indemnification agreement. Make sure that the assumption of risk section of the agreement 1) presents a detailed description of the nature of the activity, 2) contains a representative list of the risks involved, 3) explains the types of injuries that can occur – ranging from minor to catastrophic, and 4) includes an assumption of risk statement (with an assertion by the parent that he/she has explained the risks to the child and the child understands). The participant agreement should include the signature of both the parents and the minor (if the minor is above age 10 or so). While it is not always practical, get the signature of both parents/guardians if possible.

For any chance of enforcement, **a parent (preferably both) must sign this document** – and as shown earlier, even then it may not provide for protection from liability for negligence in many states. While the agreement may not protect against the minor's negligence claims in many states, it will generally protect against negligence claims of loss suffered by the parents/guardians. It is likely to protect against liability for injuries resulting from the inherent risks of the activity. This document is discussed in detail in Chapter 5.

Use an Informed Consent or Agreement to Participate

Sometimes a provider is reluctant to use a participant agreement; an option to the second recommendation is to use an agreement to participate or an informed consent agreement – depending on the nature of the activity (both are described in detail in Chapter 4).

The **agreement to participate** is frequently used in conjunction with participation in recreational activities, physical education classes, and other physical activities. *It should be noted that this agreement primarily addresses only inherent risks and is not as strong as a participant agreement.* The agreement to participate is somewhat duplicative of the participant agreement, but some agreements to participate are more detailed and provide the participant with more information regarding risks of the program and prepare the participant to be better able to make an informed decision as to whether to participate. As with the participant agreement, both the minor and parents/guardians should sign.

The **informed consent** would be particularly appropriate if the minor is to undergo some type of treatment or training regime (e.g., the minor is to be treated for an injury by an athletic trainer; the minor is to undergo a training program developed by a personal trainer). This agreement is intended to protect the provider from liability for informed treatment risks associated with the treatment or training program. The informed consent should also be signed by the parents/guardians and the minor participant.

*****

The authors feel the participant agreement gives the provider the most protection from liability. It provides:

1) the possibility of negligence protection from the minor's claims of loss;
2) the likelihood of protection from the parents/guardians negligence claims for loss;
3) the likelihood of protection for both the parents'/guardians' and the minor's claims of loss resulting from the inherent risks of the activity, and
4) the likelihood of a stronger secondary assumption of risk defense.

Chapter 4

Informed Consents
And Agreements to Participate

This chapter discusses two of the documents mentioned in earlier chapters – the **informed consent** and the **agreement to participate**[56]. The former is intended to help protect the provider from liability for injuries resulting from the informed treatment risks of a program and the latter, from the inherent risks of an activity. **Informed treatment risks** are those risks associated with the treatment the client is undergoing (e.g., diet, conditioning program, rehabilitation program, physical therapy, research project) and about which the participant has been warned. **Inherent risks** of an activity are those that are normal or natural to that activity and cannot be eliminated without changing the primary nature of the activity. An injury resulting from an inherent risk would be one caused by an accident for which no one was at fault. Neither document has as its primary purpose to protect the provider from liability for injuries resulting from the negligence of the provider, its employees, or its agents. However, the agreement to participate can in some instances protect against or ameliorate liability for the negligence of the provider. (See the section on Agreements to Participate below.)

The **agreement to participate** is an agreement by which the signer is 1) made aware of and acknowledges understanding of the inherent risks of the activity and 2) is informed of the rules of the activity and behavioral expectations and agrees to abide by them. The agreement to participate is often used when persons are about to participate in an activity, sport, or class (e.g., extreme sport participants, physical education class members, participants in intramural or recreational programs). The agreement is based in tort law and does not constitute a formal contract; therefore it is an ideal instrument for dealing with minor participants. Like the informed consent, it provides little protection from liability for negligence. The agreement differs from the informed consent in that it is not a contract and nothing is *done to* the participant. Rather, the participant is *seeking to* participate. The purpose of the agreement to participate is to inform participants of 1) the nature of the activity, 2) the risks to be encountered through participation in the activity, and 3) the behaviors expected of the participant.

The **informed consent** is a document used to protect the provider from liability for the informed treatment risks of a treatment or program to which the signer is subjected. The thing that makes the informed consent unique is that another party **does something to the participant** with the consent of the participant. It may be in the form of medical treatment, rehabilitation, therapy, fitness testing, or a training program (e.g., when one is to be treated for an injury by an athletic trainer, when a participant is to undergo a training program developed by a personal trainer). The document informs the signer of the risks, thereby enabling the signer to make an educated, informed decision. The informed consent is based in contract law, thus the signing parties must be of age. If used with a minor, both minor and parent should sign the contract. Those relying on such agreements should keep in mind that the agreements (informed consent agreements?) suffer from the same limitations as parental waivers (see Chapter 3).

---

[56] Note: a reminder, the agreement to participate is not the same as the participant agreement to be discussed in Chapter 5.

The two documents differ in three ways: 1) the agreement to participate is used with participants and the informed consent is used with subjects in a treatment or training program; 2) the agreement to participate addresses the inherent risks of the activity while the informed consent focuses on the treatment risks of the program; and 3) the agreement simply informs and is appropriate for any age while the consent is a contract and inapplicable to minors without parental consent.

They are similar in that 1) both help to strengthen the primary assumption of risk defense; and 2) *neither is intended to provide protection against liability for ordinary negligence* by the provider. *Grace v. Kent State University* (2009) exemplifies an instance when, as one would expect, an informed consent fails to protect a provider against ordinary negligence. While one can assert the assumption of risk defense without documents, the availability of documents as evidence showing that the participant was informed of the risks, understood the risks, assumed those risks, and participated voluntarily notwithstanding the risks, can significantly strengthen the defense.

Informed Consent Agreements

The doctrine of informed consent derives from two principles: 1) a person's inherent right to control what happens to his or her body and 2) the physician's fiduciary duty to the patient -- to warn the patient of risks and make certain the patient knows enough to make an informed decision regarding his or her care. It is an ethical, moral, and legal concept that is ingrained in American culture.

There are two separate, but related, components of informed consent — **disclosure** and **consent**. (Nolan-Haley, J.M., 1999). The doctrine requires that those who consent be competent (i.e., of legal age, intellectually capable of consent), sufficiently informed about the treatment to enable an educated decision, and consent voluntarily with no duress (Koeberle and Herbert, 1998; Herbert and Herbert, 2002).

Informed consents originated with and have been primarily used in conjunction with the medical profession. They also gained more widespread use in the area of human subject research. The Office of Human Subjects Research of the National Institutes of Health outlines requirements for such research. The consent should 1) be obtained in writing, 2) be understandable, 3) be obtained in non-coercive circumstances, and 4) contain no language suggesting a relinquishment of rights.

Some of the elements that should be included in the consent are: 1) purpose and duration of the research, 2) description of the procedures, risks, and discomforts involved, 3) benefits and compensation to the subject, 4) alternative procedures, 5) confidentiality policies, 6) compensation and treatment available in event of injury, 7) who to contact for questions, and 8) a statement of voluntary participation. (The Office of Human Subjects Research) Some suggest that the document should be written at a level below that of a high school graduate — making liberal use of subheads, avoiding multi-syllable words when possible, and keeping sentences short and understandable.

In recent years, informed consents have been used more frequently in sport and fitness. Service providers are becoming more aware of the necessity of utilizing informed consents for participants in certain types of programs. Injury rehabilitation programs, fitness testing, and fitness regimens directed by personal trainers are three examples of situations in which the use of informed consents is becoming standard practice.

The informed consent in the fitness setting is described as "a voluntary agreement from a client who has been informed of, appreciates, and understands the material and relevant risks associated with participation in the activity or range of activities involved in exercise testing and activity provided through prescription."(Koeberle and Herbert, 1998, p.52) They suggest that informed consents in personal fitness settings do not require consent forms in the same detail as those required of physicians. The trainer is not held to a standard as high as that of the physician since activity programs contain a very low incidence of risk when compared to even the safest medical procedures.

The following guidelines for the content and administration of the informed consent for sport, recreation, and fitness activities are drawn from four sources (Herbert and Herbert, Koeberle and Herbert, Independent Review Consulting, Inc., 2000, Olivier and Olivier, 2001).

Content

The content of the informed consent for the recreation, fitness, and sport setting should include the following concepts and is illustrated in Figure 4.1:

- Be in writing on a pre-printed form.
- Be written in plain, understandable language.
- State the purpose of the exercise program, test, or prescribed action.
- Include a general description of the exercise program, test, or prescribed action.
- List any likely discomforts that might be associated with the program, test, or activity.
- List the potential risks and potential benefits of the exercise program, test, or activity.
- Be worded to allow all staff members to have physical contact or interact with the participant.
- Have participant acknowledge voluntary participation.
- Have participant acknowledge that consent was not signed under duress.
- Have participant acknowledge an opportunity to ask and gain answers to questions.
- Have participant acknowledge that the participant read and understood the informed consent.

Administration

The administrative procedures relating to the obtaining and handling of the informed consent can make a difference in the effectiveness of the agreement.

- A separate form should be used for each type of activity (e.g., exercise program, test, rehabilitation, fitness activity).
- The professional should explain the content of the informed consent and give the participant an opportunity to ask and have his or her questions answered satisfactorily.
- The consent form should be signed by the participant and professional, and dated.
- A copy of the consent should be provided to the participant.
- The signed and dated consent should be placed in the participant's file.
- If the subject is a minor, several additional steps are critical. 1) It is imperative that one, and preferably both, of the parents sign the contract. 2) The provider should use an informed consent written specifically for parents of minor subjects. 3) The consent should contain language directed to the parent by which the parent gives permission for the activity, acknowledges an understanding of the risks, and signs the agreement.

An illustrative informed consent for personal trainers is presented in Figure 4.1. This form is for illustrative purposes only and the reader is cautioned to consult a competent attorney for legal advice regarding such a form.

Documentation

Herbert and Herbert (2002) have written extensively about informed consents. They stress the importance of documentation and record keeping when working with individuals who have consented to programs. Just as physicians now must keep detailed notes on patient visits (e.g., complaints, treatments, responses to treatment, instructions), personal trainers, therapists, and other providers utilizing informed consents should do the same. While the extent of documentation required might not be the same, all documentation and notes can serve as evidence and can help the provider recollect the facts if called upon to testify in the event of litigation --- sometimes years later. Development and use of a standardized form that includes spaces for the date, signature, and notes is suggested.

Agreements to Participate

The agreement to participate, unlike the informed consent and the waiver, is not a contract. It is simply an agreement by which the participant is informed of the inherent risks of the activity and behavioral expectations of participants and affirms his or her assumption of the inherent risks and voluntary participation in the activity. However, like the informed consent, the signer 1) must have knowledge of the nature of the activity, 2) must understand the activity in terms of his or her own condition and skill, and 3) must appreciate the type of injuries that may occur. It is important to the provider that the participant understands these inherent risks and the provider should take steps (e.g., the agreement to participate) to insure this understanding. Since the agreement is merely informative in nature, it can be used when the participant or client is a minor. The signature of a parent is desirable from a public relations standpoint, but is not mandated (Cotten, 2007; van der Smissen, 1990).

The agreement has two major purposes. First, it helps to establish the primary assumption of risk defense by establishing that participation was voluntary and that the participant was aware of and assumed the inherent risks of the activity. It further serves to provide documentary evidence that can be used in court to show the participant was informed of the inherent risks. One should keep in mind, however, that an agreement to participate or an assumption of risk does not exculpate the provider from liability for negligence (*King v. University of Indianapolis*, 2002).

The second purpose is to help establish the secondary assumption of risk defense. **Secondary assumption of risk** is a form of contributory fault that involves the voluntary conduct of the participant to encounter a known or obvious risk created by the negligence of the service provider. By establishing that the participant was aware of and had agreed to the conduct expected, the secondary assumption of risk defense is strengthened because some of the responsibility for the safety of the participant is transferred to the participant. Whether the state is governed by contributory fault or comparative fault, the participant has a duty to protect himself or herself from unreasonable risk of foreseeable harm. If the participant acted in an irresponsible manner, departing from the expected behaviors, any award the participant might be due is subject to either be reduced or barred completely. It should be noted that the only effect an agreement to participate has on liability for injury caused by the negligence of the recreation, fitness, or sport business or its employees is to reduce the award (or in some cases, actually bar recovery) through contributory or comparative fault.

What to Include

The courts require no specific wording or ironclad format. However, certain information should be in any agreement to participate and the following format (illustrated in Figures 4.2 and 4.3) would serve as a logical order for inclusion.

Section I: Nature of the Activity. Give a detailed description of the specific activity involved. The description should be specific to the activity and not generic in nature. It should include a description of the nature of the activity, giving more detail when the participants may not be familiar with the activity. Include negative or un-pleasurable aspects that the participant should expect, how much physical stress is involved, and the intensity level of the activity.

Begin the description with a general introductory statement. A typical one is "Every physical activity has certain inherent risks and regardless of the precautions taken, it is impossible to ensure the safety of the participant."

Section II: Possible Consequences of Injury. Two areas should be covered in this section. First, include some of the injuries that can occur in the particular physical activity. List some minor injuries that are common (*e.g.*, bruises, strains, pulled muscles, sprains), some more serious injuries (*e.g.*, ruptured disks, broken bones, concussions), as well as catastrophic injuries (*e.g.*, paralysis and death).

Second, the participant should be made aware of the types of accidents that may occur in the specific physical activities involved. Here one should list some insignificant accidents that are common to the activity (slips while performing aerobics), as well as some serious accidents that occur occasionally (losing control of weights so that they fall on the lifter).

Use phrases such as "some of the...", "injuries such as ...", and "including, but not limited to ..." in listing both accidents and injuries. It is critical that the accidents and injuries be specific to the activity for which the agreement applies. Generic agreements to participate are less effective because one of the purposes of the agreement to participate is to show that the participant was aware of the specific risks of the particular activity.

Section III: Behavioral Expectations of the Participant. One should list on the agreement to participate several very important safety rules to which the participant is expected to adhere. Examples might be that racquetball players are required to wear eye protection at all times and those exercising are expected to wear support belts when lifting weights.

A few rules may be listed on the front of the agreement. If there are numerous rules, the participant should be referred to the back of the sheet where they are listed. In either case, give the participant a copy of these rules. Once again, do not attempt to make the list all-inclusive. Use phrases such as "Some of the rules which the participant agrees to follow...."

Section IV: Condition of the Participant. Have the participant affirm that he or she possesses the physical condition and required competencies to participate in the activity safely. The required level of condition or skill will vary with the activity and should be described in Section I of the agreement.

Include a statement by which the participant affirms possession of no physical conditions that would preclude participation in the activity. Have the participant list any conditions of which management should be aware (*e.g.*, heart problems, seizures, asthma). Particularly for vigorous activities, include a statement that the participant should discontinue the activity if undue discomfort or stress occurs. Participant affirmation of condition is generally adequate for activities such as 5K runs and health and fitness club memberships. Other situations might require more confirmation of condition. For example, residential camps usually require health histories and schools generally demand pre-participatory physical exams prior to varsity competition.

Section V: Concluding Statement. This concluding section should contain several items. First, include a statement by which the participant affirms knowledge, understanding, and appreciation of the inherent risks of the activity. Second, the participant should also affirm that participation is voluntary, if that is the case. Third, include an assumption of risk statement. Fourth, explain the procedures to be followed in the event of an emergency and the financial responsibility of the participant for emergency actions. Insurance requirements, if any, can also be specified here. Finally, a space for the signature of the participant and the parent (if the participant is a minor) should be at the bottom of the agreement. The critical signature is that of the participant/minor; however, the parent's signature is important for public relations purposes.

Section VI: Exculpatory Clause (Optional). If an exculpatory clause is included, it should be carefully worded to release the provider from liability for injury caused by the negligence of the provider or its employees. This section should follow the signature section of the agreement to participate and provide space for a second signature by the participant relating specifically to the exculpatory clause. If the participant is a minor, provide space for the parents' signatures as well.

While noted earlier that there is no particular format or wording dictated by law, a sample format including the critical information is illustrated in Figures 4.2 and 4.3. All information in italics is specific to the type of activity. The person preparing the agreement must substitute information specific to a particular activity when using this format as a guide. Remember, relying upon a generic agreement that attempts to include many or all activities will probably fail to provide the desired protection.

Section VII: Parental Permission Form (Optional). This optional section merely gives permission for a minor to participate in the activity --- strengthening neither the primary nor secondary assumption of risk defense. Contrary to widespread belief, neither the parent nor child is giving up the right to file suit in the event of injury due to negligence. The only way the parental permission form can provide liability protection from negligence is if it includes exculpatory language. In *Sweeney v. City of Bettendorf* (2009), a permission slip was used which included the following exculpatory language: "I realize that the Bettendorf Park Board is not responsible or liable for any accidents or injuries that may occur …." (p. 2)

The permission form has some public relations value in informing the parent of the activity in which the child will be participating and can be used to gain permission for emergency medical treatment, to assign financial responsibility for such treatment, and to obtain permission for the use of the participant's name and photograph. It can be useful as a component of the agreement to participate when the participant is a minor.

Using the Agreement

The following are some suggested guidelines for using the agreement to participate. They can help to insure the effectiveness of the agreement in strengthening the assumption of risk and the contributory negligence defenses.

•   Accompany the presentation of the agreement with a verbal explanation of the risks participants will encounter through participation and inform them of their responsibility for their own safety.

•   Provide an opportunity for the signer to ask questions and gain clarification.

•   Stress the participant's duty to inform you of any dangerous practices, hazardous conditions, or faulty equipment of which they may become aware while participating. This, however, in no way reduces or relieves the provider of its duty to inspect the facility, examine the equipment, or supervise the activity.

•   Be certain the language used in both the agreement and the verbal explanation is appropriate to the age and maturity of the participant.

•   Keep in mind that the agreement to participate can serve as important evidence in the event of a lawsuit. These records should be safely stored so that they may be retrieved when needed. The time during which a person may file a timely suit varies from one to four years after the injury, depending upon the state. However, keep in mind that a minor who is injured can generally file a suit until one to four years after reaching the age of majority. So in the event of an injury, it would be helpful to make and carefully store a file on that individual which would include the agreement to participate along with all other pertinent documentation (e.g., accident report, witness statements, parental permission slips).

Disclaimer

The information in this book is intended as accurate and authoritative educational material relative to liability waivers and other protective documents. It is sold with the understanding that the authors and publishers are not engaged in rendering legal advice. Readers requiring legal advice should consult an attorney who is competent in this area.

The reader is reminded to re-read the **What do I do with this book?** section of the **Preface** before writing or modifying one of the documents discussed in this chapter. Remember, all agreements should be customized to the activity and to the laws in your state. Even then, one is never guaranteed protection. The authors do not guarantee the effectiveness of any agreements presented in this chapter or developed from the information presented.

Figure 4.1
Informed Consent Agreement
Health & Fitness Club

Introduction

This is an agreement between the client and Health & Fitness Club (hereafter referred to as H&FC) The purposes of this agreement are 1) to affirm that H&FC has fully informed the client of the risks and benefits of the H&FC Personal Fitness Training Program offered by H&FC and one of the personal fitness trainers employed by H&FC and 2) to affirm that the client voluntarily consents to the risks involved in the H&FC Personal Fitness Training Program.

Program Objectives

I understand that the H&FC Personal Fitness Training Program is individually tailored to meet the goals and objectives agreed upon by my personal fitness trainer and myself. I understand, however, that neither my personal fitness trainer nor H&FC can guarantee that I will accomplish the goals that I establish. My program goals include (please initial all that apply):

_____ Cardiovascular improvement   _____ Improved muscular endurance
_____ Increased strength   _____ Improved flexibility
_____ Decreased body fat   _____ Weight loss
_____ Other _____

_____

Description of the Exercise Program

I understand that my exercise program can involve participation in a number of types of fitness activities. These activities will vary depending upon the objectives that my personal fitness trainer and I establish, but can include:

1) Aerobic activities including, but not limited to, the use of treadmills, stationary bicycles, step machines, rowing machines, and running track;
2) Muscular endurance and strength building exercises including, but not limited to, the use of free weights, weight machines, calisthenics, and exercise apparatus;
3) Nutrition and weight control activities; and
4) Selected physical fitness and body composition tests, including but not limited to strength tests, cardiovascular fitness tests, and body composition tests.

Description of Potential Risks

I understand that neither H&FC nor my personal fitness trainer can guarantee my personal safety because all exercise programs have inherent risks regardless of the care taken by a personal fitness trainer. **I will initial the types of activities (including a sample list of their risks) that my trainer and I have selected for my program to acknowledge that I understand the potential risks of my training program.**

_____ **Aerobic Activities:** I realize that participation in any cardiovascular activity involves sustained, vigorous exertion which places stress on the muscles, joints, and cardiovascular system, sometimes resulting in injuries ranging from common minor injuries (e.g., muscular soreness, strains, and sprains) to the infrequent more serious injury (e.g., torn ligaments, torn tendons, joint injuries, heat related injuries, stress fractures) to the rare catastrophic incident (e.g., heart attack, stroke, paralysis, death).

_____ **Muscular Endurance & Strength:** I realize that participation in muscular endurance and strength building activities involves repetitive exertions and maximal exertions which can result in stress-related injuries ranging from common minor injuries (e.g., muscular soreness, strains, and sprains, ligament and tendon injuries) to the infrequent more serious injury (e.g., torn rotator cuffs, herniated disks or other back injuries, crushed fingers) to the rare catastrophic incident (e.g., heart attack, stroke, paralysis, death).

_____ **Nutrition and Weight Control:** I realize that the nutrition and weight control program may involve a dietary change, selected nutritional supplements, and regular exercise. I also understand that no nutrition and weight control program is without risk and that some of the risks range from minor concerns (e.g., failure to achieve my goals, muscle soreness, strains) to the infrequent serious injury (e.g., physical reaction to food supplements or nutritional products, adverse body reaction to weight loss, eating disorders) to the rare catastrophic incident (e.g., heart attack, stroke, paralysis, death).

_____ **Fitness and Body Composition Tests:** I realize that participation in tests can result in injuries ranging from minor injuries (e.g., muscle soreness, strains, sprains) to the infrequent serious injury (e.g., torn ligaments, back injuries, herniated disks) to the rare catastrophic incident (e.g., heart attack, stroke, paralysis, death).

Description of Potential Benefits

I understand that a regular exercise program has been shown to have definite benefits to my general health and well-being. **I will initial the types of activities (including their benefits) that my trainer and I have selected for my program to acknowledge that I understand the potential benefits of my training program.**

_____ **Aerobic Activities:** loss of weight, reduction of body fat, improved appearance, improvement of blood lipids, lowering of blood pressure, improvement in cardiovascular function, reduction in risk of heart disease, increased muscular endurance, improved posture, and improved flexibility.

_____ **Muscular Endurance & Strength:** loss of weight, reduction of body fat, increased muscle mass, improved muscle tone, improved appearance, improvement of blood lipids, lowering of blood pressure, improved strength and muscular endurance, improved posture.

_____ **Nutrition and Weight Control:** loss of weight, reduction of body fat, improved appearance, less stress on joints, improvement of blood lipids, lowering of blood pressure, improvement in cardiovascular function, reduction in risk of heart disease.

_____ **Fitness and Body Composition Tests:** learn current status and gain information regarding areas needing improvement.

Client Responsibilities

I understand that it is my responsibility to
1) fully disclose any health issues or medications that are relevant to participation in a strenuous exercise program;
2) cease exercise and report promptly any unusual feelings (e.g., chest discomfort, nausea, difficulty breathing, apparent injury) during the exercise program; and
3) clear my participation with my physician.

Client Acknowledgments

In agreeing to this exercise program:
* I acknowledge that my participation is completely voluntary.
* I understand the potential physical risks and believe that the potential benefits outweigh those risks.
* I give consent to certain physical touching by my personal fitness trainer that may be necessary to ensure proper technique and body alignment.
* I understand that the achievement of health or fitness goals cannot be guaranteed.
* I have had a voice in planning and approving the activities selected for my exercise program.
* I have been able to ask questions regarding any concerns, and have had those questions answered to my satisfaction.
* I assert that I possess sufficient skill and fitness to participate, have no disability that might prevent my participation, and have been advised to consult a physician prior to beginning this program.
○ I have been advised to cease exercise at once if I experience unusual discomfort and feel the need to stop.

My signature below affirms that 1) I have read and understand this document; 2) I understand the risks and benefits of the H&FC Physical Fitness Training Program provided by H&FC; 3) I have been able to ask questions regarding any concerns I might have; 4) I have had those questions answered to my satisfaction; and 5) I am consenting and voluntarily participating in the H&FC Physical Fitness Training Program fully understanding the risks involved in training.

_____   _____   _____   _____   _____
Signature of Client   Name of Client (Print)   Date   Signature of Trainer   Date

Emergency Contact Person _____ Phone _____

Figure 4.2
Agreement to Participate
Aerobics[57] [58]

Participation in all sports and physical activities involves certain inherent risks and, regardless of the care taken, it is impossible to ensure the safety of the participant. *Aerobics* is an activity requiring *considerable coordination, agility, and a high level of cardiovascular exertion.* It may involve *static and dynamic stretching, vigorous activity for as long as an hour or more, and sustained periods of repetitive, cardiovascular activities.* While it is a reasonably safe activity as long as safety guidelines are followed, some elements of risk cannot be eliminated from the activity.

A variety of injuries may occur during *aerobic* activities. Some examples of those injuries are:
1. Common minor injuries such as *muscle strains, sprains, and muscle soreness*;
2. More serious, but rare, injuries such as *damaged ligaments, broken bones, and concussions*;
3. The very Very rare catastrophic injuries such as *heart attacks, paralysis, and death.*
These, and other injuries, sometime occur in *aerobics* as a result of hazards or accidents such as *slips, falls from loss of balance, falling on steps or other equipment, colliding with another participant, colliding with the wall, falling to the floor, or stress placed on the cardiovascular system.*

To help reduce the likelihood of injury to yourself and to other participants, participants are expected to follow the following rules: *All participants are expected to*:
1. Follow the instructions of the instructor.   *2. Wear proper clothing and footwear.*
3. Use care when using or near equipment.   *4. Follow all posted safety rules.*
I agree to follow the preceding safety rules, all posted safety rules, and all rules common to the activity of *aerobics*. Further, I agree to report any unsafe practices, conditions, or equipment to the instructor.

I certify that 1) I possess a sufficient degree of physical fitness to safely participate in *aerobics*, 2) I understand that I am to discontinue activity at any time I feel undue discomfort or stress, and 3) I will indicate below any health-related conditions that might affect my ability to participate in *aerobics* and I will verbally inform the instructor immediately.
Circle: Diabetes   Heart Problems   Seizures   Asthma   Other _____

I have read the preceding information and it has been explained to me. **I know, understand, and appreciate the risks associated with participation in *aerobics* and I am voluntarily participating in the activity. In doing so, I am assuming all of the inherent risks of the sport.** I further understand that in the event of a medical emergency, *management will call EMS to render assistance and that I will be financially responsible for any expenses involved.*

_____	_____	_____
Name of Participant (Print)	Signature of Participant	Date

WAIVER OF LIABILITY: In consideration of being permitted to participate in *aerobics,* on behalf of myself, my family, my heirs, and my assigns, I hereby release the *club*, its agents, and its employees from liability for injury, loss, or death to myself, while *using the facility, equipment, or in any way associated with participating in the activity of aerobics now or in the future,* resulting from the ordinary negligence of the *club*, its agents, or employees.

_____	_____	_____
Name of Participant (Print)	Signature of Participant	Date

---

[57]All language indicated by italics should be modified and customized to the sport or activity involved.
[58]This agreement to participate is designed to be used with an adult client. See the next page for a modification to be used with minors.

Figure 4.3
Agreement to Participate
Annual 5K Fun Run
(For Use with Minor Participants)

All physical activities involve certain inherent risks. Regardless of the care taken, it is impossible to ensure the safety of all participants. The *5K Fun Run* is a vigorous, cardiovascular activity requiring *sustained running endurance, coordination, and running skill.* While the *Club* is using care in conducting the event, it is unable to eliminate all risk from the activity.

It is possible for *runners* to suffer common injuries such as *cramps, muscle strains, and sprains.* More serious, but less frequent, injuries such as *broken bones, cuts, concussions, heart attacks, strokes, paralysis, and death* may also occur. These injuries, and others, may result from such incidents as (but not limited to) *slips and falls, tripping, colliding with another runner, imperfections in the street surfaces, heat-related illnesses, and stress placed on the cardiovascular system.*

All *runners* are expected to follow these safety guidelines:
1. *Wear proper footwear.*   2. *Be alert for unanticipated hazards on the course.*
3. *Do not crowd other runners.*   4. *Consume adequate liquids during the run.*
5. *Follow all announced or posted rules.*
I agree to follow the preceding safety rules, all posted safety rules, and all rules common to *running.* Further, I agree to report any unsafe practices, conditions, or equipment to the *race* management.

I certify that 1) I possess a sufficient degree of physical fitness to safely participate in *the 5K Fun Run,* 2) I understand that I am to discontinue *running* at any time I feel undue discomfort or stress, and 3) I will indicate below any health-related conditions that might affect my ability to safely *complete the run* and I will verbally inform activity management immediately.
Circle: Diabetes   Heart Problems   Seizures   Asthma   Other _____

I have read the preceding information and my questions have been answered. **I know, understand, and appreciate the risks associated with *distance runs* and I am voluntarily participating in the activity. In doing so, I am assuming all of the inherent risks of the sport.** I further understand that in the event of a medical emergency, *management will call EMS to render assistance and that I will be financially responsible for any expenses involved.*

Signature of Participant	Date	Name of Participant (Please Print)
Signature of Parent	Date	Name of Parent (Please Print)
Signature of Parent	Date	Name of Parent (Please Print)

WAIVER OF LIABILITY: In consideration of being permitted to run in the *5K Fun Run,* on behalf of myself, my family, my heirs, and my assigns, **the undersigned Participant and Parent or Guardian hereby release the *club* from liability for injury, loss, or death** to the minor, while *participating in the run or while in any way associated with participating in the event now or in the future,* **resulting from the ordinary negligence of the *club*, its agents, or employees.**

Signature of Participant	Date	Name of Participant (Please Print)
Signature of Parent	Date	Name of Parent (Please Print)
Signature of Parent	Date	Name of Parent (Please Print)

Chapter 5

Steps for Writing the Stand-Alone Waiver
(Participant Agreement)

Writing or obtaining a good, enforceable waiver or participant agreement is not easy, but it is also not impossible. Note that in this book, the terms "participant agreement" and "waiver" will often be used interchangeably. The following quote from the *Cohen v. Five Brooks Stable* (2008) court provides valuable insight into the art of writing waivers.

> While it is true, as we have seen, that California courts hold releases of liability to a high standard of clarity, it does not in our view require Olympian efforts to meet the standard. An effective release is hard to draft only if the party for whom it is prepared desires to hide the ball, which is what the law is designed to prevent. A release that forthrightly makes clear to a person untrained in the law that the releasor gives up any claim against the releasee for the latter's own negligence . . . or that the releasee cannot be held liable for *any and all risks* the releasor encounters while on the former's premises or using its facilities . . . , ordinarily passes muster (p. 27-28).

However, it is important that one who is depending upon a waiver for liability protection realize that even a good waiver is not always enforced by the court. This chapter contains many guidelines that will help

---

Disclaimer

The information in this book is intended as accurate and authoritative *educational material* relative to liability waivers and other protective documents. It is sold with the understanding that the authors and publishers are not engaged in rendering legal advice. Readers requiring legal advice should consult an attorney who is competent in this area.

These guidelines, illustrative waiver language, and other illustrative agreements are based upon case law and, in the judgment of the authors, should, when customized to a specific business and situation, afford the provider with protection from liability for injuries resulting from the inherent risks of the activity and the ordinary negligence of the provider in most states and under most circumstances. *Although the authors have tried to identify and interpret the waiver law in each state, some important information could have been missed, misinterpreted, or could have changed since publication. Neither the accuracy nor the effectiveness of the guidelines or anything else in this book is guaranteed.* Further, there is no guarantee that documents developed from these guidelines will afford the sought-after protection to the provider.

If recreation, fitness, or sport professionals (or others without legal training) use this material to develop a waiver, participant agreement, or other document, the authors advise you to **consult a local attorney** who is knowledgeable about and has experience with contracts and sport, fitness, and recreation-related liability waivers. Have the attorney examine your finished agreement and make adjustments where necessary.

---

the party preparing a stand-alone waiver avoid many pitfalls, but in no way does it ensure that a waiver will be enforced (see Figure 6.1 for a comparison of waiver formats).. Adhering to the guidelines increases the likelihood that the waiver will provide liability protection if challenged.

The Participant Agreement

A current trend in waiver construction is to increase the breadth and effectiveness of the waiver by its inclusion in a document called a participant agreement. The **participant agreement** *is a document that combines a waiver, an assumption of risk agreement, an indemnification agreement and other protective language into one stand-alone document that provides for an exchange of information between provider and client and helps to establish a better rapport and friendlier relationship between the provider and client.* It is intended to protect against liability for injuries resulting from both the inherent risks of the activity and from the ordinary negligence of the provider.

Charles R. Gregg and Catherine Hansen-Stamp, former editors of the *Outdoor Education and Recreation Law Quarterly* and Program Co-Chairs of the *Recreation & Adventure Program Law & Liability Conference*, have listed several functions of the participant agreement:

1) It can serve to improve the rapport and understanding between provider and participant;
2) It increases the understanding of the rewards and activity risks of the participants, prepares them psychologically for any discomforts, and makes legal action less likely;
3) It allows participants to make more informed decisions as to participation;
4) Its mere existence can deter a party from filing a claim; and
5) If a suit is filed, it provides the potential for early dismissal of the case. If the suit proceeds, the participant agreement can serve as evidence that the participant was aware of the risk and had assumed some or all of the risks.

The participant agreement is intended to help protect the service provider from liability for two causes of injury – inherent risks and ordinary negligence. The agreement has several sections, but three are most important. First, the **assumption of inherent risks section** is intended to help protect the provider from liability for injuries resulting from the inherent risks of the activity. Generally, the provider is not liable for inherent risks and needs no protection from injuries caused by these risks *so long as participation was voluntary and the participant was aware of and appreciated the risks.* The assumption of inherent risks section informs the participant of the inherent risks of the activity and the behavioral expectations placed on the participant. It also secures an affirmation that participation is voluntary and that the participant knows, understands, and appreciates the risks of the activity. This part of the agreement helps to solidify the primary assumption of risk defense for injuries resulting from inherent risks and may also offer some protection from ordinary negligence based upon secondary assumption of risk or contributory fault (see Agreements to Participate in Chapter 4).

Second, the **waiver section** helps to protect the provider against liability for the second cause of injury – the ordinary negligence of the provider, its employees, and its agents. In the waiver, the participant relieves the provider of liability for injuries resulting from the ordinary negligence of the provider. The waiver section does not generally provide liability protection for extreme acts such as gross negligence. In the past, many providers have failed to make use of waivers, thinking they were not effective. Today, however, providers of recreation, fitness, and sport services generally recognize that such agreements can be effective in limiting liability. It is worth noting that in some cases in which a waiver does not protect against liability for provider negligence, the agreement does help protect the provider from liability for reasons other than the defendant's negligence (*Glenn v. Annunziata*, 2010).

Third, the indemnification agreement can provide added protection in many instances. An **indemnification agreement** is a contract signed prior to participation by which the participant or another party agrees to reimburse the provider for any monetary loss, including attorney's fees, incurred as a result of 1) injury to the participant or 2) injury or loss caused by the participant. For example, a parent might sign an agreement to reimburse a rafting company for loss due to litigation resulting from an injury to the minor child in exchange for the opportunity for the minor to participate in rafting. In another example, a facility operator or owner might ask the party desiring to lease the facility to agree to be responsible for any loss incurred by the facility owner resulting from injury or property damage occurring during the event. *This agreement can protect the service provider or property owner from liability for negligence by the party leasing the facility by shifting the financial responsibility to the leasing party.*

It is important to note, however, that indemnification agreements are traditionally agreements between two business entities. Courts in some states find indemnity agreements unenforceable when such agreements are between providers and participants (a business and an individual) where an individual is asked to indemnify a provider for the negligence of the provider.

Use of indemnity clauses in participant agreements may be particularly important in states that hold **loss of consortium** as an independent cause of action. In *Walsh v. Luedtke* (2005), the **Ohio** court held that the waiver signed by Walsh prior to a tractor pull contest protected against all of Walsh's claims; however, it provided no protection from the loss of consortium claim made by Walsh's wife. Fortunately for the defendant, the indemnity language within the waiver document stated clearly and without ambiguity, that Walsh would indemnify Luedtke for all claims. Consequently, any award granted to the wife would have to be repaid by the husband. In another similar case involving a go kart (*Beaver v. Foamcraft, Inc.*, 2002), the wife was injured. The court held that the waiver prevented the wife's claim, but had no effect on the **loss of consortium** claim made by the husband. The consortium claim, however, was countered by the indemnification agreement contained in the waiver in which the wife agreed to repay Foamcraft for any loss (including the claim of the husband).

Eleven Steps in Writing an Effective Stand-Alone Waiver (Participant Agreement)

The following steps include guidelines that one should consider when developing Participant Agreements or when evaluating such agreements currently in use. They have been drawn from court decisions throughout the United States. Following each set of guidelines is an example of how this step might appear in a waiver – but keep in mind that this is just an example and that there are many acceptable ways of expressing this language. While not all of the guidelines must be met for a participant agreement or waiver to be enforced, each represents an issue that has been challenged in previous cases involving waivers. And, as can be seen in Chapter 8, states differ considerably in the rigor required for a valid waiver, Rather than attempt to develop guidelines for each state, it seems more prudent and economical to develop one set of guidelines designed to withstand challenge even in the most rigorous states.

When using this book to develop a document for your business, *do not simply duplicate a waiver section from this book or any other source and use it.* One should study the guidelines and then adapt any waiver you use to your specific situation and conditions.

Step One
Understanding the Fundamentals of Waivers

The first step in developing a successful waiver or participant agreement is to learn as much as you can about liability waivers. These initial guidelines involve general concepts that one should understand.

General Guidelines

1. **Remember that all waivers are not created equal.** Copying a waiver from a book, an article, a friend, or the Internet is risky business. A waiver does not suddenly become "good" by being published. For maximum effectiveness, your waiver should be written specifically for your business. Your best chance of success is either 1) to have a person (generally an attorney) who has written sport, recreation, or fitness waivers, is up-to-date on waiver law in your state, and is knowledgeable about your type of business prepare a waiver specifically for your business, or 2) prepare a waiver yourself from information gained in this book and then have the previously described, qualified attorney examine it.

2. **Create a friendly tone or ambiance.** The participant agreement should be approached and written in such a way as to develop rapport with the client. It should be written and presented in such a way that the patron understands that the waiver benefits both the patron and the provider. It should serve as a tool for information exchange.

3. **Avoid any untrue or fraudulent statements in the agreement.** A fraudulent statement or misrepresentation within the waiver can invalidate it. In a Wisconsin case (*Merten v. Nathan*, 1982), the waiver falsely stated that the business carried no liability insurance. The court said that this constituted fraud and rendered the exculpatory agreement ineffective. In a California case (*Sevilla v. Estate of Lynn Maxey Wiley*, 2004), a company selling sky diving trips stated in the waiver that it "did not provide insurance," but later admitted the statement was false. The court concluded that the act of signing the waiver gave inference that the passengers relied upon the false statement. The waiver was not enforced.

   It is worth noting, however, that erroneous statements do not necessarily void a waiver. In a Connecticut case (*Reardon v. Windswept Farm*, 2005), the plaintiff claimed the waiver was not enforceable because it cited a General Statute that had been renumbered and because one word was mistyped to say "provided" rather than "providing." The waiver was upheld.

4. **Do not state that participants have an "opportunity to inspect" facility if they do not**. In a Delaware case (*DeVeccio v. Delaware Enduro Riders, Inc.*, 2004), the court did not uphold a waiver because the waiver stated that participants have had an opportunity to inspect the track when, in fact, they were not allowed to inspect the track in advance. The court held that the waiver did not constitute a valid understanding between the parties. Likewise in an older Delaware case (*Hallman v. Dover Downs, Inc.*, 1986), a reporter was required to sign a waiver that included language stating he had inspected the premises and knew the risks – yet he could not enter the premises until he had signed the waiver. The court found the waiver unconscionable – in part, because Hallman's job required his attendance at the race, and also, because the waiver seemed designed for race drivers, not reporters.

5. **Do not promise safe participation or make assurances of participant well-being in your participant agreement**. Such assurances are likely to lead to a claim if there is an injury. In *Chavez v. City of Santa Fe* (2011), the trial court upheld the waiver; however, the waiver was

overturned by the appellate court, partially because promises that the minor would be safe and supervised "at all times" led the court to feel that evidence was such that a jury might rule gross negligence. In *Ledgends v. Kerr* (2004), the Alaska Supreme Court affirmed a lower court ruling in which the lower court said the release was inconsistent; it said the gym would try to keep its facilities safe and its equipment in good condition, but disclaimed liability for actions that failed to meet those standards. This conflict created an ambiguity that prevented enforcement.

However, such claims (lawsuits) do not always lead to awards to the plaintiff (*Isbell v. Carnival Corporation*, 2006). In *Isbell,* Carnival employees assured the plaintiff there were no concerns relating to snakes or reptiles, but the court enforced the waiver. Likewise, in a Minnesota case (*Hanson v. Northern J & B Enterprises*, 2009), employees assured the plaintiff that the assigned horse would be "safe and gentle," she would be "just fine," and that the horse would be "ok." The waiver stated the horses were chosen for their "calm dispositions." Plaintiff alleged that these statements constituted implied and express warranties. The courts in each case held for the defendants and enforced the waivers. See Chapter 7 for more information regarding assurances.

6. **Avoid conflicting wording within the agreement.** Conflicting language within a waiver can create ambiguity and result in the failure of a waiver. In a **Florida** case, Paragraph 7 of the agreement stated that protection was for "any cause not attributable to the willful gross negligence of the Marina" while Paragraph 8 refers to "any act or neglect of the Marina." The court interpreted Paragraph 8 to include either simple or gross negligence, which would contradict Paragraph 7 (*Sunny Isles Marina v. Adulami*, 1998). Similar conflicts may be found in two **Utah** cases (*Ghionis v. Deer Valley Resort Company*, 1993; *Zollman v. Myers*, 1997).

7. **Whenever possible, avoid requiring that clients sign two different waivers**. Just as with conflicting language within an agreement in guideline number 6, conflicting language between two or more waivers can result in ambiguity and failure of the waiver. Granted, in some cases the use of more than one waiver is necessary, but care must be taken to make certain identical exculpatory language is used.

Conflict between two documents was at issue in *Bergin v. Wild Mountain, Inc*. (2014). Bergin signed a waiver contained in the season pass agreement. The waiver included exculpatory language releasing Wild Mountain from liability for negligence. When he arrived at Wild Mountain, he was given a wallet-sized ski pass card with the following language on the back:

> I agree and understand that skiing and snowboarding involve the risk of personal injury and death. I agree to assume those risks. These risks include …. I agree to always ski and snowboard in control and to avoid these objects and other skiers. I agree to learn and obey the skier personal responsibility code.

Bergin contended that the waiver was ambiguous because the waiver agreement and the language on the back of the ski pass card differed. The court explained that the season pass card listed inherent risks and did not constitute a contract; it contained no offer by which Wild Mountain was legally bound.

Two documents were used in *Gorlin v. Jacobson* (2005): a riding agreement waiver and a boarding agreement liability provision. As to the effect of the conflict in wording between the two, the court ruled that the boarding agreement did not modify the riding agreement. In this case, the waiver was enforced, but one should realize that when two or more waivers are used, problems sometimes arise regarding conflicts in wording or intent and this conflict creates the possibility of ambiguity.

In *Lotz v. The Claremont Club* (2013), Lotz signed both a membership agreement and a waiver. The waiver contained language that negated any other release – "This Agreement constitutes my sole and only agreement respecting release, waiver of liability . . . ." The waiver was inconsistent saying in one paragraph that he was giving up his right to sue on behalf of his spouse; then in another paragraph he asserted that "his participation" was voluntary and he knowingly assumed all risks. These statements could have two reasonable interpretations, thereby were ambiguous and created a triable issue of fact.

8. **Address liability for inherent risks and ordinary negligence separately.** When providers try to protect against both liability for the inherent risks and liability for ordinary negligence in one brief exculpatory section, the chances of ambiguity increase greatly. This is particularly true if a phrase like "negligence of the provider" is not included in the language. An Oregon ski pass waiver provides a good example of this problem (*Steele v. Mt. Hood Meadows Oregon, Ltd.*, 1999; see also *Brown v. Columbus All-Breed Training Club*, 2003 and *Richards v. Richards*, 1994). The language used on the Mt. Hood pass was:

- The purchaser or user of this ticket accepts and assumes the inherent risks of skiing including man-made objects, changing conditions, natural obstacles, weather, and other skiers.
- All injuries must be reported to the area medical clinic.

  Contract of Release and Indemnification Agreement:
- In consideration for lift access, the holder of this lift ticket agrees to release and indemnify Mt. Hood Meadows from any claims for personal injury and loss of or damage to property arising in connection with or resulting from the use of this ticket or the area facilities.

The court pointed out the release language was immediately preceded by a long list of risks not stemming from the negligence of the ski resort – inherent risks. Given this stress on inherent risks of skiing, the court felt the ticket holder reasonably could have understood that the phrase "any claims for personal injuries" referred only to claims for injuries arising out of inherent risks – not operator negligence.

The waiver was not upheld, in part due to the resulting ambiguity. Two things could have helped to avoid the problem: 1) the inherent risks and the ordinary negligence risks should have been handled separately so that there was no confusion regarding the intent of the parties and 2) the phrase "any claims arising from the ordinary negligence of the operator" could have been used rather than "any claims for personal injuries." Even in states not requiring the use of the term "negligence," the use of the term "negligence" will help to clarify the intent of the waiver (*McDermott v. Carie*, 2005).

It is apparent from the *Steele* case that it is important that a participant agreement not devote a preponderance of its content to the assumption of inherent risks to the detriment of the exculpatory language. One should be certain the waiver of negligence language is separate, distinct, and not to be confused with the inherent risk language. In a Missouri case (*Frank v. Mathews*, 2004) involving horseback riding, the first half of the document warns of the inherent risks while only one sentence at the bottom of the page purports to release "any and all liability." The court stated that the waiver as a whole appears to waive any and all claims resulting from only the inherent risks of riding lessons.

Keep in mind, however, that the amount of content allotted to inherent risks need not be extensive to create ambiguity. In *Thompson v. Hi Tech Motor Sports* (2008), the waiver began by saying that a motorcycle was inherently dangerous and its operation may result in injury. It then waived "any claim." The Supreme Court decided that "any claim" referred to inherent risks – not negligence. Similarly, the problem in *UCF Athletics Association, Inc. v. Plancher* (2013) was that a paragraph outlining the inherent risks of the sport was followed by the statement "I understand that the possibility of injury . . . does exist even though proper rules and techniques are followed to the fullest." This was followed immediately by exculpatory language that did not specify "negligence." The court felt the clause did not expressly inform Freck that he would be contracting away his right to sue UCF for its own negligence.

9. **Include immunity statutes when required by the statute.** Some immunity statutes in some states specifically require that the statute or a particular statement from the statute be included in any liability waiver. This is frequently true of equine statutes.

10. **Re-visit your document periodically or when circumstances change.** In *Merten v. Nathan* (1982), the waiver stated that the business did not carry liability insurance. Although this was true when the waiver was written, the business later obtained insurance and failed to amend the waiver. The waiver was not enforced due to the fraudulent statement. In *Dobratz v. Thomson* (1990), the participant had signed a waiver, but since a new water show event was added months after he signed the waiver, the court did not enforce the waiver stating that he could not have agreed to accept the risks of the new event.

11. **A contract should set out the particular conditions to which it applies.** For example, it should specify the activity, events, and facilities to which the agreement applies. In *Arnold v. Shawano County Agric. Society* (1983), the court criticized a waiver used nationwide for failing to set out any conditions concerning the nature of the race and the facility where it took place.

12. **Avoid the Use of Multi-function Documents.** Waivers are sometimes designed to serve more than one function. For instance, the exculpatory language is sometimes included on an entry form, a membership contract, or equipment rental form; also, waivers often contain the rules of the operator or event. Many courts recommend that only exculpatory materials be included on the waiver.

    In *Benavidez v. The University of Texas – Pan American* (2014), the waiver document included on the back side a list of safety policies which the University promised to follow. The plaintiff claimed the waiver was not enforceable, alleging the University breached the contract by not following all of the safety policies. The court, fortunately for the University, ruled that the list of policies was not part of the contract, there was no breach, and the waiver was enforced. Restricting the document to the relevant exculpatory information would have avoided the problem.

    In *Kolosnitsyn v. Crystal Mountain, Inc.* (2009), the document, in addition to the waiver, included a receipt for payment, personal information of the renter, place for marking equipment rented, and place to note whether returned. The court implied that the exculpatory function of a multi-purpose document is more likely to be ambiguous. In *Porter v. Dartmouth College* (2009), the court, when examining another multi-function waiver, said that a reasonable person would not interpret the agreement to be anything more than a standard equipment manufacturer liability release.

13. **Call Attention to Important Language.** When language is very important and it is crucial that the reader see it, one should highlight the language in some way. One may use **bold print**, a **different color print, underline, bold italics,** and other such methods. All **uppercase letters** are sometimes used with the intent of alerting signers to important information; however, research shows that text using all uppercase letters is very difficult to read. Experts say that lower case letters, with their differing shapes and heights, are much easier to decipher (Sullivan, 2012).

Step Two
An Informative Title

The first thing the client sees when presented with a waiver is the title. The title should be an honest, unambiguous explanation of the intent of the document.

Guidelines

1. **Precede the participant agreement with a descriptive title.** It is important that terminology such as *Waiver, Release of Liability,* or *Participant Liability Agreement* be used. Including a subhead that gets the attention of the signer can be important. Something like "This is an important legal document. Read carefully before signing." may be used. This helps to alert the signer of the document's importance. A Florida court, in upholding a waiver without a title, stated that the title was not mandatory but would provide more clarity as to the subject matter (*Gambino v. Music Television, Inc.*, 1996).

   A descriptive title can save the day for a defendant, as it did in *Blog v. Battery Park City Authority (*1996). The plaintiff argued that she thought she was signing a "sign-up" sheet, however the Court pointed out the title of the waiver – "RELEASE AND WAIVER OF LIABILITY, ASSUMPTION OF RISK AND INDEMNITY AGREEMENT (READ CAREFULLY BEFORE SIGNING)."

2. **Avoid misleading titles** such as *Sign-up Sheet, Roster, Application for Membership, Entry Blank,* and *Receipt.* Such titles can be considered deceptive and can affect the validity of the waiver. In a 2008 Utah case (*Mason v. Brigham Young University)*, the U.S. District Court ruled a waiver signed by an athlete in order to get an MRI was invalid. One of the major reasons for the decision was that the university's waiver was ambiguous because of a confusing and misleading title – "Injury and Liability Report." Another misleading title played a role in the failure of a waiver in *Applbaum v. Golden Acres Farm and Ranch* (2004). The title on the group waiver was "Stable Arrival List." In *Hobby v. Ramblin Breeze Ranch* (1984), the title of the group waiver was "Sign-In Sheet." This was the sole factor in the failure of the Tennessee waiver.

Example A:

Lucky Horseshoe Trail Rides
Assumption of Risk, Waiver of Liability, and Indemnity Agreement
(*This is an Important Legal Document: Read Carefully before Signing*)

Step Three
Assumption of Inherent Risks

Many jurisdictions today require that the waiver warn the client of the inherent risks of the activity. A strong section warning of the inherent risks of the activity is a major step toward avoiding liability. In *Parveen v. Tiki Tubing, LLC* (2012), the court stated that the waiver sheet provided the only warning of risk at the facility.

Guidelines

1. **Clearly describe the nature of the activity within the waiver.** The agreement should describe the activity including such aspects as how vigorous, fitness level required, and anything unpleasant about the activity. In general, the less familiar the participant and the public are with the activity, the more detail required in this section. In a 2010 **Colorado** case (*Wycoff v. Grace Community Church of the Assemblies of God*), the court refused to uphold a parental waiver because the waiver did not warn and inform the parent of the risks. The court pointed out that the statute requires the parent's decision to be "voluntary and informed."

2. **The agreement should clearly warn the signer of the inherent risks involved in the specific activity.** The agreement should include a representative list of risks associated with the specific activity. The list should not be comprehensive, but rather one that represents the broad scope of possible risks. Phrases such as ... *including, but not limited to* ... or *some of the inherent risks are...*should be used. Follow this with 1) a list of a few minor, common injuries, 2) a few serious injuries, and 3) a warning regarding catastrophic events, including death and paralysis.

   While the courts in many states do not require that a waiver list the inherent risks of the activity in order to be enforceable, the courts in a number of states seem to require a delineation of these risks. In **Colorado,** the *Wycoff* court required that the parent be informed of the risks (discussed in guideline 1 above). *Coughlin v. T.M.H. International Attractions, Inc.* (1995) involved a **Kentucky** spelunking death in which the court stated that the signer was unaware of the dangers in the cave. *Maurer v. Cerkvenik-Anderson Travel, Inc.* (1994) was an **Arizona** case involving a tour. The court stated that the waiver did not alert the signer to the specific dangers she was facing. Neither waiver was upheld. The *Benjamin* court in another Arizona case (*Benjamin v. Gear Roller Hockey Equipment, Inc.*, 2000) held that a general release could not absolve one of its duty to disclose unexpected and extraordinary risks known to it but not to its principals. The court added that the provider is not required to provide a specific listing of every one of the possible causes of an accident. In a third Arizona case (*Thorne v. Eaton*, 2002), the court noted that the waiver adequately notified the plaintiff that the activity was hazardous. The **Connecticut** court in *Niedbala v. S.L. – Your Partners in Health* (2002) held that a client could not be expected to assume the risks associated with equipment that was not in the club when the agreement was signed. In **Wisconsin**, the waiver in *Mettler v. Nellis* (2005) was not upheld, in part because the waiver stated that the signer assumed the inherent risks of all horse-related activities, but failed to list those risks. Similarly, the *Simeone v. Bombardier-Rotax* (2005) **Pennsylvania** court held that an order form release, couched in generalities, is not relative to the assumption of risk defense if it does not inform a purchaser of any real risks associated with the product. The **Nevada** Supreme Court ruled that a signed liability waiver was not sufficient as a matter of law to show that appellant subjectively understood the risks inherent in horseback riding and actually intended to assume those risks (*Renaud v. 200 Convention Center LTD.*, 1986).

   Illinois is another state that has strict requirements regarding listing of the inherent risks. The ruling in *Locke v. Lifetime Fitness, Inc.* (2014) emphatically addresses this requirement. Locke had a heart attack while playing basketball. The staff failed to make use of an available

AED and did nothing to help the victim; EMS arrived in 6 minutes, but it was too late. His wife filed suit alleging, among other things, failure to train the staff on how to handle emergencies. Lifetime claimed protection based on the liability waiver which named four inherent risks from which Lifetime was released. One of those risks was the inherent risk of improper emergency treatment – "injuries resulting from the actions taken or decisions made regarding medical or survival procedures." Mrs. Locke pointed out that this did not protect against a "failure to train staff"claim.

The court cited Illinois law requiring a waiver to contain clear, explicit, and unequivocal language *specifying the types of activities, circumstances, or situations* to be encompassed by the waiver. It then stated "An injury not specifically contemplated in an exculpatory clause can also still be covered if it 'fall[s] within the scope of possible dangers ordinarily accompanying the activity and therefore, reasonably contemplated by the parties.'" It explained that the waiver failed to explicitly cover the staff training issue, ruling that the wrongful death claim is not barred to the extent it is premised on the lack of staff emergency training.

When States do not Require Listing Risks. *Even in states that do not require an enumeration of the inherent risks, certainly the more prudent course would be to list them. The following cases illustrate why this might be important.* In a **New York** case (*Pineda v. Town Sports International, Inc.*, 2009) the waiver was not enforced because it violated a New York statute; however the listing of the inherent risks on the waiver helped with the assumption of risk defense, serving as evidence that the plaintiff was aware of those risks. Likewise in two other New York cases (*Duchesneau v. Cornell University*, 2013; *DiMaria v. Coordinated Ranches, Inc.*, 1988), the courts allowed redacted versions of the waivers to be presented as evidence of plaintiffs' assumption of the inherent risks. Similarly, in **Montana,** a state in which waivers were not enforced at the time, the court admitted a waiver in which the exculpatory language was redacted so that it could serve as evidence that the signer understood the risks (*McDermott v. Carie*, 2005).

In a **California** bicycling case (Coleman *v. United States of America*, 1992), the sponsors required the plaintiff to sign a waiver in which the U.S.A. was not a released party. Consequently, the waiver did not protect the U.S.A. However, U.S.A.'s assumption of risk defense benefited from the waiver since it provided evidence that the plaintiff had understood and assumed the risks of the activity. In another **California** case (*Biondi v. Motorcycle Safety Services, Inc.*, 2014), the document did not contain language exculpating the defendant from negligence; the document was admitted in order to show the plaintiff appreciated and assumed the inherent risks of operating a motorcycle. In *Hague v. Summit Acres Skilled Nursing and Rehabilitation* (2010), the **Ohio** court stated that although the waiver was ambiguous, it put the plaintiff on notice of the fitness center's intent to limit its liability for injuries due to her own negligence. In *Milne v. USA Cycling* (2007), the **Utah** court said the participant was warned of the inherent risks by the waiver.

Note, however, that waivers have failed because the court ruled that the inherent risks listed made the intent of the waiver unclear. So be certain to keep this section separate and distinct from language exculpating for negligence.

Statutory Mandates. A listing of inherent risks can also be mandated by statute. For instance, the **Ohio Equine Activity Immunity Statute R.C. 2305.321** (like many activity immunity statutes) states that to be valid, an equine activity waiver must specify at least each inherent risk of equine activity that is listed in the statute (*Markowitz v. Bainbridge Equestrian Center*, 2007). Likewise, the **Hawaii Revised Statutes sec. 663-1.54** allows waivers to protect providers from liability for the inherent risks of the activity if the plaintiff was adequately informed of those risks.

It is worth noting, however, in *Mettler v. Nellis* (2005), the waiver that the inherent risks of equine activities could be found in **Wis. Stat. δ 895.481(1)(e).** The court held that merely stating where the risks could be found did not adequately explain the risks; the risks specified in the statute must actually appear in the waiver.

3. **When the signer may participate in a variety of activities, make your description of risks and activities as representative and inclusive as is practical.** It is impossible (and unnecessary) to list all inherent risks of a single activity; it is equally impossible to list all of these risks when a multitude of activities are involved. That said, and remembering that waiver law varies from state to state, it is advisable to summarize the types of risks faced and, when possible, explain the types of activities available.

    In *Vinson v. Paramount Pictures Corporation* (2013), Vinson joined a studio club, paid a fee, and signed a waiver. When at a party that included carnival games, booths, and performances, he was injured when he fell from a rock-climbing wall due to an equipment malfunction. He alleged the waiver was ambiguous and that the waiver did not list a rock-climbing wall. The **California** court held the waiver language was clear – including the release of "any and all claims" and "any and all injuries" resulting from "any accident" arising out of his or her "participation in any of the events or activities sponsored by the Club." Regarding the failure to name the specific risk or event, the court said it is not necessary that the plaintiff have had a specific knowledge of the particular risk that ultimately caused the injury; that it is unnecessary to spell out every possible specific act of negligence of the defendant; and that it is not necessary to list every activity available to the participant. Another California court (*Lotz v. The Claremont Club*, 2013) stated that it is only necessary that the negligent act be reasonably connected to the object or purpose for which the waiver is given.

4. **Broaden the Inherent Risks.** Each activity or sport has inherent risks that are unique to the activity or to the facility. As discussed above, these risks should be listed. The following four types of risks, although some may be considered negligence risks, should be included as inherent risks. For each type, some courts have considered these to be inherent risks of the activity. If these are treated by the court as inherent risks, the liability of the provider is substantially reduced.

    - *Equipment failure*. Equipment can fail, thereby resulting in injury. It is important to specify that equipment failure is an inherent risk. In a case involving an injury on the ski lift resulting from a lift chair being out of place (*Savarese v. Camelback Ski Corp.* 2005, p. 10), the waiver read "...damages relating to skiing ... and or the use of this equipment...." The court ruled that "related to skiing" includes the use of the lift and is protected by the waiver. In *Padilla v. The Sports Club Company* (2008), the waiver stated that the use of facilities and equipment included an inherent risk of injury. The court ruled that the agreement expressly excluded liability for injury while using the equipment. In *McCune v. Myrtle Beach Indoor Shooting Range, Inc.* (2005), the waiver stated that equipment could only minimize risk. McCune claimed equipment failure was unexpected and not assumed. The court disagreed and upheld the waiver.

    - *Inability of participant to adequately operate activity equipment*. Often, equipment-related injuries are not due to equipment failure, but due to inability of the participant to safely use and manage his or her equipment. The failure of the participant to adequately control his or her own equipment or any equipment furnished to them is an inherent risk and should be added to the list of inherent risks when the activity involves equipment.

    - *Staff member (e.g., employee, guide, outfitter, teacher) judgment errors*. Persons in charge of activities can make mistakes that result in injury. Sometimes, such as in wilderness activities, decisions must be made in situations not previously encountered or anticipated. In a California case (*Lewis v. Mammoth Mountain Ski Area,* 2009), the waiver language included "... [MSA guides] might be ignorant of a participant's fitness or abilities. They might misjudge the weather, the elements, or the terrain. They may give inadequate warnings or instructions...."

Likewise, a waiver in a New Jersey health club case (*Allen v. LA Fitness,* 2011) read "The client further acknowledges that such risks, include, but are not limited to, injuries caused by the negligence of the instructor...." In a California equine case (*Pendergrass v. Diamond Bar & Circle K Horse Rentals,* 2010), the waiver named as employee-related inherent risks 1) being unaware of a participant's fitness or abilities, 2) might misjudge the weather or environmental conditions, and 3) might give incomplete warnings or instructions.

In *Donahue v. Ledgends, Inc.* (2014), Donahue sued the climbing wall facility charging negligent instruction by an employee. The employee told Donahue to drop from the wall a short distance to the surface; the drop resulted in an injury. Donahue claimed the waiver did not warn her of risk of negligent instruction. However, the court pointed out that the waiver included an assertion that the gym and the instructors "seek safety, but they are not infallible." It described some errors that instructors might make, including being ignorant of a participant's abilities and failing to give adequate warnings or instructions. The final sentence of the paragraph stated "...I acknowledge that I AM ULTIMATELY RESPONSIBLE for my own safety ...." The court said she was warned and subsequently enforced the waiver.

Obviously, if such judgment errors by employees are accepted as inherent risks of the activity, then provider exposure to liability is reduced.

- *Co-participant behavior.* It is common practice to include actions of co-participants among the listed risks. In *Moser v. Ratinoff (*2003), a participant in a long distance bicycle ride was injured when another participant swerved causing a fall. The waiver stated "The risks include, but are not limited to those caused by ... actions of other people including but not limited to participants.... I hereby assume all of the risks of participating ... in this event." **Florida Statute 744.301** specifically lists co-participant negligence as an inherent risk of activity.

- *Participant negligence.* An inherent risk of many activities is negligent actions of the participant. In fact, a number of equine statutes (e.g. South Dakota [**SDCL §42-11-1 to 5**], Florida [**F.S. 744.301**], Missouri [**M.S. 537.325**]) specifically list participant negligence as an inherent risk. The South Dakota equine statute lists participant negligence as one of seven inherent risks of equine activities and the Missouri statute lists it as one of five inherent risks.

  The potential of a participant to act in a negligent manner that may contribute to injury to the participant or others, such as failing to maintain control over the animal or not acting within the participant's ability; (S.D. 42-11-1 sec. 6e)

5. **Include within the agreement specific mention of any risks that are unique to your operation.** A unique risk in horseback riding might be the risk of being thrown from a horse or the likelihood of the horse reacting erratically to unexpected wildlife. Some waivers used for scuba divers include mention in the waiver of the absence of a decompression chamber. In one case, a bar included a statement in the waiver asserting that the signer is not under the influence of alcohol before the patron was allowed to ride a mechanical bull. Unique risks found in wilderness camping would include the possible necessity of being rescued and extreme distance

from medical care. Auto racing waivers often include language that protects the sponsoring organization from liability for negligent rescue operations (*Groves v. Firebird Raceway, Inc.,* 1994). Such unique risks should be included in the participant agreement.

6. **The possible consequences of participation should be defined and the client should affirm an understanding of the consequences.** Include both the types of actions or incidents that are common to the activity as well as the type of injuries or disabilities that can result from the injuries that might occur. These should include minor, serious, and catastrophic risks.

7. **The assumption of risk section should include an affirmation of voluntary participation.** Wording can be something like *I know, understand, and appreciate the risks involved in this activity and am voluntarily participating in....* This statement is important because the primary assumption of risk defense is effective only if the participant is aware of the risks and when participation is voluntary.

8. **Participant affirms having read and understood the above information and agrees to assume all inherent risks of the activity.** This statement usually involves such language as *I recognize that whitewater rafting is a dangerous activity and I agree to accept any and all inherent risks.* A Mississippi Court required evidence of discussion of provisions, negotiation, and understanding (*Rigby v. Sugar's Fitness and Activity Center,* 2002).

9. **Participant agrees to abide by the rules.** This can include both the rules of the sport and any rules established by the provider. This notifies the participant of the conduct expected and, thereby, strengthens the secondary assumption of risk defense (contributory fault) for injuries attributable to rule violations.

10. **Participant may be encouraged to inspect for hazardous conditions.** The act of participating would indicate that the participant found the conditions to be safe. Participants may also be asked to affirm that they will notify management of any hazards or dangerous conditions that are discovered.

Example B:

Trail riding is a popular activity enjoyed by young and old alike. It combines wholesome physical activity, adventure, powerful animals, and the natural beauty of the out-of-doors. While the pleasure of such rides is unmistakable, Lucky Horseshoe Trail Rides (hereafter referred to as LHTR) wants to make certain that all riders are fully aware of the various inherent risks involved in such an activity. LHTR feels that it is important that riders know that certain risks cannot be eliminated without destroying the unique character of this activity; that some danger is involved in trail riding; and that on occasion, riders do suffer injury. LHTR does not want to frighten riders or reduce their enthusiasm for a trail ride, but we believe it is important that you be informed of the nature of the activity.

Assumption of Inherent Risks: Risks of horseback riding include, but are not limited to: 1) falls from horses; 2) unpredictable weather changes; 3) the propensity of the horse to behave in ways that may result in injury, harm, or death to those around it; 4) the unpredictability of the animal's reaction to sounds, sudden movement, unfamiliar objects, persons, or other animals; 5) surface or subsurface conditions; 6) collisions with other animals or objects; 7) steep, uneven, or snow-covered terrain; 8) actions of the rider or other riders; 9) failure of tack or other equipment; and 10) errors in judgment of the trail guide or other employees.

These risks can result in three types of injury. *Minor injuries* are not uncommon and include, but are not limited to, being scratched by a bush or cactus, muscle soreness, bruises, sunburn, and sprains. *Serious injuries* occasionally occur and include, but are not limited to, exposure from extreme hot, cold, or wet conditions, altitude sickness, broken bones, concussions, cuts, and bites. *Catastrophic events* are very rare and can include, but are not limited to, heart attack, stroke, paralysis, serious internal or head injuries, and death. In addition, these injuries may occur in locations far from emergency medical care.

I understand that the inherent risks of horseback trail rides **are serious** and that horseback **trail riding is a dangerous activity** regardless of the care taken by LHTR and its employees. I have read the previous paragraphs and 1) **I know the nature of the activity** of horseback trail riding; 2) I **understand the demands** of this activity relative to my physical condition and riding skill level, and 3) **I appreciate the potential impact** of the types of injuries that may result from horseback trail riding. **I hereby assert that my participation at the LHTR is voluntary and that I knowingly and willingly assume all of the inherent risks of the activity.**

Step Four
Waiver of Liability for Negligence

The waiver of liability for negligence is the heart of the participant agreement and the major reason for its use.

Guidelines

1. **Denote consideration within the contract.** To have a valid contract, there must be consideration. **Consideration** is what is given up by each of the parties for the promise of the other. Contracts are not enforceable without this mutual exchange of something for something. Courts are near unanimous in ruling that the privilege of participating constitutes consideration, thus a phrase such as *In consideration of my participation, I agree to release ...* indicates that the signer is receiving the opportunity to participate in exchange for relinquishing the right to file suit. A Texas court in *Last v. Quail Valley Country Club* (2010) stated that when a party acquires a legal right to do something that is otherwise prohibited (e.g., participate in an activity), that party receives a benefit (e.g., consideration).

    In *Hall v. Bill Perry and Hidden Creek Outfitters* (2009), the waiver was signed on arrival after the hunt agreement was completed by mail. After Hall was injured, he sued claiming there was no consideration since the deal was closed prior to receiving the waiver. The Wyoming Supreme Court enforced the waiver concluding it was a part of the original agreement since the waiver had been referred to in the original agreement. *So if your waiver is not a part of the activity contract/agreement, make certain the contract/agreement refers to the release – or better yet, also attach a copy of the waiver to the original contract/agreement.*

    In a 2006 non-sport Michigan case (*Ansari v. Gold*), an attorney reduced his fee in exchange for a malpractice waiver. The court held that the plaintiff had to return the consideration in order to regain the right to sue the attorney. A Delaware case failed for lack of consideration when a racer was not allowed to inspect the track after having been promised the opportunity in the waiver (*DeVeccio v. Delaware Enduro Riders, Inc.*, 2004).

In a 2004 Connecticut case (*Brown v. Sol*), the waiver specified which parties were to be released and the court held that lack of consideration from each defendant does not invalidate a waiver. Similarly, two New Hampshire courts accepted as consideration continued employment (*Smith, Batchelder & Rugg v. Foster*, 1979) and permitting continued cheerleader practice (*Gonzales v. University System of New Hampshire*, 2005).

In an interesting Michigan decision (*Theodore v. Horenstein*, 2009), the court stated that it has recognized a waiver may bar a claim against a defendant who did not provide consideration for its signing. The court enforced the waiver signed by a volunteer worker at the racetrack.

2. **Use wording that will minimize the likelihood of ambiguity.** A Wisconsin court (*Yauger v. Skiing Enterprises, Inc.*, 1996) stated that a waiver, to be valid, "must be clear, unambiguous, and unmistakable to the layperson." It is important that the waiver clearly state that the signer is releasing the provider from responsibility for injury to the signer caused by *ordinary negligence* on the part of the provider or any of its employees or agents. The waiver should include a phrase such as *I hereby release … from any and all present and future claims resulting from ordinary negligence on the part of….* The language must be simple, straight forward, and unambiguous. The waiver should say plainly the message intended, should not include long and convoluted sentences, and should not be full of a lot of *legalese*.

An Oregon court found a waiver ambiguous because 1) the title "Liability of the Club and the Members" implied both the club and members will be assuming some sort of liability; 2) the waiver included use of equipment owned by the club and participation in physical activities organized or sponsored by the club, but did not clearly cover a member injured by a loose locker or a broken chair, and 3) did not clearly limit liability for the negligence of the club in maintaining auxiliary areas (*Landren v. Hood River Sports Club. Inc.*, 2001).

It is worth noting, however, that a waiver that is ambiguous for failing to specify coverage of negligence can sometimes provide protection from liability for injuries resulting from inherent risks (see Step Three, Guideline 3). In *Trummer v. Niewisch* (2005), the waiver did not protect the defendant from liability for negligence because the term "negligence" was not used. The court, however, found that the injury was due to an inherent risk (falling from a horse) and held that the waiver language "relinquish any and all claims" protected the defendant from liability for inherent risks.

3. **Avoid promises of "every reasonable precaution" and similar statements.** Use of such language tends to create ambiguity. In *Murphy v. Young Men's Christian Association of Lake Wales, Inc.*, (2008) the waiver stated

> "… even when every reasonable precaution is taken, accidents can sometimes still happen. Therefore, … I understand and expressly acknowledge that I release the Lake Wales Family YMCA … from all liability for any injury …. I understand that this release includes any claims based on negligence … (p. 1-2).

The court acknowledged that the waiver specifically stated that the YMCA is not liable for any claims based on negligence; however, the court pointed out the waiver also promised that the YMCA will take "every reasonable precaution" to prevent accidents. Since "every reasonable precaution" can be interpreted to mean "ordinary care," confusion was created since the waiver appeared to be promising "no negligence," yet asking to be excused from "negligence." The court went on to state that a reasonable reader might be led to believe that the waiver of liability extends only to claims for injuries that were unavoidable "even when every reasonable precaution" had been taken by the YMCA. The court held that the waiver failed to state clearly and unequivocally that the YMCA was not liable for its own negligence.

In an Alaska Supreme Court case (Kissick v. Schmierer, 2005), the court made a similar ruling. The defendant, in its waiver, promised to try to keep its facilities safe and its equipment in good condition. The waiver also disclaimed liability for actions that failed to meet such standards. The court said the language was problematic and ambiguous because the signer was not clearly notified in the waiver of its effect. The Supreme Court went on to name six characteristics required of an effective waiver. One was that *"the release agreement must not represent or insinuate standards of safety or maintenance."*

4. **Refer specifically to the "negligence" of the service provider.** Figure 2.2 lists several states in which the specific word "negligence" is required as well as a number of states in which its use is strongly encouraged. The use of the word can help to clarify the intent of the waiver in any state and subsequently will significantly reduce the likelihood of the success of an allegation of ambiguity (see Chapter 2). Be certain that the terms "negligence" or "ordinary negligence" are conspicuous. They can be made so by always placing the terms in caps or in bold letters.

   While courts differ on the issue, Florida's Judge Cohen, in a concurring opinion in *Give Kids the World, Inc. v. Sanislo* (2012), summed up the controversy beautifully when he wrote

   > The better view is to require an explicit provision to that effect.... While those trained in the law might understand and appreciate that the general language releasing a party from any and all liability could encompass the injuries suffered by Ms. Sanislo, a release should be readily understandable so that an ordinary and knowledgeable person would know what is being contracted away. I would suggest that the average ordinary and knowledgeable person would not understand from such language that they were absolving an entity from a duty to use reasonable care. Conversely, *a clause which provides a waiver of liability for one's own negligence is easily understood.* The other district courts of appeal have recognized **how simple it is to add such a clause in a release**. I suggest we do the same. [Emphasis added.]

   In light of rulings in recent cases, there are three rules one should follow in relation to the word "negligence."

   Use "ordinary negligence." Instead of simply using the term "negligence," it would be safer to specify "ordinary negligence*"* or, better yet, use "**ordinary negligence of the provider**" in order to make it clear that protecting the provider from liability for gross negligence is not the purpose of the document. Use of the term "negligence" has been deemed by an Oregon court to include both ordinary and gross negligence, whereby, the court ruled the waiver was against public policy and unenforceable (*Farina v. Mt. Bachelor*, 1995). Likewise, in *In the Matter of Pacific Adventures, Inc.* (1998), the waiver used by a scuba diving company failed to protect because the waiver called for a release of negligence and gross negligence. The court held that the part of the waiver addressing mere negligence was not severable from the gross negligence section; thus, the waiver was deemed to be in violation of public policy. In *Wheeler v. Owens Community College* (2005), the court held that "for any reason whatsoever, including negligence" was unenforceable because it was too broad.

   One plaintiff in a snowmobile case argued that the term "negligence or otherwise" was ambiguous (*Ball v. Waldoch Sports, Inc.*, 2003). The court ruled that the waiver as a whole shows a clear intent to release the sponsors from claims arising from negligence and went on to refer to 45 cases in which the phrase has been upheld.

   It is interesting that occasionally a waiver will be used which specifically excludes exculpation for the negligence of the provider. For instance, in *Zipusch v. LA Workout, Inc.* (2007), the waiver language sought to exculpate LA Fitness resulting from the negligence of anyone else using LA Workout, but stated "The member or guest will defend and indemnify LA Workout for any negligence EXCEPT the sole negligence of the club" (p. 3). In spite of the wording, LA Workout unsuccessfully attempted to use the waiver to avoid liability for its own alleged negligence.

Clearly specify whose negligence. In another 2005 case, a court held that language reading "release...from and against all claims...I may sustain or incur due to personal injury, death, or property damage, whether or not the result of negligent acts or omissions..." failed to meet the requirement that a contract must clearly state that the provider is not responsible for its own negligence (*Gonzalez v. University System of New Hampshire*). The court stated that "... whether or not the result of negligent acts or omissions..." does not clearly specify the negligent acts *of the provider* (p. 5). Language such as "...as a result of the ordinary negligence of the provider, its employees, and its agents" might show the intent of the waiver more clearly. *Hawkins v. Second KYU, Inc.* (2009) provides another example in which the negligence of the provider was not specified in the waiver. The waiver stated "... will not be liable to the member for claims, demands, injuries, and loss of property or acts of negligence" (p. 2).

Don't substitute other words for negligence. Some providers are shy about using the term "negligence," using other words such as **"fault"** instead. In a recent case, the Wisconsin Supreme Court held that the word "fault" was overly broad and all-inclusive (*Atkins v. Swimwest Family Fitness Center*, 2005). They reasoned that language such as "...I agree to assume all liability without regard to fault..." never makes clear what type of acts the word "fault" encompasses. Referring to Black's, they felt that fault included any deviation from duty resulting from inattention, incapacity, perversity, bad faith, or mismanagement and could cover reckless and intentional acts.

In *Hackett v. Grand Seas Resort Owner's Association* (2012), the exculpatory language was "will not be responsible for accidents or injury to guest ...." The Florida court did not enforce the waiver and stated that "**'Accident'** does not equate to negligent or negligence."

In a Minnesota case (*Salinger v. Leatherdale*, 2012), the court failed to enforce a waiver that used the word **"carelessness"**; the court stated that "carelessness" does not equate to "ordinary negligence."

The meaning of the phrase **"any and all"** (or the term "any" or "all") varies depending upon the state. In many states, the phrase is interpreted to be all-inclusive and include every claim, every person, and, most importantly, every risk (including both inherent risk and the risk of negligence). In those states, the use of the term "negligence" or like words is not mandated to be in a waiver of liability for negligence.

In other states, however, the term "negligence" or words of similar meaning are required in order for a waiver to relieve an actor of liability for negligent actions; in those states "any and all" is construed to include only inherent risks and not negligent acts. In **Missouri**, for instance, the Missouri Supreme Court in *Alack v. Vic Tanny International of Missouri, Inc.* (1996) ruled that to be enforceable, a waiver must contain "clear, unambiguous, unmistakable, and conspicuous language" and "must effectively notify a party that he or she is releasing the other party from claims arising from the other party's own negligence." It stressed that the words "negligence" or "fault" or their equivalent must be used so there is no doubt that the party understood what claims he or she was waiving. Another more recent Missouri court ruled similarly *(Guthrie v. Hidden Valley*, 2013).

Ohio courts generally enforce waivers containing the phrase "any and all" to apply to negligence. In *Geczi v. Lifetime Fitness* (2012), an Ohio appellate court addressed the following language in a health club case.

> ... the undersigned ... accepts this risk and agrees that *LIFE TIME FITNESS will not be liable for **any injury**,* including ... *resulting from the negligence ....the undersigned* agrees to specifically assume all risk of injury .... and *hereby waives **any and all** claims or actions which may arise against LIFE TIME....*

The court concluded the clear intent was to release Lifetime from injuries resulting from both inherent risks and negligence. Another Ohio court (*Swartzentruber v. Wee-K Corp.*, 1997) interpreted "any and all claims" arising out of "any and all personal injuries" as unambiguous and barring negligence. In 1999, an Ohio court interpreted "all liability" regarding a race car stored on another's property to include liability for negligence (*Conkey v. Eldridge*).

Not all Ohio courts, however, are as lenient in their interpretation. A First District Court held that language asserting that a member used facilities at his "own risk" and that the club would not be liable for "any injury or damage" was ambiguous and unenforceable against negligence (*Holmes v. Health & Tennis Corp of America, 1995*). A Ninth District Court found ambiguity in language that the rider assumed "full responsibility and liability" for any and all personal injury. The court said the language was so general as to be meaningless (*Tanker v. North Crest Equestrian Center*, 1993).

See Figure 2.2 for states requiring the use of "negligence" as well as states in which the use of "any and all" or similar language would be satisfactory to protect. To avoid confusion, the authors suggest the use of the term "ordinary negligence" in order to reduce ambiguity. Wording might be

> ... parties may not be held liable in any way for any injury, death, or other damage resulting from my participation, or as a result of the ordinary negligence of the provider, its employees, and agents....

5. **Specify within the waiver all parties other than the signer who are relinquishing claims by virtue of the waiver.** Additional protection may be gained by including a phrase in which the signer relinquishes, on behalf of self, spouse, heirs, estate, and assigns, the right to recover for injury or death. Be aware, however, that state laws vary and that this phrase will not be effective in all states.

In a case involving a ski injury to a minor, the parent had signed a waiver that read "... Parent(s) (and skier if 18 years of age or older) hereby release and forever discharge...." The court held that the waiver did not release any claim of the skier since she was not 18 or older (*Davis v. Sun Valley Ski Education Foundation, Inc.,* 1997).

6. **Specify within the waiver all parties who are protected by the waiver.** All classes of persons or entities that are to be protected should be listed in the agreement. It would seem that naming the protected parties would go without saying; however, it is surprising how many waivers fail for this reason. The corporate entity, employees, volunteers, agents, sponsors, independent contractors, insurance carrier, equipment manufacturers and suppliers, owners of the property you rent or use, and any others that you intend to protect should be listed. A general inclusiveness clause such as ... *and all others who are involved* may be included, but may fail to protect in some states.

Waivers Failing to Include a Category or Party. How specific one needs to be in listing parties for whom protection is intended varies from state to state. A waiver in a **Maine** case (*Amburgey v. Atomic Ski USA, Inc.,* 2007) failed to protect a manufacturer because the manufacturer was not specifically named in the waiver. The court stated that the general rule is that a contract generally does not bestow enforceable rights on a non-signatory (a signatory is one who signs a document or contract). To invoke the protection of a release on a non-signatory, one must clearly show that the protection was intended by the signers of the contract. The court stressed the importance of making certain that parties intended to benefit be conspicuous. The waiver in question failed to protect the manufacturer because 1) the manufacturer was not named, 2) the language was in fine print, 3) buried on the second page, and 4) buried within a long sentence.

In a **Georgia** Case (*Herren v. Barrin Innovations, Inc.,* 2013), a health club, the owner of the club, the personal trainer, and a dietary supplement manufacturer were sued for damages.

Summary judgment was granted for the first three, but not for the supplement manufacturer because it was not included as a protected party on the waiver.

A **Nebraska** court (*Palmer v. Lakeside Wellness Center*, 2011), in determining if an equipment manufacturer was protected by a health club waiver, stated that for not-named parties to be protected as third party beneficiaries, the waiver must expressly stipulate that such parties were intended as a protected party. Likewise, in an **Ohio** case (*Jones v. Staubli Motor Sports*, 2012), the waiver did not name nor protect the manufacturer of a defective refueling system that resulted in an injury. Similarly, an **Illinois** court ruled that a waiver did not protect the manufacturer of a race car (*Nesbitt v. National Muscle Car Association*, 2014). Among the named releasees were "equipment and parts manufacturers and suppliers"; the court ruled that the waiver was ambiguous as to whether this was meant to include the supplier of the entire car.

On the other hand, **North Carolina** courts are apparently more likely to enforce waivers intended to protect non-signatories. In *Brown v. Robins* (2007), the release language was "all other persons, firms, or corporations who are or might be liable from all claims of any kind" (p. 7). The court stated that "it is clear defendants were direct intended third-party beneficiaries of the releases" (p. 7).

In **Missouri**, when referring to parties released by the waiver in *Lunceford v. Houghtlin* (2005), the court ruled that "any and all persons" was unambiguous and enforceable to bar claims against third parties; it is not necessary that the release identify those persons by name or otherwise. More recently, an appellate court ruled that "any event sponsors" unambiguously releases all event sponsors, saying it is not necessary to name each sponsor (*Holmes v. Multimedia KSDK, Inc.*, 2013).

In a **Pennsylvania** case involving a snow tubing injury (*Tayar v. Camelback Ski Corporation*, 2012), the waiver named the corporation as a protected party, but failed to include "employees." The Supreme Court said that even though the employees were not named, they were protected because the corporation could not act "negligently, improperly, or otherwise, other than through its agents and employees."

The writers of an amusing 2010 **Texas** waiver (*Last v. Quail Valley Country Club*) used an unusual concluding inclusive term. The waiver read:

> I also release and hold harmless Bull Power, any operator, sponsor, club owner,
> managers, or landlords or anyone you can think of in connection with…. (p. 3).

Interestingly, the waiver was enforced.

Waivers Failing to Name the Party. A **Connecticut** client signed a waiver, was subsequently injured playing deck hockey in an arena, and filed suit against the arena (*Klem v. Chaplinsky*, 2002). The relevant waiver language read

> I am assuming any and all risks, hazards and injuries . . . incidental to
> participation in such a physical contact sport . . . I accept any and **all hazards of
> participation** . . . and the dangers of injury including, but not limited to, injuries
> or damages arising from the **negligence or carelessness of fellow players,
> referees, staff, spectators and others present** on or near the property on which
> the facility is located [Emphasis added.](@ 9-10).

It seems ironic that a waiver that is well-written so as to include both inherent risks and the risk of negligence of "fellow players, referee, staff, spectators, and others present" failed to list the arena as a protected party. Needless to say, the waiver failed to protect the arena.

In a **Massachusetts** case (*Powers v. Mukpo*, 2000), a client at a riding academy located on Woodlock Farm was injured while riding. The riding academy was not protected because the waiver language, "I voluntarily release Woodlock Farm, its instructors, and agents from ..." did not specify the academy. Likewise, in *Hackett v. Grand Seas Resort Owner's Association* (2012), the waiver failed to name the Association.

In *Ruppa v. American States Ins. Co.* (1979) the **Wisconsin** waiver specified that sponsors were released, but failed to identify the parties involved. None of the defendants were listed in the program in the list of sponsors. The court ruled that the defendants were not adequately identified in the waiver. In another **Wisconsin** case (*Park-Childs v. Mrotek's, Inc.* 1998), the waiver was worded so as to release the individual, but not her business, from liability. The waiver was not upheld. In **Iowa**, the *Huber v. Hovey* court (1993) ruled the waiver did not protect the insurer because the insurer, who was named in the suit for negligent inspection of the racetrack, was not named in the waiver.

Some other cases in which the failure to name the party being sued was the issue include the following: *Bailey v. Palladino*, 2006, **New Jersey** martial arts club; *Perry v. New Jersey Sports & Exposition Authority*, 2008, horse trainer; *Hague v. Summit Acres Skilled Nursing and Rehabilitation*, 2010, **Ohio** health club; *Porter v. Dartmouth College*, 2009, **New Hampshire** college ski rental; *Kolosnitsyn v. Crystal Mountain Inc.*, 2009, **Washington** ski rental.

Language that Fails to Name Party, Too Broad, and Too Narrow. A **South Carolina** case (*Fisher v. Stevens,* 2003) involved a tow truck employee (Fisher) who fell from the truck while speeding to a crash on the track. He had signed a waiver in which protected parties included "vehicle driver," "vehicle owner," and "any persons in any restricted area." Fisher's estate filed suit and the driver and owner of the tow truck claimed protection based on the waiver. The court ruled that the driver and owner were not protected because the **narrow wording** of the waiver applied to racecar drivers and owners, and the waiver **did not specifically name** tow truck operators. Next, the court held that "any persons in any restricted area" protected even unauthorized persons in the area and, as such, was **so broad** as to be against public policy. *So, uniquely, this case illustrates 1) failure to name the party, 2) too narrow language, and 3) overly broad language.*

7. **Use language that is as broad as possible without offending public policy.** In addition to care in naming all protected parties, waivers must be broad in describing what they are meant to cover. Examine the agreement for restrictive language and replace it with language that can be interpreted broadly when the court is determining what the provider meant for the exculpatory agreement to encompass. Phrases that tend to broaden include: 1) *... in all phases of the activity,* 2) *... while using the equipment and facility,* 3) *... while in, on, or about the premises,* and 4) *... any and all claims arising out of....*

The general rule is that for an agreement to be effective, it must appear that its terms were intended by both parties to apply to the particular event or conduct of the defendant that has caused the harm. The document should reference "the types of activities, circumstances, or situations that it encompasses and for which the plaintiff agrees to relieve the defendant from a duty of care" (*Garrison v. Combined Fitness Centre,* 1990). However, it is not necessary to spell out in the agreement every possible specific act of negligence. It is only necessary that the negligent act which resulted in injury be reasonably related to the purpose for which the release is given (*La Fata v. LA Fitness International, LLC,* 2008).

Reimund v. Guthrie (2008) provides an example of the use of extremely broad language in a waiver. Note the breadth of the underlined portions of the agreement.

"I/We the undersigned Boarder(s), as part of consideration for being permitted to board or keep a horse(s) at 8781 Palladay Road, Elverta, CA 95626, HEREBY RELEASE AND DISCHARGE AHE, its partners, Gloria Guthrie and Cindy Magness, Partners, their families and relatives, their agents and friends, employees, veterinarians, farriers, independent contracts or trainers or representatives (hereinafter 'Releasees') from any type or kind of liability arising out of or connected in any manner with said boarding or keeping of horses. AHE agrees to take every reasonable precaution to protect boarded horses from illness, accident, theft, fire through supervision, adequate equipment, proper feeding, etc. Nevertheless, injuries to horses sometimes do occur, as it is impossible to anticipate every contingency. Except in the event of gross negligence or willful misconduct, I/we <u>shall not hold releasees liable for any sickness, disease, estray, theft, death or injury which may be suffered by any boarded horse during the time the horse is in the care, custody or control of releasees.</u> IN ADDITION I/WE WAIVE OUR RIGHTS TO BRING ANY LEGAL ACTION AGAINST RELEASEES <u>FOR ANY ACTIONS WHATSOEVER ARISING OUT OF, OR IN ANY WAY CONNECTED WITH BOARDING, CONDITIONING, TRAINING, TRANSPORTING, SHOWING, MARKETING OR PROVIDING ANY OTHER EQUINE-RELATED SERVICE TO ME/US.</u> THIS INCLUDES, BUT IS NOT LIMITED TO, <u>ANY PERSONAL INJURY OR DISABILITY WHICH I/WE, MY/OUR FAMILY, FRIENDS, AGENTS OR EMPLOYEES, OR ANY THIRD PARTY MAY RECEIVE WHILE ON THE PREMISES</u> OF AHE. [Underline emphasis added].

The plaintiff alleged the waiver was intended to give "defendants carte blanche to maintain the premises in an irresponsible and negligent manner" and was, therefore, unconscionable. The plaintiff did not provide evidence supporting the assertion and it was deemed perfunctory. The waiver was upheld.

The *Benavidez v. The University of Texas – Pan American* (2014) case involved a waiver that contained very broad language. The plaintiff agreed to release the defendant from:

> … from <u>any cause of action, claims, or demands of any nature whatsoever, including but not limited to</u> a claim of negligence … for <u>personal injury, property damage, death or accident of any kind</u> … <u>related to my use</u> of the Climbing Wall … <u>SUPERVISED OR UNSUPERVISED, howsoever the injury or damages is caused</u> … <u>including, but not limited to the negligence</u> of the University. [Underlined emphasis added.]

The court enforced the waiver, finding no problem with the breadth of the waiver.

In *City of Hammond, Hammond Civic Center v. Plys* (2008), the waiver was broadly worded and was found to protect the defendant. The **Indiana** waiver stated "While engaging in any contact, game, function, exercise, competition, or any other activity operating, organized, arranged or sponsored by the ... Recreation Department, Civic Center, or the City of Hammond, either on or off their premises, …" In another Indiana case (*Marshall v. Blue Springs Corp.*, 1994), the waiver using the wording *... as a result of engaging in or receiving instruction in [scuba diving activities] or any activities incidental thereto wherever or however the same may occur ...* was enforced.

In *Peters v. Bally's Holiday Spa Health Clubs of California* (2004), a woman was injured by a windblown piece of umbrella while sitting in a Jacuzzi. She alleged that this was beyond the meaning or intent of the release; however, the **California** court ruled that "in, on, or about the premises" unambiguously relieved the club of liability for any injury sustained while on the premises regardless of its cause. In another California case, another aspect of breadth of a waiver related to businesses with more than one location. In *Heilig v. Touchstone Climbing, Inc.* (2007), Touchstone had facilities in more than one location. Their waiver language included "the use of any of [Touchstone's] services or facilities, at this location and all other locations."p.26 The waiver in *Padilla v. The Sports Club Company* (2008) addressed and included risks from 1) use of equipment and machines, 2) participation with others in supervised and unsupervised activity or programs, 3) injuries related to facilities, 4) accidental injuries occurring anywhere in the club, 5) slip and fall type injuries, and 6) injuries caused by other persons. The California court enforced the waiver.

8. **Insufficiently broad language can cause a waiver to fail.** Unfortunately for the defendants, not all waivers provide such broad coverage. In an **Illinois** situation that clearly demonstrated the need for broad wording, Gina Calarco (*Calarco v. YMCA of Greater Metropolitan Chicago*, 1986), was injured when weights on a Universal gym machine fell on her hand. She had previously signed an exculpatory clause included on the YMCA's application for membership that stated:

> In consideration of my participation in the activities of the Young Men's Christian Association of Metropolitan Chicago, I do hereby agree to hold free from any and all liability the YMCA of Metropolitan Chicago and its respective officers, employees and members and do hereby for myself, my heirs, executors and administrators, waive, release and forever discharge any and all rights and claims for damages which I may have or *which may hereafter accrue to me arising out of or connected with my participation in any of the activities of the YMCA of Metropolitan Chicago.* I hereby do declare myself to be physically sound, having medical approval to participate in the activities of the YMCA.

The waiver was not upheld because the wording did not include language such as "use of the said gymnasium or the facilities and equipment thereof" to clearly indicate that injuries resulting from negligence in maintaining the facility or equipment would be covered by the waiver. Further, it was impossible to determine whether the statement, "I hereby declare myself to be physically sound, having medical approval to participate in the activities of the YMCA" applied to injuries which result only from a member's own physical ailments or those resulting from participating in activities at the YMCA.

Likewise, in a **California** case (*Huverserian v. Catalina Scuba Luv, Inc.*, 2010), the scuba waiver failed because the language was too narrow. The waiver read "… scuba & snorkel gear for boat dives or multiple day rentals." It was not enforced because the plaintiff rented the equipment for a single day, wade-in dive.

Hawkins v. Second KYU, Inc. (2009) presents a very poor waiver that is much too narrow. The waiver language states "The school shall not be liable to the member for claims, demands, injuries, and loss of property or acts of negligence (p. 2)." The **Pennsylvania** court failed to enforce the waiver because it did not specify protection from negligent failure to instruct. The waiver also failed to clearly specify that the release was for the provider's negligent actions. In another Pennsylvania case (*Martin v. Montage*, 2000), the waiver specified protection against loss or injuries related to the use of a snow tube or a lift, but did not protect against negligence in the design of a snow tubing trail.

Waivers are too specific when certain classes of claims are included, but other types of claims are not included. In *Porter v. Dartmouth College* (2009), the **New Hampshire** court concluded that a reasonable person might have interpreted the waiver language to relate to claims arising from the recreational setting, but not where education or instruction is provided.

9. **Overly broad language can cause a waiver to fail.** On the other hand, one must take care not to make the waiver overly broad as that can violate public policy (see Chapter 2). The waiver language should reference the activity to which the waiver applies and not necessarily all general operations of the sport business. In an equine-related case, the *Thompson v. Otterbein College* (1996) court examined the following wavier language:

> I hereby, * * * release and discharge the owners, operators, and sponsors of THIS STABLE and their respective servants, agents, officers and all other participants of and from all claims, demands, actions and causes of action for such injuries sustained to my person, or that of my child or legal charge and/or property.

90

The **Ohio** court found the language released "essentially everyone . . . from *any* type of misconduct, whether it be negligent, wanton or willful conduct." The court did not enforce the waiver against negligence because they felt it was so general as to be meaningless.

Courts in **Wisconsin** have frequently found waivers to be too broad. In *Richards v. Richards* (1994), the court ruled that the waiver was overbroad as against public policy because it intended to release the relying party from liability for intentional acts, reckless conduct, and negligence not only by the relying party, but by a multitude of other entities and associated parties as well. Further, it released the relying party from liability for any and all injury while Richards was a passenger in any vehicle at any time and while on any and all company property at any time. The court stated "The very breadth of the release raises questions about its meaning and demonstrates its one-sidedness...." In *Mettler v. Nellis* (2005), a waiver was deemed invalid because the language was too broad. The court felt that "any liability or responsibility for any accident damage, injury, or illness" encompassed more than injuries from horse-related activities. The court also held that the waiver was too broad in terms of the number and category of parties released. It went on to quote the *Richards* Court, which stated "An exculpatory contract contravenes public policy when it would absolve the tortfeasor from any injury to the victim for any reason." Similarly, the *Atkins v. Swimwest Family Fitness Center* (2005) court said the broadness of the exculpatory language made it difficult to ascertain exactly what was within the contemplation of either party. The *Brooten v. Hickok Rehabilitation Services, LLC* court (2013) stated that the phrase "negligence or any other cause" clearly encompasses conduct beyond negligence and is unenforceable.

In a **Connecticut** case (*Rahuba v. 5 D's, Inc.,* 2004), a patron was injured in the snack bar of a skating rink after having signed a waiver. The waiver language included reference to the "condition of the premises," however, the court held that the scope of the waiver was limited to the skating area and did not include the snack bar. It went on to say that the inclusion of the snack bar in this waiver would be void on public policy grounds. A **Minnesota** court held a waiver to be unenforceable, as overly broad, because it interpreted the language, "harmless for all damages arising from personal injury or property loss," to include intentional, willful, and wanton acts (*Wu v. Shattuck-St. Mary's School,* 2005).

A **Colorado** court, commenting on waiver language they considered so ambiguously broad as to include willful and wanton negligence, said that enforcing for willful and wanton negligence would be against public policy (*Chadwick v. Colt Ross Outfitters, Inc.,* 2004). They went on to say, however, that similar language has been construed to extend only as far as would be consistent with public policy and would not render the entire document void.

A **Delaware** court (*Hallman v. Dover Downs, Inc.,* 1986) stated that to be enforced, the waiver should specifically refer to the negligence involved because an overbroad waiver is against public policy and unenforceable. Refer also to the **South Carolina** case (*Fisher v. Stevens*) discussed earlier in Guideline 6 in which the waiver was construed as both overly broad and too narrow.

But it is important to realize that the terms "overly broad" and "too narrow" are interpreted differently in courts in different states – and sometimes within a state. Take, for instance, the **Idaho** case (*Morrison v. Northwest Nazarene University,* 2012) in which the plaintiff claimed the waiver was overly broad and unenforceable. This extremely broad waiver showed that courts differ as to what is considered to be overly broad. The waiver purported to

- Exempt the University and "its members, directors, administrators, representatives, officers, agents, employees, and assigns, and each of them."
- From "any and all past, present or future claims, demands, and causes of action which the undersigned now has or may in the future have."
- For all "bodily injury, including death, however caused

- Resulting from, arising out of or in any way connected with his/her participation in or use of the Northwest Nazarene University Challenge Course Adventure Program … whether caused by the negligence of the Releasees or otherwise.

The court ruled that it was not overly broad and enforced the waiver.

10. **Waivers should be broad enough to defeat claims of "not within the contemplation of the signer" or "beyond the scope of the waiver."** These are common challenges that, if true, can defeat an otherwise good waiver. It is important to contemplate all likely *types of risks* and word the waiver to try to cover them. For instance, if the dive trip for a scuba class involves a road trip, the drafter should remember to word the waiver so that it encompasses traffic accidents or other hazards of the trip.

    In an **Illinois** case (*Locke v. Life Time Fitness, Inc.*, 2014), the plaintiff made a number of allegations, including failing to train employees to properly identify and respond to medical emergencies. The court stated that, to be valid, a waiver

    > should contain clear, explicit, and unequivocal language referencing the types of activities, circumstances, or situations that it encompasses and for which the plaintiff agrees to relieve the defendant from a duty of care.

    Thus, to be enforceable, the waiver must put the signer on notice. The court added, however, that a risk "not specifically contemplated in an exculpatory clause can also still be covered if it 'fall[s] within the scope of possible dangers ordinarily accompanying the activity and, therefore, reasonably contemplated by the parties.'" The court determined that no terms in the waiver covered the failure to train allegation; subsequently, the club's motion for summary judgment failed.

    Otherwise perfectly good waivers sometimes fail because the cause of the injury was not what was contemplated when the participant signed the waiver. For instance, in *ver Weire v. Styles* (2013), the plaintiff was a spectator at a race track when a loose plank in the bleachers caused her to fall. The waiver was well-written, but related solely to the unique and obvious dangers associated with being in the restricted area of the race track. The **Arkansas** Court of Appeals did not enforce it, stating that the negligence claim related only to the lack of care in maintaining safe bleachers for the spectators – in other words, the incident was beyond the scope of the waiver. The case was remanded in order to determine if the race track breached its duty to maintain the premises in a reasonably safe condition. A Navy SEAL was killed in a live fire drill when a bullet penetrated a "bulletproof" wall and struck him (*Ghane v. Mid-South Institute of Self Defense Shooting, Inc.*, 2014). The **Mississippi** Supreme Court stated that relieving the defendant of liability for not following even basic safety standards in the design of the ballistic wall or the failure of the wall to perform as advertised is unreasonable; it was plainly beyond the contemplation of the signer.

11. **Include within the agreement reference to property damage, loss, and theft.** Property is often stored either temporarily or on a fairly long-term basis in lockers or elsewhere on the premises during participation. Service providers need to be protected against liability in the event of damage due to fire, flood, and such, as well as against loss or theft from the locker or other area. In *Guivi v. Spectrum Club Holding Company* (2011), a patron had valuable jewelry stolen from her locker during a massage. She sued alleging negligence in failing to provide facilities and failure to train staff for the security of her property. The waiver she had signed stated the club was not responsible for valuables and recommended that they be kept on one's person at all times. The waiver was upheld.

10. **The agreement should specify the duration of the agreement.** Generally such contracts continue until terminated by one of the parties, (*Bien v. Fox Meadow Farms, Ltd.,* 1991) but it is safer to insure the ongoing nature of the agreement with such language such as "for today and on all future dates," "which may hereinafter occur" or "in present or future participation. " A waiver in a 2005 California case (*Mower v. City of Realto,* 2005) was enforced when it included the language "in said activity or any activities incidental thereto … **for whatever period said activities may continue….**" [Bold added]. The waiver in the *Heilig v. Touchstone* (2007) climbing wall case was very clear as to its duration. The language stated that the duration of the waiver is *forever.*

When Waiver is in a Membership Contract. When the exculpatory clause is a part of a **membership contract** or the waiver is signed in conjunction with a contract, the clause would generally be effective for the duration of the contract. However, it is not uncommon for an exculpatory clause to remain in effect for a time after the contractual period has ended. In a ski club case, a membership had expired before the member drowned. The club stated that it generally allowed four or five month grace periods on renewals. The court, therefore, ruled the person was still a member and the waiver was still in effect (*Finkler v. Toledo Ski Club,* 1989). Likewise, in *Johnson v. Fit Pro, LLC* (2010) and in *Mower,* the courts enforced the waiver after the contract period had ended. The *Mower* court stated that a membership agreement can expire in some respects, but remain in force in others. The court held that the member's right to use the center had expired, but that the release agreement remained in effect.

In a 2014 case (*Applegate-Rodeman v. JDK*), the plaintiff joined a health club. The membership agreement contained a waiver giving a membership expiration date and provided for renewal on a monthly basis. Her insurance provider executed a separate agreement for its members. When the original yearly contract expired, she did not renew or cancel her membership; she enrolled in the new program paid for by her insurance company, but was not required to complete a new waiver. Later that year she was injured. The court ruled that the original waiver "continued to have effect after the initial twelve-month term expired, in a manner similar to that of a holdover tenancy."

Nevertheless, waivers do not always outlive the membership. In *Nimis v. St. Paul Turners* (1994), a woman joined a health and fitness club, signed a waiver, and eventually let her membership lapse. A year later, she rejoined the club but was not required to sign a waiver and was injured. The *Nimis* court ruled that the original waiver was not in effect because it had expired when the membership lapsed.

When Waiver Contains no Duration. *While waivers are often enforced when there is no specified duration on the waiver, providers are on much safer ground when duration is on-going until cancelled* (as in *Mower* and *Heilig* above). A Pennsylvania court encountered a waiver signed six months earlier at a previous Lehigh Valley go-kart event; the waiver was silent as to the duration of the agreement (*Weinrich v. Lehigh Valley Grand Prix Inc.,* 2015). The court found that there was no **Pennsylvania** or federal authority addressing the matter. The plaintiff relied on a **Florida** case in which a waiver was not enforced because it contained no express language indicating it applied to future visits to the motocross track (*Cain v. Banka,* 2006). The Lehigh Valley waiver neither limited the time for its applicability nor specified the event or occasion to which it applied. The court stated that 1) waivers generally only encompass matters within the contemplation of the parties; 2) waivers must be construed in accordance with traditional principles of contract law; 3) that courts must not invalidate such a waiver, but must infer that the intent was to apply for a "reasonable amount of time"; 4) what constitutes a "reasonable period of time" is a question of fact and must be resolved by the fact finder – the jury; and 5) summary judgment is inappropriate when there is a genuine issue of material fact. Hence, the court denied Lehigh Valley's summary judgment motion based upon the waiver.

Likewise, in a Pennsylvania case involving an ultra light aircraft (*Simeone v. Bombardier-Rotax GMBH,* 2005), the waiver signed by the plaintiff prior to a demonstration flight was not upheld because the waiver was not written to include subsequent flights after purchase.

In contrast, in *Couch v. Lyon* (2013), Couch joined a guided deer hunt and signed a waiver. Later in the summer, he rejoined RCA Hunting Service (and Lyon) as a volunteer helper. He was accidentally shot during a pheasant hunt and filed suit. Lyon claimed protection from the waiver. The waiver, using the word "activities," did not specify the type of hunt and there was no expiration date. The **South Dakota** court ruled that the waiver barred the suit. Similarly, in an **Ohio** go-kart case (*Webster v. G & J Kartway,* 2006), a father of a participant registered his son for a race and signed a waiver to enter the restricted area. The race was rained out and rescheduled two weeks later. When the father arrived and was going to the registration window, he slipped and fell injuring himself. Defendants claimed the waiver signed two weeks earlier as a defense. The court upheld the waiver.

11. **Avoid asking questions on the waiver.** Asking questions of a participant can suggest that the waiver is valid for the day of signing only. In a **Puerto Rico** scuba case, the waiver asked several questions. They were: Last time you dove? Number of dives since you have been certified? Have you taken any medication in the last 24 hours? Recent illnesses? Pregnant? The plaintiff claimed that in light of the questions, one would reasonably conclude that the waiver was valid only for that one day. The court said that since the waiver did not include applicable dates or the number of dives for which it was applicable, it was ambiguous and not enforceable (*Sylva v. Culebra Dive Shop,* 2005). Similarly, in *Cain v. Banka* (2006), the waiver stated that the signer knew the *present condition* of the track, suggesting that the waiver was for a particular day. The plaintiff argued that if the purpose of the waiver was to cover all future times a person might be on the property, it should state that the waiver "applies to all future entrances to the premises." The court **Florida** agreed and held for the plaintiff.

12. **Avoid making the exculpatory statement too long.** Qualify and broaden the statement by adding a following statement such as:

> This agreement applies to all injuries or loss which may result from 1) use of the facility and equipment, 2) participation in any activity, class, program, instruction, or personal training, 3) use of and malfunction of equipment, 4) our supervision or dietary recommendations, and 5) slips, falls, or other mishaps on the club premises, sidewalks, parking areas, locker areas, or rest rooms.

Example C:

> **Waiver of Liability:** In consideration of permission to participate in a horseback trail ride, today and on all future dates, **I,** on behalf of myself, my spouse, my heirs, personal representatives, or assigns**, do hereby release, waive, and discharge LHTR (including its officers, employees, and agencies) from liability from any and all claims** resulting from the *inherent risks* of the activity of trail riding or from the **ordinary negligence of the LHTR.**
>
> This agreement applies to 1) personal injury (including death) from incidents or illnesses arising from horseback trail ride participation at the LHTR (including, but not limited to, all premises [including in and around the stable and corral, on trails, bleachers, the associated sidewalks and parking lots] and while mounting, dismounting, mounted, riding, during any instruction by the staff, during practice or events, and during facility or trail inspections); and to 2) any and all claims resulting from the damage to, loss of, or theft of property.

Step Five
Indemnification Agreement

An indemnity clause is language by which a participant or another party agrees to reimburse the service provider for any monetary loss resulting from an injury to the participant or an injury or loss caused by the participant. Indemnification is indicated by such language as 1) *... agrees to indemnify,* 2) *reimburse,* 3) *hold harmless,* or 4) *save harmless (Johnson v. New River Scenic Whitewater Tours, Inc.,* 2004).

An effective indemnification agreement can add additional protection against both liability for injuries resulting from the inherent risks of the activity and liability for injuries resulting from the negligence of the provider. A **Kentucky** court (*Speedway SuperAmerica, LLC v. Erwin,* 2008) has pointed out that when a party uses an indemnification clause to protect against provider negligence, the distinction between a waiver and indemnification agreement is negligible. It went on to stress that a key factor in both types of agreements is the relative bargaining positions of the parties.

Angelo v. USA Triathlon (2014) illustrates the value of an indemnity agreement. Richard Angelo died during the swim portion of the triathlon; his wife filed a wrongful death suit claiming conscious pain and suffering by the decedent, gross negligence, and negligent infliction of emotional distress suffered by the wife. Angelo had signed a waiver and indemnification agreement, The indemnification portion of the agreement read:

> I further agree that if, despite this Agreement, I, or anyone on my behalf, makes a claim for Liability against any of the Released Parties, I will indemnify, defend and hold harmless each of the Released Parties from any such Liability which any [sic] may be incurred as the result of such claim.

Based upon this agreement, USAT counterclaimed for any award and legal costs associated with the legal action[59]. The waiver protected against the pain and suffering negligence claim; the gross negligence claim was not protected by the waiver; but, of course, gross negligence must be proven. The wife indicated intent to re-file her personal negligent infliction of emotional distress claim; the court noted that USAT would be entitled to indemnification of any losses incurred due to this claim. Any award, however, would go to the plaintiff (individually, not her husband's estate), so USAT would have to seek indemnification from the estate and not from the wife.

Guidelines

1. **Include an indemnity clause within the participant agreement.** Indemnification seems to be most effective when one business entity agrees to indemnify another business entity. Courts often seem to ignore indemnification language in waivers where individuals agree to indemnify business entities for damages caused by the negligence of the business entity.

   In a houseboat rental case (*Yang v. Voyagaire Houseboats, Inc.,* 2005), the Supreme Court of **Minnesota** ruled that the waiver and indemnity agreement was against public policy since the houseboat rental company was, in effect, a resort providing a public service by furnishing sleeping accommodations to the public. It stated that to be enforceable, indemnity clauses must 1) specifically refer to negligence, 2) expressly state that the signer will indemnify the provider for the provider's negligence, or 3) clearly indicate that the renter will indemnify the provider for negligence occurring before the renter took possession of the houseboat. This ruling suggests that parties relying on indemnity agreements should clearly state the intent of the clause.

---

[59] The **Massachusetts** court stated that indemnity contracts that exempt a party from liability are not illegal and can survive the death of the signer and become an obligation of the estate. Decedent's survivors, being non-signers, are not bound by the indemnification agreement.

2. **There is no "magic" in the word indemnify**. A **West Virginia** court stated that to be effective, an indemnification clause should include language such as "I agree to hold harmless, defend, and indemnify . . . from any claims . . ." (*Johnson v. New River Scenic Whitewater Tours*, 2004). Language such as "I agree to release and indemnify. . ." is often interpreted as waiver language.

   The importance of an indemnification clause is illustrated in the following cases. In an **Indiana** case (*Beaver v. Foamcraft, Inc.*, 2002), Dorothy Beaver participated in a go-kart race and was injured when struck by padding from a foam barrier. She and her husband sued alleging willful and wanton conduct, loss of consortium, and other claims. Foamcraft claimed that a waiver and indemnity agreement protected them from liability. After considerable legal action, the court ruled that the defendant was protected from recovery of Dorothy Beaver by the waiver of liability. However, the court ruled that the waiver did not prevent the claim of the husband for loss of consortium. The court held that as a practical matter, the husband would be unable to collect damages because Dorothy had agreed to indemnify the defendant for all losses. A similar situation occurred in a previously discussed **Ohio** case (*Walsh v. Luedke*, 2005).

3. **Language must reflect the mutual intent of the parties to indemnify for indemnitee negligence**. In a **Maine** case (*Rice v. American Skiing Company*, 2000), the court held that an indemnity agreement used by the ski provider was ambiguous as it did not make clear that it provided for indemnity for provider negligence.

   > I hereby indemnify the ski areas named above, its owners, affiliates, employees and agents for all awards, legal expenses and settlements arising out of the child's participation in this clinic and the use of the ski area premises.

   The *Rice* court cited the following language as being valid and unambiguous (*International Paper Co. v. A&A Brochu*, 1995):

   > SELLER does hereby agree to indemnify and hold harmless PURCHASER from and against any and all claims, damages, debts, demands, suits, actions, attorney fees, court costs, and expenses arising out of, attributable to, or resulting from SELLER'S or any supplier's said operations ... caused or alleged to have been caused in whole or in part by the negligence of PURCHASER, its agents or employees.

   The *Walsh* case in Ohio provides another example of an unambiguous indemnification clause:

   > [I] HEREBY AGREE TO INDEMNIFY AND SAVE AND HOLD HARMLESS the Releasees and each of them FROM ANY LOSS, LIABILITY, DAMAGE, OR COST they may incur arising out of or related to the EVENT(S) WHETHER CAUSED BY THE NEGLIGENCE OF THE RELEASEES OR OTHERWISE.

   Courts in some states have less stringent requirements. In *Heilig v. Touchstone Climbing* (2007), the **California** court examined the following indemnity language:

   > Should [Touchstone] or anyone acting on their behalf, be required to incur attorney's fees and costs to enforce this agreement, I agree to indemnify and hold them harmless for all such fees and costs.

   The plaintiff argued that the indemnity applied only to third party actions, however, the court, while recognizing that indemnity did often relate to third party claims, emphasized that indemnification encompassed both parties to the agreement and third parties. It went on to point out that indemnity clauses may also serve as an attorney fee provision. In other words, in the event some action by the signing party (participant) results in injury to some third party (e.g., co-participant, instructor, rescuer, or spectator) and the provider is sued, the signing party is obligated to repay the provider for losses incurred.

4. **Use a two-pronged indemnity section.** Include at least two paragraphs or sections in the indemnity section. In the first, the participant (or parent if the participant is a minor) agrees to indemnify against claims of the participant, parent, family members, or others arising from the participant's injury or loss due to involvement in the activity. In the second, the participant (or parent if the participant is a minor) indemnifies against claims of co-participants, rescuers, and others arising from the conduct of the participant in the course of participation.

5. **Specify legal fees and investigative costs in the language.** Most states follow the American rule that requires each party to litigation to pay his or her own attorney's fees. Courts in some states, nevertheless, have exceptions such as 1) fees are recoverable if there is an express contractual obligation [as specified in a waiver] or 2) if a suit is found to have been brought in bad faith. Courts are more likely to require payment of legal fees and investigative costs if the indemnification language specifies "all expenses including court costs, legal fees, and investigative costs."

> In *Sevilla v. Estate of Lynn Maxey Wiley* (2004), the court stated that the "plain language of the indemnity provision ... supports an award of attorney fees." The waiver read, in part, "... from any and all losses.... THIS INCLUDES REIMBURSEMENT OF ALL LEGAL COSTS AND REASONABLE COUNSEL FEES INCURRED BY THE ESTABLISHMENT...." Gregg suggests wording such as "I further agree to protect and indemnify (that is, defend and pay any judgment and costs, including attorney's fees)...."

6. **Use first person language.** Language in the first person is sometimes considered to be less ambiguous than other language. Language might include "I agree to hold harmless, defend, and indemnify ...."

7. **Word the agreement broadly.** Word the agreement to include as many aspects of the activity as possible. Narrow wording can leave the provider unprotected. In *Potrzebowski v. Redline Raceway* (2011), the wife of a racecar driver was injured while walking down the staircase to the pit area. She sued the raceway for her injuries and the raceway claimed protection from the indemnity language in the waiver signed by her husband. The language read

> HEREBY AGREES TO INDEMNIFY AND SAVE AND HOLD HARMLESS the releasees and each of them from any loss, liability, damage or cost they may incur due to the presence of the undersigned in or upon the restricted area or in any way competing, officiating, observing or working for, or for any purpose participating in the event and whether caused by the negligence of the releasees or otherwise.

The court ruled that the indemnity language did not clearly and unequivocally provide that the husband indemnified the raceway for injury to his wife or any other third person.

Example D:

> **Indemnification:** **I also agree to hold harmless, defend, and indemnify LHTR** (that is, defend and pay any judgment and costs, including investigation costs, court costs, legal fees, and attorney's fees) from any and all claims of mine, my spouse, family members, or others arising from my injury or loss due to my participation in horseback trail riding (including those arising from the inherent risks of trail riding or the ordinary negligence of LHTR).
>
> **I further agree to hold harmless, defend, and indemnify LHTR** (that is, defend and pay any judgment and costs, including investigation costs, court costs, legal fees, and attorney's fees) against any and all claims of co-participants, rescuers, and others arising from my conduct in the course of my participation in horseback trail riding.

Step Six
Six Other Protective Clauses

Extra protection can be gained by including a "packet" of six protective clauses in the waiver. The clauses are a severability clause, a venue and jurisdiction clause, a covenant not to sue, a mediation and arbitration clause, an integration clause and a disclaimer.

Guidelines

1. **Always include a severability clause within the agreement.** A severability clause is a statement within the document that says, in effect, that if any part of the document is held void, this will have no effect upon the validity of the remainder of the document. Language commonly used is illustrated by *The undersigned hereby expressly agrees that this release and waiver is intended to be as broad and inclusive as permitted by the laws of the State of Missouri and that if any portion hereof is held invalid, it is agreed that the balance shall, notwithstanding, continue in full legal force and effect* (*Vergano v. Facility Mgmt. of Missouri*, 1995; *Ball v. Waldoch Sports, Inc.*, 2003). Without such a phrase, the entire waiver can be declared invalid due to one invalid phrase; in *In the Matter of Pacific Adventures, Inc.* (1998) and *Farina v. Mt. Bachelor* (1995), the **Hawaii** and **Oregon** courts failed to enforce waivers because the language was interpreted as protecting against both negligence and gross negligence, which made the waivers against public policy. A severability clause would have eliminated the offending language and allowed possible enforcement of the waivers.

    In a 2007 case before the **District of Columbia** Court of Appeals (*Moore v. Waller*, 2007), the appellant claimed that the waiver was so broad that it could be construed to exempt the club from liability for intentional torts or for reckless or grossly negligent conduct. The appellant argued that such provisions should invalidate the entire waiver. The court disagreed, holding that "A better interpretation of the law is that any 'term' in a contract which attempts to exempt a party from liability for gross negligence or wanton conduct is unenforceable, not the entire [contract]." Even though this waiver containing no severability clause was enforced, inclusion of a severability clause is strongly recommended.

2. **Always include a selection of venue and jurisdiction clause (forum selection).** Venue selection and jurisdiction merely specify in which state and county any future legal proceedings must take place, the court having the legal power to interpret and apply the law, and which state

law is to be applied. Generally, the plaintiff has the choice of venue unless a venue is specified by contract within the waiver. If the venue is specified within the contract, courts will usually enforce that venue. It helps to insure that if legal action does result, it will be in the local court rather than in a distant state and that the case will be decided by the laws of the state in which the business resides.

The wording of the venue clause can be crucial, as was indicated by the similar rulings of two **Florida** courts (*American Boxing v. Young*, 2005; *Dore v. Roten*, 2005) on the following clause:

> If any disputes arise which are related in any way to this document, then I consent and agree that jurisdiction for such dispute shall be in Bay City, Michigan.

The courts held that the venue clause did not require that a tort action be tried in Michigan because the clause specified, "... related in any way to this document." Since the tort action did not relate to the waiver document, it could be tried in Florida. The courts further stated that the clause was ambiguous because the language "consent and agree" indicated a permissive venue provision while the term "shall" signifies that the venue provision is mandatory. Since ambiguity existed, the courts interpreted the clause in favor of the plaintiff.

A **Washington** court (*Chew v. Lord*, 2008) ruled similarly in an adult scavenger hunt case in which the plaintiff fell into an abandoned mine shaft. The language of the waiver was "I understand and agree that this waiver . . . shall be governed by and construed in accordance with the . . . laws of the State of Washington." The court ruled that consent to personal jurisdiction in Washington courts is not the same as agreeing that Washington courts are the only venue in which a claim can be brought. Rather, the language means that should suit be brought in a Washington court, the defendant consents to that jurisdiction. Language such as the following should prove more effective:

> Likewise, I understand that if legal action is brought, the appropriate trial court for the county of _____ in the State of _____ has the sole and exclusive jurisdiction and that only the substantive laws of the State of _____ shall apply.

For more information on choice of law and forum selection clauses, see Choice of Law and Forum Selection in Chapter 2 and Appendix B.

3. **Include an integration clause in the agreement.** The integration clause is used to prevent either party from claiming that other promises (oral or written) were made. It states that this agreement supersedes any and all previous oral or written promises or agreements. This clause, in stating that this is the complete and final agreement, makes any oral promises unenforceable.

In a **Colorado** case (*Brooks v. Timberline Tours, Inc.* (1997), the plaintiff alleged breach of contract, claiming that an advertising brochure constituted part of the contract. The court ruled for the defendant since the last paragraph of the agreement provided: "I understand that this is the entire Agreement between myself and Timberline Tours, Inc. ... and cannot be modified or changed in any way by the representations or statements of any employee or agent of Timberline Tours, Inc.... or by me."

In *Handy-Mixon v. LA Fitness* (2007), the plaintiff signed a waiver containing the following integration clause:

> Member has read this release and waiver of liability and indemnity clause, and agrees that no oral representations, statements or inducement apart from the foregoing written agreement have been made.

The plaintiff argued that the integration clause should not apply to her because she did not understand the agreement. The **California** court considered the motion, but ruled in favor of the defendant.

4. **Consider the option of including a mediation clause, an arbitration clause, or both within the participant agreement.** Mediation and arbitration offer many advantages over going through the court system. Some are that they 1) are less expensive, 2) require less time, 3) are more private, thereby reducing the likelihood of unfavorable publicity, and 4) are more likely to result in a peaceful settlement. An argument sometimes heard in opposition to such clauses is that arbitration usually results in a monetary settlement.

While most insurance companies seems to look favorably on arbitration agreements, one should always obtain approval of his or her insurance carrier (in writing) prior to including an arbitration agreement in a waiver. Many companies will want to see the waiver and the arbitration language. Also, consult with an attorney familiar with mediation/arbitration law in your state. Your attorney can often give you good advice regarding the clause.

The participant agreement can include a clause by which the participant (or the parent of the participant if the participant is a minor) agrees to engage in good faith efforts to mediate any dispute that might arise. Any agreement reached can be formalized by a written contractual agreement at the time. The participant agreement can also include an agreement to submit any unresolved dispute to binding arbitration. Venue, source of the arbitrator, and any limitations or restrictions (e.g., time period, motions, discovery, depositions, expert witnesses) can be included in the agreement.

Language such as "I further agree that if a legal dispute arises, I will attempt to settle the dispute through mediation before a mutually acceptable mediator whose name appears in the registry of names recognized by the 'State' courts as qualified persons for mediation assignments. To the extent mediation does not result in a resolution, I agree to submit the dispute to binding arbitration through the American Arbitration Association in 'State.'" [60] Note, however that there are other arbitration organizations available.

Arbitration agreements are governed by the Federal Arbitration Act (FAA), **9 U.S.C. Sections 1-16**, enacted by Congress to embody a national policy favoring arbitration and to place arbitration agreements on equal footing with other contracts. An arbitration provision 1) is severable from the rest of the contract, 2) unless the challenge is to the clause itself, the contract's validity is considered by the arbitrator, and 3) arbitration law applies in state as well as federal courts (*Buckeye Check Cashing, Inc. v. Cardegna*, 2006).

In a 2005 case (*Hojnowski v. Vans Skate Park*), the skateboard park included provision for arbitration in a clause reading in part "If you are injured and want to make a claim, you must file a demand before the American Arbitration Association.... You agree that any dispute between you and Vans will be decided by the AAA. Vans will pay all costs of the arbitration for you..." (p. 3). The clause was held to be enforceable by the New Jersey Supreme Court.

In a non-recreation case, the language read "the Purchaser and Terminix agree that any controversy or claim between them arising out of or relating to this agreement shall be settled exclusively by arbitration" (*Troshak v. Terminix International Company*, 1998, p. 6-7). In a case arising out of medical care, the agreement provided for binding arbitration of "any claims for damages for personal injury ... arising out of the rendition of or failure to render services under this contract" (*Leong v. Kaiser Foundation Hospitals*, 1990, p. 6).

In an **Ohio** case involving an arbitration clause within a health club membership contract, the client filed suit alleging the clause was unconscionable and unenforceable (*Cronin v. California Fitness*, 2005). The clause read in part:

---

[60] Adapted from The National Outdoor Leadership School acknowledgement and assumption of risks and the agreement of indemnity and release prepared by Charles R. Gregg.

If there is any dispute over $500 ... both parties agree to submit it to binding arbitration, using the American Arbitration Rules. Arbitration means that neither you nor California Fitness can sue each other in court over the dispute and that a neutral arbitrator will decide it, not a jury or judge....

The arbitration covers ... financial obligations, facilities, representations, personal injury, and property, contract, and tort damage of any kind. If there is any dispute over the applicability of arbitration or the validity of ... waiver provision only an Arbitrator, not a court, may decide the dispute....

If the arbitration proceeds further, the Arbitrator is limited to the terms of this Agreement and whether you or California Fitness prevail in the arbitration, the maximum an Arbitrator may award is the cost of your annual membership....

The party who makes the claim must pay the costs of arbitration, including the arbitrator's fees, but each party will pay its own expenses, including attorney's fees and costs.... The parties shall not disclose the existence, contents, or results of the arbitration without the written consent of both parties (p. 1-4).

The appellate court upheld the trial court ruling that the agreement was not unconscionable. It stated 1) the signing of the agreement was knowing and voluntary, 2) the plaintiff was not in a disadvantageous bargaining position, and 3) the plaintiff was not induced to sign by adverse circumstances.

In spite of the ruling in *Cronin*, one should attempt to keep the terms of an arbitration clause from being too one-sided in favor of the provider. In *McGregor v. Christian Care Center of Springfield, LLC*, (2010) and *Lhotka v. Geographic Expeditions, Inc.* (2010) one may see two examples of unreasonably one-sided arbitration agreements. Both agreements were ruled unconscionable and unenforceable by their **Tennessee** and **California** courts.

In a case to determine if an arbitration agreement of a deceased resident of a rehabilitation center was enforceable, the **Pennsylvania** court ruled that the agreement was enforceable against the survival claims, but that such agreements are not enforceable against wrongful death claims (*Northern Health Facilities v. Batz*, 2014). But waiver law differs from state to state; a **Florida** case (*Spivey v. Challenge of Florida, Inc.*, 2013) involved a wrongful death claim of a young man in a drug and alcohol rehabilitation center. The court found that nothing in Florida or federal law forbade the enforcement of arbitration agreements in wrongful death cases.

Conflict between Arbitration and Exculpatory Language. In *Finley v. Club One, Inc.* (2012), the plaintiff argued that the provision for binding arbitration in the waiver was inconsistent with a release of personal injury claim resulting from negligence. The California court ruled that "even if the two clauses are arguably inconsistent, the presence of an arbitration clause does not impact or reduce the clarity or scope of the liability release language."

5. **The participant agreement should include a covenant not to sue.** A covenant not to sue is a contract not to sue to enforce a right of action against the provider. While some authorities view the distinction between a waiver (release) and a covenant not to sue as artificial, most see a significant difference in that 1) the waiver eliminates the cause of action while the covenant not to sue does not and 2) the waiver or release often releases joint tortfeasors while the covenant not to sue does not (*McCurry v. School Dist. Of Valley*, 1993).

A covenant not to sue is included in many, if not most, waivers – sometimes as a separate clause and sometimes it is simply listed in the waiver exculpatory language similarly to ". . . do hereby release, waive, discharge, and covenant not to sue Healthier Health Club . . . ." At times, its inclusion seems pointless because many courts generally seem to ignore the language totally.

However, in a 2004 **California** case (*Bossi v. Sierra Nevada Recreation Corporation*, 2004) involving rappelling to the floor of a cavern, a woman signed a document in which she agreed to release, waive, discharge, and covenant not to sue the service provider. The jury found that the waiver protected the provider from liability and returned a verdict for over $100,000 in damages on the defendant's cross-complaint for breach of the covenant not to sue.

6. **The Participant Agreement may include a statement of disclaimer by the provider.** A **disclaimer** is a statement in which the service provider disclaims all liability for injury and asserts that the participant is assuming all risks of injury or loss. The disclaimer may appear on a waiver, on the back of a ticket, or on a posted sign. Keep in mind, an unsigned disclaimer (as on a ticket) does not usually carry the legal weight of a signed waiver. The Uniform Commercial Code in **Pennsylvania** states that a disclaimer must be clear and conspicuous to engage the attention of a reasonable person (**RCW 62 A. 2-316[2]** and **RCW 62A. 2-179[1],[3]**). A Pennsylvania court said that whether a disclaimer on the back of a lift ticket gave adequate notice was a question of fact for the jury (*Passero v. Killington, Ltd.*, 1993). A **Michigan** court said that small print on the back of a ski lift ticket gave inadequate notice for enforcement (*Braun v. Mount Brighton, Inc.*, 1989).

    A 2008 United States District Court for the District of **Oregon** (*Silva v. Mt. Bachelor, Inc.*) enforced a waiver on a ski pass. Mt. Bachelor had posted a sign at the ticket window stating "YOUR TICKET IS A RELEASE" and warning that by using the ticket, the purchaser was releasing Mt. Bachelor from liability, including liability for negligence. Interestingly, the court stated that the plaintiff cited no cases that require that a recreational release be signed. The court ruled that the waiver was enforceable. The fact that the plaintiff had not signed the waiver, but was aware of its presence and meaning might have been a factor. It seems that such disclaimers are sometimes enforced when the disclaimer is conspicuous and has been read and understood by the plaintiff (*Beck-Hummel v. Ski Shawnee, Inc.*, 2006; *Nisbett v. Camelback Ski Corp.*, 1996; *Savarese v. Camelback Ski Corp.*, 2005).

    A disclaimer may, in some cases, add a little weight to a waiver by clarifying the purpose of the waiver. Courts in Hawaii, New York, and North Carolina have upheld disclaimers for the negligent acts of a third party supplier. Each was used by a travel agent or tour company to protect themselves from the negligent acts of a third party supplier of services (see Chapter 6 for more information on disclaimers).

Example E:

Other Protective Clauses:

Severability: I expressly agree that the foregoing Assumption of Risk, Waiver of Liability, and Indemnification Agreement is intended to be as broad and inclusive as is permitted by the laws of the State of _____ and that if any portion thereof is held invalid, it is agreed that the balance shall, notwithstanding, continue in full legal force and effect.

Venue and Jurisdiction: Likewise, I understand that if legal action is brought, the appropriate trial court for the County of _____ in the State of _____ has the sole and exclusive jurisdiction and that only the substantive laws of the State of _____ shall apply.

Integration Clause: I affirm that this *agreement supersedes any and all previous oral or written promises or agreements*. I understand that this is the entire agreement between me and LHTR and cannot be modified or changed in any way by representations or statements by any agent or employee of LHTR. This agreement may only be amended by a written document duly executed by all parties.

Mediation and Arbitration: I agree to engage in good faith efforts to mediate any dispute that might arise. Any agreement reached will be formalized by a written contractual agreement at that time. Should the issue not be resolved by mediation, I agree that all disputes, controversies, or claims arising out of or relating to this contract shall be submitted to binding arbitration in _____ County in the State of _____ in accordance with the applicable rules of the American Arbitration Association then in effect.

Covenant Not to Sue: I further covenant not to sue LHTR for any present or future claim arising directly or indirectly from my participation in horseback trail riding at LHTR. This includes claims resulting from the inherent risks of trail riding and/or the ordinary negligence of LHTR.

Disclaimer: LHTR is not liable for any injuries that may occur to riders while participating at Lucky Horseshoe Trail Rides; riders assume all risk of injury.

Step Seven
Assertions, Authorizations, and Affirmations

The assertions, authorizations, and affirmations are gathered in order to enable the provider to better address the health and safety needs of the client. This is not meant to be a comprehensive list of health affirmations, medical care authorizations, or safety agreements. The writer of the waiver may address other concerns relative to the specific situation. The comprehensiveness of the health status statement should vary with the type of activity. Certain types of activities (e.g., very strenuous activities or extraordinarily risky activities) may require securing more health information, authorizing different types of emergency care, or additional safety provisions. Also, a physical examination may be recommended or required before participation in some activities.

Guidelines
1. **Assertions of health status.** The participant affirms that he or she:
    * possesses no health problems or physical disabilities (including pregnancy) that would preclude participation in the activity.
    * does not have asthma, diabetes, anaphylaxis, epilepsy, or heart disease/high blood pressure.
    * will inform the activity leader of any health problem or disability that arises during participation.
    * possesses sufficient skills, coordination, and physical fitness to safely participate.
    * is in full command of his or her faculties and is not under the influence of alcohol or drugs.

2. **Authorizes Medical Care.** The participant affirms that he or she:
    * agrees that the provider can administer emergency first aid, CPR, and AED when deemed necessary by the provider.
    * authorizes emergency transport to medical care should that be deemed necessary by the provider.
    * authorizes the provider to secure medical care when it is deemed necessary by the provider.

- authorizes the provider to share participant medical information with emergency or medical personnel if deemed necessary by the provider.
- agrees to assume all cost of the care and transportation listed above.

3. **Affirms Agreement to follow Safety Rules.** The participant affirms that he or she:
   - agrees to wear all required safety gear during participation.
   - agrees to follow all rules of the activity and the provider.
   - agrees that the provider has authority to terminate signer's participation if the provider feels that further participation endangers the participant or others.
   - agrees to inform the provider of any conduct or environmental condition that might create a hazard for participants or others.
   - agrees not to participate in the activity while under the influence of alcohol or drugs.
   - understands that it is my responsibility to report all injuries (even minor injuries) so that we may make a record of the injury.

4. **Other Affirmations.** The participant affirms that he or she:
   - agrees to and grants permission for certain physical touching when necessary in teaching certain skills or in spotting performances.
   - Gives permission to _____ to use any photographs, videos, images, or likenesses taken of me to be used in any marketing or public relations brochures, ad, videos, or other media.

Example F:

Assertions, Authorizations, and Affirmations

Health Status – I assert that I:
- * do not have asthma, diabetes, anaphylaxis, epilepsy, heart disease, or high blood pressure.
- * have no medical problems that would contra-indicate participation in horseback trail riding.
- * possess sufficient fitness and skill to enable safe participation in horseback trail riding.

Emergency Care – I authorize or agree:
- * LHTR to administer emergency first aid, CPR, and AED if deemed necessary by LHTR.
- * LHTR to secure emergency medical care or transportation if deemed necessary by LHTR.
- * LHTR to share my medical history with medical personnel when deemed necessary by LHTR.
- * to assume all costs of emergency medical care and transportation.

Rules and Safety Equipment – I agree:
- * to abide by the rules established by LHTR.
- * to inform LHTR immediately if I become aware of rider conduct or equipment condition that presents a danger to others or myself.
- * to wear any required equipment at all times while riding.
- * that LHTR may find it necessary to terminate my participation if the supervisor judges that I am incapable of safely meeting the rigors of the activity. I accept LHTR's right to take such actions for the safety of myself and/or other riders.

Step Eight
Acknowledgement of Understanding and Signatures

The final section of the participant agreement is the concluding statements and the required signatures. This is a crucial part of the agreement and should be carefully done.

Guidelines

1. A concluding **acknowledgement of understanding** should immediately precede the signature(s), reinforcing the previous assertions and agreements.

   The acknowledgement of understanding can include:
   - Affirmation of having **read and understood** the agreement.
   - Affirmation of **relinquishing rights**.
   - Affirmation of **voluntary participation** and **voluntarily signing** the agreement.
   - Affirms the **release of liability** for injuries resulting from inherent risks and from ordinary negligence of the provider.

2. **Failure to read the waiver.** Courts generally disregard or fail to recognize claims by plaintiffs that they did not read the waiver. A Tennessee court stated that a person is under a duty to learn the contents of a contract before he signs it (*Thoni v. Duck River Speedway*, 1984). Unless there is fraud, even if the signer fails to read it, he or she is presumed to know the contents and cannot deny his/her obligation. One cannot avoid a contract pleading that the signer did not know the terms and did not read the document (*Hussein v. L.A. Fitness International, LLC*, 2013). In *Forrester v. Aspen Athletic Clubs, LLC* (2009), an Iowa court said if a party is able to and has the opportunity to read the contract and fails to do so, he or she cannot claim to be ignorant of its terms and conditions. In a 2011 California case (*Hazelwood v. L.A. Fitness International, LLC*), the plaintiff failed to read the waiver because he had forgotten his glasses. When injured three years later, the court upheld the waiver he had signed. Courts are consistent in holding that parties who cannot read have the responsibility to have it read or explained to them.

   In a California case (*Rosencrans v. Dover Images*, 2011), the court said it is not reasonable to fail to read a contract even if the plaintiff relies on the defendant's assertion that it is not necessary. California courts have said that for parties who cannot read, cannot read the language in which the waiver is written, or are blind, the general rule is that the signer cannot avoid liability on the basis of not having read the document (*Randas v. YMCA of Metropolitan Los Angeles*, 1993; *Cortez v. Ceres Unified School District*, 2003). In *Randas*, the plaintiff could not read English; she was provided a waiver which she signed. The court enforced the waiver since there was no fraud or over-reaching. Likewise, in *Cortez*, the father was unable to read the waiver sent home for him to sign. The court enforced the waiver saying the father should have had someone translate or explain it to him. The key factor is that the providers in these cases were not making assertions misrepresenting the waiver to the plaintiffs.

   Another approach was taken by the defendant in an Arizona hot air balloon case (*Thorne v. Eaton*, 2002). The waiver required the participant to write out the statement "I have carefully read this RELEASE and fully understand its contents" near the signature.

   Approach with Non-readers. In some of the preceding cases, waivers were enforced when the plaintiff was a non-reader. In spite of this, when developing your policy regarding non-readers, one should be aware of the **California** case, *Jimenez v. 24 Hour Fitness USA, Inc.*, 2015. The employee knew Jimenez could not speak or read English and made gestures toward the computer showing the price and gestures indicating exercise – seeming to indicate for that price, the plaintiff could use the facility. Additionally, the employee did not call for a Spanish-speaking

105

employee to help – which was his customary procedure. The court stated that an agreement is not enforceable if the releaser is under a misapprehension induced by the misconduct of the provider. The court felt that reasonable persons could find that the employee's actions constituted fraud and misrepresentation; thus this constituted a fact issue and should be determined by the jury. The court reversed the trial court summary judgment ruling and remanded it for trial. *Thus, the safest policy, from both legal and humane standpoints, would be to make certain non-readers have the effect of the waiver explained to them. Best practice might be to have the waiver read to English speakers and explained to those who speak another language by a speaker of that language.*

3. The **signature area** should provide for the 1) signature of the client, 2) printed name of the client, 3) date of the waiver, and 4) name and contact information of a party to contact in the event of an emergency. See also Step 10 for a discussion of signatures when dealing with minor clients.

4. Common practice includes the **requirement of one signature** at the end of the waiver. Some agreements include a space for a signature after each major section of the agreement (i.e., assumption of risk section, waiver section, and indemnity section). Others require an **initial** following each section. The court in *Stelluti v. Casapenn Enterprises, LLC* (2009) suggested that this might help to draw the reader's attention to significant passages, particularly if the agreement is exceptionally long.

    However, if several signatures or initials are required, it behooves the provider to inspect to see if all spaces have been addressed. An issue of intent may arise if one blank is inadvertently left blank; however, in *In re Aramark Sports and Entertainment Services, LLC* (2012) and *Grijalva v. Bally Total Fitness Corporation* (2015), the courts found no problem with waivers on which one blank was not checked.

    In contrast, in *Strickert v. Neal* (2015), the most important language in the waiver, "It is my intention by this instrument to exempt, release, and hold harmless Scuba Shack . . . from all liability. . .", was not checked. The court said the absence of Strickert's initial next to the paragraph cuts against the defendant's argument that Strickert clearly intended to release the defendant from liability. For that, and other reasons, summary judgment was not granted.

    Nevertheless, most waivers require only one signature. Requiring additional signatures or initials does not seem important in a stand-alone waiver and could create a problem where no problem exists.

5. When the participant is a **very young minor** (perhaps under 12 years old), the language should allow the parent to assert that the parent has explained the danger to the child and that the child understands that he or she could suffer injury. Obviously, the major burden of acceptance falls upon the parent in this situation; this makes the signature of a five- or six-year-old less important.

6. The **location of the signature** is important. If the agreement consists of only one page, the signature can be at the bottom of the page at the end of the agreement. When the agreement consists of two or more pages, it is good practice to make certain the signer knows that there is an exculpatory agreement and that he or she is agreeing to it. There are several ways to accomplish this: 1) require a signature on each page, 2) make clear at the signature that the agreement includes a waiver of liability, or 3) summarize the exculpatory language again immediately prior to the signature. The court in *Putzer v. Vic Tanney-Flatbush Inc.* (1964) did not uphold an exculpatory agreement appearing on the back of a document when the document was signed only on the front.

    In a similar case (*Kubisen v. Chicago Health Clubs,* 1979), the document was signed on the front, the exculpatory agreement was on the back, and there was no reference to the exculpatory agreement on the front page. The court ruled that the location of the exculpatory agreement was relevant only if the plaintiff was unaware of the exculpatory language. In this case, the waiver was upheld because the plaintiff had made no such assertion. Similarly, the court in *Lin v. Spring Mountain Adventures, Inc.* (2010) enforced the waiver because the plaintiff was made aware of the waiver by numerous references to the waiver language on the back of the sheet. In fact, the line directly above the signature referred specifically to the location of the waiver on the back of the document.

In a 2015 New Hampshire case (*Serna v. Lafayette Nordic Village, Inc.*), the waiver was challenged in part because the signature line was on the front of the page and the waiver was on the back of the page. Just above the signature line was the following statement: "I have read the agreement on the back of the form, releasing the inn from liability. I voluntarily agree to the terms of that agreement." The waiver on the reverse side consisted of seven paragraphs and lines for the signature and date. The court held that although the defendant did not sign the waiver on the reverse side, she signed the front of the document; by doing so, she agreed to the release on the back.

7. The question sometimes arises as to whether a **witness signature** is needed on a waiver. The simple answer is "No;" however, a question occasionally is raised about the validity of the signature – in which case a witness would help. Nevertheless, a witness signature is not required on a waiver. One exception is found in Hawaii statute **H.R.S. 663 – 10.95** which states that parental waivers for motorsports participants are enforceable provided in writing and signed by a parent *and a witness*.

8. The waiver should be **dated when it is signed**. In *Cruz v. Atco Raceway, Inc.* (2013), the waiver was not dated so the issue arose as to whether it had been signed on the date of the accident. The court ruled that the absence of the date helped to create an issue of material fact and denied defendant's motion for summary judgment.

Example G:

Acknowledgment of Understanding: I **have read** this 2-page Participant Agreement (Assumption of Risk, Waiver of Liability, and Indemnity) and **fully understand** its terms. I understand that I am **giving up substantial rights**, including my right to sue LHTR for injuries resulting from the inherent risks of horseback trail riding or the ordinary negligence of LHTR. I further acknowledge that I am participating and signing this agreement **freely and voluntarily**, and intend my signature to be a complete and unconditional release of all liability, including that due to ordinary negligence by LHTR, to the greatest extent allowed by the laws of the State of _____.

_____ _____ _____

Printed Name of PARTICIPANT   Signature of PARTICIPANT   Date

Emergency Contact: _____   Phone_____

Step Nine
Physical Appearance of the Agreement

The physical appearance of the agreement can be crucial to its success when challenged in court. Courts in most jurisdictions examine the document to determine whether the signer knew or should have known the importance of and the effect of the agreement. The appearance of the agreement can have a significant influence on that determination. The most extreme departure from this step was illustrated in *Mangels v. Yale* (2007) in which a professional wrestler was asked to sign a hand-written waiver.

Guidelines

1. **Make the document a one- to two-page, stand-alone agreement if possible.** A stand-alone waiver is one which has protection of the provider as its only objective. It does not include entry information, a membership agreement, a list of company rules, or other such information that might be of use to the provider. It is more difficult for the plaintiff to allege that he or she did not realize the function of the document when it is not overly long and contains nothing other than the protective agreement. Do not make the document any longer than is necessary, but include everything that is necessary for broad protection.

   The use of a stand-alone waiver is much preferred over those that are contained within another document. The *Holzer v. Dakota Speedway, Inc.* (2000) court stated that a pre-injury waiver is much more likely to be found valid and enforceable when it is written as a separate document.

2. **Number each page.** Numbering the pages in a manner such as (Page 1 of 3) helps to insure that a page is not missing when the client signs the waiver.

3. **Be certain that the print size is large enough to be easily read.** Courts do not usually specify minimal size; however, an Arizona statute (**ARS 12-556**) does specify 8 point or greater in motorsport waivers. By using a 10-point type size or greater, the provider can eliminate the issue if the agreement is challenged, but be certain that the key exculpatory language is at least as large as that of the remainder of the document.

   One California court (*Link v. National Association for Stock Car Racing*, 1984) commented, "The five-and-one-half-point print is so small that one would conclude that defendants never intended it to be read. Moreover, the lengthy fine print seems more calculated to conceal and not to warn the unwary." They noted that the Civil Code generally restricts type size in contracts to 8- to 10-point type and suggest, "As a matter of public policy, the typeface size of the crucial language in a release should be no smaller." In contrast, courts in several California cases ruled that 5 1/2–point type was sufficiently conspicuous and legible (*Bennett v. United States Cycling Federation*, 1987; *Okura v. United States Cycling Federation*, 1986; *Mower v. City of Rialto*, 2005).

   The Supreme Court of Texas failed to enforce a waiver in a case in which print size was the primary issue (*Littlefield v. Schaefer*, 1997). The waiver consisted of 30 lines of text compressed into a 3-inch by 4.25-inch rectangle located in the lower left hand corner of the form. The heading was in four-point font and contained 28 characters per inch. The main text used an even smaller font and contained 38 characters per inch. The court ruled that when the terms of a contract are unreadable, the contract is in violation of the Texas fair notice requirement and conspicuousness test.

4. **Make the exculpatory language conspicuous in the agreement.** It is important that the exculpatory language (the specific statement that the participant will not hold the provider liable

108

for ordinary negligence) be featured in such a way as to bring attention to it. The court in *Kolosnitsyn v. Crystal Mountain, Inc.* (2009) defined "conspicuous" as meaning 1) clearly displayed and 2) with clear and unambiguous meaning. The test is that the language should be so conspicuous that reasonable persons could not reach different conclusions as to whether the document was unwittingly signed. The following factors are used to determine conspicuousness: 1) heading is clear; 2) set off in capital letters or bold type; 3) signature line below the waiver provision; 4) clear that the signature is related to the waiver; 5) what the language above the signature line says; and 6) whether the waiver is set apart. Three other ways to make language conspicuous were given by the court in *Akin v. Bally Total Fitness Corporation* (2007): 1) use of an easily-read print size, 2) use of contrasting colors, and 3) use of underlining.

Some courts seem to give weight to wording that asserts that the signer has read the document, especially when the wording is near the signature line. An Illinois court (*Bien v. Fox Meadow Farms, Ltd.*, 1991) ruled that the notice "CAUTION: READ BEFORE SIGNING" preceding the signature coupled with a caption "RELEASE" were sufficiently conspicuous to overcome a claim of fraudulent inducement. The issue of conspicuousness of an exculpatory agreement at the top of a sign-up sheet was at issue in cases in Washington and Indiana (*Conradt v. Four Star Promotions, Inc.*, 1986; *LaFrenz v. Lake Cty. Fair Bd.*, 1977). The courts found the documents to be sufficiently conspicuous especially in light of the fact that "I have read this release" or "THIS IS A RELEASE" was printed above each signature line.

5. **Avoid large sections of upper case text.** The use of upper case to emphasize a word, phrase, or a sentence can make text stand out; extensive use of upper case text is much more difficult to read and results in text that is less likely to be understood by the reader. The following illustrates part of a waiver that was all in upper case type:

> 9. READ CAREFULLY THE FOLLOWING WAIVER AND RELEASE OF LIABILITY: HAVING RECEIVED A SAFETY TALK BY A MEMBER OP LESSOR'S STAFF, AND HAVING READ THE SAFETY PRECAUTIONS AND RECOMMENDATIONS ON THE REVERSE SIDE HEREOF, LESSEE(S) HEREBY ACKNOWLEDGE THAT HE/SHE/THEY FULLY UNDERSTAND(S): (a) THAT OUTDOOR RECREATIONAL ACTIVITIES HAVE INHERENT RISKS, DANGERS, AND HAZARDS, AND THAT SUCH EXISTS IN MY USE OF THE EQUIPMENT ABOVE DESCRIBED AND MY PARTICIPATION IN WHITE WATER RAFTING AND RELATED ACTIVITIES; (b) THAT MY PARTICIPATION IN SUCH ACTIVITIES AND/OR THE USE OF SUCH EQUIPMENT MAY RESULT IN INJURY OR ILLNESS, INCLUDING, BUT NOT LIMITED TO, BODILY INJURY, DISEASE, STRAINS, FRACTURES, PARTIAL AND OR TOTAL PARALYSIS, DEATH, OR OTHER AILMENTS THAT COULD CAUSE SERIOUS DISABILITY; (c) THAT SAID RISKS AND DANGERS MAY BE CAUSED BY (i) THE NEGLIGENCE OF THE OWNERS, EMPLOYEES, OFFICERS, OR AGENTS OF LESSOR, (ii) THE NEGLIGENCE OF PARTICIPANTS, (iii) THE NEGLIGENCE OF OTHERS, (iv) ACCIDENTS, (v) BREACHES OF CONTRACT, AND (vi) THE FORCES OF NATURE OR OTHER CAUSES. . . (*Wroblewski v. Ohiopyle Trading Post, Inc.*, 2013).

6. **Texas Guidelines for Conspicuous Waivers.** One Texas court (*Charbonnet v. Shami*, 2013) stated that a waiver "is conspicuous when it draws the attention of a reasonable person looking at the face of the document such that the person ought to notice it." The court made the following suggestions:

109

Considerations:

1. Whether the waiver is set off by a heading in capital letters and
2. Whether it is a different size, type, font, or color than the surrounding text.
3. Whether the document is clearly identified as a waiver
4. When the exculpatory language appears on the front side of the page and is not hidden under a separate heading or surrounded by unrelated terms
5. When the entire document is a single page
6. Whether it is set-off from the surrounding text by symbols or marks that call attention to the language.
7. Whether the text of the waiver is large enough to be easily legible

Although these guidelines are tailored to Texas, they would constitute good practice in any state.

Step Ten
If the Client is a Minor

When the client is a minor, another step (Step Ten) is necessary. Chapter 3 examined waiver law when the client is a minor and the information makes clear that waivers for minor clients are currently enforceable in several states. Still, such a waiver, even if not enforced, may be of value in showing that the client understood the inherent risks. Here are a few special guidelines that one should follow when the client is a minor.

Guidelines

1. **Limit your expectations.** Keep in mind that parental waivers are not enforced in every state. Do not rely solely upon such a waiver for liability protection.

2. **Address the rights of the minor and the rights of the parent.** Have the parents or guardians release the provider from liability from any claims made by or on behalf of the minor participant. Then in the same agreement, have the parents or guardians release the provider from any claims made by or on behalf of the parents or guardians. While a waiver may not protect the provider against the claims of the minor, the waiver will generally protect against claims made by or on behalf of the parent. (See Example H for illustrative language in a waiver written for both adults and minors.)

3. **One should place particular emphasis on the description of the activity, the nature of the activity, the inherent risks, and the possible consequences of participation.** If the waiver does not protect you against liability, the waiver can effectively show that the participant was aware of the inherent risks of participation.

4. **Have both the minor and the parents or guardians sign the waiver.** Both parents and the minor should sign the agreement. Have spaces for the signatures of the minor and both parents or guardians. It is best to require the signatures of both parents or guardians, but, be certain that at least one parent or guardian signs. Keep in mind that while in some states the signature of one parent binds both parents, in many states the non-signing parent is not bound by an agreement he or she does not sign. (See Example H below for illustrative assumption of risk language in a waiver or participant agreement written specifically for minor clients.)

110

Example H:

> **Assumption of Risk:** I, the minor client and the parents or guardians of the minor client, understand that the inherent risks of physical conditioning and training (including strength-building and cardiovascular activities) vary with the activity, the muscle group involved, and with the exercise equipment used. Common minor risks include minor muscle strains, muscle sprains, muscular fatigue, contusions, and post-exercise soreness. More serious, but less frequent, risks include joint injuries, torn muscles, heat-related illnesses, eye injuries, and back injuries. There are also the more remote risks of a catastrophic incident (e.g., stroke, heart attack, paralysis, or death).
>
> I, the minor client and the parents or guardians of the minor client, have read the previous paragraphs and **I know and understand the nature of the activities** at H&FC; **I understand the demands** of those activities relative to my physical condition and skill level (that of my son or daughter); and **I appreciate the types of injuries** that may occur as a result of activities made possible at H&FC and their potential impact on my well-being and lifestyle (that of my son or daughter). I, the minor client and the parents or guardians of the minor client, **hereby assert that the participation of the minor client is voluntary and that I**, the minor client and the parents or guardians of the minor client, **knowingly assume all such risks.**

5. **The agreement should allow the minor participant to affirm** 1) having had either the provider or the parent explain the document, 2) that he or she understands the agreement, and 3) having an opportunity to ask questions regarding the agreement.

6. **Give the parent or guardian responsibility for explaining the risks and safety rules to the child (particularly with very young children).** Include language in the waiver by which the adult verifies 1) having explained the risks of the activity and the safety rules, and 2) that the child understands the risks and rules. This is particularly important for children under age 10.

7. It is preferable that providers **who cater to both adult and minor participants use two agreements** – one for adult participants and one for minor participants. If only one waiver form is used, it should be carefully worded to make it clear that 1) it is intended to be in effect whether the client is a minor or adult and 2) the parent(s) or guardian(s) is waiving both the rights of the child and the rights of the parent(s). (See Example I below for illustrative language in a waiver written for **both adults and minors.**)

Example I:

> **Waiver of Liability:** In consideration of permission to use the property, facilities, and services of the MCSP, today and on all future dates, **I, the ADULT PARTICIPANT or** the MINOR PARTICIPANT AND PARENT/GUARDIAN, on behalf of myself, my heirs, personal representatives, or assigns (hereafter referred to as *Releasing Parties*) **do hereby release, waive, and discharge MCSP**, its officers, employees, and agencies (hereafter referred to as *Protected Parties*) **from liability from any and all claims resulting from the inherent risks of the activity of skateboarding or from the ordinary negligence** of the *Protected Parties*.
>
> This agreement applies to 1) personal injury (including death) from incidents or illnesses arising from or incidental to skateboarding participation at the MCSP (including, but not limited to, organized training activities, practice, competition, events, classes, assisting other skaters, observation, individual use of facilities or equipment, shower/locker room area, and all premises including bleachers, the associated sidewalks and parking lots); and to 2) any and all claims resulting from the damage to, loss of, or theft of property.

Acknowledgment of Understanding: I, the PARENT OR GUARDIAN**,** affirm that I **have explained the activity risks and the safety rules to my child** and that the **child understands both the risks and the rules.**

I, the **ADULT PARTICIPANT** or MINOR PARTICPANT AND PARENT/GUARDIAN have read this **Assumption of Risk, Waiver of Liability, and Indemnification Agreement** and fully **understand its terms. I understand that I am giving up substantial rights, including the right to sue** of the ADULT PARTICIPANT or the MINOR PARTICIPANT and the PARENT(S)/ GUARDIAN(S). I further acknowledge that **I am signing the agreement freely and voluntarily, and intend my signature to be a complete and unconditional release of all liability**, including that **due to ordinary negligence by** *Protected Parties*, to the greatest extent allowed by law of the State of Florida.

Printed Name of PARTICIPANT	Signature of PARTICIPANT	
Printed Name of Parent/Guardian #1	Signature of Parent/Guardian #1	Date
Printed Name of Parent/Guardian #2	Signature of Parent/Guardian #2	Date

Emergency Contact: _____ _____ _____
Name   Relationship   Phone Number

Step Eleven
Waivers Guidelines for Unsupervised Fitness Facilities

When the waiver is to be used for participation at an unsupervised fitness facility, another step (Step Eleven) is necessary. While most would agree that participation in a supervised fitness facility setting is safer than that of an unsupervised facility, the fact is that there is a growing demand for unsupervised facilities (e.g., apartment complexes, motels/hotels, senior centers). There are a number of risks that are created or enhanced by the lack of supervision and these should be addressed in a waiver or participant agreement. Since the gravity of these risks may not be readily apparent to the average client, it is critical that the risks and their potential impact on the client be dealt with in detail.

Below are five important risks that are either unique to an unsupervised facility or are greatly enhanced by the lack of supervision. These should be addressed in detail in the waiver. While many facilities continue to rely on brief one- or two-paragraph waivers for liability protection, it is the opinion of the authors that these would be totally inadequate for unsupervised facilities. A participant agreement such as that discussed in this chapter would be much more likely to provide the needed protection. The participant agreement should contain extensive information on the risks of the activities, how they are enhanced by the absence of supervisory personnel, and address fully their potential impact on the client.

Guidelines
1. The waiver should make it clear that during certain hours of operation **no trained staff member is on duty for emergencies.** Further, at times there may not be anyone – staff or other client – on hand to assist, and that even if other clients are present, they would most likely be untrained in emergency care. The waiver should emphasize that some emergencies demand immediate care in order to prevent death or permanent damage to the individual.

112

2. The waiver should stress that **all ordinary risks are enhanced**. Make it clear to the client that the absence of a trained staff member tends to increase the risks associated with fitness and conditioning activities. The waiver should emphasize that both ordinarily minor risks and major risks are enhanced by the absence of trained support staff. Clients should understand that severe head injuries, serious arterial lacerations, strokes, heart attacks, or other such serious conditions could become life threatening when there is no emergency care or when emergency care is delayed. In addition, minor injuries can become more serious when treatment is delayed or an inappropriate treatment is applied.

3. The waiver should accentuate the fact that **satisfactory emergency care may be unavailable**. The waiver should stress the fact that there will be no trained party available to utilize the AED in the event of sudden cardiac arrest (and quite possibly, no one at all available). Likewise, there will be no trained staff member to administer CPR if needed. In fact, there may be no one to call EMS for help.

4. The client should be informed that the **danger of getting infections is increased**. The waiver should make it clear that the chance of getting infections such as colds, influenza, and staph are enhanced since no staff will be on hand to clean or sanitize equipment on a periodic basis.

5. The waiver should point out that **dangers resulting from entry by unauthorized persons are increased**. Regardless of the security method used by the facility, the opportunity for unauthorized entry is greater than that of a supervised facility. It should be mentioned that in the event of altercations, threats, or violent acts (e.g., assault or rape), there may be no one who can or will be of assistance.

Chapter 6

Writing Waivers in Other Formats

Waivers and protective tools come in all shapes and sizes. Many service providers choose to use a format other than the participant agreement or stand-alone waiver to secure liability protection. The common formats are the 1) waiver within another document (such as a membership agreement or an entry form), 2) the group waiver (such as a team waiver or a health club "sign-in" waiver), and 3) the disclaimer (often on the back of a ticket or displayed as signage). While none is as consistently effective as the stand-alone format, all can provide protection under certain circumstances and when carefully written and administered (see Figure 6.1 for a comparison of waiver formats). *However, regardless of the care taken, none of these alternate formats is as reliable and effective as the stand-alone waiver/ participant agreement discussed in Chapter 5.*

Waiver Formats and Situations

The format chosen can be important because some are more likely to be enforced than others. Figure 6.1 compares the four commonly used formats. By examining the figure and by carefully reading the discussion on each format, one can learn much about the four types of waiver formats discussed in this book. The provider can then make a more informed decision regarding the type of waiver format to use.

1) A **Stand-alone document** containing only the waiver and related protective language is probably the most commonly-used format and certainly the most recommended. In *Holzer v. Dakota Speedway, Inc.* (2000), the court stated that 1) waivers are more likely to be deemed valid and enforceable when they appear as a separate document and not as part of another document and 2) the more inherently dangerous or risky the recreational activity, the more likely the waiver will be held valid. Courts in *Yauger v. Skiing Enterprises, Inc.* (1996) and *Johnson v. Rapid City Softball Association* (1994) had similar comments. This format was discussed in detail in Chapter 5.

2) **Part of another document** (e.g., within a membership contract or as part of a registration form) is another commonly-used format (see Figure 6.2). This format is popular with health clubs and for special events.

3) A **Group waiver** (see Figure 6.3) is a waiver that is signed by several persons (e.g., team roster, sign-in waiver sheet at a health club). It, too, is a frequently used format.

4) A **Disclaimer** (e.g., on the back of a ticket, on a posted sign) is an unsigned statement by which the provider renounces any responsibility or liability for injury.

Figure 6.1
Comparison of Waiver Formats

	Stand-Alone Waiver Or Participant Agreement	Waiver Within Another Document	Group Waiver	Disclaimer
Physical Characteristics	One or more pages containing only the waiver & related information.	Exculpatory language (often just a paragraph) included within a contract or application	Exculpatory language (often just a paragraph) at the top of the sheet with spaces below for all members of the group to sign)	Language usually appearing on the back of a ticket or sign disclaiming liability for injury to the participant or spectator
Advantages	1) Longer, easier to achieve clarity of intent. 2) Conspicuousness of the waiver is increased. 3) Can include more information (e.g., inherent risks, severability). 4) Some courts advise that providers use this waiver format.	1) One document to retain per client. 2) Less paperwork to retain.	1) One document to retain per group. 2) Less paperwork to retain.	1) Dispersal achieved with ticket or signage. 2) Little or no cost. 3) Little or no paperwork to retain.
Disadvantages	1) More paper to file and retain. 2) Providers may fear it will scare away participants.	1) Language is often inconspicuous. 2) Susceptible to a claim that client was unaware of the waiver. 3) Generally, it must be kept brief and some critical language may be omitted 4) If contract is ruled invalid, this makes the waiver invalid.[61]	1) Person administering the waiver may not explain its function. 2) Language is often Inconspicuous. 3) Susceptible to a claim that client was unaware of waiver. 4) Generally, must be kept brief and some critical language may be omitted.	1) Activity ticket disclaimers or signage usually not enforced due to difficulty in showing a meeting of the minds existed. 2) Least likely format to be enforced.
Validity	Stand-alone waivers are enforceable in at least 45 states. They are the most commonly used. For information on their validity, see Chapter 8. Some courts encourage this format.[62]	This format has been found enforceable in many cases, but provides less protection and is less likely to be enforced than the stand-alone waiver.[63]	This format has been found enforceable in many cases, but provides less protection. Is often found invalid due to ambiguity or administrative problems.[64]	Activity ticket disclaimers generally not enforceable because meeting of minds must be shown. Cruise line disclaimers of Line's negligence invalid by statute.

---

[61] *Dunlap v. Fortress Corporation*, 2000.

[62] *Holzer v. Dakota Speedway, Inc.*, 2000; *Yauger v. Skiing Enterprises, Inc.*, 1996; *Johnson v. Rapid City Softball Association*, 1994.

[63] *Stokes v. Bally's Pacwest, Inc.*, 2002; *Reed v. U. of North Dakota*, 1999; *Ko v. Bally Total Fitness Corp.*, 2003.

[64] *Del Raso v. United States of America*, 2001; *Pulliam v. Pocono International Raceway, Inc.*, 1996; *Johnson v. Rapid City Softball Ass.*, 1994; *Reuther v. Southern Cross Club, Inc.*, 1992.

Waiver within another Document

The **waiver within another document** format is the most popular format used by health and fitness clubs. The waiver within another document consists of relatively brief protective language located within a document that serves another purpose (e.g., a membership contract, a 5-K run application, and rental agreements). Many health clubs include an exculpatory paragraph within the membership contract. Generally, the participant or client signs the primary document and is considered to have agreed to the waiver conditions. See Figure 6.1 for a concise summary this format, including its advantages and disadvantages.

This format has been found to provide the desired protection in a large number of cases. In fact, the *Stokes* court (*Stokes v. Bally's Pacwest, Inc.*, 2002) specifically stated that an exculpatory clause did not have to be contained in a separate document to be enforceable so long as the language is conspicuous. However, while a brief paragraph or two can include the basic exculpatory language, it obviously cannot offer the breadth of protection that is provided by the preceding guidelines suggested for the stand-alone Participant Agreement.

In a 2009 case, a Connecticut court (*Schneeloch v. Glastonbury Fitness & Wellness, Inc.*) actually compared a brief waiver included in another document with a longer, stand-alone waiver, discussing why a longer document was less likely to be ambiguous.

The waiver within another document format has several significant problems. The first problem is that if it is in a contract (e.g., membership agreement) and if the **contract is deemed invalid**, it can invalidate the included waiver. In a Tennessee case (*Dunlap v. Fortress Corporation*, 2000), the waiver was contained within a standard membership agreement. The membership agreement, however, was in violation of a state statute regarding notification of the buyer's right to cancel and the contract and the waiver were found unenforceable. Similarly, California has a statute referred to as the *California Health Studio Services Act* which has many regulations regarding the requirements for valid health club contracts. These include rules regarding length of contract term, print size, cancellation rights, listing of the name and address of the club, the facilities, and the hours during which the club is open. Contracts that violate even one of these regulations could possibly be deemed invalid and unenforceable. This is particularly important to the club because if the club waiver is contained within the contract, the waiver becomes invalid when the contract is ruled invalid.

One located in a state other than Tennessee or California might feel this is irrelevant because he or she works in another state; however, most states have statutes relating to health club contracts. Why take the chance?

The second problem is that plaintiffs often **claim that the waiver was inconspicuous**; therefore the signer did not see the waiver and did not voluntarily and knowingly relinquish the right to sue for injuries resulting from negligence.

A third problem with including waivers within other documents is that some courts are **reluctant to enforce waivers that serve more than one purpose.** The Wisconsin Supreme Court has rejected several waivers that attempted to serve two purposes because it becomes less certain that the signer is fully notified of the nature and significance of the document (*Atkins v. Swimwest Family Fitness Center*, 2005; *Yauger v. Skiing Enterprises Inc.*, 1996; *Richards v. Richards*, 1994). In *Atkins*, the waiver failed because it served as a registration and a liability waiver; in *Yauger*, the document served as a waiver and a ski pass; and in *Richards*, it was an authorization to ride and a waiver. The *Atkins* court said that a clear distinction between the two and space for two separate signatures could have avoided the confusion while the *Richards* court suggested a clear title.

A fourth problem is that an increasing number of states are requiring that the **client be informed of the inherent risks** of the activity. Waivers using this format usually are limited in length and generally stick to the most basic waiver language; consequently, a number of what might be called "critical ingredients" of a comprehensive waiver are usually excluded from this format. Also, as discussed earlier, waiver law is not static. As the standard for an effective waiver required by the courts in any particular state changes, a complete, stand-alone waiver is less likely to be found lacking a necessary component.

Increasing the Likelihood of Enforcement

Providers can increase the likelihood that waivers within another document will be enforced by using additional care. In a 2015 Texas case (*Grijalva v. Bally Total Fitness Corporation*), a Texas court of appeals explained why the waiver located within a membership agreement was considered to be conspicuous. The agreement consisted of five pages; at the bottom of the first page, the agreement stated, "This is Page 1 of 5 of your Contract. Please count these pages." The second page contained several notices including the statement: "WAIVER AND RELEASE. This Contract contains a WAIVER AND RELEASE in Paragraph 1 which applies to you. . . . BY SIGNING BELOW, YOU ACKNOWLEDGE RECEIPT OF A FULLY COMPLETED COPY OF THIS CONTRACT EXECUTED BY BOTH YOU AND THE COMPANY." The first paragraph of the third page included detailed exculpatory language as well as an acknowledgement of having read and fully understood the agreement. The Membership Agreement further stated, approximately one inch above Grijalva's signature: "WAIVER AND RELEASE. This Contract contains a WAIVER AND RELEASE in Paragraph 1 which applies to you. . . . BY SIGNING BELOW, YOU ACKNOWLEDGE RECEIPT OF A FULLY COMPLETED COPY OF THIS CONTRACT EXECUTED BY BOTH YOU AND THE COMPANY."

The court explained that the Texas requirement of conspicuousness mandates "that something must appear on the face of the [contract] to attract the attention of a reasonable person when he looks at it." The court defined "conspicuous" as "so written, displayed, or presented that a reasonable person against which it is to operate ought to have noticed it;" it noted that this may be satisfied by appearing in larger type, contrasting colors, or otherwise calling attention to itself. The court enforced the membership agreement waiver.

Similarly, a California waiver that appeared in a multi-page "retail installment contract" was challenged in *Lund v. Bally's Aerobic Plus, Inc.* (2000). Several factors influenced the decision to enforce the waiver. First, near the signature line, the contract stated: **"NOTICE TO BUYER: 1. DO NOT SIGN THIS AGREEMENT BEFORE YOU READ IT OR IF IT CONTAINS ANY BLANK SPACES TO BE FILLED IN...."** A few lines later, the contract states: "**WAIVER AND RELEASE**: This contract contains a **WAIVER AND RELEASE** in Paragraph 10 to which you will be bound." In addition to these warnings, the waiver listed each of the activity areas that were covered (e.g., locker room, pool, whirlpool, sauna, sidewalks). Finally the waiver included possible injuries resulting from use of exercise equipment (which may malfunction or break), the club's improper maintenance of exercise equipment or facilities, negligent instruction or supervision, or slipping or falling on the premises.

Why Some Waivers Within Another Document Fail

Although there are many cases illustrating the failure of such waivers, none illustrates "how not to do it" better than *Hinkal v. Gavin Pardoe & Gold's Gym, Inc.* (2015). The Pennsylvania membership agreement was printed on a single, two-sided page in a carbon copy packet with the signature line located at the bottom of the front side. The first line in the paragraph above the signature line provides, "[d]o not sign this [a]greement until you have read both sides. The terms on each side of this form are a part of this [a]greement;" the language is not set off from the rest of the paragraph and is not in bold typeface, capital letters, or larger font. On the reverse side of the agreement are 13 additional items printed in light gray ink on pink carbon paper. The court said that points worth noting are 1) All of these items are single-spaced and printed in the same font size; 2) The "Waiver of Liability; Assumption of Risk" clause at issue is the 12th item, located approximately three-quarters of the way down the page, and is not differentiated in any manner from the surrounding paragraphs; 3) The reverse side of the agreement does not have any space for a signature or for initials where a signatory may acknowledge notice of the additional items; 4) The front side of the agreement does not require separate confirmation that the signatory has read and accepted the additional terms on the reverse side; 5) Furthermore, it is undisputed that Appellant did not read the waiver of liability language on the reverse side of the agreement; and 6) No employee verbally informed her that the terms of the agreement included a waiver. The court held the waiver to be inconspicuous and did not enforce the waiver. The *Hinkal* court contrasted the waiver and agreement

117

with that used in *Chepkevich v. Hidden Valley Resort, L.P.* (2010); the *Chepkevich* waiver consisted of a full page titled "RELEASE FROM LIABILITY" in capital letters in a large font. The Pennsylvania Supreme Court stated that "we cannot agree that a full-page, detailed agreement, written in normal font and titled "RELEASE FROM LIABILITY" constitutes an insufficient effort on [the part of the ski resort] to inform [the appellees] of the fact that, by signing and purchasing a lift ticket, she was giving up any right . . . ."

Another good example of "how not to do it" may be found in *Alack v. Vic Tanny International of Missouri, Inc.* (1995). The waiver failed for multiple reasons. It was the seventh paragraph of a 19 paragraph, two-page membership contract entitled "Retail Installment Contract." While the type size of the waiver paragraph was the same as that of the remainder of the contract, it was only about half the size of common newspaper print. Further, the waiver language was not made to stand out from the remainder of the contract in any way and was located on the back side of the contract while the signature was required on the front. Likewise, the exculpatory language in a Washington golf cart rental agreement (*Baker v. City of Seattle*, 1971) was in the middle of the agreement in the same size type and not distinguished in any way. The court said the language was not conspicuous and failed to relieve the provider from liability.

Guidelines for Waivers within another Document

The following guidelines will help to insure that brief waiver language placed within another document will be found valid if challenged in court. As noted earlier, it is common practice for clubs or other businesses to include one or two waiver paragraphs within a contract. In light of some court cases in several states, the authors suggest that all providers using a waiver within another document include a more inclusive section – in effect, an abbreviated participant agreement that the authors will refer to as a mini-participant agreement. *A **mini-participant agreement** is a slimmed-down participant agreement that addresses the inherent risks, liability for negligence, and indemnity for loss in a bare-bones approach.* Figure 6.2 is an illustrative waiver that addresses most of the guidelines for preparing a waiver within a document. To avoid unnecessary duplication, these guidelines include less detail than those in Chapter 5 addressing the stand-alone waiver. Consequently, one should review the guidelines for the stand-alone waiver.

1. The mini-participant agreement section should account for as many as possible of the **Participant Agreement guidelines** presented in Chapter 5. Attempt to include an assumption of inherent risk, a waiver of liability for negligence, and an indemnity agreement.

2. Make the language of the agreement **understandable** to the average person. Avoid legal jargon.

3. When the waiver is within another document (e.g., membership agreement), include the space for the signature immediately following the exculpatory language (*Ormiston v. Calfornia Youth Soccer Association*, 2011).

4. When the waiver is within another document (e.g., membership agreement), place the exculpatory language and the signature blank within a box, setting it apart from the remainder of the document (*Ormiston*).

5. Establish assumption of risks by specifying that the signer
    a. **Knows, understands, and appreciates the inherent risks** of the activity.
    b. Is **assuming the inherent risks** of the activity.
    c. Affirms **voluntary participation.**

6. Include a waiver paragraph which clearly:

    a. **Specifies all parties who are releasing** the provider from liability.
    b. **Specifies all parties that are being released** from liability.

    c.   Specifies that the signer is releasing the provider from liability for injuries or loss resulting from the **ordinary negligence of the provider**.

    d.   Makes the **exculpatory language stand out** (e.g., bold, underline).

7.   Include **indemnification language** that clearly shifts the financial responsibility to another party for 1) claims of the participant, parent, family members, or others arising from the participant's injury or loss due to involvement in the activity and for 2) claims of co-participants, rescuers, and others arising from the conduct of the participant in the course of participation.

8.   The **structure of the agreement** is most effective if:

    a.   The mini-participant agreement section **consists of three paragraphs**. The inherent risk paragraph informs the signer of the inherent risks and allows the signer to assert that he or she assumes the inherent risks. The waiver paragraph protects the provider from liability for injury or loss due to the negligence of the provider. The indemnification paragraph shifts the financial responsibility to the participant or another party.

    b.   The mini-participant agreement section is separated from the other topics covered in the contract and **stands out** from the remainder of the contract. The operative language must be placed in a position that compels notice, distinguishable from other sections of the document (*Lockett v. Flying U Rodeo Company*, 2004).

    c.   **No other information** (e.g., club rules, safety rules) should be included in the mini-participant agreement.

    d.   The mini-participant agreement section appears either at the **beginning or end of the contract**. In any event, a **signature space** should immediately follow this section of the contract.

    e.   The contract has a statement immediately above the signature space that says "**I am aware that this agreement contains a release of liability**" (*Intriligator v. PLC Santa Monica*, 2002).

    f.   The mini-participant agreement section **appears on the front** (as opposed to the back) of a one page contract. If the contract has multiple pages, the mini-participant agreement should be placed on the first page. If for some reason the mini-participant agreement must appear on a page other than the first, the reader should be given clear and obvious notice of its existence on the first page and the agreement should be **referenced** near the signature section (*Ko v. Bally Total Fitness Corporation*, 2003; *Lockett v. Flying U Rodeo Company*, 2004).

9.   Key aspects regarding the **appearance** of the agreement include:

    a.   The **title of the document** should include descriptive language. For example, *Membership Contract and Waiver of Liability* would describe a health club membership contract more accurately than *Membership Contract*.

    b.   Use a separate, **descriptive heading** preceding the mini-participant agreement of the contract. A descriptive heading such as *Waiver of Liability, Waiver and Assumption of Risk,* or *Liability Release* would be preferable. It is important that the heading draws attention to the mini-participant agreement by use of bold print, color, upper case, underlining, or some other technique.

    c.   Make the mini-participant agreement **stand out from the remainder of the document**. When the exculpatory language is buried in the middle of a membership contract, the organization is risking invalidity because of inconspicuous language. Placing the mini-participant agreement in a box is effective or one of the highlighting techniques listed previously can be used. An effective combination involves placing the mini-participant agreement in a box with the critical waiver language in bold print. (Do not overuse any technique designed to make language stand out. A paragraph in which 80% of the words are bolded does not emphasize any of the language and loses its effect.)

    d. Use a **print size** that is at least as large as that in the remainder of the document. Ten or twelve point type is desirable. Certainly, use type that is no smaller than 8 point.

10. The **signature area** can be very important.

    a. The **location of the signature** is particularly important when the exculpatory agreement is a part of a membership contract. It is important that a signature space appear immediately following the mini-participant agreement (even if it is in the middle of the contract) in addition to the signature required at the end of the contract as a whole.

    b. Near the membership agreement signature line, the contract should state: **"NOTICE TO BUYER: 1. DO NOT SIGN THIS AGREEMENT BEFORE YOU READ IT OR IF IT CONTAINS ANY BLANK SPACES TO BE FILLED IN...."**

    c. Also near the signature line, the contract should state: **"WAIVER AND RELEASE**: This contract contains a **WAIVER AND RELEASE** to which you will be bound."

    d. **Signature spaces should be provided for all adults** who are to be covered by the contract. If the contract for membership is designed for a married couple, both spouses should be required to sign the waiver.

Figure 6.2
Model Mini-Participant Agreement within another Document
Your Health Club

Assumption of Risk, Waiver, and Indemnity Agreement: I acknowledge that I know, understand, and appreciate the inherent risks of using fitness facilities and equipment. I know that these risks range from minor scrapes, strains, and bruises to significant injuries such as broken bones, loss of vision, and concussions to catastrophic events like paralysis or death. I hereby assert that I am voluntarily participating in such activities and fully assume the inherent risks associated with the use of Your Health Club.

In consideration of being permitted to use the Your Health Club facilities and equipment, on behalf of myself, my family, my heirs, and my assigns, I hereby release Your Health Club (its owners, employees, and agents) from all liability claims arising from injury, death, or property loss including those resulting from the **ordinary negligence** of Your Health Club, its employees, or agents. This waiver includes claims resulting from injury in the facility, using the equipment, on the grounds, or in any way associated with Your Health Club activities now or in the future.

I further agree to hold harmless, defend, and indemnify Your Health Club from any and all claims (including the **ordinary negligence** of Your Health Club, its employees, or agents) arising from my activities in the facility, using the equipment, or in any way associated with my membership in Your Health Club now or in the future. I further agree to pay all costs and attorneys' fees incurred by Your Health Club in investigating and defending a claim brought by me, on my behalf by my heirs, personal representatives, or assigns.

In summary, *I acknowledge that I have carefully read this Waiver and fully understand that it is a release of liability. I further acknowledge that it is my intent to waive any right that I may have to bring a legal action to assert a claim against Your Health Club, its employees, or agents for injury or loss resulting from either the inherent risks of the activity or from the negligence of Your Health Club, its employees or agents.*

_____   _____
Signature   **Date**

Group Waivers

Another popular format used for waivers is the **Group Waiver.** The group waiver usually consists of a brief exculpatory paragraph, often even briefer than that in the waiver within another document. The paragraph is placed at the top of a sheet of paper above a number of blanks to be signed by a number of participants. A waiver of this sort is frequently used in health and fitness clubs for visitors (drop-ins) or members to sign prior to participation. Recreation departments also frequently choose this format for use with teams. A staff member or a team captain is asked to secure the signatures of all participating team members. Figure 6.1 provides a concise summary of this format.

The advantages of this format are obvious. You have one sheet of signatures for a number of participants and it can be administered to a large number of participants in a short time period (This can also be a disadvantage because the less time required often correlates with inadequate explanations and failure to inform of the true purpose of the document.).

A major weakness of this format is the susceptibility to the claim that the signer was unaware of the import of the document because of the way in which it was presented. Similarly, another disadvantage is that the function of the waiver may not be explained, or understood, by the person administering the waiver (often a team captain). The waiver is sometimes inconspicuous; a number of cases have involved a group waiver on a clipboard with the clip concealing the waiver language. The waiver is also sometimes administered under rushed conditions that are not conducive to reading and understanding the waiver. Also, this waiver is often very brief, failing to include needed information. Finally, a California court (*Storer v. E Street MX, Inc.*, 2015), expressed concern that the group waiver offers no opportunity for any individual customer to negotiate terms of the contract.

Waivers utilizing this format have been upheld in court and can often provide protection when carefully written and properly administered. Proper administration is somewhat more difficult here. Such waivers have failed when presented as a "sign-in sheet;" when used under conditions that prevented the signer from reading the exculpatory language (e.g., when the waiver was folded so that the signer could see only the signature area); and when the person collecting the signatures purposely or accidentally misled the signers regarding the intent of the document.

Although the group waiver format is different from that of the waiver within another document, the protective language itself can be identical or very similar to the **mini-participant agreement** found in the waiver within another document and discussed earlier in this chapter. Since each format usually is restricted by a limited amount of space for the protective language, it makes sense, then, that the content requirement of the two formats is quite similar.

A sign-in sheet was examined and enforced in a drowning case in Ohio (*Bishop v. Nelson Ledges Quarry Park, Limited,* 2005). The following group waiver was used.

Nelson Ledges Quarry Park Liability
Waiver Form

Persons under 19 years of age must have an adult/guardian sign for them.
CUSTOMERS AND COMPANY AGREE: When you enter Nelson Ledges Quarry Park, LLC, you agree that it is at your sole risk; that you will abide by all the park rules; that you will retain care and control of your car: its parts and contents. Company is not responsible for your car, articles left in your car, loss of use; all liability for any loss including but not limited to, any loss arising from bodily injury, personal injury or drowning. We the company do not accept responsibility of any personal injury or loss caused due to the influence of alcohol or other mind altering substances, or food consumed from private vendors. **NO ILLEGAL SUBSTANCES ARE PERMITTED IN THE CAMPGROUND.** I /We hearby (sic) release Nelson Ledges Quarry Park LLC and J&E Management from any liability whatsoever arising from use of the park. No employee may modify any of the terms herein (p. 2-3).

The Ohio Supreme Court stated that there was no genuine issue of fact regarding the validity of the waiver. The sheet was clearly labeled in bold type. Furthermore, it stated that the customer agrees the company is not responsible for "all liability for any loss, including, any loss arising from drowning." While the court found no problem with the waiver, be aware that the courts in Ohio have very lenient requirements for the enforcement of a waiver. Even though the waiver would usually be enforceable in Ohio, it would not be effective in many states which maintain stricter standards.

Why Some Group Waivers Fail

Some group waivers are not enforced because the waiver does not make it clear that the signer is releasing the provider from liability for provider negligence. The following waiver was examined in a Michigan case (*Xu v. Gay*, 2003) involving a health club patron who suffered a head injury when he fell from a treadmill. The waiver appeared at the top of a "**sign-in sheet**."

> I understand that Vital Power Fitness Center reserves the right to revoke my membership for failure to respect the center's rules and policies. I also understand that Vital Power Fitness Center assumes no responsibility for any injuries and/or sicknesses incurred to me or any accompanying minor person as a result of entering the premises and/or using any of the facilities....

The court did not interpret the waiver as releasing the defendant from liability stemming from negligence for several reasons. First, it did not inform the reader that he is solely responsible for injuries incurred or that he waives the right to sue. Second, it did not contain the words "waiver" or "disclaim" or similar language that would clearly indicate that the reader is giving up the right to a negligence claim. The court stated that the waiver should explicitly inform the reader of the effect of waiver.

Other group waivers fail because the signer was unaware of the purpose or import of the document. One case (*Connors v. Reel Ice, Inc.*, 2000) illustrates this problem very well. The plaintiff was presented the waiver by his team captain and required to sign just prior to competition. Plaintiff claimed he was unaware that he was giving up rights. Similarly, in *Lee v. Dreamdealers USA, LLC* (2014), when Lee was signing up for a "driving experience," he was in line, was given a group waiver, told to sign here, and he signed thinking it was a "sign-in" sheet. Summary judgment was denied because there was an issue of fact as to whether the signature was fraudulently induced.

Also, such waivers can fail because they do not include all information required by the courts in a particular state. For instance, courts in some states have ruled that liability waivers must inform the signer of the inherent risks of the sport or activity. In a Kentucky spelunking case (*Coughlin v. T.M.H. International Attractions, Inc.*, 1995) involving the death of a participant, the brief group waiver read:

> We the undersigned hereby accept the following special conditions and in recognition that speeology is an inherently dangerous recreational activity, we voluntarily assume all risks and shall indemnify and hold the owners, operators, and employees of Buzzards Roost Historic Cave harmless from all claims, suits, actions, damages and costs of every name and description arising out of or resulting from the privileges granted by this permit including damages caused by or resulting from the sole or joint negligence of the owners, operators, or employees of Buzzards Roost Historic Cave. Additionally I accept and understand the aforementioned conditions apply to any minor we escort.

The court determined that the deceased participant was an inexperienced caver who knew little about the activity. Pointing out that he did not know of the dangers inside the cave and that the waiver read more like an enticement than a warning of the specific risks to be confronted, the court did not uphold the waiver and the defense motion for summary judgment was denied.

As was evident in the Quarry Park waiver, a waiver does not always have to be perfect to be enforced. In a 2013 California case, the waiver violated a number of the guidelines presented here (*Jones v. City of Ukiah*). The heading of the document read "2008 Fall Men's Softball League Softball Roster Form; the waiver appeared on the back of the sheet; the form did not provide an acknowledgement of the waiver by the signature blank; and no one informed the signer that it was a waiver. The California court enforced the waiver because the plaintiff was given plenty of time to read the waiver and no one prevented him from reading it. Nevertheless, both administrative procedures and exculpatory language are important factors in group waiver enforcement.

Group Waiver Guidelines

The following guidelines will help to increase the likelihood that the protective language used in a group waiver will be found valid if challenged in court. Group waivers have been challenged in a number of cases (*Del Raso v. United States of America*, 2001; *Hornbeck v. All American Indoor Sports, Inc.*, 1995; *Reuther v. Southern Cross Club, Inc.*, 1992; *Jeute v. Jarnowski*, 1968; *Carpenter v. American Honda Motor Co., Inc.*, 2004). Based on rulings and comments in court cases in several states, the authors suggest that all service providers using a group waiver use the **same approach as was suggested for the waiver within another document** – that is, develop a **mini-participant agreement**. As already discussed, the document should provide a minimum of 1) inherent risks protection, 2) protection from negligence, and 3) indemnification (see Figure 6.2).

In order to avoid unnecessary duplication, the reader will find only seven guidelines below.[65] The reader should refer back to the guidelines for stand-alone Participant Agreements and the guidelines for waivers within another document. Many of these are relevant.

1. The mini-participant agreement section should be placed at the **top of the page** immediately following the title. Signature spaces should be placed below the mini-participant agreement. The mini-participant agreement should appear at the top of each page that contains signature lines.

2. Use a **descriptive title** for the mini-participant agreement. Titles such as "Waiver of Liability" and "Assumption of Risk, Waiver, & Indemnity Agreement" are encouraged. The term "Participant Agreement" may be used if the terms "Assumption of Risk, Waiver, & Indemnity Agreement" follow immediately below. Avoid such titles as Team Roster, Sign-in Sheet, and other misleading, non-descriptive titles.

3. Each signature blank should **include a statement** by which the signer acknowledges acceptance of the preceding mini-participant agreement (See Figure 6.3). Such statements help to ensure the conspicuousness of the waiver, thereby enhancing the likelihood that the waiver will be upheld if challenged in court.

4. Include a space for the **date at the top** of each group waiver. This helps in filing and in the retrieval of the waiver when needed.

5. At the end of each day, someone should collect all group waiver sheets, staple them together if there is more than one, **file them**, and then prepare and date sheets for the next day.

6. Take care not to write anything on the waiver or use a clipboard that **might cover part** of the waiver language (*Jenks v. New Hampshire Motor Speedway*, 2010).

7. The person in charge of having the roster/waiver completed should **explain to each signer** that it is a release of liability.

Group waivers used by Nelson Ledges Quarry Park and T.M.H. International Attractions were reproduced in this chapter. Take this opportunity to compare these two waivers with the model group waiver in Figure 6.3. Evaluate the two waivers based upon the guidelines for waivers within another document and guidelines for group waivers.

---

[65] The State of Florida has a statute (FS 549.09) which states that group waivers are enforceable provided three requirements are met. The waiver language must be 1) at the top of the page, 2) located on the same side of the sheet as the signatures, and 3) in 8 point type or larger.

Figure 6.3

Model Group Mini-Participant Agreement for Group Waiver
Club Aerobics Marathon
(Assumption of Risk, Waiver, and Indemnity Agreement)

Date _____

I acknowledge that I know, understand, and appreciate the inherent risks of participating in an aerobics marathon. I know that these risks range from minor injuries such as blisters, muscle strains, and sprains to significant problems such as knee injuries, heat-related illness, and collision-related injuries to the very rare catastrophic events like heart attacks, paralysis, or death. I hereby assert that I am voluntarily participating in the Club Aerobics Marathon and that I fully assume the inherent risks of such participation.

In consideration of being permitted to participate in the Club Aerobics Marathon, **I hereby release** (on behalf of myself, my family, my heirs, and my assigns) **Club**, its employees, agents, and sponsors **from liability for any and all claims involving injury, death, or property loss** suffered by me including those **which result from the ordinary negligence** of Club, its employees, agents, or sponsors. This includes incidents that occur while participating in the Club Aerobics Marathon, while using the facilities, or while engaging in any activities incidental thereto, wherever, whenever, or however the same may occur.

I further agree to hold harmless, defend, and indemnify Club from any and all claims (including the ordinary negligence of Club, its employees, or agents) arising directly or indirectly from my participation in the Club Aerobics Marathon. I further agree to pay all costs and attorneys' fees incurred by Club in investigating and defending a claim brought by me or on my behalf by my heirs, personal representatives, or assigns, or by a third party.

	Printed Name	**Signature**
I have read, understand, and agree to the above:	_____	_____
I have read, understand, and agree to the above:	_____	_____
I have read, understand, and agree to the above:	_____	_____
I have read, understand, and agree to the above:	_____	_____
I have read, understand, and agree to the above:	_____	_____
I have read, understand, and agree to the above:	_____	_____
I have read, understand, and agree to the above:	_____	_____
I have read, understand, and agree to the above:	_____	_____
I have read, understand, and agree to the above:	_____	_____
I have read, understand, and agree to the above:	_____	_____
I have read, understand, and agree to the above:	_____	_____

Disclaimers

A **disclaimer** is a statement in which the service provider disclaims all liability for injury and asserts that the participant is assuming all risks of injury or loss. Disclaimers are often used on the back of event admission tickets, on signage posted at facilities, in some contracts, or on equipment. *As a general rule, these disclaimers are not enforced because courts agree that there must be a meeting of the minds and the disclaimer must be clear and conspicuous enough to constitute adequate notice.* Disclaimers when included in signed contracts can provide some protection in certain circumstances. For instance, they have been enforced allowing tour operators to protect themselves from the liability of independent contractors whom they employ. In other instances, such as those in a cruise ship contract, they fail to protect the cruise lines from liability to passengers injured aboard ship due to federal statute. For additional information regarding cruise line contracts, see **Appendix B**, **Cruise Line Contracts**.

Some disclaimers also include other information such as warnings and enumeration of some of the inherent risks of the activity. Disclaimers by entities such as tour operators and cruise ship lines generally address other legal issues as well. The participant does not generally sign a disclaimer and, in general, *disclaimers used instead of waivers in recreation, fitness, and sport activities provide less protection from liability.* See Figure 6.1 for a concise summary this format.

A major difference between the disclaimer and the signed waiver form is that the signed waiver form is likely to result in summary judgment and avoid the necessity and expense of a trial. In the case of a disclaimer, however, the case would probably be sent to trial for a jury decision as to whether there was adequate notice, conspicuousness, and a meeting of the minds. The jury, after examining the disclaimer and the circumstances under which it was used, might well deem the disclaimer to be an enforceable contract and result in a verdict for the defendant.

Activity Ticket Disclaimers

Disclaimers are frequently found on the backs of tickets for such activities as baseball games, amusement parks, and ski lifts. The validity of such disclaimers has been at issue in a number of states.

Ticket Disclaimer Law. Courts in many states have addressed the issue of unsigned ticket disclaimers. Most states seem to hold that unsigned disclaimers are enforceable only when 1) the language is clearly exculpatory, 2) it is clear that the participant was made aware of the agreement on the ticket, and 3) there was a meeting of the minds. However, these criteria are difficult to achieve because the disclaimer is not signed and there is often no evidence of awareness or a meeting of the minds.

Consequently, with infrequent exceptions, disclaimers fail to protect the provider. Two things are worth noting: 1) Except for the cases in Pennsylvania and Oregon, most of the following cases are quite old. It may be that most providers are becoming aware that disclaimers have limited effectiveness. 2) No cases have been found in most states. Cases addressing disclaimers have been in **Pennsylvania** (*Duffy v. Camelback Ski Operation*, 1992; *Missar v. Camelback Ski Resort*, 1984; *Passero v. Killington*, LTD, 1993; *Beck-Hummel v. Ski Shawnee, Inc.*, 2006; *Checket v. Tuthill Corporation*, 2001; *Tayar v. Camelback Ski Corporation* (2008), *Savarese v. Camelback Ski Corp.*, 2005); **Massachusetts** (*Lee v. Allied Sports Assocs., Inc.*, 1965; *Brennan v. Ocean View Amusement Company*, 1935; *O'Brien v. Freeman*, 1937; *Kushner v. McGinnis*, 1935); **Wisconsin** (*Hackel v. Whitecap Recreations*, 1984), **Alabama** (*Vines v. Birmingham Baseball Club*, 1984); **Vermont** (*Pitasi v. The Stratton Corp.*, 1992); **Illinois** (*Yates v. Chicago National League Ball Club Inc.*, 1992; *Coronel v. Chicago White Sox, LTD*, 1992; *Moore v. Edmonds*, 1942; *Russo v. The Range, Inc.*, 1979); **Oregon** (*Steele v. Mount Hood Meadows Oregon, LTD*, 1999; *Silva v. Mt. Bachelor, Inc.*, 2008)); **Michigan** (*Braun v. Mount Brighton, Inc.*, 1989; *Falkner v. John E. Fetzer, Inc*, 1982); **Ohio** (*Broome v. Ohio Ski Slopes, Inc.*, 1995); and **Colorado** (*Hook v. Lakeside Park Company*, 1960)

Ticket disclaimers are also prohibited in **Oklahoma** where a statute (**15 O.S. 1991 @ 212.1**) holds that unsigned, un-bargained-for disclaimers of liability are against public policy and unenforceable. Additionally, such disclaimers would not be enforceable when they conflict with state sport safety statutes or other statutes (*Phillips v. Monarch Recreation Corp.*, 1983). Of course, ticket disclaimers would not be enforceable in **Virginia** or **Louisiana** since those states do not even enforce signed waivers exculpating providers from negligence.

Examples of Activity Ticket Disclaimers. The following are actual disclaimers taken from court cases. *The fitness, recreation, and sport professional should note that none of these disclaimers were enforced when challenged in court.* After reading the guidelines in Chapter 5 and earlier in this chapter, it is easy to observe why they failed to provide protection for the relying service provider. The recreation and sport manager is again urged not to rely solely on such disclaimers and to make use of one of the other three waiver formats.

This **ski lift ticket disclaimer** was not enforced by a Pennsylvania court (*Missar v. Camelback Ski Resort*, 1984). It was printed with a 9-point heading and a 5-point text.

NO REFUND – NO TRANSFER

The purchaser and user of this ticket assumes and understands that skiing is a hazardous sport and that bare spots, variations in snow, ice and terrain along with bumps, moguls, stumps, forest growth and debris and rocks and many other hazards or obstacles exist within this ski area. In using the ticket in skiing at this area, such dangers are recognized and accepted, whether they are marked or unmarked. The skier realizes that falls and collisions do occur and injuries may result, and therefore, assumes the burden of skiing under control at all times.

This **baseball ticket disclaimer** appeared on the reverse side of the entry ticket. The validity of the disclaimer was not addressed in the case (*Costa v. The Boston Red Sox Baseball Club*, 2004).

The holder assumes all risk and danger incidental to the game of baseball including specifically (but not exclusively) the danger of being injured by thrown bats and thrown or batted balls and agrees that the participating clubs, their agents and players are not liable of injuries resulting from such causes.

These **amusement park ride ticket disclaimers** appeared on the reverse side of the tickets. The first failed in an Illinois court and the second in a Massachusetts court.

The person using this ticket so assumes all risks of personal injury... (*Russo v. The Range, Inc.*, 1979).

The Management will not be responsible for injury to anyone who goes through the device (or devices) (*Kushner v. McGinnis*, 1935).

Activity Disclaimers Not on Tickets. A **Massachusetts** court enforced a disclaimer involving a liability and indemnification disclaimer for a golf cart rental (*Post v. Belmont Country Club, Inc.*, 2004). The following disclaimer was located in the club membership handbook:

Each person using a cart does so at his/her own risk. Each person renting or driving a cart is responsible for any personal injury or property damage caused, including without limitation, injury to him/herself and damage to the cart, and agrees to indemnify the Club against all loss, claims, or expenses resulting from use of said cart.

In spite of the fact that the disclaimer was more or less buried among many rules, regulations, and provisions within the handbook; the section was not highlighted as other sections were; was not pointed out; and there was no evidence the plaintiff had read or knew of its existence, the court upheld the disclaimer. The court reasoned that when plaintiff became a member of the club, he entered into an obligation to be bound by the club's rules and by-laws.

In contrast, a **Minnesota** court held that the trial court erred in admitting evidence that "skate at your own risk" signs were posted. The disclaimer signs read: Because of the normal risks of maintaining balance on skates and the probability of occasional contact between skaters, accidents can and do happen. You must voluntarily assume the risk of injury when you skate" (*Wagner v. Obert Enterprises,* 1986).

Disclaimer Suggestions. Whenever possible, providers should use waivers rather than disclaimers when seeking liability protection. This recommendation is based on two factors. First, while disclaimers may provide some liability protection in a few states, no cases have been found addressing the issue in the vast majority of states. In comparison, waivers can provide protection in almost all states. Second, the waiver can achieve a summary judgment, while the disclaimer often cannot do so.

Providers electing to use disclaimers on activity tickets can increase the likelihood of enforcement by following a few simple suggestions (Note: one is still better protected by a waiver.).

- Be certain to take measures to point out the existence of the disclaimer.
- Include a notice emphasizing the disclaimer such as "Please Read" or "Important Information."
- Post large, conspicuous signs where the tickets are sold.
- Make the disclaimer wording as large and as conspicuous as possible.
- Remember, if the disclaimer is to be effective, the basics that are included in a mini-participant agreement must be addressed.
- Utilize additional risk management procedures to protect against liability.

Tour Operator Disclaimers

Travel agents and tour operators generally utilize disclaimers to limit their liability. Tour operators typically include disclaimers in one or more of the following documents: contracts, itineraries, brochures, travel guides, and invoices. In *Giuffra v. Vantage Travel Service, Inc.* (2015), a tourist was mugged and robbed. The court ruled that a travel agent or tour operator 1) is not an insurer or guarantor of a customer's safety; 2) has no legal duty to protect clients against criminal acts; 3) has no duty to warn clients of a possible hazardous condition on property it does not own or occupy; and 4) owes no duty to inform clients of hazardous conditions on the property of others. It went on to add that Vantage would not be liable in this case even if the tour guide was negligent in telling the client the area was safe because the guide was an employee of an independent subcontractor hired by Vantage.[66]

Validity of Tour Operator Disclaimers. A federal regulation (**14 C.F.R. sec. 380.32(x) [1998]**) governs the validity of disclaimers or exculpatory clauses used by tour operators. The regulation provides that exculpatory clauses in contracts between tour operators and participants, drawn in accord with the regulation, may expressly provide that the charter operator is not responsible for personal injury or property damage caused by any direct air carrier, hotel, or other supplier of services in connection with the charter unless the tour operator is negligent. *This regulation preempts state law and cannot be contravened by any state policy prohibiting exculpatory clauses from taking effect (Powell v. Trans Global Tours, Inc.,* 1999). The disclaimer or exculpatory clause is enforceable even if the plaintiff has not signed it *(Powell; Wilson v. American Trans Air, Inc.,* 1988). Thus, the independent tour operator or travel agent cannot be held responsible for the negligence of its principal where the agent simply makes the reservation or packages the tour (*Loeb v. United States of America,* 1992).

In an Alabama case (*Harden v. American Airlines,* 1998), the plaintiff sued the travel agent, the airline, and the cruise operator alleging damage because a flight delay caused them to miss two days of their cruise. The travel agent was granted summary judgment on the basis that the agent is not liable if the principal breaches the contract. Under agency law, the principal is liable for the acts that the agent does within the actual or apparent authority from the principal.

In contrast, in a Pennsylvania case the court was unable to conclude that the disclaimer was brought to the attention of the plaintiff. It appeared in an advertising brochure and in inconspicuous print on the back of an invoice. The court noted that the issue could be revisited at trial if additional evidence was forthcoming *(Rudisill v. Grand Circle Travel Inc.,* 1999).

---

[66] The choice-of- law in the agreement was Massachusetts law, but the court seemed to be applying New York law.

An exception occurred in a Minnesota case when a travel agent was injured while on a promotional trip for which the agent pays only a nominal fee (*Walton v. Fujita Tourist Enterprises Co.*, 1986). The court ruled that the disclaimer relied upon by the defendant was unenforceable as against public policy because 1) it was not bargained for and was unilateral in nature, 2) such trips are necessary for the business success of travel agents, thus is a necessary service that is unavailable elsewhere, and 3) the clause was ambiguous.

The law regarding cruise line contracts is quite different from that of tour operators. For information regarding cruise line contracts, see Appendix B, Cruise Line Contracts.

Tour Operators and Third Parties. Tour operators frequently use disclaimers to protect themselves from liability for the negligence of third parties beyond the control of the operator. These disclaimers are generally effective in providing liability protection for the tour operator (*Sova v. Apple Vacations*, 1997; *Wilson v. American Trans Air, Inc.*, 1989; *Bailey v. United States of America*, 2003; *Honeycutt v. Tour Carriage, Inc.*, 1996). The language has been viewed as evidence of a lack of intention on the part of the defendant tour operator to assume a contractual obligation to guarantee or warrant the safety of the participant. The disclaimer generally precludes liability either on a theory of breach of contract or negligence (*Loeb v. United States of America*, 1992; *Bryant v. Cruises, Inc.*, 1998).

A Minnesota court stated that the tour operator is not liable for third party negligence even when the optional tour is included in the tour operator brochures. It should be noted, however, that a travel agent or tour operator can be held liable where its own negligent failure to select a competent contractor caused the injury (*Wilson v. American Trans Air, Inc.*, 1989). It is well established that a tour operator meets its duty of reasonable care to investigate an independent contractor when it makes a generalized inquiry into the contractor's reputation and safety record (*O'Keefe v. Inca Floats*, 1997).

A waiver used by another tour operator in Minnesota was found to be enforceable (*Catalano v. N.W.A. Inc.*, 1998). The operator was not liable for the negligence of the hotel used by the tour. The court found no disparity of bargaining power and no violation of public policy.

Joint Enterprises and Joint Ventures. Plaintiffs often allege that the travel agent, tour operator, hotel, and common carrier are engaged in a joint enterprise or venture and are jointly liable. The elements necessary for a joint enterprise are 1) mutual undertaking for a common purpose and 2) a right to some voice in the direction and control of the means used to carry out the common purpose (*Powell v. Trans Global Tours, Inc.*, 1999). The elements necessary for a joint venture are 1) contribution (parties must combine money, property, time, or skill), 2) joint proprietorship and control, 3) sharing of profits by express or implied agreement, and 4) a contract showing that a joint venture was entered into. Generally, tour operators, travel agents, and hotels do not qualify as joint enterprises or ventures (*Wilson v. American Trans Air, Inc.*, 1989; *Meyers v. Postal Fin. Co.*, 1979; *Walton v. Fujita Tourist Enterprises*, 1986; *Powell v. Trans Global Tours, Inc.*, 1999).

Duty to Warn. A tour patron was injured when she slipped and fell while disembarking from the tour bus onto desert sand and sued alleging the company brochure had promised a safe trip and that the company failed to warn of the inherent dangers of bus travel in Morocco (*Davies v. General Tours, Inc.*, 2001). The court held that while there may be a duty to warn of a known, dangerous condition unknown to the traveler, the travel agent or tour operator has no general duty to warn tourists as to general safety precautions or to warn of obvious and apparent dangers. Courts in *Honeycutt v. Tour Carriage, Inc.* (1996) and *Passero v. DHC Hotels & Resorts, Inc.* (1996) ruled similarly. The court further held that the tour operator and the Moroccan tour company that conducted the tour were not partners in the venture – but that the Moroccan company was an independent contractor and no agency relationship existed. Finally, the court ruled that the brochure assuring plaintiff of a smooth, comfortable, and safe trip did not constitute a warranty, but rather was puffery and advertising rhetoric.

Numerous courts have ruled that language promising a safe trip does not constitute a guarantee that no harm will befall the patron (*Wilson v. American Trans Air, Inc.*, 1989; *Passero v. DHC Hotels & Resorts, Inc.*, 1996.; *Sova v. Apple Vacations*, 1997). However, in *Stevenson v. Four Winds Travel, Inc.*

(1972), the brochure language was considered to be a guarantee. The language however was very specific stating, "Four Winds also guarantees that every tour will be escorted by a qualified professional tour director. Our tour directors have been carefully selected and trained.... Your escorts (tour directors) are also informative, they know precisely what you will be seeing and doing every day." It went on to say "they've been there before," "fully escorted from start to finish," and "from the moment you leave until your journey ends, you are cared for by a carefully selected Four Winds Tour escort." Further, the defendant was responsible for all management matters regarding the tour.

In an Arizona case, the court held that the travel agent serves as a special agent of the traveler and that this agency relationship imposes duties upon the agent (*Maurer v. Cerkvenik-Anderson Travel, Inc.*, 1994). The agent has a duty to act with care, skill and diligence as well as a duty to disclose material dangers known to the agent. The agent is not an insurer and can't be expected to divine and forewarn of all dangers in foreign travel, but he does have a fiduciary duty to warn of those dangers of which he is aware, or should be aware in the exercise of due care. While the court stated that the agent could be discharged from duty by an effective waiver, summary judgment based on a disclaimer contained in the invoice and in the itinerary was not granted because the waiver was too general and failed to alert the patron to the specific risks that were being waived. The itinerary and disclaimer contained a certification that the customer has read, agreed to, and understands the terms of the itinerary and disclaimer.

Sample Tour Operator Disclaimer. The following are two typical tour operator disclaimers. This one is used by Vantage Travel and yielded a ruling of summary judgment in favor of Vantage in *Giuffra v. Vantage Travel Service, Inc.* (2015). The other helped to protect Unique Vacations in *Santoro v. Unique Vacations, Inc.* (2014).

Responsibilities & Liability

The responsibility of Vantage . . . is strictly limited. As a tour operator, Vantage organizes, promotes and sells tour programs consisting of certain travel services, including surface, air and water transportation, sightseeing excursions, and cruise/hotel accommodations, that Vantage purchases or reserves from various suppliers (collectively, "Suppliers"). Vantage does not own or operate any of these Suppliers. The Suppliers providing travel services for Vantage's tour programs are independent contractors, and are not agents or employees of Vantage. As such, Vantage is not responsible for direct, indirect, consequential, or incidental damage, injury, loss, accident, delay, or irregularity of any kind occasioned by reason of any act or omission beyond its control, including, without limitation, any negligent or willful act or failure to act of, or breach of contract by, any Supplier or any other party. . . . By utilizing the travel services of the Suppliers, you agree that you will look only to such Suppliers in respect of any accident, injury, property damage, or personal loss to you or to those traveling with you, and that neither Vantage nor any representative of Vantage shall be liable.

Limitation of Damages: Unique Vacations, SRI [Sandals Resorts International, Ltd.], any hotel or hotel management company, their affiliates, subsidiaries, directors, officers, and employees, shall not be liable to guest in any circumstances, for: (A) any personal injuries or property damage arising out of *or caused by any act or omission on the part of any air carrier or ground transportation carrier;* (B) emotion distress, mental suffering, or psychological injury of any kind; or (C) any consequential, incidental, punitive, or exemplary damages.

Chapter 7

Administering Waivers
And Participant Agreements

The major hurdle to overcome in using a participant agreement to protect the recreation, fitness, or sport business from liability is the development of a well-written agreement. Nevertheless, even well- written agreements have been overturned in court when they are not administered properly. This chapter offers some guidelines that will help recreation, fitness, and sport professionals administer participant agreements effectively.

Electronic or Online Waivers

The most significant change in liability waivers over the twenty years since the first edition of this book has been the employment and growth in the use of electronic and online waivers. In using earlier editions of this book, many questioned whether electronic or online waivers would be enforceable in court. Today, such waivers are in widespread use and there is no question as to their validity. This writer has found no cases in which a waiver has failed simply because it was not a paper waiver. In fact, in *Berenson v. USA Hockey, Inc.* (2013), a waiver was enforced by a **Colorado** court without the waiver or a print screen of it being presented in court to show that it was signed by the plaintiff. Testimony provided by an employee of USA Hockey that the plaintiff could not have registered for the event online without signing the waiver proved adequate for the court.

In a 2013 **Washington** case (*Johnson v. Spokane to Sandpoint, LLC*), the court examined an online waiver to determine if it could protect the defendant. One complaint was lack of conspicuousness; the court listed six factors in determining if language is conspicuous. The court said the waiver was conspicuous in that it was set apart from the rest of document, was in italics or in capitals, had an informative title, and warned Johnson of the effect of the waiver. An electronic waiver was used in *Locke v. Life Time Fitness, Inc.* (2014). The **Illinois** court failed to enforce the health club waiver, but only because the offending risk was beyond the scope of the waiver. The court stated the fact that the waiver was displayed on a computer screen and the client signed on an electronic keyboard is insufficient to show the waiver is against public policy. In a **Massachusetts** wrongful death case (*Angelo v. USA Triathlon*, 2014), the decedent renewed his membership and electronically signed a waiver and indemnity agreement. They were upheld regarding the ordinary negligence claim, but not against the gross negligence claim. Also, Massachusetts law enforces waivers requiring clicks on an online checkbox (*Pazol v. Tough Mudder Incorporated*, 2015).

At least three courts in **Florida** have dealt with electronic waivers. In *Hinely v. Florida Motorcycle Training, Inc.* (2011), a woman registered for a motorcycle training school on an internet site, signing an electronic waiver of liability. She was injured during the training program. The waiver was enforced by the court without mention of the fact that it was an electronic waiver. In two Florida cases (*Johnson v. Royal Carribean Cruises*, 2011; *Magazine v. Royal Caribbean Cruises, LTD*, 2014), cruise ship passengers signed electronic waivers for onboard activities. Both waivers ultimately failed, but in neither case was it because the waivers were electronic.

Similar rulings were handed down in two **Minnesota** cases (*Waltz v. Life Time Fitness, Inc.*, 2010; *Bergin v. Wild Mountain, Inc.*, 2014), in two **New York** cases (*Stephenson v. Food Bank for New York City*, 2008; *Zuckerman v. City of New York*, 2011), and in a **Vermont** case (*Littlejohn v. Timberquest Park at Magic, LLC*, 2015). None of the courts had any problem with the fact the waivers were electronic. The *Stephenson* court stated that electronic signatures are valid under New York law (**NY CLS State Technology Law sec. 304 [2]**). The law states that waivers with electronic signatures shall have the same validity and effect as the use of a signature affixed by hand. The Zuckerman waiver was executed on the New York Road Runners website; the court stated the electronic waiver is a release within the meaning of **PCPLR 321(a)(5)**.[67] A **Pennsylvania** court in *Scott v. Altoona Bicycle Club (*2010) upheld both an online waiver and a waiver signed when the plaintiff entered the event. The court, in evaluating the waivers, did not distinguish between them in terms of validity or effectiveness.

Based on a limited number of cases in these states, it appears that electronic and online waivers are valid. Two important points should be remembered. First, the waiver should be well-written. Secondly, the full name of the participant should be required. If the participant is a minor, both the parents/guardians and the minor should sign electronically. The reader should remember, however, that waiver law varies from state to state. Therefore, parties considering the use of such waivers should consult legal counsel regarding their use in their state.

Avoiding Allegations of Fraud

Black (1990) defines fraud as "an intentional perversion of truth for the purpose of inducing another in reliance upon it to part with some valuable thing belonging to him or to surrender a legal right." As mentioned previously, false statements within the agreement can be construed as fraud and can invalidate the agreement (*Sevilla v. Estate of Lynn Maxey Wiley*, 2004; *Merten v. Nathan*, 1982). In addition, certain actions taken while administering the agreement can also invalidate the document on the same grounds.

Courts have failed to uphold liability agreements when claims were made by the person administering the agreement that the agreement was for some other purpose than relieving the business of liability for injury (*e.g.*, for check-in, for records only, for insurance purposes). The agreement is sometimes deemed fraudulent if the signer is induced to sign by false representations of the relying party (*Walsh v. Luedtke*, 2005). Similarly, fraud may also exist in cases in which material facts are withheld from a signer (*Cabellero v. Willow Springs International Raceway, Inc.*, 2004). In addition, fraud may occur when the exculpatory language is hidden from the signer by the paper being folded, covered, or simply missing (*Sexton v. Southwestern Auto Racing Ass'n*, 1979; *Talbert v. Lincoln Speedway*, 1984; *Johnson v. Robert Dunlap and Racing, Inc.*, 1981; *Hobby v. Gilpin*, 1984).

Fraudulent trade practices was alleged in a 2006 horseback riding case in Hawaii (*Courbat v. Dahana Ranch, Inc.*, 2006) because the provider sold tickets to a horseback riding tour months in advance, but made no mention of a required waiver until the day of the tour. The appellate court remanded the case to the trial court to determine if the action constituted an unfair trade practice. The court indicated that the waiver should not be enforced if it was determined that the practice was deceptive.

In a 2007 health club case (*Handy-Mixon v. LA Fitness*, 2007) the plaintiff read the waiver and asked the employee to explain it to her. He assured her that it applied only to injuries she might inflict upon herself such as overexertion or pulled muscles. After signing the waiver, she was injured by a defective bike while in a spinning class. She sued alleging, among other things, that the waiver was unenforceable because of fraud through misrepresentation. The court relied on waiver language that included "no oral representations, statements, or inducements apart from the foregoing written agreement have been made." It went on to state that in order to establish fraud in the inducement, plaintiff would need to show an independent promise (e.g., that "LA Fitness promised her that in spite of the language in

---

[67] A New York statute including "release" as valid criteria for dismissal of a cause of action.

the Agreement, it would agree the liability waiver would not apply to her, when in fact, it had no intent to perform such a promise.") The court found no evidence of fraud. In another case (*Pena v. The Roladium,* 2002), a waiver was misdated (inadvertently used the previous year in January), but was enforced.

It is important that agreements be administered in a straightforward, honest manner. If the signing party does not know the purpose of the agreement, the agreement may well be invalidated and fail to protect the business.

For more information on fraud, see Fraudulent Language section in Chapter 2.

Time to Read

Agreements are often challenged alleging that insufficient time was given for reading the document, the signer was rushed, or long lines created pressure to sign without reading. While not having read a waiver is seldom considered by courts to be reason to not enforce a waiver, waivers are sometimes not enforced when the signer was rushed or pressured to sign the waiver quickly (*McCorkle v. Hall,* 1989; *Lombardo v. Maguire Group Inc.,* 1997; *Delk v. Go Vertical, Inc.,* 2004). The *Delk* court found no evidence that the plaintiff was rushed, but stated that evidence that she was rushed and deprived of an opportunity to read the waiver would have been reason to deny the motion for summary judgment. Claims have also been made that the conditions were not conducive to reading the document (*e.g.,* bad lighting).

It is worth noting that waivers are sometimes enforced even when participants were rushed to sign (without reading) the waiver (*Wroblewski v. Ohiopyle Trading Post,* 2013). In this case, a whitewater rafter was running behind her group; she was told to sign this and hurry to catch up with your group. No fraud was involved. Plaintiff did not try to negotiate the contract, did not ask for more time to read it, and was compelled to rush only by her personal desire to meet up with her group. Under Pennsylvania law, the failure to read a contract does not nullify a contract's validity.

It is suggested that whenever possible, participants be informed in advance that a waiver is required. It is good practice in some situations to make waivers available in advance of the day of participation. For instance, if a group has advance reservations for whitewater rafting, many providers send the participatory agreements to the rafters in advance or post them on their website and, thereby, avoid "springing it" on them at the last minute. Clients joining a health club could be given the agreement to take home and read.

To be safe, always allow the client ample time or opportunity to read the agreement and make certain that conditions do not prevent the client from reading the agreement.

Oral Explanation

One action that could strengthen the procedural context of the execution of the waiver would be to have a staff member provide an oral explanation of the agreement to the signer prior to signing to emphasize the intended breadth and effect of the document (*Stelluti v. Casapenn Enterprises, LLC,* 2009). Care must be taken to insure that it is explained properly; a video explanation screened by an attorney would be ideal.

Non-readers

Occasionally persons who cannot read or persons who cannot read English are required to sign a waiver. In general, courts hold that persons signing waivers are responsible for what they sign, even if the person cannot read.

A participant, who could not read English, signed an exculpatory agreement which included a statement, "I HAVE READ THIS WAIVER" (*Randas v. YMCA of Metropolitan Los Angeles,* 1993). The court noted that the general rule is one who signs cannot escape liability on the ground he has not read a document. The court said that if he cannot read, it is his responsibility to have it read or explained to him. Another California court (*Cortez v. Ceres Unified School District,* 2003) ruled similarly when there was a question regarding a father's ability to read the participant form he signed allowing his son to go on a field trip.

In a New Jersey case (*Cruz v. Atco Raceway, Inc.*, 2015), a question was raised about a waiver which the spouse signed for an illiterate husband. The court stated that "there is no evidence that she read the document to him or that he affirmatively indicated that he agreed to the waiver's terms." Summary judgment was denied.

In an Iowa case (*Adams v. Frieden, Inc.*, 2002), a legally blind woman challenged a waiver protecting against liability for injuries incurred in the pit area of an auto racetrack The court stated that the state supreme court had not carved out a disability exception to the rule that people are bound by documents they sign even if they have not read them. This, coupled with the fact that she could read with a magnifying glass, led the court to uphold the waiver.

While courts consistently rule that one is responsible to understand what one signs, best practice for a provider is to have someone read and/or explain the waiver to any non-reader. In *Jimenez v. 24 Hour Fitness USA, Inc.* (2015), the California health club discovered that the provider is on safer ground to make sure the non-reader understands what he or she is signing. The employee failed to call for a Spanish- speaking employee to assist even though this was his usual policy. The court ruled that non-verbal gestures could be considered affirmative misrepresentation when parties did not speak the same language. The court felt that reasonable persons could find that the employee's actions constituted fraud and misrepresentation; thus this created a fact issue and should be determined by the jury. The court reversed the trial court summary judgment ruling and remanded it for trial.

Staff Education

Comprehensive employee training conducted on a regular basis can help to reduce a number of waiver problems. Some of the most important considerations follow.

Explanation of the Agreement

There have been numerous cases in which the employee has told the participant that the waiver is meaningless, just a formality, used only for sign-in purposes, or just something required by the insurance company. When employees in some way misrepresent the purpose or significance of waivers or participant agreements, the possibility that the agreement will not be enforced because of fraudulent inducement is increased.

Courts have ruled that "allegations of verbal assurances contrary to a writing signed by a claimant will defeat summary judgment despite the clear and unambiguous language of the document signed" (*Weatherby v. Beechridge Speedway Inc.*, 1994). *Weatherby*, an auto racing case, involved both verbal assurances and written statements at issue. Likewise, in a California case (*Valentine v. Leisure Sports, Inc.*, 2006) a health club employee pressured Valentine to sign the membership agreement telling him not to "worry about" the waiver of liability. The trial court ruled the contract and the waiver were unenforceable because they were entered into on the basis of misleading information and representations. The jury then found that Leisure Sports had not been negligent. The appellate court, in light of a showing of no negligence, ruled the waiver issue to be moot.

It is essential that all employees understand the importance of waiver agreements and that they be trained to properly introduce and administer the document.

Make Certain Everyone Signs

Training your staff to take care that everyone signs the waiver is important. In *Soucy v. Nova Guides. Inc.* (2015), a mother and her two daughters (one a minor and one a 20 year-old signed waivers for a jeep tour. The next day they purchased and went on an ATV tour, for which the mother signed for all three of them. No one told the 20 year-old to sign; she was subsequently injured and filed suit. Interestingly, the plaintiff admitted signing the jeep waiver and said she though it applied to the ATV tour as well; she also admitted she would have signed the ATV waiver had she been instructed to. The fact was, Nova Guides did not have a signed ATV waiver, but depended on the waiver signed by the mother and the fact that they claimed it was an oral agreement. The court ruled that an oral agreement requires mutual assent… and Nova had never claimed that it thought the jeep waiver applied to the ATV trip. The waiver was not enforced and summary judgment was denied.

Waivers Signed After the Incident

Many businesses require post-injury releases be signed prior to agreeing to a monetary settlement. In a Florida case in which a man was injured by a large wind-blown balloon, the providers responsible for the balloon had the injured party sign a **pre-injury** waiver after he was injured. Why he would agree to sign it was not given. When the defendants (one of whom was Walt Disney Parks and Resorts U.S. Inc.) tried to claim the waiver as protection, the court said the waiver language did not protect the defendants from liability from injuries occurring prior to signing the agreement (*Peterson v. Flare Fittings, Inc.,* 2015).

Impaired Signers

Under common law, certain groups of individuals lack the ability, competence, or capacity to enter into binding contracts (*Ervin v. Hosanna Ministry, Inc.*, 1995). One such group is those who lose their capacity through the consumption of alcohol or drugs. Waivers signed by persons who are intoxicated to the extent that they are unaware of the effect of their actions are generally voidable by that person and will not protect the business from liability.

Provider management and staff should be certain all persons signing contracts or agreements are aware of the impact of such agreements.

Group Agreements

The group waiver should be administered by an employee of the service provider and NOT by a team captain or group leader. The employee should orally explain to the signers what the waiver is and its function. An opportunity should be given in which the signers can ask questions. A team captain could neither explain the function nor adequately answer the questions.

Be certain the waiver language above the signature spaces is plainly visible to all. Also, be certain that lighting and conditions are such that the signer has the opportunity and time to read the waiver prior to signing. In *Jenks v. New Hampshire Motor Speedway* (2010), a group waiver was not upheld, in part because of flaws and inconsistency in the ways in which waivers were administered. It is vital that the operator train the employees who will administer the waiver.

Mandatory Signing

Staff should be trained to understand that **all participants** must sign the waiver prior to participation and that there must be no exceptions. If a party refuses to sign the waiver, they must not be allowed to participate. In a horseback riding case, the waiver was not signed. The court said that it would have been valid had it contained a proper signature (*Millan v. Brown*, 2002). For rationale, see *Storing and Locating Agreements* section later in this chapter.

Cross Outs

It is not unusual for a client to read a waiver and wish to cross out part of the language. For two reasons, it is important that this not be allowed. 1) The cross out might delete important exculpatory language, thereby negating the intended effect of the agreement and 2) It is important that the waiver be consistently administered to all participants. In fact, waivers that were lost or destroyed have been enforced when the provider could show that they always required the waiver prior to participation (see *Storing and Locating Agreements* section later in this chapter).

Alternatives to Signing

In some states, the availability of certain alternatives for the signer can increase the likelihood that a court will enforce a waiver. Courts in some states hesitate to enforce a waiver that is offered on a "take it or leave it" basis. The following are possible alternatives.

Additional Fee for Avoiding Waiver

Some providers offer the participant the option of signing a waiver or paying a higher price to participate. Two California ski providers (*Solis v. Kirkwood Resort Company*, 2001; *Poulos v. Alpine Meadows Ski Corporation*, 2002) used a mid-week, less expensive season pass that included a waiver while it did not require a waiver for those buying day passes. In each case, the plaintiff was injured while using a day pass on a weekend and the courts ruled that the waiver applied only when the discounted mid-week pass was used. In a Washington ski case (*Chauvlier v. Booth Creek Ski Holdings, Inc.*, 2001), a skier was injured while using a discounted Spring season pass which required a waiver. In that case the waiver was upheld.

In *Boucher v. Riner* (1986) a parachuting school allowed students the option of signing a waiver or paying an additional fee of $300 to exempt oneself from the waiver and indemnification agreement. In another case involving skydivers (*Sevilla v. Estate of Lynn Maxey Wiley*, 2004), the waiver contained the option of signing the waiver or paying $900. Parties chose to sign the waiver.

Tunkl's guidelines (*Tunkl v. Regents of University of California*, 1963) for determining if a contract is of public interest seemed to suggest that a standardized adhesion contract would be more acceptable to the court if the signer had the option of paying an additional reasonable fee to avoid signing the waiver. For maximum protection, waivers should be used for both full price and discounted admissions. One is not less likely to be injured simply because one paid full price. (For more information, see the *Unequal Bargaining Power* section in Chapter 2).

Refund of Pre-payment to Non-Signers

On occasion, clients have pre-paid a fee in part or whole and then are required to sign a waiver upon arrival at the site. Some courts might determine that a waiver signed under such circumstances was not freely signed and, as such, is unenforceable. In *Booth v. Santa Barbara Biplanes* (2008), the company policy was to require a waiver, but to refund the client's money if they decided not to sign the waiver. The court upheld the waiver.

Retention of Agreements

Businesses generally do not have an unlimited amount of storage space and the questions arise: Which records do I need to keep? Moreover, how long must I keep them?

How Long Should Waivers be Retained?

One might think that if no injury has occurred at the conclusion of the individual's participation, the business would be safe in discarding the waiver at that point. This is not the case because many times injuries are not reported at the time of occurrence. The participant may not realize an injury has occurred, may not realize the seriousness of an injury until a later date, or has not yet decided to file suit against the provider. So do not discard a stack of waivers simply because you think no injury has occurred.

In previous editions, the authors have recommended that agreements should be retained until the statute of limitations (the legal restriction on the length of time an injured party has in which to file suit) has expired. Upon the recommendation of Gary Eaton, an attorney and balloonist, *we would now recommend that one keep waivers forever*. There are several reasons for this:

135

1) Claims in California (and possibly other states) must be filed during the statute of limitations period, but you may not be notified of the suit until much later;

2) Confusion may exist because of the varying lengths of the statutes of limitations and the complexity presented by minors; and

3) If one has taken the trouble to use waivers, the comparative effort to retain them is minimal. The increased peace of mind should be worth the extra effort.

The situation one must avoid is to need a waiver and no longer have it. Being able to access a needed waiver would outweigh any inconvenience.

Which Agreements Should be Kept?

The answer to this question is simple. Keep them all! Then you do not need to worry about whether a client was injured or when the statute of limitations expires. Many may ask, "Where will I keep all those waivers?" A solution to the problem of waiver storage space is presented below.

Storing and Locating Agreements

When an injury occurs or when you receive notice of a legal action against you, the most important question to ask is not "Did he sign a waiver?" It is not "Did I save the waiver?" The most important question is "Can I locate the waiver?"

Locating and Identifying

The best waiver in the world may not provide protection if the provider cannot produce it when needed. Most providers use more than one type of agreement (e.g., participation agreement, rental agreement, informed consent agreement) or use different agreements for different activities (e.g., snowmobiling, skiing, snow-shoeing). Color-coding, by using a different color paper for each different type of agreement or activity involved, can be very helpful in filing and locating the agreement needed. Much time can be saved if you know that all rafting waivers are green and all overnight hike waivers are yellow.

Storage

As with any important business records, safe storage of waivers is very important. Stored waivers should be well organized (e.g., by year, activity, name) for easy access and should be stored in a safe location. Being able to produce a waiver signed by the plaintiff can help to protect the business from liability.

For a business that deals with a large number of clients, the space needed for storage of waivers can become immense very quickly. *A convenient solution to the problem is to scan each waiver and store them on CD or DVD.* This conversion might be done periodically (e.g., monthly, end of season). It would also be good practice to make a copy of each disk and store them in different buildings just in case a facility burns or is otherwise destroyed.

Lost Waivers

Lost or missing waivers can be costly to the service provider. In a New York case (*Schaeffer v. Wenk*, 2001) involving a health club, no waiver was found and summary judgment failed. In a Georgia speedway case (*Seibers v. Dixie Speedway, Inc.*, 1996), the defendant speedway produced five waivers signed by the plaintiff, but none for the date in question. They were not upheld. A stable (*Millan v. Brown*, 2002) was unable to produce a waiver signed by a plaintiff injured while horseback riding. The court said that the waiver would have been valid had one been found. In Idaho (*Davis v. Sun Valley Ski Education Foundation, Inc.*, 1997), a ski operator was not allowed to present an unexecuted waiver as evidence in place of a destroyed waiver. In a tanning bed case (*Oliver v. Tanning Bed, Inc.*, 2008), the operator was unable to produce a signed waiver. This created an issue of whether the client was adequately warned of the danger and resulted in the court denying summary judgment.

However, courts do enforce missing waivers under certain circumstances. In a 2005 Connecticut case (*Corso v. United States Surgical Corporation*, 2005), the court enforced a waiver in spite of the fact that the defendant fitness center could not produce a signed waiver. The defendant established that all members were required to read and sign a waiver prior to using the center and that no exceptions were made to the rule. The court stated that Connecticut law has long recognized that a party may use secondary evidence to establish the existence of a document that no longer exists.

In a Washington ski case (*Lunt v. Mount Spokane Skiing Corporation*, 1991), the court enforced a missing waiver stating that when an original document is lost and a diligent search is made, secondary evidence of its content may be admissible provided there is no bad faith. A waiver destroyed by fire was enforced when evidence indicated one had been signed (*Daddario v. Snow Valley, Inc.*, 1995). In another case of a lost waiver (*Nishi v. Mount Snow, LTD.*, 1996), the court enforced the waiver because the application form stated that a waiver was required. Another missing waiver was upheld in an Indiana auto racing case (*Beaver v. Grand Prix Karting Association, Inc.*, 2001). In a Minnesota case (*Moore v. Minnesota Baseball Instructional School*, 2009), the defendant could not produce the signed release or the online enrollment form, but the court upheld the waiver because no one is allowed to participate until the release is signed.

Importance of a No Exception Waiver Policy. When a waiver is enforced even though it cannot be physically produced, invariably a major factor in the decision is that the provider has a firm "no exception" policy. No one participates until a waiver is signed. The organization should develop a waiver acquisition "process" that helps to insure that all patrons have signed a waiver. Failure to require all parties to sign the waiver contributed to the failure of the waiver to be enforced in *Jenks v. New Hampshire Motor Speedway* (2010). In *Porter v. Dartmouth College* (2009), the school was not protected, in part, because only students renting equipment were required to sign waivers. Those having their own equipment did not. A guest of a club member did not sign a club waiver prior to his injury (*Tabrizi v. L.A. Fitness International*, 2011). The club tried to rely upon the waiver of the club member, but the court ruled in favor of the plaintiff and denied summary judgment.

Store waivers using a system that allows easy accessibility to the waivers, store them in a secure (and preferably fireproof) setting, and, whenever possible, store copies in more than one place.

Chapter 8

State Waiver Law

Waiver law in each state is specific to that state and frequently differs from the law in surrounding states. Courts in some states look more favorably upon waivers and are much more likely to enforce a waiver than are courts in states that do not favor waivers. In fact, a waiver that is enforced in one state may not be enforced when the same exact waiver is used by a business in another state.

Readers familiar with previous editions of this book will note that the classification system has changed since the 8th edition. Previously, the classification was based on how strict courts were when enforcing waivers. The authors feel, however, that readers really are interested in **how likely a waiver is to be enforced**.

In this chapter, each state is categorized into one of four groups, based upon case law and/or legislation passed by the legislature of that state (see Figure 8.1). The categories describe the authors' judgment as to the likelihood that the courts in each state will enforce a well-written waiver which is challenged in court: **Poor**, **Fair**, **Good**, and **Excellent**.

The likelihood of enforcement of waivers in seven states has been classified as **Poor**. In these states, Supreme Court rulings or statutes either declare that waivers are against public policy or maintain such stringent requirements for validity that enforcement of a waiver in that state is very unlikely. Ten states have been categorized as **Fair**; courts in these states do uphold some waivers, but waivers frequently fail when challenged in court because of the strict standards of enforcement. The likelihood of enforcement of waivers in twenty-six states, Puerto Rico, and the Virgin Islands is categorized as **Good**. Courts in these states regularly enforce waivers; requirements for validity might be called average or reasonable. The likelihood of waivers being enforced in seven states, the District of Columbia, and federal admiralty law is **Excellent**. Courts in these states tend to favor waivers and are inclined to enforce them on a regular basis. Courts in these states generally hold that waivers promote public policy.

Each state or territory has been subjectively categorized. Some have had dozens of sport- and recreation-related cases, while others have had only one or two such cases. The reader is cautioned, however, that 1) the classification is a subjective standard and is based upon the judgment of the authors; and that 2) the law is not static, but, rather, is always subject to change by the courts or legislature of each state.

To make this information on state waiver law more user-friendly, it is presented in three formats. First is Figure 8.1 which simply lists the states by classification – so the reader can look and quickly see how any state is classified. Second is Figure 8.2, from which the reader can at a glance learn much about the views toward waivers held by the courts and legislatures in each state. And finally, is the summary of state waiver laws where the waiver law of each state is organized and summarized. The summaries vary in length –from a paragraph to several pages – depending upon the number of relevant waiver cases in the state. In addition, Chapter 3 contains more information regarding the state waiver law for minors.

The authors want to point out that hundreds of relevant cases are cited in this book. We suggest that you take the time to find the cases, read them, and draw your own personal conclusions regarding waiver law in the state. That way, you minimize any errors contained in this secondary source.

Figure 8.1
Likelihood of Courts to Enforce a Liability Waiver
For Adult Participants

POOR	FAIR	GOOD		EXCELLENT
Alaska	Arkansas	Alabama	New York[68]	Admiralty Law
Arizona	Delaware	Florida	North Carolina	California
Connecticut	Maine	Idaho	Oklahoma	Colorado
Hawaii	Mississippi	Illinois	Pennsylvania	District of Columbia
Louisiana	Nevada	Indiana	Puerto Rico	Georgia
Virginia	New Hampshire	Kansas	South Carolina	Iowa
Wisconsin	Oregon	Kentucky	South Dakota	Michigan
	Rhode Island	Maryland	Tennessee	North Dakota
	West Virginia	Massachusetts	Texas	Ohio
		Minnesota	Utah	
		Missouri	Vermont	
		Montana	Virgin Islands	
		Nebraska	Washington	
		New Jersey	Wyoming	
		New Mexico		

Tabular Summary of Waiver Law in Each State

This information regarding waiver law is based on recreation-, fitness-, and sport-related waiver cases from throughout the country. The waiver law for each state is presented in two formats – tabular and commentary. For a quick, overall view of waiver law in any state, inspect the chart shown in Figure 8.2. Here, the recreation and sport professional can compare states at a glance. Then for detailed commentary, including references to statutes and case law for a particular state, turn to the summary of waiver law presented alphabetically by state later in this chapter. Additional state law regarding agreements for minor clients may be found in Chapter 3.

Explanation of Figure 8.2

Column 1: Name of the the State or Government Entity.

Column 2: Approximate Number of Cases from that State. The number of cases in a state falls within the range shown in the table. More cases generally means that more information is available regarding waiver law in that state. One can generally be more confident of conclusions based on many cases than those from a few cases.

Column 3: Statutes and Significant Supreme Court Rulings <u>Restricting the Use of Waivers</u>. The more significant statutes and Supreme Court rulings are presented in bold print.

Column 4: State Statutes and Court Public Policy Positions <u>Allowing Enforcement of Waivers</u>. These provide information regarding the general attitude of the legislature and courts toward waivers.

Column 5: History of Waiver Enforcement in the State. Indicates whether the courts of a state have a history of enforcing waivers; also, indicates if there has been a change in the practice in recent years.

Column 6: Court Attitude toward Use of the Term "Negligence." Courts in some states Require the term "negligence" or its equivalent. Others Recommend or Strongly Recommend its use. Others have no requirement.

Column 7: Likelihood of Enforcement of Parental Waivers. Author judgment of likelihood: Not Enough Information, Poor (Indicates Not Enforced or Extremely Unlikely), Fair, Good, Excellent.

Column 8: Likelihood of Enforcement of Adult Waivers. Author judgment of likelihood: Poor (Indicates Not Enforced or Extremely Unlikely), Fair, Good, Excellent.

---

[68] Likelihood of enforcement is poor if G.O.L. 5-326 applies.

Summary of Waiver Law in Each State

Figure 8.2

A Comparison of State Waiver Laws

State	Based on Approx. Number of Cases	STATUTORY/SUPREME COURT RESTRICTIONS ON WAIVERS Major Statutes & Rulings (Bold Face) Limited Restrictions (Normal Face)	PUBLIC POLICY (PP) Court PP Positions and State Statutes Allowing Enforcement of Waivers	Courts Currently Tend to Uphold Waivers	Requirement Of the Term 'Negligence'	Likelihood of Enforcement of Parental Waivers	Likelihood of Enforcement of Adult Waivers
Admiralty Or Maritime Law	21-40	**46 U.S.C. § 30509 Bars Cruise Ship Waivers**	Yes Businessmen must be free to bargain regarding who bears risk of damage.	Yes Waivers are generally enforced.	Not Required	*NOT ENOUGH INFO*	EXCELLENT POOR (if by cruise line)
AL	6-20		Yes S. Ct. .Holds Waivers Are in the Public Interest. **A.C. 12-21-109** Calls for enforcement of waivers.	Yes except when gross or wanton	Not Required	*POOR*	GOOD
AK	1-5	A.S. § 05.45.120 Prohibits Ski Operator waivers	Yes S. Ct. strictly construes waivers and requires high standards for enforcement. **AS 09.65-202** Allows enforcement of parental waivers.	No In the past; **Yes** Recently S.Ct. upheld 2014 waiver.	Required	*EXCELLENT*	POOR
AZ	6-20	**S. Ct. (*Phelps v. Firebird Raceway*, 2005) interprets Arizona Constitution XVIII § 5 to Forbid Summary Judgment Based on Waiver**	Yes Waivers can be used in court, but cannot be used to determine summary judgment. **ARS 5-706** Enforces Ski Operator Waivers **ARS 12-556** Enforces Motorsports Waivers **ARS 12-553** Enforces adult and parental equine waivers	Yes In the past; **No** No cases found since 2005 *Phelps* S.Ct. ruling.	Highly Advised	*NOT ENOUGH INFO* *(EQUINE ALLOWED)*	POOR (No Summary Judgment)
AR	6-20		Yes S.Ct. stated that waivers are disfavored, but they are not invalid *per se*. To avoid liability for negligence, the waiver must make clear what negligence liability is to be avoided.	No In the past; **Yes** Most are enforced in recent years.	Not Required	*POOR*	FAIR
CA	76+	CCC §1668 Bars Senior Care Provider Waiver CC 1542 Bars Childcare Provider waiver	Yes Waivers are not contrary to PP or Public interest Enforces Sport & Recreation waivers; but strict standards are required.	Yes Most waivers are enforced, but standards are high.	Required in Some Districts	*EXCELLENT*	EXCELLENT

State	Based on Approx. Number of Cases	STATUTORY/SUPREME COURT RESTRICTIONS ON WAIVERS Major Statutes & Rulings (Bold Face) Limited Restrictions (Normal Face)	PUBLIC POLICY (PP) Court PP Positions and State Statutes Allowing Enforcement of Waivers	Courts Currently Tend to Uphold Waivers	Requirement Of the Term 'Negligence'	Likelihood of Enforcement of Parental Waivers	Likelihood of Enforcement of Adult Waivers
CO	21-40		Yes Unambiguous Waivers that that do not involve a public duty are not against PP. **CRS 13-22-107** Allows enforcement of Parental Waivers	Yes Most waivers enforced.	Highly Advised	*EXCELLENT*	EXCELLENT
CT	41-75	*Hanks v. Powder Ridge* and *Reardon v. Windswept* **Supreme Court rulings calling for rigid criteria make enforcement unlikely.** CGS § 29-211 Prohibits ski operator waivers	No Few waivers have been enforced since the S.Ct. decisions.	Yes In the past; **No** Few waivers are valid now.	Required	*POOR*	POOR
DE	6-20		Yes PP provides that waivers are valid & enforceable when the intent is crystal clear and unequivocal. Few waivers are enforced.	No Strong Require-ments for Clarity and Intent	Highly Advised	*GOOD*	FAIR
DC	6-20		Yes PP provides that waivers are valid & enforceable when the intent is clear.	Yes Most waivers enforced	Highly Advised	*NO INFO*	EXCELLENT
FL	76+		Yes PP in Florida is to not interfere lightly with the freedom to contract. Clear & unequivocal waivers not involving a statutory duty are enforceable. **F.S. 549.09** Allows parental motorsports waivers.	Yes Waivers are frequently enforced.	Not Required But Highly Advised	*GOOD-non-profit POOR-Commercial* *(MOTORSPORTS ALLOWED)*	GOOD
GA	21-40		Yes The paramount PP is that courts will not lightly interfere with the freedom to contract unless it, in some manner, violates PP; a contract is not against PP unless declared so by the General Assembly. **O.C.G.A. § 4-12-1**; *Mays v. Valley View Ranch*, 2011 Allows equine waivers	Yes Weak standards	Not Required	*FAIR* *(EQUINE ALLOWED)*	EXCELLENT
HI	6-20	**H.R.S. 663-1.54 Bars Waivers of Negligence by Recreational Activity Providers**	Yes S.Ct. has stated that there is no PP prohibiting the enforcement of waivers so long as there is no conflict with a statute or public interest and bargaining power is equal. **§663-10.95** Allows Parental Waivers for Motorsports	Yes A few waivers have been enforced since statute	Required	*POOR* *(MOTORSPORTS ALLOWED)*	POOR

State	Based on Approx. Number of Cases	STATUTORY/SUPREME COURT RESTRICTIONS ON WAIVERS Major Statutes & Rulings (Bold Face) Limited Restrictions (Normal Face)	PUBLIC POLICY (PP) Court PP Positions and State Statutes Allowing Enforcement of Waivers	Courts Currently Tend to Uphold Waivers	Requirement Of the Term 'Negligence'	Likelihood of Enforcement of Parental Waivers	Likelihood of Enforcement of Adult Waivers
ID	6-20	IC 6-1103(10) Prohibits Ski Operator Waivers IC 6-1204 Prohibits Guides &Outfitters Waivers	Yes S.Ct. says freedom to contract is fundamental to free enterprise system; Waivers are upheld if bargaining is equal and no public duty is involved.	Yes S.Ct. has enforced waivers	Not Required	NOT ENOUGH INFO	GOOD
IL	41-75		Yes Courts strictly construe waivers to give effect to the intention of the parties. Though waivers are not favored, parties may allocate risk of negligence. 745 ILCS 47/1-15 Allows parental equine waivers.	Yes Courts enforce most waivers – even some weak ones	Not Required	POOR (EQUINE ALLOWED)	GOOD
IN	21-40		Yes, If no contrary statute, providers' use of waivers is not against PP. I.C. 34-28-3 Allows parental motor sports waivers.	Yes Courts have strict require-ments	Required	EXCELLENT (MOTORSPORTS ALLOWED)	GOOD
IA	6-20		Yes Waivers for sporting events do not violate PP; the PP of freedom to contract is best served by enforcing liability waivers.	Yes Most waivers are enforced	Highly Advised	POOR	EXCELLENT
KA	6-20		Yes Waivers are valid and enforceable if they do not involve settled PP or matter of public interest. PP supports waivers because they play a vital role in allowing participation in recreation.	Yes Enforced for negligence; No gross recognized.	Not Required	NOT ENOUGH INFO	GOOD
KY	6-20		Yes Waivers for ordinary negligence are not against PP if there is no public interest, public duty, or statutory duty. Waivers play a vital role in recreational activities. KRS 247.4027(2)(a) Allows parental waivers for equine activities	Yes Most recent waivers have been upheld.	Highly Advised	NOT ENOUGH INFO (EQUINE ALLOWED)	GOOD
LA		La.Civ.Code art. 2004 Bars All Waivers	No	*	*	POOR	POOR
MD	6-20		Yes Absent a contrary statute no PP prevents parties from contracting as they see fit, if the signer knows and agrees to the terms.	Yes Waivers are usually enforced.	Not Required	EXCELLENT	GOOD

State	Based on Approx. Number of Cases	STATUTORY/SUPREME COURT RESTRICTIONS ON WAIVERS Major Statutes & Rulings (Bold Face) Limited Restrictions (Normal Face)	PUBLIC POLICY (PP) Court PP Positions and State Statutes Allowing Enforcement of Waivers	Courts Currently Tend to Uphold Waivers	Requirement Of the Term 'Negligence'	Likelihood of Enforcement of Parental Waivers	Likelihood of Enforcement of Adult Waivers
MA	21-40	ALM GL Ch. 93 sec. 80 Prohibits Health Club waivers	Yes PP favors the enforcement of waivers; allocation of risk by agreement is not contrary to PP. **MA ST 128 § 2D**; *Powers v. Mukpo*, 1999 Allows equine waivers	Yes Enforces good waivers.	Highly Advised	*EXCELLENT* *(EQUINE ALLOWED)*	GOOD
ME	6-20		Yes While disfavored, the S.Ct. holds that a waiver is enforceable and not against PP provided it violates no PP, is equally bargained for, intent is clear, and terms are brought home to the client.	Yes Standards seem to be getting stricter.	Highly Advised	*POOR*	FAIR
MI	41-75		Yes Waivers for ordinary negligence are not against PP, but the language must be clear and unequivocal. **MCLA 691.1661 – 1667** Allows Equine waivers	Yes Even weak waivers are usually upheld.	Not Required	*POOR* *(EQUINE ALLOWED)*	EXCELLENT
MN	21-40		Yes S.Ct.: Enforcement of waivers supports the public interest in freedom to contract. Recreational waivers do not involve a public service and are not against PP. **MN ST 604.055** Allows enforcement of adult and parental waivers of ordinary negligence.	Yes Waivers are generally upheld.	Not Required	*EXCELLENT*	GOOD
MS	6-20	**S.Ct. Ruling Stresses that Waivers Are to be Enforced Only if Fairly and Honestly Negotiated.**	Yes Waivers are disfavored but upheld if: close scrutiny; clear and precise; honestly negotiated; & understood by signer. Courts stress opportunity to negotiate.	Yes But most waivers are not enforced.	Highly Advised	*POOR*	FAIR
MO	6-20		Yes Waivers are disfavored & strictly construed, but are not against PP except when a disparity in bargaining power or an essential public service. **MO ST 537.325** Allows Equine waivers	Yes Enforces good waivers.	Required	*NOT ENOUGH INFO* *(EQUINE ALLOWED)*	GOOD
MT	6-20		**MCA 27-1-753** and **28-2-702** This 2015 statute allows the use of liability waivers in and sport and replaces **MCA 28-2-702** which prohibited waivers.	No cases involving waivers since statute.	Required By Statute	*NOT ENOUGH INFO*	GOOD

143

State	Based on Approx. Number of Cases	STATUTORY/SUPREME COURT RESTRICTIONS ON WAIVERS Major Statutes & Rulings (Bold Face) Limited Restrictions (Normal Face)	PUBLIC POLICY (PP) Court PP Positions and State Statutes Allowing Enforcement of Waivers	Courts Currently Tend to Uphold Waivers	Requirement Of the Term 'Negligence'	Likelihood of Enforcement of Parental Waivers	Likelihood of Enforcement of Adult Waivers
NE	6-20		Yes Waivers are not against PP and are valid unless clearly repugnant to public conscience. Courts are reluctant to void contracts on a PP basis. Waivers promote PP since they inform signer of risks.	Yes But based on few definitive cases.	Not Required	*NOT ENOUGH INFO*	GOOD
NV	1-5		Yes Liability waivers are a valid exercise of freedom to contract if signer understands the risk and appreciates the danger.	Yes Enforced about half the time.	Highly Advised	*NOT ENOUGH INFO*	FAIR
NH	6-20		Yes Waivers are generally prohibited, however they can be enforced if they do not violate PP and the meaning of the waiver was clearly understood.	No Has very strict standards and enforces few waivers.	Required	*NOT ENOUGH INFO*	FAIR
NJ	21-40	N.J.S.A.5-13 Prohibits Ski Operator Waivers	Yes Waivers are disfavored & strictly construed, but are enforceable if not against PP. Strict standards.	Yes Majority of waivers upheld.	Required	*POOR*	GOOD
NM	1-5	NMSA 1978, sec. 42-13-4 [1993]; Prohibits equine waivers	Yes The S.Ct. (*Berlangieri v. Running Elk Corp.*, 2003) Waivers not affecting public interest are enforceable, but must be strictly construed, be clear, unambiguous, & inform the signer of its effect.	Yes Insufficient Cases.	Not Required	*NOT ENOUGH INFO*	GOOD (few cases)
NY	76+	**G.O.L. 5-326 Prohibits Enforcement of Waivers At Places of Recreation and Amusement that Charge an Admission fee** NYSCL, GB 30, sec. 623(3); Prohibits Health Club Waivers	Yes In general, NY waiver law calls for the enforcement of waivers that do not conflict with a statute (including **G.O.L. 5-326**) or violate PP. Standards for enforcement, however, are high.	**Yes** Standards are high; most are upheld; No Most fail if GOL 5-326 applies.	Required	*POOR*	GOOD POOR (if GOL 5-326 applies)
NC	6-20	NCGS §99C-1-5 Prohibits Ski Operator Waivers	Yes Courts enforce waivers under freedom to contract principle; waiver is valid if there is no conflict with PP or statute; it must be unambiguous and involve parties with equal bargaining power.	Yes Most waivers have been enforced.	Not Required	*GOOD (for non-profit)*	GOOD
ND	1-5		Yes While waivers are disfavored, courts enforce waivers that are not against PP; courts do not seem to hold waivers to a high standard for enforcement.	Yes Even weak waivers are enforced.	Highly Advised	*GOOD (for non-profit)*	EXCELLENT

State	Based on Approx. Number of Cases	STATUTORY/SUPREME COURT RESTRICTIONS ON WAIVERS Major Statutes & Rulings (Bold Face) Limited Restrictions (Normal Face)	PUBLIC POLICY (PP) Court PP Positions and State Statutes Allowing Enforcement of Waivers	Courts Currently Tend to Uphold Waivers	Requirement Of the Term 'Negligence'	Likelihood of Enforcement of Parental Waivers	Likelihood of Enforcement of Adult Waivers
OH	41-75		Yes The paramount PP is that courts are not to lightly interfere with the freedom to contract. Clearly worded waivers are generally not contrary to PP. **R.C. § 2305.321**; *Markowitz v. Bainbridge Eq. Center*, 2007 Allows equine waivers.	Yes Most waivers enforced – even weak waivers.	Highly Advised	*EXCELLENT*	EXCELLENT
OK	6-20	15 O.S. 1991 @212.1 Forbids Enforcement of Un-bargained for Disclaimers (e.g., signs)	Yes Waivers are not against PP and people are free to contract as they see fit; they must be unambiguous, involve bargaining equals, and not violate PP.	Yes Strict require-ments are enforced.	Not Required	*POOR*	GOOD
OR	6-20	***Bagley v. Mt Bachelor*, 2014 Supreme Court Rulings Make Enforcement of waivers Unlikely**	No In 2014 (*Bagley v.Mt Bachelor*), S.Ct. set bar for enforcement (PP & unconsionability) so high as to seemingly make most waivers unenforceable.	Yes In the past; **No** 2014 S.Ct. makes validity doubtful.	Not Required	*POOR*	FAIR
PA	41-75	Unsigned Ticket Disclaimers are Enforceable only if Clearly Exculpatory and Client was Made Aware	Yes Waivers violate PP only if an overriding PP or public interest. They are not favored, but are enforced if they meet the standards.	Yes Strict standards but most are enforced.	Highly Advised	*POOR*	GOOD
PR	1-5		Yes Waivers are enforceable, but must meet the clarity, intent, and PP requirement.	Yes Tend to enforce waivers.	Required	*NOT ENOUGH INFO*	GOOD (few cases)
RI	1-5		Yes Few recreation cases, but S.Ct. does uphold waiver if it is unambiguous and clear; they are not favored and are strictly construed.	Yes Few cases, but seems to have strict standards.	Not Required	*POOR*	FAIR (few cases)
SC	1-5		Yes Waivers for sporting events and activities are in the public interest and are enforceable. Private parties are free to contract as they please.	Yes Most waivers have been enforced.	Highly Advised	*NOT ENOUGH INFO*	GOOD
SD	6-20		Yes Courts have held that recreational waivers are in the public interest and enforceable because they enable providers to offer sporting events; waivers are not void as a matter of PP.	Yes Most waivers have been enforced.	Yes	*NOT ENOUGH INFO*	GOOD

State	Based on Approx. Number of Cases	STATUTORY/SUPREME COURT RESTRICTIONS ON WAIVERS Major Statutes & Rulings (Bold Face) Limited Restrictions (Normal Face)	PUBLIC POLICY (PP) Court PP Positions and State Statutes Allowing Enforcement of Waivers	Courts Currently Tend to Uphold Waivers	Requirement Of the Term 'Negligence'	Likelihood of Enforcement of Parental Waivers	Likelihood of Enforcement of Adult Waivers
TN	21-40	TCA 44-20-101-105; *Teles v. Big Rock Stables*, 2006 Prohibits some equine waivers	Yes The PP of the state favors freedom to contract except for professionals in an area of public interest. Waivers are NOT construed against the relying party.	Yes Even weak waivers are sometimes enforced.	Not Required	*POOR*	GOOD
TX	21-40	**Courts Require that Waivers Meet <u>Fair Notice Requirement</u> Which Includes Conspicuousness and Express Negligence Doctrine**	Yes Sport-related waivers are not against PP. Waivers are valid and enforceable if they satisfy the Fair Notice Requirement pertaining to conspicuousness and clear and unambiguous intent.	Yes Waivers that meet strict require-ments are enforced.	Required	*POOR*	GOOD
UT	6-20	UCA 78-27-51-54; *Rothstein v. Snowbird Corporation*, 2007 Prohibits Ski Resort Waivers; S.Ct.. ruling Prohibits Summary Judgment on Issue of Gross Negligence	Yes Enforcement of waivers is PP; to declare a waiver against PP, evidence must be absolutely free from doubt. Waivers must be clear and unambiguous. **UCA78-27b-101-103.** Allows adult & parental waivers for equine activities.	Yes Strict standards but many are enforced.	Not Required	*POOR* *(EQUINE ALLOWED)*	GOOD
VT	6-20	In *Dalury v. S-K-I, Ltd.*, (1995) S.Ct. Ruling Declares Most Ski Operator Waivers Violate P.P. because it affects large numbers of people	Yes Waivers are disfavored & strictly construed, but do not generally violate PP. The exception seems to be activities affecting large numbers of participants (e.g., skiing).	Yes Strict standards but most are upheld.	Highly Advised	*NOT ENOUGH INFO*	GOOD
VA	6-20	**S.Ct. in *Hiett v. Lake Barcroft*, (1992) ruled that waivers protecting against liability for personal injury due to negligence are against PP and are unenforceable**	No S.Ct. stated that a waiver allows provider to put the signer at the mercy of provider's misconduct and cannot be lawfully done. However a state circuit court & a federal court have upheld a few pre-injury waivers. **VCA § 3.1-796.132(B)** Allows adult & parental waivers for equine activities.	No But 3 cases, (2 auto racing; 1 scuba) have been enforced.	*	*POOR* *(EQUINE ALLOWED)*	POOR
VI	1 - 5		Yes To be enforceable, the waiver must be broad and unambiguous; further, it must not violate PP. There is a strong PP for enforcement of contracts.	Yes Most waivers are enforced.	Highly Advised	*NOT ENOUGH INFO*	GOOD

State	Based on Approx. Number of Cases	STATUTORY/SUPREME COURT RESTRICTIONS ON WAIVERS Major Statutes & Rulings (Bold Face) Limited Restrictions (Normal Face)	PUBLIC POLICY (PP) Court PP Positions and State Statutes Allowing Enforcement of Waivers	Courts Currently Tend to Uphold Waivers	Requirement Of the Term 'Negligence'	Likelihood of Enforcement of Parental Waivers	Likelihood of Enforcement of Adult Waivers
WA	21-40		Yes Waivers are enforceable if they do not involve the public interest, are conspicuous, & apply only to ordinary negligence.	Yes Most waivers are enforced, but must meet the criteria.	Not Required	*POOR*	GOOD
WV	6 - 20	WVC 20-3B-1-8 Prohibit Outfitters & Guides Waivers W.Va.C. 20-3A-1 to 8 Prohibits ski operator waivers	Yes Waivers that do not violate PP or a safety statute are generally enforceable. They must be clear and the action must be within the contemplation of the parties.	Yes Few are upheld; very strict standards & PP.	Not Required	*POOR*	FAIR
WI	21-40	*Atkins v. Swimwest* and other Supreme Court Rulings Set Standards That Prohibit the Enforcement of Almost all Waivers	No Appellate courts have often enforced recreational waivers, but the S.Ct. has never enforced one – although it states that waivers are enforceable. The court places such severe restrictions on waivers that enforcement is very unlikely.	Yes In the past; No Few waivers are valid now.	Highly Advised	*POOR*	POOR
WY	6-20	Wyo.Con., Art. 19, sec. 7 prohibits employer/employee waivers	Yes Waivers are valid and enforceable if not in violation of PP. Recreational activity waivers are not generally against PP unless they are not fairly entered into. **WY ST § 1-1-122-123**; *Street v. Darwin Ranch* 1999 Allows equine waivers.	Yes Most waivers are enforced.	Not Required	*NOT ENOUGH INFO*	GOOD

Summary of Waiver Law in Each State

Admiralty Law (Maritime Law)
EXCELLENT
POOR – For Cruise Lines

A Word of Explanation

Admiralty law (also called Maritime Law) is "that system of law that particularly relates to marine commerce and navigation, to business transacted at sea or relating to navigation, to ships and shipping, to seamen, to the transportation of persons and property by sea, and to marine affairs generally" (Black, 1990, p. 47). Admiralty law is federal law and trumps state law when the two conflict; however, when there is an absence of well-developed admiralty law regarding an issue, courts may adopt state law or incorporate general common-law principles so long as there is no conflict with federal admiralty law (Smolnikar v. Royal Caribbean Cruises LTD., 2011).

Admiralty law is addressed in this book because it is the appropriate law in many sport, recreation, and fitness waiver cases. Federal courts have original jurisdiction over civil cases in admiralty jurisdiction; admiralty law applies to activities on any navigable waterway (e.g., lakes, rivers, canals, seashores, bays, oceans), not solely to activities on the high seas. Some examples of recreational activities to which admiralty law has been applied include swimming, body surfing, wakeboarding, snorkeling, snuba, scuba diving, jet skis, sailing, whitewater rafting, charter fishing, pleasure boating, powerboat riding, parasailing, and any recreational activities on cruise ships. In fact, admiralty law even extends to cruise ship excursions on shore (e.g., city tours, zip line expeditions, hikes, jungle float trips).

While admiralty law has traditionally disfavored waivers, today *liability waivers, disclaimers, and exculpatory clauses are usually deemed to be enforceable so long as they are not overreaching.*

Public Policy. The rationale for upholding liability waivers and other exculpatory tools is that businessmen must be free to bargain over which party is to bear the risk of damage. This enables the businessman to be able to provide a risky activity at a more reasonable price. Owners of recreational vessels and providers of recreational activities, therefore, are free to use written waivers to disclaim liability for recreational activities in navigable waters so long as the waiver is (1) clear, unambiguous, (2) does not violate federal public policy, and (3) is not a contract of adhesion (a waiver for recreational sporting activities is not adhesionary because recreational activities are not essential services) (*Charnis v. Watersport Pro LLC*, 2009).

To be enforceable, such clauses must 1) clearly and unequivocally indicate the intentions of the parties, and 2) not involve a monopoly, or a party with excessive bargaining power. The liability waiver can protect the provider from liability for injuries resulting from the provider's ordinary negligence, but there are limitations to liability waivers. They will not (1) provide protection from liability for acts of gross negligence; (2) exempt a party from liability arising from that party's failure to comply with a safety statute (no private individual has the power to waive such an obligation) (*Tassinari v. Key West Water Tours, LC*, 2007); (3) be enforced against employees of the provider; and (4) protect when a critical public service is involved.

Admiralty law requires that, in interpreting a waiver, the document (1) should be read as a whole and its words given their plain meaning unless the provision is ambiguous; (2) should be construed to cover all losses, damages, or liabilities which reasonably appear to have been within the contemplation of the parties; (3) should not turn on whether it expressly mentions the word "negligence." Phrases such as "from any and all causes of action" unambiguously show the intention of the parties to exempt the defendants from liability for plaintiff's claims based on negligence. For example, in *Piche v. Stockdale Holdings, LLC* (2009), the court stated that the waiver language ". . . hereby hold harmless and release forever ... from all rights, claims, demands, damages, costs and causes of action of whatever kind or nature arising from any damages, liabilities, or injuries I may sustain . . ." clearly and unequivocally indicated that the parties intended to shift the risk of loss to plaintiff and indemnify the defendants against his personal injury claims under any theory of recovery.

With respect to bargaining power, it is not sufficient to assert that one party was less sophisticated than the other; the plaintiff must show evidence that the party holding the superior bargaining power used the power in an overreaching manner, such as engaging in fraud, coercion, or by insisting on an unconscionable clause (*Piche*). Regarding a release that clearly states that the signer is relinquishing rights, 1) the contract is not invalid simply because it is a form contract; 2) the signer has the responsibility to read the document prior to signing; and 3) failure of the signer to read the contract does not mean he will not be held to the terms of the contract. These, coupled with the fact that signers generally have other options regarding their choice of recreational activities, indicate that such a clause is neither overreaching nor unconscionable.

The prevailing rule in American courts limits punitive damages to cases in which a defendant's conduct is outrageous due to gross, willful, wanton, and reckless indifference for the rights of others. The United States Supreme Court has stated that a plaintiff may recover punitive damages under admiralty law consistent with the common-law rule unless specifically limited by Congress (*Atlantic Sounding Co., Inc. v. Townsend*, 2009). Likewise, authorities agree that victims can recover damages for pain and suffering in maritime personal injury cases (*Lobegeiger v. Celebrity Cruises, Inc.*, 2011).

It should be noted that **assumption of risk** is not an available defense in admiralty law personal injury cases. However, this does not preclude the use of liability waivers since an express waiver and assumption of risk are two distinct affirmative defenses. (*Cobb v. Aramark Sports and Entertainment Services, LLC* (2013a).

Electronic waivers, including those using a click on an online checkbox to indicate assent, are enforceable in federal courts (*Pazol v. Tough Mudder Incorporated*, 2015).

Arbitration Clause. A written provision affording arbitration in any maritime contract shall be valid, irrevocable, and enforceable except when there are legal grounds for the revocation of any contract (*Pazol*).

"Negligence." A waiver does not have to specifically use the word "negligence" to be enforceable.

Gross Negligence. Waivers will protect against ordinary negligence, but not against gross negligence.

Statutes. Waivers will not exempt a party from liability arising from that party's failure to comply with a safety statute.

Cruise Line Exception. Cruise lines, like other common carriers, are held to a standard of reasonable care. Federal statute **46 U.S.C. § 30509** expressly voids any contract provision purporting to limit the liability of a cruise line for injuries resulting from its negligence; subsequently, use of disclaimers and liability waivers to protect the cruise line from liability for its own negligence is prohibited by admiralty law. This prohibition also applies to waivers protecting the cruise line from negligence liability for recreational activities aboard the ship, in the water, and on shore excursions.

Parental Waivers. One court has ruled that parental waivers involving a for-profit business are not enforceable; the court seemed to indicate that it would have been enforceable if it had been used by a school or a community provider (*Cobb v. Aramark Sports and Entertainment Services, LLC* (2013a,). The father had signed the waiver on behalf of his minor son in order for the boy to ride a jet ski.

Alabama
GOOD

The general rule is that a release is valid absent public policy consideration and releases are not against public interest (*Young v. City of Gadsden*, 1985). **In fact, the Alabama Supreme Court indicated that waivers were in the public interest because they enabled promoters to hold sporting events.**

Public Policy. Waivers in Alabama are supported by both statute and case law. Alabama Code (Section 12-21-109, Ala. Code 1975) provides

> All receipts, releases, and discharges in writing, whether of a debt of record, a contract under seal or otherwise, and all judgments entered pursuant to *pro tanto* settlements, must have effect according to their terms and the intentions of the parties thereto

Where no ambiguity exists, "a court's only function is to interpret the meaning and intentions of the parties as found within the four corners of the document" (*Minnifield v. Ashcraft*, 2004). The courts will uphold an unambiguous release, supported by consideration. If voluntary agreements were not upheld, the effect would increase liability for organizers so that no one would be willing to undertake to sponsor a sporting event, thus the court suggests that waivers may be in the public interest. Participation in auto races is a voluntary undertaking of a hazardous activity and releases, when voluntarily entered, should be enforced.

When a patron sued after being injured when he fell from a mechanical bull, the court did not rule on the waiver, declaring that the danger was "open and obvious." The waiver was used as evidence that the danger was "open and obvious" as the court stated that the patron 1) had seen two previous riders fall off, 2) had seen a thick floor mat beneath the bull, and 3) had signed a release that explicitly stated that there were inherent risks and that injury was a possibility (*Lilya v. The Greater Gulf State Fair*, 2003).

"Negligence." The word "negligence" does not have to appear in the waiver in order for it to be enforceable.

Willful/Wanton Conduct. Waivers seeking to provide protection from liability for willful or wanton actions and intentional acts are against public policy (*Barnes v. Birmingham International Raceway, Inc.*, 1989; *Minnifield v. Ashcraft*, 2004).

Parental Waivers. Alabama applies the firmly-entrenched common law rule that a minor may void or disaffirm contracts, except regarding contracts for necessaries. The purpose of this rule is to protect minors from being taken advantage of due to the improvidence and incapacity of the minor (*Thode v. Monster Mountain, LLC*, 2010). Courts also hold that parents may not sign binding contracts on behalf of a minor (with rare exceptions such as health care plans) and may not sign post-injury settlements on behalf of the minor without court approval. The *Thode* Court ruled that pre-injury parental waivers in favor of a for-profit activity sponsor are voidable. It did not address whether or not waivers used by non-profit school or community organizations are enforceable.

In one case (*Harden v. American Airlines,* 1998), the enforceability of a **forum selection clause** on airline tickets used by minors was at issue. The court declared that if the minor chooses benefits under the contract, he may not avoid his contractual obligations.

Alaska
POOR

The Supreme Court of Alaska maintains that waivers are to be strictly construed against the party seeking immunity and sets a high bar for the enforcement of such waivers. The document is only valid to the extent it reflects a "conspicuous and unequivocally expressed" intent to release from liability (*Moore v. Harley Motors, Inc.,* 2001). **In addition, the legislature has passed two important statutes relating to waivers: 1) AS 05.45.010-.210 prohibiting the use of waivers by ski facility operators; 2) AS 09.65-202 allowing enforcement of parental waivers.**

Public Policy. The Supreme Court of Alaska has relied on *Tunkl* (*Tunkl v. Regents of the University of California,* 1963) in determining whether a waiver is against public policy (*Moore v. Hartley Motors, Inc.,* 2001). Waivers must be strictly construed and courts have very strictly enforced standards requiring that the waiver be clear, explicit, and comprehensible in each of its details. When read as a whole, it must clearly notify the signer of the effect of signing the agreement and that the terms are applicable to the particular misconduct of the relying party (*Kissick v. Schmierer,* 1991; *Ledgends Inc. v. the Alaska Rock Gym,* 2004). In addition, the Supreme Court stated that "a conspicuous and unequivocal statement of the risk waived is the keystone of a valid release" (*Donahue v. Ledgends, Inc.,* 2014).

The *Donahue* Supreme Court discussion confirmed a lower court list of six characteristics required for an effective waiver. They are:

- The risk being waived must be specifically and clearly set forth (e.g. death, bodily injury, and property damage).
- A waiver of negligence must be specifically set forth using the word "negligence."
- These factors must be brought home to the releaser in clear, emphasized language by using simple words and capital letters.
- The release must not violate public policy.
- If a release seeks to exculpate a defendant from liability for acts of negligence unrelated to inherent risks, the release must suggest intent to do so.
- The release agreement must not represent or insinuate standards of safety or maintenance.

The Alaska Supreme Court holds waivers to a very high standard of clarity. In *Kissick,* passengers, prior to a plane crash and the wrongful death of Kissick, signed a waiver promising not to sue. Death was not specifically disclaimed in the waiver and the court ruled the term "injury" to be ambiguous; the court construed the waiver against the drafter and ruled that it did not apply to claims for wrongful death. Similarly, in *Ledgends v. Kerr* (2004), the Alaska Supreme Court affirmed a lower court ruling in which the lower court said the release was inconsistent; it said the gym would try to keep its facilities safe and it equipment in good condition, but disclaimed liability for actions that failed to meet those standards. This conflict created an ambiguity that prevented enforcement.

In a case involving an error in the telephone book published by the Anchorage Telephone Utility, the Supreme Court ruled that a business granted monopoly status by the state might not limit its liability by contract. The Court cited rulings of courts from other jurisdictions that held it unconscionable to enforce limited liability clauses in such cases and held that ATU had a decided advantage in bargaining with the advertiser (*Municipality of Anchorage v. Locker,* 1986). In *Moore,* however, the court ruled that there was no advantage in bargaining power because ATV riding was a service that was neither essential nor regulated by a statute.

The Alaska legislature **(AS 05.45.010-.120)** has prohibited the use of liability waivers by ski facility operators to protect against liability for negligence. A ski operator may not require a skier to sign an agreement releasing the operator from liability in exchange for the right to ride a ski area tramway and ski in the area. Such a waiver is void by statute. The ski operator may require waivers of special event coaches, participants, spectators or customers. Special event includes an event, pass, race, program, rental program, or service that offers competition or other benefits in addition to a ticket representing the right to ride a ski area tramway or ski ..., whether or not additional consideration is paid.

"Negligence." It is necessary to use the word "negligence" in order to avoid liability for negligence (*Kissick v. Schmierer*).

Parental Waivers. The state legislature has passed a statute (**A.S. 09.65-202**) allowing the enforcement of parental waivers. See Chapter 3 for more information.

Arizona
POOR

The **Supreme Court of Arizona** (*Phelps v. Firebird Raceway, Inc.*, 2005) **has interpreted the Arizona Constitution to mean that assumption of risk is "in all cases whatsoever" and "at all times" to be treated as a question of fact for the jury. This ruling either negates waivers or seriously reduces the effectiveness of waivers. As a consequence, the enforceability of waivers is in question and will probably remain so until further court rulings occur.**

Public Policy. When interpreting the **Arizona Constitution XVIII § 5** in a 2005 case, the supreme court interpreted the article to include both implied assumption of risk and express assumption of risk (including waivers). This in effect prohibits a judge from granting summary judgment based on liability waivers. Thus the validity of an express contractual assumption of risk is a question of fact for a jury, not a judge. The court went on to say that during the trial, the defendant "is entitled to have the jury instructed both as to the enforceability of contracts and as to the substance of the statute governing race track liability as long as it is clear that the ultimate decision as to the enforceability of the Release and Waiver signed by Phelps is for the jury" (*Phelps* p.25). The court later stated that "juries will consider express contractual assumptions of risk in a rational manner, as the framers of our constitution clearly contemplated when they approved Article 18, Section 5" (*Phelps* p.26, 36). Thus, it appears that juries will continue to address factual questions about the scope of waivers as they often have in the past and the waiver can still help to protect the provider from liability for negligence. The difference is that the jury will always make this decision – not the judge by way of summary judgment.

In light of this Supreme Court decision, the status of waivers is unclear. The following describes the status prior to the ruling, including statutes affecting waivers. The authors cannot predict how much of these statutes and this case law still applies.

Releases are against public policy in Arizona 1) when there is an employment relationship between defendant and plaintiff and 2) when there is an unequal bargaining position making the release unconscionable (*Valley National Bank v. National Ass'n for Stockcar Auto Racing, Inc.*, 1987). The legislature has passed a statute (A.R.S. 12-556) allowing motor sport facility operators to require waivers of spectators and participants entering the non-general spectator area (pit area and other restricted areas) of the facility.

Absent any public policy to the contrary, Arizona allows parties to agree in advance that one party shall not be liable to the other for negligence. Waivers are not looked upon with favor since waivers would tend to encourage carelessness. The law disfavors contractual provisions by which one party seeks to immunize himself from the consequences of his own torts (*Bothell v. Two Point Acres, Inc.*, 1998). Three requirements must be met for an enforceable waiver: (*Morganteen v. Cowboy Adventures, Inc.*, 1997) 1) There must be no public policy impediment to the limitation of liability; 2) The parties must have, in fact, bargained for the limitation – an actual bargain rather that the use of a preprinted release is necessary; 3) The limiting language must be construed most strictly against the relying party. Courts construe waivers strictly against the relying party and look more closely at agreements when one of the parties is not a business entity, as with recreation-related waivers.

Although it may sometimes be possible to absolve oneself of liability for negligence, agreements must be strictly construed and use clear and unequivocal language. They must alert the party that it is giving up a substantial right. Arizona law 251 Ariz. Adv. Rep. 17 states that "In any action brought by a skier against a ski area operator, if the ski area operator proves that the skier signed a valid release, the ski area operator's liability shall be determined by the terms of the release."

"Negligence." Some courts suggest that waivers must alert signers to the specific risks that are being waived and must reflect the clear intent to release the relying party from liability for negligence. A 2000 court (*Benjamin v. Gear Roller Hockey Equipment, Inc.*, 2000), however, upheld a release in which the risks were not specified. Interestingly, that same court stated that a release cannot absolve one of the duty to disclose unexpected and extraordinary risks known to its principals. Courts do not specifically require the use of the word "negligence," but strongly imply it (*Sirek v. Fairfield Snowbowl, Inc.*, 1990).

Parental Waiver. The court ruled that a waiver affecting a minor was not enforceable due to ambiguity of wording (*Bothell v. Two Point Acres, Inc.*). Parents of a 10-year old signed the waiver prior to an accident involving a horse. The court made no mention that a waiver signed for a minor by a parent was unenforceable. In view of the nature of the ruling, *it may be* that a waiver signed by a parent on behalf of a minor participant is enforceable in Arizona. The matter is made even more confusing by the state equine statute (A.R.S. 12-553 A2) which says that equine operators can avoid liability by a waiver signed by the parent of a minor. However, another court (*Gomez v. Maricopa Co.*, 1993) has held that neither parents nor other adults may make a binding post-injury settlement on behalf of the minor without court approval.

Arkansas
FAIR

The Supreme Court stated that two rules of construction apply to waivers: 1) They are to be strictly construed against the relying party. 2) It is possible to avoid liability through such a contract, but the contract must at least clearly set out what negligent liability is to be avoided. While, this sounds strict, the court went on to say a court *"is not restricted to the literal language of the contract,"* and we *"will also consider the facts and circumstances surrounding the execution of the release in order to determine the intent"* of the parties. (*Jordan v. Diamond Equipment & Supply Co.*, 2005)

Public Policy. Contracts that exempt a party from liability for negligence are not favored by the law. This disfavor is based upon the strong public policy of encouraging the exercise of care. However, such exculpatory contracts are not invalid *per se*. Two rules of construction apply for an enforceable waiver: (1) They are to be strictly construed against the party relying on them. (2) It is not impossible to avoid liability for negligence through contract; but to avoid such liability, the contract must at least clearly set out what negligence liability is to be avoided. Further, the court *is not restricted to the literal language of the contract*, and we *will also consider the facts and circumstances surrounding the execution of the release in order to determine the intent* of the parties.

An exculpatory clause may be enforced: (1) when the party is knowledgeable of the potential liability that is released; (2) when the party is benefitting from the activity which may lead to the potential liability that is released; and (3) when the contract that contains the clause was fairly entered into (*Jordan v. Diamond Equipment & Supply Co.*, 2005).

While the Arkansas Supreme Court uses language that indicates strict standards for enforcement of waivers, the U.S. District Court's recent application (*Kotcherquina v. Fitness Premier Management*, 2012) of language used by the Arkansas Supreme Court in *Jordan v. Arkansas Development Finance Authority* (2003) seems to be in conflict. *Jordan* stated that the court *is not restricted to the literal language of the contract* but will *also consider the facts and circumstances surrounding the execution of the release in order to determine the intent* of the parties. A more common approach to determine the intent of the parties is that the intent must be discerned *from the four corners of the document*, and not from other sources or witnesses. The proper application of this language is unclear. At first thought, this interpretation of waivers seems likely to result in more lenient enforcement, but in the following *ver Weire* case, the court applied the reasoning and it seemed to have the opposite effect.

In a 2013 raceway case (*ver Weire v. Styles*), a spectator signed a waiver to enter restricted areas at the racetrack. Later a loose plank in the bleachers caused her to fall and suffer an injury. The waiver specified coverage for negligence while the "undersigned is in or upon restricted area, and/or competing, officiating in, observing, working for, or for any purpose participating in the event." The appellate court questioned whether the waiver "pertained only to the risks associated with racing as opposed to the common duties owed to a business invitee." It added that to enforce the waiver would "exonerate the appellees and the racing industry in general from all liability anywhere on the grounds." The court reversed and remanded the case ruling that "such a release must be limited to injuries that are rationally associated with the dangerous nature of the activity."

In *Plant v. Wilbur* (2001), the Supreme Court enforced a sport waiver that completely avoided liability for ordinary negligence for the first time. The waiver involved a regular participant in auto racing who was familiar with the risks of the sport. The waiver was conspicuous, comprehensive, and specifically referred to the negligence of the releasees. The court felt that auto racing affected only a narrow segment of society and, as such, did not involve a public interest. In *Kotcherquina*, a U.S. District Court enforced a waiver that in most states would be ruled to be inadequate and ambiguous; in addition, the waiver did not contain the word "negligence" which has been a requirement in Arkansas courts. It seems, however, that federal courts often err in interpreting state law.

Parental Waivers. In a case involving a minor under the supervision of the Government, the Supreme Court held a waiver invalid due to its language and public policy. The court stated "To permit the Government to assume the care . . . of school children without an underlying policy encouraging the exercise of reasonable care would violate basic principles of fairness." (*Williams v. U.S.*, 1987)

"Negligence." The *Williams v. U.S.* (1987) court ruled the waiver insufficiently clear since the word "negligence" did not appear in the waiver. However, the *Kotcherquina* court more recently enforced a waiver that did not contain the word.

California
EXCELLENT

California courts have uniformly held that waivers of ordinary negligence for injuries arising from sport or recreational activities are not against public policy and that such waivers are not contrary to the public interest in that the public as a whole benefits from such waivers since they allow groups to sponsor recreational and sports activities (*City of Santa Barbara v. The Superior Court of Santa Barbara County*, 2006). **Courts, however, maintain stringent requirements that waivers be well-written and unambiguous** (*Paralift, Inc. v. Superior Court*, 1993).

Public Policy. California courts consistently hold that recreation does not implicate the public interest, therefore courts have consistently ruled that recreation-related waivers are not against public policy (*Eriksson v. Nunnink*, 2015). A waiver of future liability is an express assumption of the risk that negates the defendant's duty of care. Since the plaintiff has expressly consented to relieve the defendant of an obligation of conduct toward him, the defendant is relieved of a legal duty to the plaintiff and cannot be charged with negligence (*Knight v. Jewett*, 1992).

According to the U.S. District Court for the Northern District of California (*R.H. v. Los Gatos Union School District*, 2014), a valid waiver may exculpate a provider from future negligence or misconduct. These agreements take one of two forms: 1) an **advance waiver of liability** or 2) an **express assumption of risk**. With an advance waiver of liability, a client promises not to exercise the right to sue if injured as a result of a negligent act by the provider – thereby, eliminating a remedy for wrongdoing. With an express assumption of risk, the client agrees not to expect the potential defendant to act carefully -- thereby, eliminating the provider's duty of care. Both types of agreements permit behavior that normally would be actionable as tortuous. The advance waiver of liability negates the duty element of a negligence claim; the express assumption of risk goes further in that it acts as a complete bar to recovery.

A waiver may violate public policy when it exhibits some of the six factors listed by *Tunkl* (*Tunkl v. Regents of University of California*, 1963); however, no specific public policy opposes private, voluntary transactions in which one party agrees to waive rights to redress (*Allen v. Snow Summit, Inc.*, 1996).

There are three elements necessary for a valid waiver (*Kendall v. USA Cycling, Inc.*, 2005). They are: 1) It must be clear and unambiguous; 2) It must not violate public policy; and 3) The injury at issue must be reasonably related to the release's object and purpose. The waiver, read as a whole, must clearly notify the releaser or indemnitor of the effect of signing the agreement (*Rothman v. Heart Consciousness Church, Inc.*, 2011). "An ambiguity exists when a party can identify an alternative, semantically reasonable, candidate of meaning of writing" (*Ericksson*). If the scope of the waiver is ambiguous, it should normally be construed against the drafter.

A release is valid and need not achieve perfection as long as it is clear and unequivocal with specific reference to a defendant's negligence (*Paralift, Inc. v. Superior Court*, 1993). It must clearly, unambiguously, and explicitly express the intent of the parties and will be strictly construed against the relying party. A valid release must be simple enough for a layperson to understand and additionally give notice of its import. When the signer expressly consents to relieve the relying party from a known risk, the relying party is relieved of any duty and cannot be charged with negligence. In California, it is critical that the waiver distinguish between injuries due to negligence and those due to the inherent risks of the activity. It is a good idea to make certain these are clearly distinguished in the document and good practice would suggest a signature space for each.

Waivers do not have to list the exact negligent action with which the defendant is charged. In order to be within the scope of the waiver, the action needs only to be related to increasing the risk of the included activity of the plaintiff (*Parco v. Snow Summit, Inc.*, 2009). The waiver must be applicable to the particular negligence; however every possible act of negligence does not need to be spelled out in the waiver (*Egan v. YMCA*, 2011). The document must not require a layperson to plow through complex language to learn that he or she is relinquishing legal rights (*Rothman*).

The *Vinson v. Paramount Pictures Corporation*, 2013 court gave the following powerful opinion regarding the breadth of liability waivers in California.

> Here, the plain language of the Release is explicit as to its breadth. According to its terms, the signer was releasing "any and all claims" against appellants based on "any and all injuries" resulting from "any accident" arising out of his or her "participation in any of the events or activities sponsored by the Club." Vinson argues the specific activity involved here, inflatable rock wall climbing, was not comprehended by the release. Similarly, the trial court relied on the theory that the Release failed to identify the specific risk involved or that the risks were unknown to Vinson when he signed it. However, "[w]hen a release expressly releases the defendant from any liability, it is not necessary that the plaintiff have had a specific knowledge of the particular risk that ultimately caused the injury." "While it is true that the express terms of any release agreement must

be applicable to the particular misconduct of the defendant, that does not mean that every possible specific act of negligence of the defendant must be spelled out in the agreement or even discussed by the parties." Furthermore, "[t]he inclusion of the term 'negligence' is simply not required to validate an exculpatory clause."[Citations omitted.]

A waiver is not enforceable if it is not easily readable. Also, the important exculpatory language should be placed so that it compels notice and must be distinguished from other sections of the document (*Rothman v. Heart Consciousness Church, Inc.*, 2011).

A plaintiff provided evidence of her lack of understanding of a release she signed. The court stated "because the release is not ambiguous, her subjective understanding is not relevant" (*Shephard v. Bear Valley Ski Company*, 2005).

"Negligence." While courts in some California jurisdictions have suggested that the word "negligence" must be used to protect against "active" negligence, others have ruled that the intent of the parties and not the presence or absence of the word "negligence" is the key (*Sanchez v. Bally's Total Fitness Corp.*, 1998). Regardless of whether "negligence" is used, courts are consistent in requiring that the language be clear, explicit, and comprehensible (*Rothman*). In a 2008 case (*Cohen v. Five Brooks Stable*), a California appellate court stated that the waiver must clearly and unequivocally make specific reference to a defendant's negligence, but emphasized this did not mean the word "negligence" must appear. It proceeded to rule against a waiver seeking to avoid liability with the language "… as a result of those inherent risks and dangers and of my negligence in participating in this activity" p.22. It stated that nothing in the waiver clearly indicates that it applies to risks attributable to the provider's negligence.

Statutes. Civil Code section 1668 provides that all "contracts which have for their object, directly or indirectly, to exempt anyone from responsibility for his own fraud, or willful injury to the person or property of another, or violation of law, whether willful or negligent, are against the policy of the law." Both intentional and negligent misrepresentation are included within the meaning of "fraud" and are not barred by waivers (See the Fraudulent Language section in Chapter 2.). Likewise, breach of fiduciary duty and negligent violations of statutory law are prohibited by **Civil Code 1668** (*Dieu v. McGraw*, 2011).

Of concern to some in California is **Civil Code 1542** which deals with waiver law. Though there is no clear evidence that it helps, some authorities recommend that language should be included in the waiver such as:

> I acknowledge that I hereby waive on my behalf and on behalf of my Heirs and Assigns, and fully understand the effect of such waiver, all benefits flowing from any state statute that would otherwise limit the scope of this Agreement, including but not limited to **Section 1542 of the California Civil Code**, which provides: "A general release does not extend to claims which [a person] does not know or suspect to exist in his or her favor at the time of executing the release, which if known by him or her must have materially affected his or her settlement with the [released parties]."[69]

Gross Negligence. The California Supreme Court (*City of Santa Barbara v. Superior Court*, 2007) has held that a waiver will not protect a defendant against claims of gross negligence. It stated that the use of language such as "any and all negligence" and "all forms of negligence" are unenforceable as contrary to public policy since those terms would encompass gross as well as ordinary negligence. In a subsequent case involving biplane tours, a California appellate court enforced the waiver in question, but cited the *City of Santa Barbara* ruling in stating that had the appellants sued for gross negligence or recklessness, the waiver would not be a bar to recovery (*Booth v. Santa Barbara Biplane tours, LLC*, 2008).

Interestingly, in *Jiminez v. 24 Hour Fitness USA, Inc.* (2015), the original claim was gross negligence, but the court held that since California does not recognize a distinct common law cause of

---

[69] Personal correspondence with Alexander Pendleton, 10/5/10.

action for gross negligence (gross negligence being a degree of negligence), gross negligence is pleaded by alleging the traditional elements of negligence. The court denied summary judgment and declared it was a fact issue for the jury.

Parental Waiver. Minors may enter into contracts in California (Fam. Code, § 6700), but waivers signed only by a minor are of little value since they may be disaffirmed by the minor before majority or within a reasonable time afterwards. However, it is well-established in California that waivers signed by parents on behalf of the minor may not be disaffirmed (*Eriksson*). Parental waivers have been enforced for high risk sports, less risky recreation, and for children's recreational activity. The court in *City of Santa Barbara v. The Superior Court of Santa Barbara County* (2006) stated that the public as a whole receives the benefit from such waivers since they allow groups like the Boy Scouts, Girl Scouts, and Little League Baseball to operate with less risk of litigation. The court held that Section 35 of the Civil Code prohibiting the enforcement of waivers signed by minors

> . . . does not apply to contracts between adults and is therefore not controlling of the question of a parent's power to bind his child to arbitrate by entering into a contract of which the child is a third party beneficiary.

Thus a minor cannot disaffirm a contract signed by a parent or guardian on behalf of the minor.

Childcare Programs. An exception to enforcement of parental waivers is found in *Gavin v. YMCA of Metropolitan Los Angeles* (2003). A waiver was at issue in a case involving a childcare program. The court ruled that waivers signed by parents in the YMCA *child care* program were unenforceable as against public policy. The court stated that permitting a child care provider to contract away its duty of ordinary care is antithetical to the very nature of such services. In a more recent case (*Lotz v. The Claremont Club*, 2013), the appellate court failed to enforce a parental waiver relating to a child in a childcare program. The court cited *Gavin*, remanding the case for trial.

Colorado
EXCELLENT

While waivers are disfavored and are strictly construed against the drafter, waivers relating to recreational activities are enforced when the intent is clearly expressed and public interest is not involved.

Public Policy. Waivers should be carefully scrutinized to see that "the intent of the parties is expressed in clear and unambiguous language and that the circumstances and the nature of the service involved indicate the contract was fairly entered into" (*Chadwick v. Colt Ross Outfitters, Inc.*, 2004). Language should be free from legal jargon and not inordinately long and complicated. It is reasonable to interpret the broad language of a release to cover claims based on negligence; otherwise, the agreement would be essentially meaningless.

Colorado uses four factors to determine the validity of a waiver (*Jones v. Dressel*, 1981):

1) whether a duty to the public exists;
2) the nature of the service performed;
3) whether the contract was fairly entered into;
4) and whether the intention of the parties is expressed in clear and unambiguous language.

When dealing with recreation-related waivers, Colorado courts have ruled that such services are not necessary and do not implicate a **public duty**. Further, the courts have determined that recreational activities do not provide an **essential service**, thus waivers are not prohibited. A contract is fairly entered into if the **bargaining imbalance** does not place one party at the mercy of the other's negligence. Since the activity is not of an essential activity, one is not at the mercy of the negligence of the other. Colorado courts are called upon to give effect to the plain meaning of the waiver, examining the entire document to determine if the intent of the parties is **clear** (*Hamill v. Cheley Colorado Camps, Inc.*, 2011).

In determining whether the intent of the parties has been clearly and unambiguously expressed, the Colorado Supreme Court (*Salazar v. On the Trail Rentals, Inc.*, 2012) looks to:

- whether the agreement is written in simple and clear terms that are free from legal jargon;
- whether the agreement is inordinately long or complicated;
- whether the release specifically addresses the risk that caused the plaintiff's injury;
- whether the contract contains any emphasis to highlight the importance of the information it contains;
- and whether the plaintiff was experienced in the activity making risk of that particular injury reasonably foreseeable.

It is not necessary to describe in detail each specific risk that might be encountered (*Lahey v. Covington*, 1996). In a 2013 skiing case involving a minor with severe physical disabilities, the court ruled that a waiver did not have to list every activity included in a program of scheduled activities; the important factor is that the waiver clearly expresses the intent to release (*Squires v. Breckenridge Outdoor Education Center*).

Regarding a disadvantage in bargaining power, the *Chadwick* court stated that even "take-it-or-leave-it" contracts are not considered adhesionary unless they involve a service that cannot be readily obtained elsewhere or is of great importance to the public; only then are adhesionary contracts void (*Espinoza v. Arkansas Valley Adventures*, 2014; *Hamil v. Cheley*, 2011).

In a 2012 case (*Eburn v. Capitol Peak Outfitters, Inc.*), a federal court, addressing the issue of ambiguity, explained some of its reasoning as to why it enforced a waiver.

- It said the language was relatively simple and used clear, non-legal terms;
- The document comprised less than two pages and was not very complicated;
- It specifically addressed the fact that tack equipment can fail;
- It specifically stated that the signer assumes all risk of the activities ... even that arising from negligence;
- Important information appeared in upper case.

Colorado courts have consistently upheld broad waivers for equine activities (*Chadwick*, 2004). Unlike with negligence, the Colorado Supreme Court has ruled that waivers do not protect the manufacturer against **strict products liability** claims (Boles, 2010).

Indemnity. Indemnity agreements are also strictly construed under Colorado law (*Lahey*, 1996). To be enforceable, the agreement must contain clear and unequivocal language that manifests the parties' intent that the indemnitee be indemnified for the expenses at issue.

"Negligence." Under Colorado law, use of the term "negligence" is not required, but the intent to extinguish liability must be clearly and unambiguously expressed.

Reckless Conduct. Colorado courts have ruled that waivers seeking to protect against reckless conduct or willful and wanton acts are not enforceable.

Parental Waivers. After the Colorado Supreme Court ruled that waivers signed by parents on behalf of minors were not enforceable (*Cooper v. The Aspen Skiing Company*, 2003), the Colorado legislature passed a statute (**CRS 13-22-107**) that allows the enforcement of such waivers. The 2003 statute states that entities need a measure of protection against lawsuits; parents have a fundamental right to make such decisions for their children; parents make choices daily regarding schooling, medical treatment, and religious education; and it is the intent of the legislation to encourage affordability of youth activities by permitting a parent to release a prospective negligence claim of the child against certain persons and entities providing such activities ". . . *[s]o long as the [parent's] decision is voluntary and informed."*

A 2010 case (*Wycoff*), however, illustrated that court interpretation of a statute and the intent of a statute do not always go hand-in-hand. The court did not enforce a parental waiver because the parent's decision was not an informed decision as specified in the statute – "So long as the decision is voluntary and informed . . . ." The waiver did not list the risks involved in the activity. In two subsequent cases

(*Hamill v. Cheley Colorado Camps, Inc.*, 2011; *Squires v. Breckenridge Outdoor Education Center*, 2013), the appellate courts ruled that the waivers did adequately inform the mothers of the risk and enabled the mothers to make an informed decision. Both waivers were enforced.

Connecticut
POOR

The Connecticut Supreme Court has made two important rulings regarding the validity of recreational waivers in snow tubing and horseback riding cases (*Hanks v. Powder Ridge Restaurant Corporation*, 2005; *Reardon v. Windswept Farms, LLC*, 2006). In them, the Court seemed to rule that waivers in those activities as well waivers in many, if not all, recreational activities are now invalid. At this point the ultimate effect and breadth of the ruling are not clear, but it is clear that some kinds of waivers are still enforceable. In addition, *Reardon* did not rule that indemnification agreements are unenforceable as a matter of law (*Reilly v. Leasure*, 2010).

Public Policy. In the 2005 *Hanks* case, the Supreme Court ruled that the waiver in a snow tubing case was against public policy even though the waiver met the standard of unambiguousness required. The court held that the waiver affected the public interest adversely and violated public policy for several reasons. They included: 1) the public expectation in trusting providers to provide a safe ride, 2) patrons are placed in the care of the provider, 3) the public lacks the knowledge and experience to discern whether an operation is maintained in good condition, 4) the waiver would remove an incentive for safe operation, and 5) the contract is a standardized adhesion contract with no opportunity for bargaining. The court indicated that the ruling applied to voluntary recreational activities and gave 11 examples.

In *Reardon*, the Supreme Court seemed to apply the ruling to all recreational activities saying "… it would be impossible for us to identify all of the recreational activities controlled by the *Hanks* decision" p.22. Snow tubing, skiing, basketball, soccer, football, racquetball, karate, ice skating, swimming, volleyball, and yoga were named as illustrative recreational activities to which the ruling would apply. The Court seemed to use eight factors in determining whether any particular recreation, fitness, or sport activity is included in this ruling. They were whether: 1) the public is generally invited to the facility, regardless of ability; 2) patrons are under the care of the entity as a result of paying a fee; 3) the facility had the superior knowledge of the facility, maintenance, staff, and equipment; 4) the entity can better insure against loss than the patron; 5) a waiver would remove the incentive of the entity to use reasonable care; 6) it was a "take it or leave it" adhesion contract; 7) the entity had a superior bargaining position; and 8) the business is suitable for public regulation. The court said that these factors combine to determine if a waiver is against public policy. Any recreation, sport, or fitness business that meets a number of these criteria should operate on the assumption that a waiver will not grant liability protection.

Some have interpreted these Supreme Court rulings to mean that all liability waivers are against public policy in Connecticut; however, others have interpreted the rulings as a tightening of the requirements, but not as a death knell to waivers in that state. **Certainly, many waivers involving a large number of activities will fail as a result of these rulings.** Time will tell as further rulings clarify the stance of the court. In the meantime, providers should be aware that their waivers may not provide the protection previously provided and should institute appropriate risk management measures.

Later in 2006 in *Adams v. Whitewater Mountain Resorts* (2006) an appellate court considered another waiver in another snow tubing case. The defendants counterclaimed that the injuries resulted from risks inherent in the activity of snow tubing, therefore Hanks' ruling did not apply since the Hanks court specifically stated that its ruling did not extend to the inherent risks of snow tubing. The court rejected this reasoning saying that the case rested on a contractual agreement similar to a contract ruled to be against public policy. It stated that it would not validate in any manner certain individual provisions of a contract similar to the one which has been determined to violate public policy.

In another 2006 Supreme Court decision (*Brown v. Soh*, 2006), the court addressed the issue of whether a waiver required of an employee by her employer releasing the employer from liability for its negligent actions is against public policy. The court noted that waivers exempting an employer from all liability for negligence toward his employees are almost universally rejected as being against public policy. Reasoning that employers have an advantage in bargaining power, that employees are under the control of employers, and the enforcement of such waivers would reduce the incentive to manage risks, the court held that waivers in the **employment context** are against public policy. In a related non-sport case involving a newspaper carrier and the newspaper company (*Colagiovanni v. New Haven Aquisition Corp.*, 2006), a Connecticut appellate court relied on the *Brown v. Soh* decision in holding that a waiver signed by an **independent contractor** was against public policy and not enforceable. The court felt that the parties did not bargain from equal footing due to the economic relationship and likened it to a waiver in the employment context.

In a 2009 case (*Schneeloch v. Glastonbury Fitness & Wellness, Inc.*), a Connecticut appellate court examined a waiver in a health club case. The court ruled that the waiver in question was unenforceable both because of ambiguity and because it violated public policy (as specified by *Reardon*). The court pointed out that the Supreme Court had stated that "the totality of the circumstances surrounding the recreational activity of horseback riding and instruction ... demonstrates that the enforcement of an exculpatory agreement in their favor from liability for ordinary negligence violates public policy..." (p.12). The appellate court went on to say that the health club case was similar in that 1) the club provided the facilities, the instructors, and the equipment, 2) the activity was open to the general public regardless of skill level, 3) the provider had the greater expertise, 4) the waiver was a classic contract of adhesion, and 5) health clubs are suitable for public regulation. Some of the reasoning seemed to indicate the appellate court did not interpret the *Reardon* and *Hanks* decisions as banning all recreation waivers. Likewise, in another 2009 case involving a health club (*McNamara v. Healthtrax International*), the court held a waiver unenforceable relying on the *Hanks* ruling.

While *Hanks* and *Reardon* obviously hold that certain waivers are against public policy, several cases since have indicated that some types of waivers are still effective. In *Roman v. City of Bristol* (2007), the court indicated that waivers between "sophisticated business entities" were enforceable, and in *Dow-Westbrook, Inc. v. Candlewood Equine Practice* (2010), the court upheld a hold-harmless agreement when a horse was injured while in the care of a clinic. Of course, this case involved economic damages to a commercial enterprise rather than a public health and safety issue. In *Furlani v. Town of East Lyme* (2010), *Robinson v. Chapel Haven, Inc.* (2010), and *Mangels v. Yale* (2007), waivers involving a high school sprinter, a sexually assaulted disabled child in an institution, and a professional wrestler were not enforced because the waiver did not contain required language based on *Hyson v. Whitewater Mountain Resorts of Connecticut* (2003). No reference was made to *Hanks* or *Reardon*.

In more recent cases (*Butler v. Saville*, 2014; *Lecuna v. Carabiners Fairfield, LLC*, 2014), two Connecticut appellate courts addressed waivers used in a health club and in a climbing facility. Both courts referred to the Supreme Court rulings and deemed the waivers unenforceable. The *Butler* court stated that it is well established in Connecticut that waivers may violate public policy if certain conditions are met.

Indemnity. Indemnification agreements have been interpreted similarly to waivers prior to the *Reardon* and *Hanks* rulings. *Reardon*'s court did not rule that indemnification agreements involving equestrian activities are unenforceable as a matter of law (*Reilly*, 2010). The court, however, went on to agree that the same analysis the Supreme Court applied to waivers between parties of unequal bargaining power should apply to the validity of indemnity agreements between such parties. In *Roman*, the court contrasted the rulings in two previous cases. They cited the *B & D Associates v. Russell*, (2002) ruling stating that when the parties are "sophisticated business entities," less precise language is required for a valid exculpatory clause. In contrast, the court in *Hyson* concluded that "in a recreational setting in which there is a distinct inequity in bargaining power . . ., imprecise hold-harmless language is fatal to the legal merit of the agreement. . . ." The *Reilly* court noted that the same analysis used in *Hanks* and *Reardon* regarding waivers between parties of unequal bargaining power would apply in determining the validity of indemnification agreements of such parties.

The following section describes the status of waivers prior to the ruling, including statutes affecting waivers. Obviously the value of waivers has been curtailed, but it is still not clear how far the Supreme Court rulings go.

Courts, even prior to the *Reardon* and *Hanks* cases, did not favor waivers because they tend to allow conduct that falls below the acceptable level of care (*Potts v. Whitewater Mountain Resorts of Connecticut*, 2001), but agreements are generally valid if they are unambiguously written. Although agreements are not favored by law and, if possible, are construed to not insure immunity from liability, such strict scrutiny is relaxed in a purely commercial setting (*Malin v. White Water Mountain Resorts of Connecticut*, 2001). The terms of the waiver must be fairly and honestly negotiated. The general rule, however, is that when a person of mature years and who can read and write, signs a formal written contract, it is his duty to read it and notice its contents (*Longley v. Whitewater Mountain Resorts, Inc.*, 2002). This rule, however, is subject to qualifications including fraud or mistake not due to negligence and applies only if nothing has been said to mislead the signer.

The court in a ski injury case (*Ehrenreich v. Mohawk Mountain Ski Area, Inc.*, 2004) seemed to consider a ski lift ticket disclaimer enforceable. The ticket, however, referred only to the inherent risks of skiing. While ticket contracts are not invalid *per se*, the law does not favor such provisions attempting to relieve a party from the consequences of its own negligence. They are particularly disfavored when used by a professional service provider in the course of business with the public. To be effective, the ticket must expressly absolve the party from responsibility for negligent conduct.

Another ski injury case addressed the issue of whether a waiver could supersede a statutory duty placed on ski operators by the **state ski statute**. The statute imposed the duty to conspicuously mark trail maintenance vehicles (CGS δ 29-211) and the court held that such waivers could not undermine statutorily defined duties (*Laliberte v. Whitewater Mountain Resorts*, 2004).

"**Negligence.**" In cases prior to *Reardon* and *Hanks*, some Connecticut courts did not require the use of the word "negligence;" however, most courts required that the negligence of the provider be specified in the waiver (*Klem v. Chaplinisky*, 2002). In *Bashura v. Strategy Plus, Inc.*, 1997), the court stated that ". . . it imposes no great burden on sports facilities . . . to require that their exculpatory agreements include the language . . . caused by the operator's negligence."

Gross Negligence. In *Hanks*, the Court explained that one reason for not enforcing waivers was that Connecticut law does not distinguish between ordinary negligence and gross negligence. It reasoned that were waivers enforced, they would apply to both ordinary and gross negligence.

Parental Waivers. The *Fisher* court (*Fisher v. Rivest*, 2002) held that parental waivers were enforceable so that youth activities could be provided. In view of *Hanks* and *Reardon*, it now seems doubtful whether a parental waiver would be enforced for voluntary recreational activities. In *Munn v. Hotchkiss School* (2013), the court did not address the fact that the case involved a parental waiver; based on *Reardon* and *Hanks*, the court ruled the waiver was against public policy.

Delaware
FAIR

Waivers that are crystal clear and unequivocally indicate that both parties contemplated release from liability are not against public policy and are enforceable (*Tucker v. Albun, Inc.*, 1999).

Public Policy. Waivers are to be construed strictly against the relying party, but should not be construed contrary to the plain and ordinary meaning of the words and probable intent. A waiver is invalid if 1) it is ambiguous, 2) it is unconscionable, or 3) it violates public policy (*Tucker v. Albun, Inc.*, 1999).

In general, waivers are not against public policy unless 1) they are too broad, 2) the entity owed a duty of public service, 3) it exempts one charged with the duty of public service from liability for negligence, or 4) if the language exempting the benefiting party is not "crystal clear." Waivers will not be set aside if the language is clear and unambiguous; however if the release is ambiguous, it must be construed strongly against the drafting party (*McDonough v. National Off-Road Bicycle Association*, 1997).

To determine if a waiver is free of ambiguity, the intent of the parties is controlling. The court will attempt to determine the intention from the overall language of the document, and when it is "clear and unambiguous, it will not lightly be set aside" (*Tucker v. Albun, Inc.*, 1999, p.8). Through the waiver, the signer may assume all risks, known and unknown, but it must appear that the signer (or that a reasonable person in his position would have) understood the terms of the agreement. Where ambiguous, language must be construed against the drafting party. Further, evidence must establish that the parties intended the release to apply to the particular conduct that caused the harm.

Waivers that are signed carry more legal significance than unsigned disclaimers contained within a document and distributed to patrons.

"Negligence." Waivers do not have to specifically state the word **"negligence,"** but must be such that the meaning is expressed in unequivocal language (*Hallman v. Dover Downs, Inc.*, 1986). Language that is not crystal clear and unequivocal in showing the intent would be unenforceable.

Parental Waiver. The only court addressing this issue (*Hong v. Hockessian Athletic Club*, 2012) enforced a waiver signed by the parent of an injured 3-year-old. The child fell from play equipment at the club.

District of Columbia
EXCELLENT

Waivers intended to protect providers from liability are not against public policy and are valid and enforceable when the language makes the intent of the parties clear (*Maiatico v. Hot Shoppes, Inc.*, 1961; *Wright v. Sony Pictures Entertainment, Inc.*, 2005).

Public Policy. Waivers of liability for negligence are enforceable; however, waivers of strict liability are not (*Jaffe v. Pallotta Teamworks*, 2004). District of Columbia law specifies that a waiver is a form of contract and is enforceable where the terms of the document leave no room for doubt as to the intent of the parties. The waiver must be spelled out with such clarity that the intent to relieve one of the parties of liability for negligence is made plain. The fundamental requirement of any exculpatory provision is that it be clear and unambiguous (*Mero v. City Segway Tours of Washington DC, LLC*, 2013).

In *Moore v. Waller* (2007), the court enforced a waiver in which the parties did not have equal bargaining power since the plaintiff presented no evidence that he objected to the provisions or tried to bargain for different terms. The court also pointed out that the contract did not involve a necessary service. The Court held that the contract was not an adhesion contract because the plaintiff did not show that 1) there was disparate bargaining power, 2) there was no opportunity for negotiation, or 3) that services could not be obtained elsewhere.

"Negligence." The appearance within the waiver of the word "negligence" or specific words of comparable meaning is not mandatory; however the intent to waive negligence must be clear (*Jaffe v. Pallotta Teamworks*, 2003). For a waiver to be enforced for negligence, the consequences of the provider's negligence must be clearly and unambiguously expressed (*Wright v. Sony Pictures Entertainment, Inc.*, 2005).

Reckless Conduct. While D.C. courts will enforce waivers protecting against negligence claims, no case law exists regarding reckless or intentional conduct. The Court of Appeals has adopted the Restatement when statutory or case law is silent and the Restatement provides that waivers that would exempt one from liability for reckless or intentional conduct are against public policy (*Wright*, 2005).

Florida
GOOD

Waivers are valid and enforceable if the intent to relieve a party of its own negligence is so clear and unequivocal as to inform an ordinary and knowledgeable person that he or she is contracting away rights (*Sunny Isles Marina v. Adulami*, 1998; *Cain v. Banka*, 2005).

Public Policy. The Florida Supreme Court has stated that public policy disfavors waivers because they relieve one party of the obligation to use due care and shift the risk of injury to the party who is probably least equipped to take the necessary precautions to avoid injury and bear the risk of loss; however, because of a countervailing policy that favors the enforcement of contracts, waivers are enforceable unless they contravene public policy. Waivers in which 1) the intention to be relieved from liability was made clear and unequivocal and 2) the wording was so clear and understandable that an ordinary and knowledgeable person will know what he or she is contracting away are unambiguous and enforceable (*Sanislo v. Give Kids the World, Inc.*, 2015).

In general, Florida courts do not enforce contracts when one party occupies a superior bargaining position. However, courts hold that bargaining power is not considered unequal in settings outside of the public utility or public function context even if the contract is a "take it or leave it" offer (*Give Kids the World, Inc. v. Sanislo*, 2012). Relative bargaining strength is irrelevant when there is no compelling state interest (*Hopkins v. The Boat Club, Inc.*, 2004).

Waivers are to be strictly construed against the party seeking to be relieved of liability (*Tatman v. Space Coast Kennel Club*, 2009). A waiver releases all sponsors or parties, even if not named in the waiver.

A Florida court did not uphold a disclaimer in a cruise ship contract of carriage. The court relied on the Federal Statute 46 U.S.C. sec. 183c (1958) that prohibits defendants from including exculpatory language in contracts of carriage to protect themselves from liability for injuries due to their own fault (*Carlisle v. Ulysses Line LTD.*, 1985). In a 2007 case (*Cook v. Crazy Boat of Key West, Inc.*, 2007), the court of appeals held that U.S.C. app. 183c(a) which prohibits limitations of liability for any vessel transporting passengers between U.S. ports or to a foreign port did not apply to "crazy boat" rides (a recreational, thrill-providing boat ride).

While it is the public policy in Florida to not interfere lightly with the freedom to contract, waivers attempting to relieve one of a positive **statutory duty** are void as contrary to public policy.

Damages of parents for loss of **filial consortium** are limited to the period of a child's minority (*Cousins Club Corp. v. Silva*, 2004).

In a case involving a seamanship school, a federal district court applying Florida law held that exculpatory clauses are ineffective in cases of **negligence *per se*** since they violate a statute or other legal pronouncement (*Knarr v. Chapman School of Seamanship*, 2000).

"Negligence." The Florida Supreme Court in *Sanislo v. Give Kids the World, Inc.* (2015) ruled that that the absence of the terms "negligence" or "negligent acts" in a waiver does not render the agreement *per se* ineffective to bar a negligence action.

The court went on to clarify, saying that the ruling "is not intended to render general language in a release of liability *per se* effective to bar negligence actions." The court stated that a waiver is enforceable only "where the language unambiguously demonstrates a clear and understandable intention to be relieved from liability so that an ordinary and knowledgeable person will know what he or she is contracting away;" it noted that the better practice is to expressly refer to "negligence" or "negligent acts" in the waiver. Failure of the waiver in *UCF Athletics Association, Inc. v. Plancher* (2013) to specify "negligence" resulted in ambiguity and failure of the waiver to protect.

Indemnity Agreements. In *Sanislo*, the Supreme court distinguished between indemnity agreements and waivers and explained that indemnification case law was not applicable to waivers. The court

> reasoned that its 'basic objective in construing the indemnity provision is to give effect to the intent of the parties involved. . .' and that the use of the general terms 'indemnify . . . against any and all claims' does not disclose an intention to indemnify for consequences arising solely from the negligence of the indemnitee.'

Hence the court ruled that indemnification agreements must use the term "negligence."

Gross Negligence. At least one Florida court has indicated that waivers will protect against ordinary negligence and gross negligence, but will not protect against intentional acts. In *Theis v. J&J Racing Promotions* (1990), the court ruled that the waiver was so clear, unambiguous, unequivocal, broad, and specific enough to protect against both negligence and gross negligence. The waiver included both the phrase "from all liability" and the phrase "by the negligence of the releases(Check) or otherwise."

Parental Waivers. In a 2008 ruling, the Florida Supreme Court (*Kirton v. Fields*, 2008) ruled that parental waivers are unenforceable when used by for-profit businesses, but the court did not rule on parental waivers for school or community activities. An appellate court (*Gonzalez v. City of Coral Gables*, 2004) upheld a waiver used for a school program, ruling that it "fell within the commonplace child oriented community or school supported activities for which a parent may waive his or her child's litigation rights..." and was enforceable.

In 2005, the Florida Supreme Court enforced a **parental arbitration agreement** in a waiver signed by a parent on behalf of a minor (*Global Travel Marketing, Inc. v. Shea*, 2005). The court reasoned that there is no Florida statute forbidding such agreements.

In *Applegate v. Cable Water Ski, LC* (2008), an appellate court refused to enforce a waiver of the rights of a minor, but did enforce the waiver against the rights of the parents.

Florida Statute 549.09 provides that the operator of a motorsport event can make use of a liability waiver for protection from liability for injuries to minor motorsport competitors resulting from negligence. Florida statutes (**F.S. 744.301; F.S. 744.387**) allow natural guardians to settle claims of minors of $15,000 or less, however a legal, court-appointed guardian is required for claims exceeding that amount.

F.S. 744.301 also provides that the natural guardian, on behalf of the minor, may waive in advance any claim against a commercial activity provider resulting from the *inherent risks* of the activity. It defines inherent risks to include the failure of the provider to warn of the risks, negligent acts by other participants, and negligent acts by the minor child.

Georgia
EXCELLENT

"In Georgia, a party may exempt itself from its own simple negligence through exculpatory clauses as long as the clause is not 'void as against public policy'" (*Flood v. Young Woman's Christian Association of Brunswick, GA, Inc.*, 2005). **"The paramount public policy of Georgia is that courts will not lightly interfere with the freedom of parties to contract unless they in some manner violate public policy"** (*Lovelace v. Figure Salon*, 1986, p. 52).

Public Policy. A contract is not against public policy unless the General Assembly has declared it to be so or unless the consideration of the contract is contrary to good morals and contrary to law. No Georgia statutes forbid waivers in sporting or recreational events and waivers in fitness club contracts do not violate public policy. Further, it is well settled that public policy does not prohibit the inclusion of waivers in health club membership contracts (*Hembree v. Johnson*, 1997).

A person may waive or renounce what the law has established in his favor when he does not thereby injure others or affect the public interest (*Lovelace*, 1996). Exculpatory clauses must be clear, unambiguous, and specific in what they purport to cover. Further, any ambiguity will be strictly construed against the drafter.

In Georgia, one asserting an assumption of risk defense (as with a waiver) must establish that the plaintiff 1) had actual knowledge of the danger, 2) understood and appreciated the risks associated with the danger, and 3) voluntarily exposed himself to the risks (*Trustees of Trinity College v. Ferris*, 1997).

"Negligence." The use of the word "negligence" is not necessary for clarity in a waiver. Waivers effectively protect against liability for ordinary negligence. The use of the term "any and all liabilities" will bar a negligence claim (*Flood v. Young Woman's Christian Association of Brunswick, Ga., Inc.*, 2005).

Gross Negligence. Waivers are ineffective in protecting against liability for gross negligence and willful and wanton conduct (*McFann v. Sky Warriors, Inc.*, 2004).

Parental Waivers. In *Mays v. Valley View Ranch, Inc.* (2012), the court stated that the equine waiver was effective because it contained the warning required by the equine statute (**OCGA § 4-12-4**). In two more recent cases involving minors, the validity of the waiver was not addressed and the ruling was based on assumption of risk in one case (*Christian v. Eagles Landing Christian Academy*, 2010) and Recreation Property Act immunity in the other (*Cooley v. City of Carrollton*, 2001). The first case involved a cheerleader injured while performing a stunt and the second involved a disabled minor in an afterschool recreational and swimming therapy program.

Hawaii
POOR

H.R.S. 663-1.54 plainly states that a waiver may protect owners or operators of businesses providing recreational activities from liability for the injuries resulting from *inherent risks*, but not for those resulting from negligence of the provider. The statute also provides that the determination of what is an inherent risk may not be decided by summary judgment. This statute seems to make waivers for certain types of recreational activities unenforceable; however, the results of two subsequent court decisions seem to indicate that waivers for certain other activities are still enforceable provided they meet certain qualifications (*Bailey v. United States of America*, 2003; *Courbat v. Dahana Ranch, Inc.*, 2006).

Public Policy.[70] "The general rule of contract law is that one who assents to a contract is bound by it and cannot complain that he has not read it or did not know what it contained." Furthermore, "'[p]arties are permitted to make exculpatory contracts so long as they are knowingly and willingly made and free from fraud. No public policy exists to prevent such contracts.'" Therefore, as a general rule, "'[e]xculpatory clauses will be held void if the agreement is (1) violative of a statute, (2) contrary to a substantial public interest, or (3) gained through inequality of bargaining power.'"

While recreational waivers may be contracts of adhesion, in that they are presented on a "take-it-or-leave-it" basis, they are not unconscionable . . . and are generally held to be valid." They are unenforceable, however, if two conditions are present: "(1) the contract is the result of coercive bargaining between parties of unequal bargaining strength; and (2) the contract unfairly limits the obligations and liabilities of, or otherwise unfairly advantages, the stronger party." In the context of a recreational sport or adventure activity, freely undertaken for pleasure, "coercive bargaining" and "an absence of alternatives" are terms that hold little meaning. Recreational activities are generally not suitable to public regulation, do not usually involve disparate bargaining power, and are not essential in nature.

Recreational Sport Waiver Statute. The Hawaii legislature attempted to leave no doubt as to where it stands on at least certain types of recreational waivers of liability for negligence. **Hawaii Revised Statutes sec. 663-1.54** states:

> (a) Any person who owns or operates a business providing recreational activities to the public, such as, without limitation, scuba or skin diving, sky diving, bicycle tours, and mountain climbing, shall exercise reasonable care to ensure the safety of patrons and the public, and shall be liable for damages resulting from negligent acts or omissions of the person which cause injury.
>
> (b) Notwithstanding subsection (a), owners and operators of recreational activities shall not be liable for damages for injuries to a patron resulting from inherent risks associated with the recreational activity if the patron participating in the recreational activity voluntarily signs a written release waiving the owner or operator's liability for damages for injuries resulting from the inherent risks. No waiver shall be valid unless:
>
>> (1) The owner or operator first provides full disclosure of the inherent risks associated with the recreational activity; and
>>
>> (2) The owner or operator takes reasonable steps to ensure that each patron is physically able to participate in the activity and is given the necessary instruction to participate in the activity safely.
>
> (c) The determination of whether a risk is inherent or not is for the trier of fact. As used in this section an "inherent risk":
>
>> (1) Is a danger that a reasonable person would understand to be associated with the activity by the very nature of the activity engaged in;
>>
>> (2) Is a danger that a reasonable person would understand to exist despite the owner or operator's exercise of reasonable care to eliminate or minimize the danger, and is generally beyond the control of the owner or operator; and
>>
>> (3) Does not result from the negligence, gross negligence, or wanton act or omission of the owner or operator.

Further, in 1997, the Hawaii legislature attempted to clarify the statute by publishing the following statement regarding the intent of the statute:

---

[70] Taken from *Courbat v. Dahana Ranch, Inc.*, 2006; citations omitted.

Your Committee finds that this measure is necessary to more clearly define the liability of providers of commercial recreational activities by statutorily invalidating inherent risk waivers signed by the participants. Your committee further finds that these inherent risk waivers require providers to disclose known risks to the participant, but these waivers do not extend immunity to providers for damages resulting from negligence. Thus, it is the intent of your Committee that this clarification in the law will appropriately reduce frivolous suits without increasing risks to participants. (Haw. Stand. Comm. Rep. No. 1537, 1997 Senate Journal, at 1476.)

The statute has a significant impact on service providers of the relevant recreational activities from four standpoints.

- *First*, it states that selected **recreational providers cannot gain protection from liability for their negligent acts from liability waivers**; it also prohibits waiver protection against gross negligence or wanton acts or omissions. There is a question, however, regarding for which sports the statutes is intended by ". . . providing recreational activities to the public, such as, without limitation, scuba or skin diving, sky diving, bicycle tours, and mountain climbing . . . ."

- *Second*, provisions include that the owner or operator **must provide full disclosure of the inherent risks** of the activity, must take reasonable steps to ensure that each patron is physically able to participate in the activity and is given necessary instruction to participate safely. If the participant voluntarily signs a written release for a recreational activity such as a bicycle tour, sky diving, mountain climbing, or scuba (and presumably other recreational activities of similar kind), it seems clear that the provider is not liable for injuries resulting from the *disclosed, known inherent risks of the activity*.

- *Third*, what constitutes an inherent risk is not specified and can only be **determined by the trier of fact** – meaning a court cannot determine on summary judgment whether a written waiver constitutes a valid waiver of liability since a statutorily-imposed issue of fact precludes summary judgment as a matter of law. Thus, even protection from liability for inherent risks may be illusionary.

- *Fourth*, the statute **does not define recreational activities** beyond scuba or skin diving, sky diving, bicycle tours, and mountain climbing.

The Hawaii Supreme Court applied the statute in a 2004 case involving horseback riding (*King v. CJM Country Stables*, 2004). The court denied summary judgment based on the waiver stating

Under Section 663-1.54, the Court must deny Defendant's Motion for Summary Judgment for two reasons. First, Defendant argues that the Release Form validly waives Plaintiffs' negligence claims but Section 663-1.54(a) explicitly precludes waiving liability for negligence. Thus, paragraph three (3) of the Release Form is void as to negligence.

Secondly, Section 663-1.54(c)'s provision that the "determination of whether a risk is inherent or not is for the trier of fact" automatically creates a genuine issue of material fact as to whether the horse-biting incident was an inherent [risk] of the horseback riding activity in which Plaintiffs participated. This statutorily-imposed genuine issue of fact precludes summary judgment as a matter of law. The trier of fact will have to decide whether the Release Form constitutes a valid waiver of Defendant's liability.

Case law since the statute is somewhat mixed. In a 2015 case (*Hambrook v. Smith*), the court declared that a waiver protecting a SCUBA business was not enforceable, but that the waiver did protect PADI because PADI was not a "business providing recreational activities to the public." So it would appear that waivers used by organizations that are not recreation providers would be enforceable. In addition, a waiver might also protect an employee of a business providing recreational activities.

An appellate court (*Madoff v. America's Adventure, Inc.*, 2013) did not rule on the enforceability of a waiver signed by a parent on behalf of a minor. The issue was choice of law – Hawaii (where the death occurred) or Colorado (where the business was located). While it made no ruling, it seemed apparent that the Hawaii court will not enforce the parental waiver because of **H.R.S. 663-1.54**; perhaps, due to the fact the deceased died on a kayaking/hiking tour. In a 2014 case in which the plaintiff was injured on an ATV tour (*Mohler v. Kipu Ranch Adventures, LLC*), the U.S. District Court for the District of Hawaii held that the statute precludes a waiver of liability for negligence and allows only waivers for loss resulting from inherent risks; further, it noted that the determination of whether a risk is inherent is for the trier of fact and not appropriate for summary judgment.

It should be noted, however, that the statute has not always been enforced even in adventure type recreation. In another horseback riding case (*Courbat v. Dahana Ranch, Inc.*, 2006), the Hawaii Supreme Court remanded the case for determination if deceptive trade practices were involved. The court did not consider **H.R.S. 663-1.54** and instructed the lower court to enforce the waiver if no deceptive trade practices were found. The court stated that the public interest was not at stake. Likewise, three years earlier, a United States District Court enforced a disclaimer on an air tour ticket voucher saying the tour company, Big Island Adventures, was not liable for the actions of Big Island Air (*Bailey v. United States of America*, 2003).

It is unclear, however, whether the statute applies to activities such as health clubs, less adventurous recreation, instructional classes, and non-commercial school and community recreational activities. It also is not clear whether waivers for other sports and activities need to list the inherent risks and are eligible for summary judgment rulings.

Waivers and Indemnity Agreements for Motorsports Participants. H.R.S. §663-10.95 provides than any waiver or indemnity agreement used by operators of a motorsports facility which releases or waives any claim by a participant or anyone claiming on behalf of the participant, signed by the participant in any motorsports or sports event involving motorsports shall be valid and enforceable against any negligence claim for personal injury of the participant. The waiver and release shall be valid notwithstanding any claim that the participant did not read, understand, or comprehend the waiver and release, waiver of liability, or indemnity agreement if the waiver or release is signed by both the participant *and a witness*. Such waiver or indemnity agreement is enforceable provided it is executed in writing by a parent or legal guardian.

"Negligence." In a 2001 decision (*Faronda v. Hawaii International Boxing Club*, 2001), a court failed to support a waiver that referred to "for any and all injuries" and did not expressly identify claims for "negligence" stating that the document only showed that the signer assumed the risks associated with boxing. The Supreme Court has not addressed this issue.

Parental Waivers. The motor-sport waiver statute (**H.R.S. 663-10.95**) states that a parental waiver for minors who are motorsports participants is valid and enforceable provided it is executed in writing and is signed by both a parent *and a witness*. It seems likely the courts will elect not to enforce parental waivers for other activities in light of **H.R.S. 663-1.54.**

Gross Negligence. Attempts to gain protection against liability for gross negligence or **strict liability** (*Wheelock v. Sport Kites, Inc.*, 1993) are against public policy and such contracts are void unless the waiver is severable (*Courtney v. Pacific Adventures, Inc.*, 1998).

Idaho
GOOD

While waivers are to be strictly construed, waivers that do not violate public policy are to be upheld (*Collins v. Schweitzer*, 1991). **Statutory duties may not be absolved by contract (Idaho Statutes prohibit waivers of negligence for ski operators, outfitters, & guides); however, no courts have ruled that waivers in sporting events such as auto racing or horseback riding are against public policy.**

Public Policy. The Idaho Supreme Court has said that freedom to contract is a fundamental element of contract law and the free enterprise system. Waivers of negligence are to be upheld unless 1) one party is at an obvious disadvantage in bargaining power or 2) a public duty is involved. The Supreme Court has stated that parties to a transaction may agree by contract to limit liability for negligence or contractually waive rights and remedies, subject to certain exceptions (*Lee v. Sun Valley Co.*, 1984; *Morrison v. Northwest Nazarene University*, 2012). The very purpose of a release of this nature is to immunize the entities and individuals hosting dangerous activities from being held liable for negligent conduct or failure to meet any specified standard of care. The *Morrison* court also stated that the general rule is that waivers of liability for injuries in the context of recreational activities are enforceable against adult participants.

Idaho courts have enforced very broadly worded waivers. For example, the Supreme Court in *Morrison* enforced a waiver containing the following language.

> . . . release and waive any and all past, present or future claims ... which the undersigned now has or may in the future have against . . . for any and all past, present or future loss or damage to property, and/or bodily injury, including death, however caused, resulting from, arising out of or in any way connected with his/her participation in or use of the Northwest Nazarene University Challenge Course Adventure Program.

The court held that waivers do not have to describe the specific conduct or omission alleged to be negligent in order to protect against liability. In *Morrison*, it stated that the waiver language ". . . from any loss, liability, damage or cost . . . whether caused by the negligence of the releases or otherwise" was adequate to protect.

The Idaho ski statute **IC 6-1103 (10)** provides that operators have a duty "Not to intentionally or negligently cause injury to any person...." Since this constitutes a statutory duty of ordinary care, the use of waivers to avoid such a duty would be prohibited.

Additionally, Idaho outfitters statute **IC 6-1204** requires guides and outfitters to "conform to the standard of care expected of members of his profession." The court held that where the legislature has addressed the rights and duties pertaining to personal injuries arising out of the relationship between two groups (i.e., outfitters and guides/participants) and has granted limited liability to one group in exchange for adherence to specific duties, then such duties become a "public duty" within the exception to the general rule validating exculpatory contracts. So a waiver will not protect when the actions of outfitters and guides do not meet the standard of care expected of members of their profession (*Lee v. Sun Valley Co.*, 1984).

"Negligence." Wording of a release need not use the word "negligence" to be deemed valid.

Parental Waivers. In the one Idaho case involving a minor, the court did not address the issue of whether a pre-injury release of a minor's claim is enforceable and the court gave no indication that a properly worded waiver would not have been upheld (*Davis v. Sun Valley Education Foundation, Inc.*, 1997). While the question remained unanswered, there is the possibility that a properly worded waiver would have protected the provider since the court made no indication to the contrary.

Illinois
GOOD

While waivers are not favored by law and are to be strictly construed, Illinois courts have long held that one may contract to avoid liability for his or her negligence. The language of the contract must be clear, explicit, and unequivocal to absolve a party from liability for negligence (*Garrison v. Combined Fitness Centre, LTD.*, 1990).

Public Policy. Illinois courts construe contracts to give effect to the intention of the parties as expressed in the language of the agreement. Illinois law construes contracts as a whole, and generally disallows extrinsic evidence unless an ambiguity exists within the contract's four corners. Illinois permits parties to contract away liability for their own negligence (*Cox v. US Fitness, LLC*, 2013).

A waiver constitutes an express assumption of risk wherein one party consents to relieve another party of an obligation. Though they are not favored and must be strictly construed against the benefiting party, parties may allocate the risk of negligence as they see fit (*Platt v. Gateway International Motor Sports Corporation*, 2004).

Waivers are enforceable if they do not violate the public policy of the state and there is no social relationship which mitigates enforcement of the agreement (*Johnson v. The Salvation Army*, 2011). Further, Illinois courts have declined to "invalidate a waiver on public policy grounds unless it is 'clearly contrary' to what our statutes or court decisions have declared to be public policy, or unless it is 'manifestly injurious to the public welfare'" (*Cox v. US Fitness*).

Waivers are against public policy and are not to be enforced if there is 1) fraud, 2) willful and wanton conduct, 3) legislation to the contrary, 4) public policy to the contrary, 5) a substantial disparity in the parties' bargaining position, 6) a social relationship that militates against upholding the agreement. The *Johnson* court supplements this list with 1) an employer – employee relationship and 2) when there is a duty of public service (e.g., public carrier or public utility). Absent the above factors, enforcement depends on whether or not defendant's conduct and the risk of injury inherent in said conduct was of a type intended by the parties to fall within the scope of the clause (*Masciola v. Chicago Metropolitan Ski Council*, 1993).

The exculpatory language of a waiver must be clear, explicit and unequivocal; *general language* is not sufficient to show clear intention to release a party from liability for negligence. The plaintiff must be **put on notice** of the range of dangers for which he or she assumes the risk of injury; this, thereby, can enable the plaintiff to minimize the risk by exercising a greater degree of caution. It is not, however, necessary that the plaintiff have contemplated the exact nature of the incident resulting in injury at the time he or she signed the waiver; it is only important that the cause of the injury falls within the scope of possible dangers ordinarily accompanying the activity and that the parties would have reasonably contemplated the possibility (*Cox v. US Fitness*).

At least some Illinois courts have stated that even broad waivers do not encompass all accidents without limit. In *Simpson v. Byron Dragway, Inc.* (1991), the court concluded that the danger of a deer running onto a racetrack was not the type of risk that is intended by racetrack waivers. Likewise, in *Hawkins v. Capital Fitness, Inc.* (2015), the court held that a mirror falling from a health club wall injuring a patron was a question of fact as to whether this constituted an ordinary risk of health club participation; consequently, the court did not grant summary judgment on the basis of the waiver.

The importance of language being clear, explicit and unequivocal was illustrated in *Locke v. Lifetime Fitness, Inc.* (2014) when a client died, partly because improper emergency treatment – which was covered by the waiver. The wife, however, alleged negligence in failing to train the staff for emergencies. The court rejected the waiver stating that the wrongful death claim is not barred to the extent it is premised on the lack of staff emergency training.

The relevant question is whether plaintiff knew or should have known the incident was a risk encompassed by the waiver; not whether plaintiff foresaw defendants' exact act of negligence. The scope of the waiver depends upon the foreseeability of a specific danger (*Cox v. US Fitness*).

Absent fraud, one signifies by signing an agreement that the signer had an opportunity to read and comprehend the terms of the document. One who had an opportunity to read and contract, but signs before reading cannot plead a lack of understanding of the agreement and may not avoid the legal consequences of the contract; failure to read an agreement is no excuse for the signer (*Hawkins v. Capital Fitness, Inc.*, 2015).

"Negligence." Courts make clear that ambiguity may be avoided without use of the word "negligence."

Gross Negligence. In Illinois, at least one appellate court states clearly that waivers can protect against liability for both negligence and gross negligence (*Maness v. Santa Fe Park Enterprises, Inc.*, 1998). The waiver in *Maness* clearly specified that the plaintiff was releasing liability for both negligence and gross negligence.

It should be noted, however, that the authors are not totally convinced that Illinois courts will enforce waivers attempting to protect against gross negligence since no waiver case enforcing or addressing gross negligence has been found since the 1998 case. Several courts have stated that absent fraud or **willful and wanton negligence**, waivers are enforceable when they meet certain requirements (*Hellweg v. Special Events Management*, 2011; *Oelze v. Score Sports Venture, LLC*, 2010). In an earlier case, the court ruled that waivers will not protect one from liability for **reckless conduct** as well (*Downing v. United Auto Racing Association*, 1991).

Parental Waivers. A minor is a ward of the court when involved in litigation, thus releases signed by adults on behalf of minors could not be valid. The court has the duty and discretion to protect the interests of the minor (*Wreglesworth v. Arcto, Inc.*, 2000). A parent does not have the right to release the rights of the minor before or after an injury (*Meyer v. Naperville Manner, Inc.*, 1994). **745 ILCS 47/1-15** allows parental equine waivers.

Parental arbitration agreements and **parental forum selection clauses** have been ruled enforceable against minors in Illinois (*Burns v. Wilderness Ventures, Inc.*, 2012).

Indiana
GOOD

In general, parties may contract to limit liability for negligence. Waivers, however, should specifically and explicitly refer to the negligence of the party seeking release from liability (*Powell v. American Health Fitness Center*, 1998).

Public Policy. Where there is no statute to the contrary, waivers are not against public policy as courts have repeatedly upheld the validity of waivers in connection with voluntary recreational activity, even when it prevents the injured party from recovery. A party may agree that that the acting party owes no obligation of care for the other; this leaves the acting party not liable for the consequences for actions that would otherwise be considered negligence (*Wabash County YMCA v. Thompson*, 2012).

However, releases are deemed void as against public policy where 1) there is unequal bargaining power such that the signer did not knowingly (understanding its contents) and willingly (while under no economic or other duress) sign the release, 2) there is evidence of fraud or misrepresentation, or 3) if they affect public interest (*Clanton v. United Skates of America*, 1997). In addition, any agreement that exculpates one from performing a statutory duty is against public policy (*Pruett v. American Motorcycle Assn.*, 1995).

A contract may be **unconscionable** if a great disparity in bargaining power leads the lesser party to contract unwillingly. An unconscionable contract "must be one that no sensible person not under delusion, duress or in distress would make…" (*Beaver v. Grand Prix Karting Association, Inc.*, 2001). The court in *Clanton v. United Skates of America* (1997) stated that it failed "to see how a contract to engage a voluntary and purely recreational activity could be unconscionable."

A release of liability is sufficient to exculpate the organizers of a racing event for all injuries sustained as a result of their negligence, even if the precise cause of the accident is not specified in the release and is extraordinary (*Pruett v. American Motorcycle Assn.*, 1995).

Indiana courts deem waivers in **loss of consortium** claims to be unenforceable against the non-signing spouse (*Beaver v. Foamcraft, Inc.*, 2002). The court determined that the non-signing spouse had an independent cause of action; however, the court stated that pursuing the activity was pointless since the indemnity agreement signed by the injured wife was also enforceable and would counter the consortium claim.

"Negligence." Where the use of the term "negligence" is required seems to depend on where the trial takes place; for that reason, the safest practice would be to always include the term in a waiver. Some Indiana courts hold that the use of the term "negligence," "fault," or some similar term is mandatory to protect against liability for negligence (*Powell v. American Health Fitness Center of Fort Wayne, Inc.*, 1998; *Stowers v. Clinton Central School Corporation*, 2006; *Wabash County YMCA v. Thompson*, 2012). These courts specified that waivers will not absolve one of liability for negligence unless it "specifically" and "explicitly" refers to the negligence of the party seeking release.

Other courts have enforced waivers and indemnity agreements that do not include "negligence" (*Avant v. Community Hospital*, 2005; *City of Hammond v. Plys*, 2008). Each court stated that the inclusion of terms like "liability," "damages," "actions,""omissions," and "any and all loss" made it obvious that negligence was intended.

The *Wabash* court and the court in *Anderson v. Four Seasons Equestrian Center, Inc.* (2006) found that waivers not containing the term "negligence" were enforceable against liability for injuries resulting from the *inherent risks* of the activity.

Gross Negligence. Waivers seeking to protect against gross negligence, reckless conduct, and willful and wanton acts are invalid in Indiana (*Beaver v. Foamcraft, Inc.*, 2002).

Parental Waivers. The *Wabash* court held that pre-injury parental waivers are valid (*Wabash County Young Men's Christian Association v. Thompson*, 2012). Based on *Wabash* and *Sauter v. Perfect North Slopes* (2014), Indiana appears to enforce both commercial and non-profit parental waivers. In addition, motorsport waivers signed by emancipated minors are enforceable (**I.C. 34-28-3**).

Iowa
EXCELLENT

Iowa courts enforce waivers exempting providers from liability for negligence. They are not against public policy; in fact, the public policy of freedom of contract is best served by enforcing liability waivers (*Bashford v. Slater*, 1959).

Public Policy. The *Bashford* court stated that no statutory prohibition or public interest opposes such agreements except when the employer-employee relationship is concerned. The Supreme Court (*Grabill v. Adams County Fair & Racing Association*, 2003) stated that waivers assented to by participants in hazardous activities are enforceable. An exception to the enforcement of waivers, however, is a professional providing a service of great importance to the public (e.g. physicians seeking protection from negligent medical treatment) (*Baker v. Stewarts' Inc.*, 1988). The Iowa Supreme Court has clearly stated that waivers for sporting competitions do not violate public policy and may be enforced in the state of Iowa (*Huber v. Hovey*, 1993). That court also ruled that there was no difference between spectator waivers and participant waivers.

A signed waiver is a contract and contract law governs its enforcement. In construing a contract, the cardinal principle is that the intent of the parties must control when the contract is not ambiguous and that intent is determined by what the contract itself says (*Huber v. Hovey*, 1993). Also, the waiver must be strictly construed against the relying party (*Bashford v. Slater*, 1959). Iowa courts have repeatedly held that contracts exempting one from liability for negligence are enforceable. The signer need not be knowledgeable and informed about the risks of an activity in order for a release to be valid. The Iowa Supreme Court in *Grabill* clarified the scope of waivers saying:

> a releasing party does not need to have contemplated the precise occurrence that caused injury as long as the occurrence was within the broad range of events that might transpire with respect to the matter being undertaken.

In *Forrester v. Aspen Athletic Club, LLC* (2009), the court enforced a health club waiver even though the waiver was buried near the end of the membership agreement. Iowa courts hold that one is bound by documents they sign. One who has the opportunity to read a contract, but signs without reading is held to the contract.

It is well established that a waiver signed by the injured spouse does not affect the rights of a non-signing spouse in a **loss of consortium** claim. The non-signing spouse has an independent cause of action (*Huber v. Hovey*, 1993).

"Negligence." The word "negligence" is not necessary if the clear intent of the language is to provide for such a release (*Korsmo v. Waverly Ski Club*, 1988). The validity of language such as "from all liability arising out of (the activity) whether caused by the negligence of releasees or otherwise" is not affected by the fact it is broadly worded (*Lathrop v. Century, Inc.*, 2002).

Parental Waivers. In *Galloway v. State of Iowa* (2010), the Supreme Court of Iowa held that a parental waiver for an educational field trip was not enforceable because it was against public policy. The court stated that the strong policy in favor of protecting children trumps the interest of parents and tortfeasors in their freedom to contractually nullify a child's injury claim.

Kansas
GOOD

Waivers are valid and enforceable as long as they do not involve a public interest or settled public policy; courts have ruled that voluntary sporting competitions are not matters of important public interest (*Fee v. Steve Snyder Enterprises, Inc.*, 1986; *Walton v. Oz Bicycle Club of Wichita*, 1991).

Public Policy. Courts recognize the validity of waivers except when they violate established public interests or settled public policy. Public policy supports the application of waivers since they play a vital role in allowing participation in voluntary recreational activities. Still, these waivers have an inherent potential for abuse and overreaching and must be subject to strict scrutiny. Public policy supports individual free choice and waivers help to make this possible. Recreational waivers make possible many recreational opportunities that would otherwise be impossible (*Walton v. Oz Bicycle Club of Wichita*, 1991).

To be enforceable, waiver language must be specific and clearly understood; general language or all-inclusive language exempting one from liability is not sufficient. The agreement must be "fairly and honestly negotiated and understandingly entered into" and the court may consider the totality of the circumstances surrounding the formation of the agreement. One consideration can be whether the relying party pointed the clauses out to the signer or whether the clauses were conspicuous in the contract. Failure to read a contract prior to signing, however, is no excuse and does not prohibit the enforcement of the contract (*Ko v. Bally Total Fitness Corporation*, 2003).

Waivers in Kansas will not limit liability for a breach of express or implied warranty. Such waivers are void by statute (**K.S.A. 84-9-109; K.S.A. 84-2-719(3); K.S.A. 50-639(a) and (e)**).

"Negligence." Waivers are to be strictly construed and apply only to situations plainly within the language of the agreement. The intention to waive liability for negligence must be clear and unequivocal, but it is not necessary to list each act of possible negligence or to expressly refer to "negligence" in the waiver (*Fee v. Steve Snyder Enterprises, Inc.*, 1986).

Wanton Conduct. Kansas does not recognize degrees of negligence, but distinguishes between ordinary negligence and wanton conduct. Wanton conduct is a product of defendant's mental attitude, not of particular negligent acts. For wanton conduct, one must show 1) a realization of the imminence of danger and 2) a reckless disregard, complete indifference or lack of concern for the probable consequences of the wrongful act (*Wagner v. SFX Motor Sports, Inc.*, 2006).

Kentucky
GOOD

It is well-established motorsports participant waivers are enforced. While disfavored, a waiver for other recreational activities may be enforced as a valid contractual agreement if it does not exempt liability for intentional conduct [or willful and wanton negligence] or allow one to breach a duty owed to the public (*Estate of Edwin Peters v. United States Cycling Federation*, 1991; *Brotherton v. Victory Sports, Inc.*, 2014).

Public Policy. Waivers for **motorsports** participants have long been enforced in Kentucky. Some of the reasons for this are that 1) races affect only private interests, 2) participation is voluntary, 3) parties possess equal bargaining power, and 4) races could not be held without such liability protection. Still, to be enforced, the waiver must be clear, involve no fraud, and must not involve willful or wanton negligence (*Brotherton v. Victory Sports, Inc.*, 2013).

For years, Kentucky law supported a public policy that disfavored and barred non-motorsports waivers from enforcement (*Coughlin v. T.M.H. International Attractions, Inc.*, 1995). In recent years, however, Kentucky courts have enforced waivers involving basketball (*Cabbage Patch Settlement House v. Wheatley*, 1999), bicycling (*Estate of Edwin Peters v. U.S. Cycling Federation*, 1991), rodeo (*Davis v. 3 Bar F Rodeo*, 2007), and paintball (*Bowling v. Asylum Extreme, LLC*, 2011). The general rule is that waivers of liability must be interpreted narrowly and against the protected party. Waivers are not valid 1) if public interest is involved, 2) if parties are not on equal footing, or 3) if the conduct was intentional. Further, in a non-sport case, the Supreme Court ruled a party cannot contract away liability for damages caused by that party's failure to comply with a duty imposed by a **safety statute**. "Any attempt by a negligent party to exculpate himself for a violation of a statute intended for the protection of human life is invalid" (*Hargis v. Baize*, 2005).

The *Hargis* court also specified that a pre-injury release will be upheld only if (1) it explicitly expresses an intention to exonerate by using the word "negligence; or (2) it clearly and specifically indicates an intent to release a party from liability for a personal injury caused by that party's own conduct; or (3) protection against negligence is the only reasonable construction of the contract language; or (4) the hazard experienced was clearly within the contemplation of the provision. Thus, an exculpatory clause must clearly set out the negligence for which liability is to be avoided.

The court in *Speedway SuperAmerica, LLC v. Erwin* (2008) stated that, generally, neither waivers nor indemnification agreements are against public policy. However, in each case, they are against public policy if one of the parties has a clearly inferior bargaining position. Additionally, if there is doubt as to the meaning of an indemnification clause, it should be interpreted by the court against a finding of indemnification (*Wisdom Fishing Camp Company v. Brown*, 2007).

The Supreme Court in *Cabbage Patch*, in upholding a waiver, indicated "the generation of funds for charitable purposes was in the public interest, that participation in sporting events was clearly voluntary, and that without a valid release charitable organizations would likely be unwilling to sponsor such fund-raising events, which would be against the interest of the public" The use of waivers is allowed in such events because waivers promote the public interest in allowing sporting competition to occur.

Gross Negligence. A U.S. Court of Appeals, Sixth Circuit, has indicated *in dicta* that waivers can protect against negligence and gross negligence (*Donegan v. Beech Bend raceway Park, Inc.*, 1990). The court cited a non-sport Kentucky Supreme Court case in which the court upheld the waiver and stated "For mere carelessness, however gross, short of wantonness or willfulness, [the defendant] will not be liable" (*Greenwich Ins. Co. v. Louisville & N.R.R.*, 1902). The *Hargis* court stated that an exculpatory contract for exemption from future liability for negligence, whether ordinary or gross, is not invalid *per se*. However, such contracts are disfavored and are strictly construed against the parties relying upon them. The wording of the release must be so clear and understandable that an ordinarily prudent and knowledgeable party to it will know what he or she is contracting away; it must be unmistakable.

"Negligence." The waiver language must be "so clear and understandable that an ordinarily prudent and knowledgeable party to it will know what he or she is contracting away; it must be unmistakable" (*Hargis*). Kentucky courts do not require the use of the word "negligence" for the waiver to be enforceable.

Parental Waivers. Parental waivers for **equine activities** that contain the warning specified in the equine statute and signed by the parent/guardian are enforceable for inherent risks, but not for negligence **(KRS 247.4027(2)(a).** No cases have been found indicating how courts will react to parental waivers in other activities.

Louisiana
POOR

Waivers intended to protect against liability for physical injuries are prohibited in Louisiana by La.Civ.Code art. 2004 (West 1987).

Public Policy. While waivers have been valid in the past, **La.Civ.Code art. 2004** (West 1987) provides "Any clause is null that, in advance, excludes or limits the liability of one party for causing physical injury to the other party." Likewise, it also specifically prohibits the limitation of liability for intentional or gross fault that causes damage to the other party. In a 2015 case (*Fecke v. The Bd. of Supervisors of L.S.U.*), the court declared a waiver of all liability unenforceable and illegal. The court did state, however, that the remainder of the document could have been admitted to show understanding of the risks and other information.

In a 1994 case, a client had signed a "Release and Hold Harmless Agreement" by which the client assumed the inherent risks in horseback riding (*Easterling v. English Point Riding Stables Inc.*, 1994). The court did not issue summary judgment because of issues of fact pertaining to risks not inherent in horseback riding saying that the client had not assumed such risks of negligence in the agreement. A 2008 case (*Ostrowiecki v. Aggressor Fleet, LTD*) involved a death on the high seas. The waiver in question was enforceable according to Maritime law, but was not enforceable under Louisiana state law.

Parental Waivers. Parental waivers, like other personal injury waivers, are not enforced pursuit to **La. Civ. Code art. 2004.**

Maine
FAIR

While traditionally disfavored, Supreme Court of Maine has held that releases and indemnity agreements exempting one from liability for his or her own negligence are enforceable and are not against public policy (*Lloyd v. Sugar Loaf Mountain Corp.*, 2003; *Doyle v. Bowdoin College*, 1979).

Public Policy. Prior to enforcing a waiver, a court must examine the waiver to determine 1) if it violates public policy, 2) if a special relationship or disparity in bargaining power exists, 3) whether the contract spells out the intention of the parties with the greatest of particularity, and 4) whether the terms were fully brought home to the plaintiff (*Weatherby v. Beechridge Speedway Inc.*, 1994). Additionally, waivers are not valid if they are shown to be the product of fraud, misrepresentation, or overreaching (*McGuire v. Sunday River Ski Corp.*, 1994).

Waivers are disfavored and must be strictly construed; there is heightened judicial scrutiny when interpreting language that exempts a party from liability for his or her own negligence. The intention of the parties to contractually extinguish liability for negligence must be clear (*Doyle v. College*, 1979).

Indemnity. Likewise, indemnification agreements that require indemnification of a party for injury caused by that party's own negligence are looked upon with disfavor (*Doyle* cited *Brogdon v. Southern Railway Co.*, 1967). The court said that such indemnity agreements should not be extended to indemnify the indemnitee's own negligence unless the language is clear and unambiguous. However, in *Lloyd v. Sugarloaf Mountain Corp* (2003) the court held that indemnification agreements within two waivers were enforceable and resulted in the plaintiff being held responsible for the defendant's legal fees.

A waiver is a contract that can bar a claim only if the plaintiff was a party to the agreement (*Hardy v. St. Clair*, 1999). Thus, a waiver signed by one spouse does not bar a **loss of consortium** claim by the other party. The claim of the non-signing spouse is an independent cause of action.

"Negligence." Documents with no express reference to defendants' liability for their own "negligence" may fall short of the requirement that the intention to extinguish negligence liability be spelled out "with the greatest particularity" (*Doyle v. College*, 1979).

Parental Waivers. Courts have held that even a well-worded parental waiver would not protect the provider because a parent or guardian cannot release the child's cause of action (*Doyle v. College*, 1979; *Rice v. American Skiing Company*, 2000).

Courts may uphold a **parental indemnification** agreement that expressly indemnifies the indemnitee against its own negligence in a manner that clearly reflects the mutual intent of the parties. "A clear reflection of mutual intent requires language from the face of which the parties unambiguously agree to indemnification for indemnitee negligence" (*Rice v. American Skiing Company*, 2000, p.13). (See Chapter 3 for more information.)

Maryland
GOOD

There is no public policy preventing parties from contracting as they see fit, provided the signer knows and agrees to the terms of the agreement (*Durrell v. Parachutes Are Fun, Inc.*, 1987; *Seigneur v. National Fitness Institute, Inc.*, 2000).

Public Policy. Absent legislation to the contrary, there is no public policy preventing parties from contracting as they see fit (*Durrell v. Parachutes Are Fun, Inc.*, 1987; *Seigneur v. National Fitness

Institute, Inc., 2000). Exceptions include: 1) when there is unequal bargaining power, 2) when the transaction involves a public interest (e.g., public utilities, common carriers, innkeepers), or 3) when there is intentional harm by acts of reckless, wanton, or gross negligence (*Winterstein v. Wilcom*, 1972). Even when the contract is an adhesion contract, that fact alone does not invalidate the contract (*Seigneur v. National Fitness Institute, Inc.*, 2000).

Additionally, if an agreement exempting a defendant from liability for his or her negligence is to be enforced, the terms of the agreement must be known to the plaintiff. If the plaintiff did not know of the provision in the contract and a reasonable person in his position would not have known of it, it is not binding – failing the requirement of mutual consent (*Winterstein v. Wilcom*, 1972).

Claims for **loss of consortium** by the non-signing spouse are dependent upon the claim of the signing spouse (*Winterstein v. Wilcom*, 1972).

"Negligence." The term "negligence" is not essential for validity. Of primary concern is the intention of the signing parties. The party is protected from liability for one's own negligence if the language clearly and specifically indicates the intent to release the defendant from liability for injury resulting from the defendant's negligence (*Adloo v. H.T. Brown Real Estate, Inc.*, 1996). Of primary concern when interpreting a contract is to effectuate the intentions of the two parties (*Seigneur v. National Fitness Institute, Inc.*, 2000).

Gross Negligence. A waiver does not bar an action for any extreme forms of negligence --- gross negligence, reckless conduct, or willful and wanton conduct (*Durrell v. Parachutes Are Fun, Inc.*, 1987).

Parental Waivers. The highest court of the state said that a parental waiver was not a "transaction affecting the public interest." On that basis, the Court elected to enforce liability waivers signed by parents on behalf of minor children (*BJ's Wholesale Club, Inc. v. Rosen, 2013*). The Court also stated that the distinction between commercial and non-commercial entities (a distinction held in many jurisdictions) is without support in Maryland

Massachusetts
GOOD

Waivers protecting against liability for ordinary negligence are not against public policy. In fact, Massachusetts public policy favors the enforcement of waivers (*Sharon v. City of Newton*, 1993; *Webb v. Peak*, 2002).

Public Policy. The general rule is that a person is free to contract to limit his or her liability. The allocation of risk by agreement is not contrary to public policy – in fact, Massachusetts law favors the enforcement of releases (*Sharon v. City of Newton*, 1993). Waivers addressing ordinary negligence are not violative of public policy as a matter of law (*Webb v. Peak*, 2002). They will be upheld unless there is 1) fraud, 2) willful and wanton conduct, 3) legislation to the contrary, 4) unequal bargaining position, 5) a social relationship of the parties which militates against upholding the agreement, 6) public policy to the contrary or 7) if there is violation of a statutory duty. The *McBride* court gave four more factors which can help determine validity: 1) the existence of a public duty, 2) the nature of the goods or services provided, 3) the contract was fairly entered into, and 4) the intentions of the parties are expressed in clear and unambiguous terms (*McBride v. Minstar, Inc.*, 1994).

A service provider may validly exempt itself from liability it might subsequently incur as a result of its own negligence. Essential terms of contracts must be definite and described in clear and unambiguous language. Whether the agreement is called a release, covenant not to sue, or indemnification agreement, it represents a practice that Massachusetts courts have found acceptable (*Sharon v. City of Newton*, 1993).

In *Angelo v. USA Triathlon* (2014), the plaintiff sued after signing a waiver and indemnification agreement. *USA* countersued based on the indemnification agreement. The court stated that **indemnity agreements** that exempt one from liability for his ordinary negligence are enforceable. They should be fairly and reasonably construed to ascertain the intention of the parties. Further the agreement can survive a decedent's death and become an obligation of a decedent's estate. Indemnity agreements are not enforceable in the event of gross negligence.

Two statutes seem to invalidate waivers employed by health clubs. The first (ALM GL Ch. 93 sec. 80) states that health clubs may not require waivers absolving themselves of liability. The second (ALM GL Ch. 93 sec. 85) states that any health club contract violating this provision or other in the statute shall be rendered void and unenforceable. These statutes have been enforced in at least one case (*Holiday Universal, Inc. v. Haber*, 1990).

Electronic waivers, including those using a click on an online checkbox to indicate assent, are enforceable in Massachusetts.

"Negligence." If the term, "negligence," is not specified, the intention of the parties to waive liability for negligent acts must be explicit and unambiguous.

Gross Negligence. Waivers do not bar an action for any extreme forms of negligence --- gross negligence, reckless conduct, or willful and wanton conduct (*Zavras v. Capeway Rovers Motorcycle Club, Inc.*, 1997; *Angelo*, 2014).

Parental Waivers. Waivers signed by minors are voidable, however those signed by a parent on behalf of a minor are clearly enforceable (*Sharon v. City of Newton*, 1993). Another court (*Eastman v. Yutzy*, 2001) recently held that an **indemnification agreement** signed by a parent on behalf of a minor was enforceable if no statute was violated. The requirement of releases as a condition of voluntary participation in extracurricular sports activities and the enforceability of such releases signed by parents on behalf of a minor are "consistent with and further the public policy of encouraging athletic programs for the Commonwealth's youth" (*Sharon v. City of Newton*, 1993, p.109).

Michigan
EXCELLENT

Generally, one may contract to limit one's liability for one's own acts of negligence if the waiver is not in violation of public policy (*Skotak v. Vic Tanny International*, 1994) **and the waiver is fairly and knowingly made** (*Xu v. Gay*, 2003).

Public Policy. Courts generally state that it is not against public policy for a party to contract against liability caused by ordinary negligence, but the language must be clear and unequivocal and will be strictly construed by the court. However, courts are actually quite lenient in enforcing this rule. For example, in *Faranso v. Cass Lake Beach Club, Inc.* (1998), the court enforced a brief waiver used by a tanning salon containing the following exculpatory language:

> "I have read the instructions.... I agree to use them at my own risk and hereby release the Sontegra operator, salon owner and manufacturer of the equipment from any damage I might incur due to use of said facility."

The scope and validity of the waiver is governed by the intent of the parties as expressed in the waiver. If the text is unambiguous, the parties' intentions are determined from the plain, ordinary meaning of the language of the release. "A contract is ambiguous only if its language is reasonably susceptible to more than one interpretation" (*Xu v. Gay*, 2003).

Summary judgment is proper disposition where a valid waiver exists (*Ansari v. Gold*, 2006). The validity of a waiver depends upon several factors: 1) it is controlled by the intent of the parties, 2) it must be fairly and knowingly made, 3) the releasor must not be dazed, in shock, or under the influence of drugs, 4) the nature of the waiver must not be misrepresented, 5) there must be no fraudulent or overreaching conduct (*Duncan v. Ryba Company*, 1999), and 6) the release must not tend to induce a tortious act (*White v. Estate of Lawrence J. Neuland*, 1988). The scope of a waiver is controlled by the language of the waiver. If it is unambiguous, the waiver is construed as written. Absent fraud or misrepresentation, a waiver is valid even 1) if it is not labeled "release," 2) if the signer failed to read it, or 3) if the signer misunderstood its terms. (*Oran v. Fair Wind Sailing, Inc.*, 2009).

In general, Michigan courts do not view favorably **disclaimers** located in small print on the back of tickets. The language limiting liability does not provide adequate notice to the patron (*Braun v. Mount Brighton, Inc.*, 1989).

Gross Negligence. Waivers are not enforceable in instances of gross negligence, reckless misconduct, willful and wanton actions, or when intent is involved (*Lucas v. Norton Pines Athletic Club, Inc.*, 2010; *Miranda v. Shelby Township*, 2003). The court in *Gonzalez v. Rusty Wallace Racing Experience, SITYS, LLC* (2015) stated that that one is grossly negligent when "conduct is so reckless as to demonstrate a substantial lack of concern for whether an injury results." It went on to say that an allegation that one should have done things differently or done more is insufficient to constitute gross negligence.

"Negligence." The term "negligence" is not essential for validity. The term "any and all" is interpreted to include negligence (*Gara v. Woodbridge Tavern*, 1997). Further, many courts have reiterated the statement that there is no broader classification than the word "all" (*Oran v. Fair Wind Sailing, Inc.*, 2009).

Parental Waivers. It is well-settled Michigan law that a parent has no authority, merely by virtue of being a parent, to waive claims by or against the parent's child. The minor can repudiate the contract upon reaching the age of majority (*Smith v. YMCA of Benton Harbor/St. Joseph*, 1996; *Woodman v. Kera d/b/a Bounce Party*, 2010).

Minnesota
GOOD

Minnesota courts hold that recreational services are not essential public services, thus waivers involving them are not against public policy (*Walton v. Fujita Tourist Enterprises Co.*, 1986).

Public Policy. The Minnesota Supreme Court has decided that the "public interest in freedom of contract is preserved by recognizing exculpatory clauses as valid..." (*Schlobohm v. Spa Petite, Inc.*, 1982). It is well-settled Minnesota law that under certain circumstances, parties to a contract may, without violation of public policy, protect themselves against liability resulting from their own negligence (*Waltz v. Lifetime Fitness, Inc.*, 2010). While not favored, contracts are valid and enforceable if they pass a test for public policy considerations. The rule of strict construction (*Schlombohm*) is applied and a waiver may be unenforceable if: 1) it is ambiguous in scope, 2) purports to release a party from liability for intentional, willful, or wanton acts (*Beehner v. Cragun Corporation*, 2001), 3) there is a disparity in bargaining power between the parties, or 4) the type of service being offered or being provided is either a public service or an essential service (*Schlombohm v. Spa Petite, Inc.*, 1982).

In addition, Minnesota Statute **604.055** provides that agreements for recreational activities that purport to release, limit, or waive liability of a party for damage, injuries, or death resulting from conduct that *exceeds ordinary negligence* is against public policy and is void and unenforceable. The statute does provide, however, that "The agreement, or portion thereof, is severable from a release, limitation, or waiver of liability for damage, injuries, or death resulting from conduct that constitutes ordinary negligence or for risks that are inherent in a particular activity." Attorney Allison Eklund, a Minnesota equine attorney, recommends that Minnesota waivers include language such as:

"Pursuant to **Minn. Stat. § 604.055**, effective August 1, 2013, nothing in this agreement purports or intends to waive liability for damage, injuries, or death resulting from conduct that constitutes greater than ordinary negligence."

The statute "does not prevent a court from finding that an agreement is void and unenforceable as against public policy on other grounds or under other law."

Courts find a disparity in bargaining power when 1) the service is necessary or unavailable elsewhere, 2) there is a compulsion to participate, and 3) when there is no opportunity to negotiate (*Beehner v. Cragun Corporation*, 2001). Equal bargaining position exists if there are more providers of the service and if it is not an essential service.

The *Bergin v. Wild Mountain, Inc.* court (2014) discussed ambiguity when there are two or more parts to a waiver contract (i.e., a season pass card and a season pass agreement). It stated that it is well-established that all documents will be read together when more than one document relates to a transaction; they are to be construed in relation to each other. In this case, the court concluded that the season pass card was not a contract. Even though it included an emphasis on the inherent risks of skiing, it did not contain an offer; thus, it created no ambiguity with the season pass agreement. The court added that even if accepted as a contract, the season pass card created no ambiguity because terms in a contract should be read together and harmonized when possible.

In *Walton v. Fujita Tourist Enterprises Co.* (1986), plaintiff was on a tour with other travel agents to become familiar with sites. The court did not uphold a pre-injury waiver because it was not bargained for, unilaterally prepared, and presented on a take it or leave it basis. In addition, the court considered the trip necessary for business purposes (and necessary for plaintiff's livelihood) and unavailable elsewhere.

In *Yang v. Voyagaire Houseboats, Inc.* (2005), Voyagaire had rented a houseboat to Yang and required that Yang sign an indemnity agreement. After six members of Yang's party suffered injury from carbon monoxide poisoning, Yang and others filed suit against Voyagaire, however Voyagaire claimed protection based on the waiver and indemnity agreement signed by Yang. The Supreme Court of Minnesota ruled that the waiver and indemnity agreement were against public policy since Voyagaire was, in effect, a resort providing a *public service* by furnishing sleeping accommodations to the public.

Indemnity Law. "Agreements seeking to indemnify a party for losses resulting from the party's own negligence are not favored in Minnesota" and such agreements will be strictly construed against the party seeking indemnification (*Yang v. Voyagaire Houseboats, Inc.*, 2004). In *Yang* (2004), the appellate court held that "all claims, actions, proceedings, damage and liabilities, arising from or connected with Renter's possession, use and return of the boat" was sufficiently broad to include negligence claims. The Supreme Court (*Yang v. Voyagaire Houseboats, Inc.*, 2005) overturned the appellate court decision, holding the agreement was not enforceable because the resort provided a public service by furnishing sleeping accommodations to the public. It also stated that the indemnity clauses were unenforceable because they do not contain language that 1) specifically refers to negligence, 2) expressly states that the renter will indemnify Voyagaire for Voyagaire's negligence, or 3) clearly indicate that the renter will indemnify Voyagaire for negligence occurring before the renter took possession of the houseboat. This ruling suggests that parties relying on indemnity agreements must take care to clearly state the intent of the clause.

Disclaimers. The validity of non-signed disclaimers is sometimes at issue. Federal regulations governing tour operators preempt state law and case law indicates that exculpatory clauses drafted in accord with 14 C.F.R. sec. 380.32 are enforced even when the clause is not part of a signed contract or is received after partial payment has been made (*Powell v. Trans Global Tours, Inc.*, 1999).

"Negligence." The use of the word "negligence" is not necessary for an unambiguous waiver (*Saude v. Red River Racquet Club, Ltd.*, 1989).

Gross Negligence and Reckless Conduct. Waivers will not protect a service provider from liability for reckless conduct, or willful and wanton acts (*Dailey v. Sports World South, Inc.*, 2003). Minnesota law does not recognize gross negligence.

Parental Waivers. Appellate courts in two cases have enforced waivers for ordinary negligence signed by parents on behalf of minors (*Moore v. Minnesota Baseball Instructional School*, 2009; *Salinger v. Leatherdale*, 2012). In addition, Subdivision 2 of **MN ST 604.055** defines "party" to include "a minor or another who is authorized to sign or accept the agreement on behalf of the minor." Thus, the statute provides for the enforcement of parental waivers.

Mississippi
FAIR

Mississippi courts do not favor waivers and construe them strictly against the relying party. Although some recreational waivers have been upheld, in actual practice, the language of such waivers must be clear and precise, not overly broad, and fairly and honestly negotiated.

Public Policy. The law does not look with favor on waivers of liability for one's own negligence; however, they are generally enforceable. They are subject to close judicial scrutiny and will be enforced only if the intent of the parties is expressed in clear and unmistakable language. The waiver must be honestly negotiated and understandingly entered into. Mississippi courts do not sanction broad, general waivers of negligence and construe them against the relying party. The Supreme Court recognizes that waivers are often used in certain activities in order to control the liability for negligence; however, they have stated that the provider must do so in specific and unmistakable terms (*Turnbough v. Ladner*, 1998).

Exculpatory contracts will not be enforced unless the limitation is fairly and honestly negotiated and understood by both parties (*Rigby v. Sugar's Fitness & Activity Center*, 2002; *Quinn v. Mississippi State University*, 1998). The *Rigby* court, in failing to uphold the waiver, noted that the plaintiff did not "recall any discussion of this waiver because she did not remember signing it" (p. 3). The court said there was nothing in the record to indicate that the contract was fairly and honestly negotiated and understood. While *Rigby* rejected the waiver because of a failure to negotiate, *Quinn* failed to enforce because of ambiguity and being overly broad. The meaning of the term "honestly negotiated and understood" is not clear.

The Mississippi Supreme Court stated that a pre-printed contract, the terms of which were not negotiated, must be strictly construed against the relying party. The same court stated that even an unambiguous waiver will not protect against liability unless the waiver was fairly negotiated and understood by both parties. It went on to say that a party cannot use an anticipatory release to escape liability for tortious acts (*Quinn v. Mississippi State University*, 1998).

The wording of a waiver should express as clearly and precisely as possible the *extent* to which a party intends to be absolved from liability. The Supreme Court does not sanction broad, general "waiver of negligence" provisions and strictly construes them against the relying party (*Turnbough*).

In a wrongful death action in which a soldier was killed in a live fire drill when struck by a bullet that went through ballistic wall it was revealed that the manufacturer did not follow safety standards. The Supreme Court ruled that it was not reasonable that the decedent intended to release the defendants from following basic safety standards in the design of the ballistic wall (*Ghane v. Mid-South Institute of Self Defense Shooting, Inc.*, 2014).

A release, waiver of liability, and **indemnity agreement** may constitute a complete defense against liability for negligence. One may contract to indemnify for one's own negligence, but the intent to indemnify must be clearly and unequivocally expressed. The U.S. Supreme Court has stated that an indemnity agreement should not be construed to permit indemnification for one's own negligence unless the mutual intent of the parties is clearly expressed (*Butler v. United States*, 1984).

Loss of Consortium. A waiver in a loss of consortium claim by a non-signing spouse is derivative of the claim of the signing spouse – thus, if the signer has waived his or her right to sue, the non-signing spouse has no claim (*Byrd v. Mathews*, 1990).

Parental Waivers. A 1998 Supreme Court ruling held that the waiver signed by both minor and parent was not enforceable because of ambiguity of language (*Quinn*). No mention was made of the fact that the injured party was a minor, and apparently the court would have upheld an unambiguous waiver in this case. In *Quinn*, a dissenting judge pointed out that a 12 year old cannot be bound by his signature and that a minor's representatives can waive nothing on behalf of the minor. He stated that for more than a century, the court has zealously protected the rights of minors and has held that they cannot waive any of their rights.

Missouri
GOOD

Courts have found waivers exempting operators of amusement devices from liability for ordinary negligence to be valid and enforceable (*Hornbeck v. All American Indoor Sports, Inc.*, 1995). **Language must be unambiguous, explicit, unequivocal, conspicuous, and within the contemplation of the signer.**

Public Policy. Waivers releasing one from liability for his or her own future negligence are disfavored in Missouri; however, they are not against public policy (*Alack v. Vic Tanny International of Missouri, Inc.*, 1996). Missouri courts consider on a case-by-case basis whether a waiver violates public policy. Courts use a two-pronged test asking 1) whether there is a disparity of bargaining power; and 2) whether the type of service offered or provided is an essential public service.

A waiver should contain clear, explicit, unequivocal, and conspicuous language referencing the types of activities it encompasses. Such acts cannot lie beyond the reasonable contemplation of the parties and the document must notify the signer that he is releasing the other party from liability for its own negligence. Waivers must be strictly construed against the party relying on the waiver; in construing a contract, one must meet the reasonable expectations of the average member of the public who accepts it. The waiver is enforceable only when it is expressed in understandable and unambiguous language (*Alack v. Vic Tanny International of Missouri, Inc.*, 1996) and properly notifies the signer of the effect of the agreement (*Hornbeck v. All American Indoor Sports, Inc.*, 1995). Courts have emphasized that general language will not suffice; the *Roe* court stated that under Missouri law, a waiver of negligence will never be implied, but must be stated clearly and explicitly (*Roe v. Saint Louis University*, 2012).

Waivers are ambiguous only if there is more than one reasonable interpretation of the language; because the parties disagree on the meaning does not make it ambiguous. Courts should focus on the plain language of the contract rather than speculating on the intent of the parties. The court added that the waiver stating release "from any and all liability" even if the injury was "the result of negligence" on the part of the defendant could have only one reasonable interpretation (*Guthrie v. Hidden Valley Golf and Ski, Inc.*, 2013).

Indemnification Agreements. An indemnity agreement will not exonerate a party from future acts of their own negligence unless it is clear and unambiguous. General language will not suffice (*Hornbeck v. All American Indoor Sports, Inc.*, 1995).

"Negligence." The Missouri Supreme Court has ruled that a waiver must use the word "negligence," "fault," or their equivalents so that the shifting of risk is clear and unmistakable (*Alack v. Vic Tanny International of Missouri, Inc.*, 1996; *Hornbeck v. All American Indoor Sports, Inc.*, 1995). Additionally, the contract must use clear, unmistakable, unambiguous, and conspicuous language. The *Alack* court also said that the waiver did not properly notify the signer since the waiver had no descriptive title and was at the bottom in 5-point print. The court went on to say that a document that would extinguish liability "should not compel resort to a magnifying glass and lexicon."

Gross Negligence. Missouri does not recognize degrees of negligence. In *DeCormier v. Harley-Davidson Motor Company Group, Inc.* (2014), the plaintiff could not avoid the enforcement of the waiver by claiming gross negligence. The court added that the bar for reckless conduct was not reached because reckless conduct comes close to **intent**.

Willful Acts. Waivers will not protect against liability for intentional torts, willful acts, or gross negligence (*Hatch v. V.P. Fair Foundation, Inc.*, 1999). There is reckless disregard of others if one intentionally acts or fails to act while knowing or having reason to know that such conduct creates an unreasonably high degree of risk of harm (*DeCormier*).

Parental Waivers. Indemnity agreements signed by a parent on behalf of a minor are not favored. Since parties are of unequal bargaining position, the agreement must show a clear and unequivocal intent of the father to act as the insurer of negligent acts of the provider (*Salts v. Bridgeport Marina, Inc.*, 1982).

Montana
GOOD

The 64th Montana Legislature (2015) revised Statutes 27-1-753 and 28-2-702 to allow the use of liability waivers by recreation and sport providers to protect them against liability for provider negligence; it declares that recreation and sport participants assume the inherent risks of the activity.

Waivers, to be enforceable, must state known inherent risks of the sport or recreational opportunity and must include the following statement in boldface type:

By signing this document you may be waiving your legal right to a jury trial to hold the provider legally responsible for any injuries or damages resulting from risks inherent in the sport or recreational opportunity or for any injuries or damages you may suffer due to the provider's ordinary negligence that are the result of the provider's failure to exercise reasonable care.

The statute also spells out that a provider is not required to eliminate, alter, or control the inherent risks within the particular sport or recreational opportunity that is provided.

The statute also provides that waivers can still be challenged on any legal grounds. Two major limitations of waivers are noted: 1) the statute allowing waivers does not apply to causes of action based on design, manufacture, provision, or maintenance of sports or recreational equipment or products or safety equipment used in the sport or recreational activity; and 2) under the statute, waivers do not exempt one from responsibility for his or her own fraud, willful injury to person or property of another, or for willful or negligent violation of law.

Indemnity Agreements. The Montana Supreme Court distinguishes between exculpatory clauses, releases, or disclaimers of liability in contracts and indemnity agreements. The former aim to deny the victim any redress by canceling liability altogether, while the indemnity agreement shifts the liability from one party to another. Thus, contracts of indemnification are not against public policy (*Haynes v. County of Missoula*, 1973).

Gross Negligence. Waivers do not protect the provider from liability for gross negligence or willful acts.

Nebraska
GOOD

The Nebraska Supreme Court has stated that waivers are not against public policy and are enforceable unless they are clearly repugnant to the public conscience (*Mayer v. Howard*, 1985).

Public Policy. Exculpatory contracts are valid unless contrary to public policy (*Mayer v. Howard*, 1985). Courts should be cautious in holding contracts void on the basis of public policy. To be void as against public policy, a contract must be clearly repugnant to the public conscience. A clear and unambiguous contract must be enforced according to its terms. The court must read the terms according to the "plain and ordinary meaning as ordinary persons would understand them (*Wiese v. Hjersman*, 2006).

The *Mayer* Court implies that the inclusion of a warning of the risks within the waiver helps the signer make an informed decision and strengthens the agreement. Informing the signer of risks to be encountered may actually serve or reflect public policy.

The *Mayer* Court made it clear that, in the absence of fraud, one who signs a waiver without reading it, when there is opportunity to read, cannot avoid its consequences on the basis that he or she was not informed of the contents of the document.

According to the Supreme Court in *Palmer v. Lakeside Wellness Center* (2011), when a third party, unnamed in the waiver, wishes to be a beneficiary of the waiver, it must appear by express stipulation that the rights and interest of such unnamed parties were contemplated when the agreement was made. It is the burden of the third party to show that the provision was made for his or her benefit.

Indemnification Agreements. In Nebraska, one may be indemnified against his own negligence if the agreement contains express language to that effect or if it contains clear and unequivocal language indicating indemnification is the intent of the parties (*Wiese*). In *Wiese*, a participant, Hjersman, signed an indemnity agreement and subsequently struck a pedestrian. In the agreement Hjersman agreed to:

> . . . release, discharge, and agree to hold harmless and indemnify The Alliance Motocross Association . . . of and from all liability, loss claims demand and possible causes of action that may otherwise accrue from any related to: . . . the negligence of other persons.

The court found the indemnity language clear and unambiguous.

Gross Negligence. When gross negligence or willful and wanton misconduct is alleged, the *Palmer* court made it clear that a court can look at the evidence in deciding whether there was action that reached gross negligence.

Parental Waivers. No cases involving waivers for minors have been found. One case did involve a parental indemnification agreement. All motions were denied and no ruling or discussion of the enforceability of the indemnity agreement was given because the party at fault had not been identified. At no point, however, did the court suggest that parental indemnity agreements were not enforceable.

Nevada
FAIR

Contractual exculpatory provisions which seek to relieve a person for negligence are "generally regarded as a valid exercise of the freedom to contract" under Nevada law (*Moffitt v. 24 Hour Fitness USA, Inc.*, 2013). **The Nevada Supreme Court has held that waivers are enforceable only if the signer understands the risk and fully appreciates the danger** (*Renard v. 200 Convention Center, Ltd.*, 1986).

Public Policy. The comparative risk statute has subsumed the assumption of risk doctrine, with the single exception of express assumption of risk (waiver of liability). A party signing an express assumption of risk (waiver) has consented to bear the consequences of a voluntary exposure to a known risk (*Mizushima v. Sunset Ranch, Inc.*, 1987). Contractual waivers are generally regarded as a legitimate exercise of the freedom of contract. Nevertheless, waivers are disfavored by law and Nevada courts must strictly construe such clauses against the relying party. (*Moffitt*)

An express assumption of risk is a contractual undertaking that expressly relieves a presumed defendant from a duty of care to the injured party since the injured party consented, by waiver, to assume the exposure to the risk (*Moffitt*). To be enforceable, waivers must "set forth the contracting parties' intentions with 'the greatest particularity' and expressly state the intent to release liability." Further, the *Moffitt* court adds that such intent may not be inferred from "words of general import."

A person voluntarily assumes a risk only when 1) the risk is known to the signer and 2) the signer fully appreciates the danger (*Renard v. 200 Convention Center, Ltd.*, 1986). The *Renard* Court said one must evaluate the circumstances as they existed at the time the release was obtained – including 1) the nature and extent of the injuries, 2) the haste or lack thereof with which the release was obtained, and 3) the understanding and expectations of the parties at the time of signing. In *Lee v. Dreamdealers USA, LLC* (2014), Lee claimed he thought he was signing a sign-in sheet and alleged fraudulent inducement because there was no instruction as to the fact it was a waiver of liability.

The *Renard* Court seems to indicate that an enumeration of the risks of the activity, providing actual knowledge of and appreciation of the danger to be encountered is necessary for a waiver to be valid. In the opinion, the court points out that a Florida court found a waiver that failed to show that the appellant subjectively understood the inherent risk of horseback riding to be unenforceable (*Renard* citing *O'Connell v. Walt Disney World Co.*, 1982).

A waiver may be found to be unenforceable if it is deemed **unconscionable**. Both procedural and substantive unconscionability must be present in order for an agreement to be deemed unconscionable. There is procedural unconscionability when a party lacks a meaningful opportunity to agree to the clause terms because of 1) unequal bargaining power, 2) an adhesion contract, and 3) its effects are not readily ascertainable from a review of the contract. Substantive unconscionability focuses on the one-sidedness of the contract terms (*Burnett v. Tufguy Productions, Inc.*, 2010).

"Negligence." To be enforceable, a waiver must express intentions with "the greatest particularity" and expressly show the intent to release liability for negligence. "Words of general import" do not sufficiently communicate negligence; one would be well advised to use the word "negligence" *Moffitt*).

New Hampshire
FAIR

New Hampshire courts generally prohibit waivers. However, they are enforced provided 1) they do not violate public policy, 2) the signer understood the import of the agreement, and 3) the claim was within the contemplation of the parties (*Barnes v. N.H. Karting Assoc.*, 1986).

Public Policy. While waivers are not favored in New Hampshire, they are enforced if 1) they do not violate public policy, 2) the signer understood the import of the agreement, and 3) the claim was within the contemplation of the parties (*Barnes v. N.H. Karting Assoc.*, 1986).

The New Hampshire Supreme Court has stated that a waiver violates public policy if 1) it is injurious to the interests of the public, 2) it violates some public statute, or 3) it tends to interfere with the public welfare or safety (*McGrath v. SNH Development, Inc.*, 2009). Further, the test for public policy is met if there is: 1) no special relationship between the parties and 2) no disparity in bargaining power (e.g.

innkeeper, common carrier, public utility, or other charged duty of public service) (*Barnes v. N.H. Karting Assoc.*, 1986). A disparity in bargaining power exists when the plaintiff may not be deemed to have freely chosen to enter into the contract (e.g., from a monopoly in a service, there is no possible alternative source of the service, physical or economic compulsion, or an essential service (*McGrath*).

The signer is deemed to have understood the import of the agreement 1) if the waiver is strictly construed against the defendant and 2) if the language clearly and specifically indicated the intent to release the defendant from liability for injuries resulting from the negligence of the defendant (*Porter v. Dartmouth College*, 2009), (*Porter v. Dartmouth College*, 2009). The agreement must be such that a reasonable person in signer's position would have known of the exculpatory provision. The waiver must clearly state that the relying party is not responsible for the consequences of his or her negligence (*Dean v. McDonald*, 2001).

The claim is considered to be within the contemplation of the parties 1) if the waiver clearly identifies the with sufficient clarity the parties being released (by name or job function), 2) if the waiver makes clear the types of claims covered (*Porter*), and 3) if the waiver specifically indicates the intent to release the defendant from liability for defendant's own negligence (*McGrath*). The clarity of the contract must be assessed by evaluating the contract as a whole – not by examining isolated words and phrases.

New Hampshire courts require that waivers be well-written and clear. In *Audley v. Melton* (1994), a model was injured while being photographed with a lion. The photographer in charge claimed the waiver for protection when sued for negligence. The waiver stated "I . . . realize that working with the wild and potentially dangerous animals . . . can create a hazardous [sic] situation . . . . I take all responsibility. . . . I hold Bill Melton and T.I.G.E.R.S . . . free of any or all liability." The Supreme Court ruled that the waiver could protect against liability for injuries inflicted by wild animals, but did not protect against injury due to the negligence of the defendant. The general release language did not clearly release the defendant from liability for his own negligence.

While the *Audley* waiver failed because it was too general, one year later the Supreme Court showed that waivers can fail for being too specific (*Wright v. Loon Mountain Recreation Center*, 1995). After four paragraphs dealing with the inherent risks of horseback riding, the waiver states "I **therefore** [emphasis added] release . . . from any and all liability for . . . personal injury to myself . . . resulting from the negligence of Loon Mountain . . . ." The court felt that the "therefore" (commonly meaning "for that reason") means the following language would relate back to the preceding discussion of inherent risks. The waiver language also said "to include negligence in selection, adjustment or any maintenance of any horse." The court felt this language could lead the signer to believe the negligence related only to upkeep and did not apply to control of the horse.

In *McGrath*, the New Hampshire Supreme Court, in addressing a claim questioning the contemplation of the defendants, stated that "[w]e judge the intent of the parties by objective criteria rather than the unmanifested states of mind of the parties." It added that defendants are not required to have contemplated the exact type of incident causing the injury if the language of the waiver includes a broad range of accidents involving negligence of the defendants.

Loss of Consortium. A claim by a non-signing spouse is wholly derivative of the claim of the signing spouse (*Rubin v. Loon Mountain Recreation Corporation*, 1985).

"Negligence." Courts have stated that no "magic words" (such as "negligence") are required, but that the intent to release for negligence must be very clear (*Audley v. Melton*, 1994). The *Audley* Court held that "any and all liability" does not protect against liability for negligence. In *Gonzalez v. University System of New Hampshire* (2005), the court held that the inclusion of the word "negligence" was not adequate and stated that the language must clearly state the defendant is not responsible for the consequences of *the defendant's negligence*.

Gross Negligence. New Hampshire law does not distinguish between causes of action based on ordinary and gross negligence. The doctrine of definitive degrees of negligence is not recognized as a part of New Hampshire common law (*Barnes v. N.H. Karting Assoc.*, 1986).

New Jersey
GOOD

While New Jersey law does not favor waivers (*Gershon v. Regency Diving Center, Inc.*, 2004) **and requires that they must be strictly construed against the relying party, such waivers are enforceable if they do not violate public policy** (*Mechanic v. Princeton Ski Shop, Inc.*, 1992).

Public Policy. A waiver is undoubtedly enforceable if it does not contravene any policy of the law (i.e., if it is not a matter of interest to the public or the state, but merely an agreement between persons relating entirely to their private affairs) (*Mechanic v. Princeton Ski Shop, Inc.*, 1992). Waivers are against public policy when 1) there is legislation intended for the protection of human life or 2) when they attempt to override statutory duties (*Stelluti v. Casapenn Enterprises, LLC*, 2010). The court in *Steinberg v. Sahara Sam's Oasis, LLC* (2014) stated that the general rule "is that competent persons shall have the utmost liberty of contracting and that their agreements voluntarily and fairly made shall be held valid and enforced in the courts."

The following factors have been deemed to affect the validity and enforceability of waivers: 1) public policy, 2) existence of a public duty or public interest, 3) nature of the goods or services provided, 4) whether the contract was fairly entered into, 5) intentions of the parties are expressed in clear and unambiguous terms, 6) existence of a statutory duty, 7) does not involve a public utility or common carrier, and 8) equal bargaining power (*McBride v. Minstar, Inc.*, 1994; *Pietroluongo v. Regency Diving Center, Inc.*, 2004).

While the law does not favor waivers because they encourage a lack of care and must be strictly construed against the relying party, parties can be bound by agreements relieving liability. **Non-signing parties** cannot be bound by such agreements (*Gershon v. Regency Diving Center, Inc.*, 2004).

New Jersey law (*Stelluti v. Casapenn Enterprises, LLC*, 2009; 2010) describes a contract of adhesion as one that is non-negotiable, offered on a take-it-or-leave-it-basis, and on a standardized printed form. Under New Jersey law, contracts of adhesion are enforceable if they do not violate public policy and are not unconscionable in nature. Four factors are used to determine if a contract is unconscionable: 1) the nature of the contract, 2) relative bargaining positions of parties, 3) whether economic compulsion is involved, and 4) whether public interest is affected by the contract.

New Jersey has a strong policy disfavoring shifting of attorney's fees. Since the shifting of attorney's fees discourages the average recreational participant from pursuing claims, it is deemed to be against public policy (*Dare v. Freefall Adventures, Inc.*, 2002).

In another case, a court failed to enforce a waiver at a ski resort because it conflicted with a state ski statute (*Brough v. Hidden Valley, Inc.*, 1998). The resort violated **N.J.S.A. 5:13-1 to 11** that specified the ski provider has a duty to post signs and remove obvious, man-made hazards as soon as practicable.

One signing a liability waiver has no legal authority to bind his or her heirs. A waiver in which the signer signs on behalf of his heirs does not bar potential heirs from instituting and winning a **wrongful death** claim. New Jersey Wrongful Death Act (N.J.S.A. 2A: 31-1) prescribes rights of heirs and is not overcome by a waiver signed by the deceased. A release agreement signed by decedent and defendant can only bar signers of the contract (*Pietroluongo v. Regency Diving Center, Inc.*, 2004).

"Negligence." Clear and explicit language, stating in precise words that the signer exempted the relying party from liability for its own "negligence," is required to absolve one from liability for negligence. The *Marcinczyk v. State of New Jersey* court (2009) enforced a waiver that did not contain the word "negligence" stating that "any claim or suit" expressly encompasses the word "negligence."

Parental Waivers. The New Jersey Supreme Court has ruled that a parent has no authority to compromise or release claims or causes of action belonging to a minor child unless the parent has been appointed guardian (*Colfer v. Royal Globe Insurance Co.*, 1986). The court said that "one who pays the parents to settle a minor's claim without judicial approval or statutory authority remains liable to the minor..." p.2. Additionally, the indemnification of a provider by a parent of the plaintiff is not enforceable because it places the interests of the parent and child in conflict (*Fitzgerald v. Newark Morning Ledger Company*, 1970).

The New Jersey Supreme Court has ruled a parent can sign a **binding arbitration** agreement on behalf of the minor. The public policy of the state favors arbitration and this represents a change of forum rather than a relinquishment of the rights of the minor (*Hojnowski v. Vans Skate Park*, 2005).

New Mexico
GOOD

In the one recreation, fitness, or sport-related waiver case found (*Berlangieri v. Running Elk Corporation*, 2003)**, the New Mexico Supreme Court said that waivers that do not affect public interest are enforceable, but are to be strictly construed.**

Public Policy. The Supreme Court of New Mexico named two factors that can void a waiver (*Berlangieri v. Running Elk Corporation*, 2003). Regarding the first, strict construction – the court said that any such document must be strictly construed against the drafting party. The specific language must be clear and unambiguous so as to inform the signer (without legal training) of its meaning. Additionally, the exculpatory language should be conspicuous to the signer. Factors such as location on the front of the contract, appropriately labeled, or whether surrounded by unrelated terms help to determine if language is conspicuous. Regarding the second, public interest – the New Mexico court relied on the *Tunkl* factors (*Tunkl v. Regents of University of California*, 1963) in determining if the waiver concerned a matter of public interest. Waivers that affect the public interest or violate a statutory duty are against public policy.

The Appellate Court (*Berlangieri v. Running Elk Corporation*, 2002) distinguished between cases involving monetary loss and those involving serious physical injury or death. It agreed with the Virginia Supreme Court and held that releases exculpating sponsors of liability for injuries in recreational activities to be void as against public policy. Subsequently, however, the New Mexico Supreme Court in *Berlangieri* (2003) said that it couldn't accept such a sweeping approach because it fails to take into account all the policy interests that favor allowing some releases to be enforced. The court went on to say that New Mexico has a strong public policy of freedom to contract that serves public policies that are no less important to society than those served by the law of tort. The court went on to conclude that while waivers should be strictly construed, that it would be inappropriate to invalidate all recreational releases.

The New Mexico Equine Liability Act (NMSA 1978, sec. 42-13-4 [1993]) expresses that equine operators should not be held liable for equine behavior; but reads "unless the acts or omissions of the ... operator ... constitute negligence." The Supreme Court in *Berlangieri* (2003) interpreted the intent of the statute to be that equine operators should be accountable for their negligence – thus prohibiting waivers from protecting operators from their own negligence.

"Negligence." The waiver does not have to expressly refer to the **negligence** of the provider. The key is whether the intent to release is clearly expressed (*Berlangieri v. Running Elk Corporation*, 2003).

New York
GOOD[71]

Liability waivers used by sport, recreation, and fitness providers that fall under G.O.L. Sec. 5-326 are not enforceable in New York. Where G.O.L Sec. 5-326 does not apply, waivers absolving recreational operators, including auto racing operators, from liability for their negligence are upheld provided certain qualifications are met (*Beardslee v. Blomberg* 1979). **In the absence of public policy to the contrary, exculpatory provisions in a contract, although disfavored by law and closely scrutinized by the courts, are generally enforceable.**

Public Policy. New York courts look with disfavor on disclaimers or releases of liability; however, absent conflict with statute or public policy, courts will enforce such contracts. Factors used in determining enforcement include: 1) intent of the parties, 2) clearness and comprehensibility of the language, 3) parties' awareness of the agreement, and 4) the frequency with which the releases appear in the type of transaction under consideration. The release must use "unmistakable language;" specifying that language such as "claim for any loss" is inadequate. Courts require that the waiver be in a language easily understandable to a lay person (*Rice v. Harley Davidson, Inc.*, 2005).

The release will not bar claims outside the contemplation of the signing party (*Beardsiee v. Blomberg*, 1979). The language of the agreement must express in unequivocal terms the intention of the parties to relieve the relying party of liability for negligence. The agreement must make its terms unambiguous and understandable (*Blanc v. Windham Mountain*, 1982). This does not mandate the use of "any simple or monosyllabic language," however; it does demand that such provisions be clear and coherent.

New York courts take a strong stance regarding the **assumption of risks** encountered by those choosing to engage in sport and recreational activities. Plaintiffs are "barred from recovering damages for injuries sustained during a voluntary sporting activity if it is established that the injury-causing conduct, event or condition was known, apparent or reasonably foreseeable" (*Viteritti v. Baseball Heaven, LLC*, 2013). Courts stress, however, risks are not assumed if the signing party has not been made aware of the risks involved in the activity (*Gross v. Sweet*, 1979).

G.O.L. Sec. 5-326. G.O.L. Sec. 5-326, passed in 1976, deems waivers void as against **public policy** under specific circumstances. The General Obligations Law provides:

> [e]very **covenant**, agreement or understanding in or in connection with, or collateral to, any contract, membership application, ticket of admission or similar writing, entered into between the owner or operator of any pool, gymnasium, **place of amusement or recreation or similar establishment** and the **user** of such facilities, pursuant to which such owner or operator receives **a fee or other compensation for the use** of such facilities which exempts the said owner or operator from liability for damages caused by or resulting from the negligence of the owner, operator or person in charge of such establishment, or their agents, servants or employees, shall be **deemed void as against public policy** and wholly unenforceable (emphasis added).

G.O.L. Sec. 5-326 was established by the legislature to provide consumer protection based on the belief that the general public was either unaware of exculpatory language on admission tickets or membership applications or did not understand the legal consequences of such language (*Owen v. R.J.S.Safety Euipment, Inc*, 1992). It appears, however, that the Second and Third departments have interpreted the statute quite differently. Since the Second Department is interpreting the statute restrictively (resulting in more situations in which the provider is exempt from the statute), more waivers are being found to be

---

[71] Likelihood is poor if G.O.L. 5-326 applies.

enforceable. The Third Department, using a more expansive view of the statute, applies the statute and rejects waivers in certain circumstances where the Second Department would likely enforce them. Thus, in many cases, whether a waiver is enforceable or not depends upon the department that reviews the case (*Rosenfeld and Nicolaou*, 2009).

Therefore, while waivers are generally valid and enforceable in New York, in light of G.O.L. Sec. 5-326, businesses charging a fee for recreational activities (e.g., health clubs, scuba diving clubs, riding stables) do not generally enjoy the protection of waivers. For example, health clubs would be places of amusement and recreation and a fee or compensation is charged for their use – suggesting that waivers would generally be unenforceable as against public policy. Hence, under normal circumstances, providers falling into this category should probably continue to use waivers, but should not be surprised if they fail to protect against their negligence; for best practice, such providers should definitely employ additional means of liability protection.

Types of Settings Where G.O.L. 5-326 has Applied

The following is a partial list of settings or activities in which G.O.L. 5-326 applied and prevented the enforcement of waivers:

- Motocross or dirt bike racing (*Sisino v. Island Motocross of New York, Inc.* 2007; *Torres v. Long Island Motocross Association, Inc.*, 2014; *Petrie v. Bridgehampton Road Races Corporation*, 1998)
- Health & fitness clubs (*Jafri v. Equinox Holdings, Inc.*, 2014; *Connolly v. The Penninsula Group*, 2008; *Debell v. Wellbridge Club Management, Inc.*, 2007; *Guerra v. Howard Beach Fitness Center, Inc.*, 2011; *Mellon v. Crunch*, 2011)
- Recreational horseback riding or trail rides (*DiMaria v. Coordinated Ranches, Inc.*, 1988; *Applebaum v. Golden Acres Farm and Ranch*, 2004; *Brancati v. Bar-U-Farm, Inc.*, 1992; *Filson v. Cold River Trail Rides*, 1997; *Vanderbrook v. Emerald Springs Ranch*, 2011)
- Parachuting or sky diving (*Bacchiocchi v. The Ranch Parachute Club, LTD*, 2000; *Tiede v. Frontier Skydivers, Inc.*, 2013)
- Go-kart racing (*Garnett v. Strike Holdings, LLC*, 2009; *Vanborkulo v. Keller's Motorsports, LTD*, 2008)
- Fun day at cycle park (*Tuttle v. TRC Enterprises Inc.*, 2007)
- Community swimming pool (*In the Matter of Winston v. Sharfstein*, 2009; Leftow v. Kutsher's Country Club Corp., 2000)
- Flag football league (*Williams v. City of Albany*, 2000)
- Fencing tournament (*O'Connor v. The United States Fencing Association*, 2003)

Keep in mind, however, that circumstances can play a role in whether the statute applies. For instance, with health clubs the general rule is that G.O.L. will apply and waivers will not be enforceable. However, in a 2014 case (*Kim v. Hanson*), Hanson operated a one-on-one training facility and engaged in personal training. When Kim was injured, the court held that the facility was clearly instructional and not recreational. G.O.L. 5-326 did not apply and the waiver was enforced.

Settings or Conditions in which G.O.L. 5-326 Usually Does Not Apply

When one or more of the following 10 conditions exist, New York courts will usually rule that the statute does not apply; in these cases, a waiver that meets New York common law criteria will generally be enforced.

- when equipment is rented or purchased and removed from the controlled environment;
- when applied to businesses which are not "similar" to a place of amusement or recreation;
- when the party was not a "user" of the facility;
- when no fee was charged;

- when the fee was paid by someone other than the signer;
- when the fee paid was paid to a party other than the facility owner or operator;
- when the waiver only waived liability for inherent risks;
- when the fee charged was for instruction;
- when the statute conflicts with federal admiralty law;
- when boarding a horse at a stable.

Each of these settings or conditions is discussed in detail below. It is important to keep in mind that in settings in which waivers are sometimes enforced, court rulings have not always been consistent, sometimes within departments and sometimes among departments.

1) G.O.L. Sec. 5-326 does not apply when the waiver is required for the **purchase or rental of equipment**. *Chieco v. Paramarketing, Inc.* (1996) involved the purchase of paragliding equipment for which the plaintiff signed a waiver. After injury, Chieco claimed that the waiver had no effect because of G.O.L. Sec. 5-326. The court ruled that the law did not apply to equipment purchases since no entry fee was paid. *Perelman v. Snowbird Ski Shop, Inc.* (1995) had similar results. G.O.L. Sec. 5-326 did not apply because Snowbird was determined to be a retail establishment that rents and sells ski equipment and accessories --- not a place of amusement.

In *Dumez v. Harbor Jet Ski* (1982), the court noted that the statute is intended for "controllable environments" and that waivers are valid when the equipment is rented and removed from the environment controlled by the business. Likewise, courts ruled that the statute neither applied in a Segway rental case (*Deutsch v. Woodridge Segway, LLC*, 2014) nor in a canoe rental case (*Farrari v. Bob's Canoe Rental, Inc.*, 2014).

2) When the business is **not similar to a place of amusement or recreation**, the statute generally does not apply. The court ruled that a hair salon with a tanning bed (*Ward v. Dunn*, 1987) was not similar to a place of amusement or recreation. In a lawsuit involving a bicycle tour (*Tedesco v. Triborough Bridge and Tunnel Authority*, 1998), the statute did not apply because the court said it was not a place of amusement or recreation. Likewise, when Conning was injured while biking along a highway, the court ruled the statute did not apply because that was not a place of amusement or recreation (*Connolly v. Dietrich*, 2013). When a runner in a 5-K race on a college campus collapsed and died (*Fazzinga v. Westchester Track Club*, 2008), the court ruled that the statute did not apply since the decedent was "not a member of the general public patronizing a proprietary recreational or amusement facility."

In *Gallant v. Hilton Worldwide, Inc.* (2014), the court ruled that a kettlebell class in a hotel was not a place of amusement or recreation. Interestingly, the waiver was not enforced because it did not plainly and precisely state that it protected against negligence. Similarly, in the *Perelman* case, the court also said that a ski equipment shop was not a place of amusement or recreation.

3) When the party was **not a "user" of the facility**, the statute may be inapplicable. *McDuffie v. Watkins Glen International, Inc.* (1993) held that a professional racecar driver was not a user. Likewise, the court in *Kazmierczak v. Lancaster Motor Sports, Inc.* (1995) held that Kazmierczak was a volunteer at the racetrack and not a user. The statute did not apply and the waiver was enforceable.

In a 2015 case (*Stevens v. Payne*), the court said that a spectator or observer who enters a racetrack is a user and is entitled to protection from G.O.L. 5-326, but that someone who actually participates in a race-related event is a participant and does not qualify as a user. The court cited several other cases that ruled similarly. In *Stevens*, the plaintiff signed two waivers so that he could help in the pit area. At one point in the race, he left his seat in the bleachers, helped to change a flat tire, and returned to his seat. Shortly thereafter, he suffered a heart attack and fell from the bleachers which had no guardrail, and suffered serious injury. The court ruled that the release was not voided by the statute because Stevens was not a user; interestingly, the court did not enforce the waiver because the waiver was written to protect against risks in the pit area – not negligence related to the bleachers.

In contrast, in *Gilkeson v. Five Mile Point Speedway, Inc.* (1996), Gilkeson paid a fee to enter the pit, falsely claiming to be a crew member. The defense argued he was not a user but the Third Department court ruled he was a user, applied the statute, and rejected the waiver. In the 2013 *Torres* case, the court determined that Torres, a motocross competitor, was a "user" of the facility; hence, the court said the statute applied and the waiver failed.

4) The statute does not apply when **no fee is paid for admission**. In *Chieco v. Paramarketing, Inc.* (1996), Chieco purchased a paragliding unit from the defendant and was given free lessons on how to use the unit. The statute did not apply and the waiver was upheld because Chieco paid no fee for the lessons. Likewise, in *Long v. State of New York* (1990), Long was injured when he dived into a pool of gelatin in a charity fund-raising contest. The waiver signed by the plaintiff was not made void by G.O.L. Sec. 5-326 because no fee was paid. Howell (*Howell v. Dundee Fair Association*, 1988) entered the racetrack to serve as a volunteer on the fire and ambulance crew and Stone, in *Stone v. Bridgehampton Race Circuit* (1995), entered claiming to be a member of a pit crew. The statute did not apply in either case because neither paid a fee for admission.

In contrast, in *Brookner v. New York Roadrunners Club, Inc.* (2008), the plaintiff signed a waiver in order to participate in a marathon. The court distinguished between an admission or entry fee and a fee to participate when it ruled that G.O.L. Sec. 5-326 did not invalidate the release. The court said the statute

> . . . . does not invalidate the release, since the entry fee the plaintiff paid to the NYRRC was for his participation in the marathon, and was not an admission fee allowing him to use the City-owned public roadway over which the marathon was run. Further, the public roadway in Brooklyn where the plaintiff alleges he was injured is not a "place of amusement or recreation."

Similarly, the court in *Schwartz v. Martin* (2011) enforced the waiver because the fee paid was for a racing license from USA Cycling and not for admission. Likewise, in the *Connolly* bicycling case, G.O.L. 5-326 did not apply because the fee was paid for instruction and training – not admission.

Interestingly, in the 2014 *Torres* motocross case, Torres paid an entry fee to the provider. The court found that the statute applied and did not enforce the waiver.

5) Who pays the admission fee may prove to be important. New York Departments have differed regarding this issue. In a case involving a softball injury (*Stuhlweissenburg v. Town of Orangetown*, 1996), the plaintiff was injured while sliding. The court ruled the waiver to be enforceable because the plaintiff had paid no fee to enter; the team entry fee was not relevant.

The court ruled differently in *Williams v. City of Albany* (2000). Williams' team paid a $550 fee to compete in a flag football league, but Williams paid no fee. The Third Department appellate court stated that the *statute applies to an owner or operator who receives a fee, regardless of who pays the fee.* The court ruled that G.O.L. Sec. 5-326 applied and the waiver was unenforceable. Likewise, the *Rice v. Harley Davidson, Inc.* (2005) court held that the statute applies regardless of who paid the fee.

6) The fee must be paid to the owner/operator of the business for G.O.L. 5-326 to apply. In *Bufano v. National Inline Roller Hockey Association* (2000), Bufano paid $25 annual dues to play in the league. The court ruled that G.O.L. Sec. 5-326 did not apply since the payment was paid to the league and not to the owner or operator of the recreational facility. Likewise, *Lago v. Krollage* (1991) involved a fee paid for a mechanics license, not for admission to the racetrack. Interestingly, both of these were Second Department cases.

7) Waivers can sometimes **protect the provider from the inherent risks of the activity** even when G.O.L. 5-326 applies. Sometimes waivers are intentionally or unintentionally worded in such a way they do not protect the provider from liability from negligence. When a waiver does not clearly indicate intent to protect against negligence G.O.L. 5-326 does not apply; the waiver cannot protect against negligence, but it still may be enforceable to protect against the inherent risks of the activity.

In *Pineda v. Town Sports International, Inc.* (2009), the broad sweeping language of the release did not include language relieving defendant of any liability arising from its own negligence. It was, however, enforceable to protect Town Sports from liability for injuries resulting from accidents or injuries not involving Town Sports' negligence. Likewise, the waiver in *Glenn v. Annunziata* (2010), did not protect the stable from its negligence, but was enforceable against liability for reasons other than defendant's negligence. The waiver from liability was enforceable to the extent that it protected the defendants from liability for injuries resulting from a fall from a horse caused by reasons other than the stable defendants' negligence.

A waiver can sometimes be useful even after the court rules that the exculpatory language meant to protect against negligent acts is inadmissible or unenforceable. In some cases the court has allowed the jury to see a **redacted version of the waiver** (a version in which all language regarding exculpation for negligence has been blacked out). This can serve as evidence that the participant was aware of the risks inherent in the activity. In *DiMaria v. Coordinated Ranches, Inc.* (1988), a woman fell from her horse and was injured. A redacted waiver contained notification of the inherent risks and evidence that the plaintiff had expressly assumed all risks. Likewise, in a case involving a Cornell University student who was injured in a tumbling activity (*Duchesneau v. Cornell University*, 2013), **G.O.L. § 5-326** applied so the waiver was inadmissible; the court did allow a redacted version, by which the defense was able to show that the plaintiff had assumed the inherent risks of the activity.

8) G.O.L. Sec. 5-326 does not apply when **the fee is paid for instruction** and not for recreation or amusement. In many cases, it is obvious that the fee paid was for instruction and not for recreation; G.O.L. 5-326 is no real issue in these cases. *Lerner v. The Society for Martial Arts Instruction* (2013) was such a case; the plaintiff attended a martial arts school specifically to learn the martial art. *Boateng v. Motorcycle Safety School* (2008) involved a similar situation in which the business was strictly educational. A third case (*Gallant v. Hilton Hotels Corp.*, 2014) involved a party who attended an instructional course that taught kettlebell techniques in a hotel. Again, it was apparent this was not a fee paid to a place of recreation or amusement, but rather, a fee for instruction. G.O.L. did not apply in each case and the waiver protected in the first two cases; in *Gallant* the waiver failed because it did not clearly indicate that the intent of the waiver was to protect against negligence.

In most circumstances involving fees, however, there is a question as to whether the fee was for instruction or recreation. This question generally arises in one of two settings – when the facility is a mixed-use facility or when there is no permanent site.

When the site is a **mixed-use facility** (facilities that provide both recreation and instruction), courts usually use one of two approaches in addressing claims that the activity was instructional. The first approach is to focus on *why the person was at the facility*: for amusement/recreation or for the purpose of receiving instruction. The second approach focuses on *what is the primary function of the facility*: to provide amusement/recreation or to provide instruction[72].

First Approach. A client was injured when she was thrown from a horse during a riding lesson (*Myers v. Doe*, 2014). Plaintiff claimed that G.O.L. 5-326 prohibited enforcement of the waiver since the facility was mixed: it provided lessons, but also offered pony rides, face painting, picnics, and birthday celebrations. The court noted that the defendant did offer recreational service, but enforced the waiver because the plaintiff was on the premises specifically for instructional riding lessons and evidence indicated that instructional riding was the primary function of the farm.

---

[72]Technically, if one examines the language of the statute closely, it would seem that the second approach more closely follows the letter of the law: ". . . contract, membership application, ticket of admission or similar writing, entered into between the owner or operator of any pool, gymnasium, **place of amusement or recreation or similar establishment** and the **user** of such facilities. . . ." The statute seems more concerned with the *function of the facility* than with *why the person was at the facility*.

In *Scrivener v. Sky's the Limit* (2003), Scrivener purchased sky diving *lessons*; the court held that the statute did not apply since the plaintiff was there for lessons. In *Gross v. Sweet* (1979), the business, Stormville Parachute Center Training School, was operated for the purpose of providing instruction in the sport. In a 1994 case (*Baschuk v. Diver's Way Scuba, Inc.*) the issue was whether a waiver signed as part of a scuba diving course was valid under G.O.L. Sec. 5-326. The court ruled that the pool was used for instructional, not recreational or amusement, purposes. Further the fee paid was for a course of instruction and is not analogous to a user fee for recreational facilities. Other cases in which the activity was instructional in nature include when a plaintiff was injured while taking horseback riding lessons (*Salazar v. Riverdale Riding Corporation*, 1999) and when the incident occurred while plaintiff was learning to scuba dive (*Murley v. Deep Explorers, Inc.*, 2003). Likewise, in *Lux v. Cox* (1998), the plaintiff was injured at Watkins Glen International Race Course while taking driving lessons. In each case, the plaintiff was on the premises specifically for lessons; G.O.L. 5-326 did not apply and the waiver was enforced.

A waiver challenged in a 2004 health club case (*Evans v. Pikeway, Inc.*) was enforced because the court held that G.O.L Sec. 5-326 did not apply. The plaintiff was injured while under the supervision of a certified personal trainer and the manager of the fitness center. The waiver read:

> I, John N. Evans have volunteered to participate in a program of physical exercise under the direction of Janet Kaiser, which will include, but may not be limited to, weight and resistance training. In consideration of Janet Kaiser's agreement *to instruct, assist, and train me*, I do hereby and forever release and discharge and hereby hold harmless ... (emphasis added). p.2

The court found that the G.O.L. Sec. 5-326 did not apply because the plaintiff was at the fitness center for instructional purposes. Similarly, Thiele attended a go-kart driving class at a mixed use facility (*Thiele v. Oakland Valley, Inc.*, 2010). The court stated there was no evidence to indicate the statute applied; the court granted summary judgment in favor of the defendant.

Second Approach. In four skydiving cases, the courts found that instruction was ancillary to recreation and failed to enforce the waivers. In *Tiede v. Frontier Skydivers, Inc.* (2013), plaintiff took a one-hour skydiving course and was injured in a plane crash. To determine if G.O.L. 5-326 applied, the court examined 1) the certificate of incorporation; 2) the statement of purpose; 3) the services for which the plaintiff paid a fee (i.e., whether payment was for instruction or for use of the facilities); as well as other evidence submitted by the defendants. The court concluded that the facility is not used solely for instruction purposes; it determined the statute applied and did not uphold the waiver. Likewise, in *Nutley v. Skydive the Ranch* (2009), G.O.L. Sec 5-326 was found to apply because the primary purpose of the business was to provide an opportunity to skydive. Any instruction was ancillary to the recreational aspects and it was irrelevant that the plaintiff was injured during the instructional phase. The waiver was not enforced. In *Wurzer v. Seneca Sport Parachute Club* (1978), the waiver was not enforced for a mixed use facility since Wurzer paid for lessons and the use of the facility. The *Bacchiocchi v. Ranch Parachute Club* (2000) court ruled similarly, stating that "It is evident that the club does not restrict the use of its facilities to instruction but promotes sport parachuting as a recreational pursuit, to which instruction is provided as an ancillary service." The statute applied and the waiver failed to protect.

A plaintiff was injured while working with a personal trainer at a health club (*Connolly v. The Peninsula Group*, 2008). The court ruled that G.O.L. 5-326 applied since the training sessions received were ancillary to the recreational activities provided by the spa. In a similar 2007 case (*Debell v. Wellbridge Club Management, Inc.*), the appellate court overturned a trial court ruling that G.O.L. 5-326 did not apply because the plaintiff was undergoing instruction in strength-training exercise when the injury occurred. The appellate court stated that it was of no consequence that the training session was arguably instructional in nature because the trial court should have focused on *whether the primary purpose of the spa was recreational or instructional – not the plaintiff's activity at the time of the injury.*

The court said G.O.L. Sec. 5-326 applied because all evidence indicated the business was recreational and the plaintiff had been a member for nine months before taking a training session.

A different ruling resulted in *LeMoine v. Cornell University* (2003). The Third Department court held that the statute did not apply in a case involving a rock climbing class at the university and upheld the waiver. It is important to note that in determining if the facility was recreational or instructional, the court examined 1) the organization's name, 2) its incorporation certificate, 3) its statement of purpose, and 4) whether payment is tuition or a fee for use of the facility. The court found that the primary function of the facility was education.

Where there is **no permanent site** (as in parachuting activities), whether G.O.L. 5-326 applies depends upon whether the primary function of the business is educational or recreational. In *Scrivener v. Sky's The Limit, Inc.* (2003), the plaintiff skydiver was injured during a jump that was part of an instructional program. In *Gross v. Sweet* (1979), the business, Stormville Parachute Center Training School, was operated for the purpose of providing instruction in the sport. In each case, G.O.L. Sec. 5-326 was ruled inapplicable since the injured party was involved in an instructional program.

In contrast, the court ruled that Seneca Sport Parachute Club (*Wurzer v. Seneca Sport Parachute Club*, 1978), by its name and its certificate of incorporation was a recreational facility. Likewise, another court (*Bacchiocchi v. Ranch Parachute Club*, 2000) ruled that *Ranch* was a place of amusement and recreation because it advertised itself as a place for having a good time with a relaxed atmosphere and its certificate of incorporation stated that its purpose was to promote sport parachuting.

Based on these cases, it is apparent that in order to gain protection from waivers, management should take steps to make certain that it is clear that the business has a distinct educational function. To determine its applicable function, courts look at 1) the name of the organization and its certificate of incorporation, 2) its statement of purpose, and 3) whether it charges tuition for instruction or a fee for use of the facility (*LeMoine v. Cornell University*, 2003). Language in advertising and brochures as well as regular availability of instruction might help to show that instruction is more than just an ancillary service.

9) G.O.L. 5-326 does not apply to a waiver when the statute **conflicts with federal admiralty law**. In a 2011 case (*Brozyna v. Niagara Gorge Jetboating, LTD.*, 2011), Diane Brozyna was injured when the jetboat she was riding came down hard in a rapids. She sued for negligence and the defendant claimed a waiver of liability as a defense. Since the incident occurred in navigable waters, the case fell under admiralty law jurisdiction. Admiralty law provides that operators of inherently risky marine recreational activities may contract to disclaim liability for their own negligence. The plaintiff contended, however, that the waiver is void as against public policy under **General Obligations Law § 5-326**. The court responded stating that federal law trumps state law and ruled that the enforcement of **G.O.L. 5-326** would be detrimental to the maritime industry by disrupting the uniformity of admiralty law.

10) A **boarding fee for a horse at a stable** is not analogous to a user fee for a recreational facility so G.O.L. Sec. 5-326 does not apply. In *Strauss v. Stoneledge Farms* (1998), a horse was injured while being boarded at a stable. The court said G.O.L. Sec. 5-326 did not apply in such instances and enforced the waiver signed by the owner of the horse.

***

Statutes. Two health club statutes (**NYSCL, GB 30, sec. 623 (3)**; **NYSCL, GB 30, sec. 627**) quite similar to the Massachusetts statutes, seem to invalidate waivers employed by health clubs. The first statute states that health clubs may not require waivers absolving themselves "of any claim or defense arising out of the health club services contract." The second states that any contract for services failing to comply shall be rendered void and unenforceable. The authors have found no case law relating to these statutes, so it seems that they are not currently being enforced.

Disclaimers. Disclaimers are often included in contracts relating to **tours**. A disclaimer on a ticket was upheld following an accident on a tour to the Grand Tetons, a bicycle tour agreement requiring arbitration was upheld, and a cruise ship agreement specifying forum selection was upheld even though the plaintiff was a minor (*Loeb v. United States of America*, 1992; *Igneri v. Carnival Corp.*, 1996; *Milgrim v. Backroads, Inc.*, 2001). In a very old case, a New York court did not uphold a disclaimer in a cruise ship contract of carriage. The court relied on the Federal Statute 46 U.S.C.A. sec. 183c that prohibits defendants from including exculpatory language in contracts of carriage to protect themselves from liability for injuries due to their own fault (*Moore v. American Santic Line. Inc.*, 1941). The court also said the disclaimer was not upheld because the plaintiff had struck out the word "negligence" when he signed the contract.

"Negligence." The word "negligence" or words conveying the same import, such as "caused by the neglect or fault of the relying party," must appear in the agreement. Here are just a few of the numerous cases in which waivers have failed for lack of the word "negligence" (*Hilliard v. Sony*, 2012; *Rich v. Teebar*, 2013; *Tadmor v. NY Jiujitsu*, 2012; *DiMaria v. Coordinated Ranches*, 1988; *Layden v. Plante*, 2012). The waiver in *Gillette v. All Pro Sports, LLC (*2014) clearly specified the assumption of the inherent risks, but made no reference to the relief of liability for negligent acts. The one exception is *Walker v. Young Life Saranac Village* (2012) in which a U.S. District Court strangely enforced a waiver both failing to indicate "negligence" and signed by a parent on behalf of a minor.

Gross Negligence. Waivers will not shield a party from liability for gross negligence or willful and wanton acts (*Gross v. Sweet*, 1979).

Parental Waivers. In a recent case involving a summer camp (*Walker v. Young Life Saranac Village*, 2012), a U.S. District Court enforced a parental waiver. In light of previous state court rulings, this was surprising and may not accurately reflect state law. While not completely clear, case law tends to indicate that neither waivers nor indemnification agreements signed by parents are enforceable against the interest of the minor.

North Carolina
GOOD

A waiver and indemnity agreement is enforceable against ordinary negligence in North Carolina provided it does not conflict with public policy or a statute. Bargaining power must be equal and the document must be unambiguous (*Strawbridge v. Sugar Mountain Resort, Inc.*, 2004; *Del Raso v. United States of America*, 2000; *Andrews v. Fitzgerald*, 1993).

Public Policy. As a general rule, North Carolina courts enforce waivers under the principle of freedom of contract (*McMurray v. United States of America*, 2012). Generally contracting parties may agree to limit liability for ordinary negligence. Such waivers, however, are disfavored and must be strictly construed against the relying party.

A waiver is against public policy if 1) a party seeks to protect himself from liability for negligence in the performance of a duty of public service, 2) a public duty is owed, or 3) a public interest is involved (*Strawbridge v. Sugar Mountain Resort, Inc.*, 2004). Waivers will be held void if the agreement 1) is violative of a statute; 2) contravenes public policy; 3) is gained through inequality of bargaining power (*Del Raso v. United States of America*, 2000); or 4) is contrary to a substantial public interest (*Andrews v. Fitzgerald*, 1993). Unequal bargaining power exists only when one must accept an offer to obtain an important service which, for all practical purposes, is not available elsewhere (M*cMurray*). The fact that a waiver is non-negotiable does not mean there is unequal bargaining power.

A release and hold harmless agreement is a complete defense to personal action for damages in North Carolina (*Del Raso v. United States of America*, 2000). In a racing case, the court held that motor sport waivers did not violate public policy because no public interest is involved. The court added that public interest is applicable only in highly regulated activities (e.g., medicine, cosmetology) and that waivers are enforceable when the party has the opportunity to see and read the exculpatory contract (*Bertotti v. Charlotte Motor Speedway, Inc.*, 1995).

Though not favored and requiring strict scrutiny (*Andrews v. Fitzgerald,* 1993), waivers are enforceable unless there is a "public interest" exception (*Del Raso v. United States of America*, 2000). The public interest exception to the enforceability of waivers applies only to heavily regulated activities (e.g., doctor-patients, participants in motorcycle training program, cosmetology services); it does not apply to activities that are not heavily regulated such as races (*Brown v. Robbins*, 2007).

A comprehensively phrased 'general release' in the absence of proof of contrary intent, is usually held to discharge *all* claims . . . between the parties" (*Brown v. Robbins*, 2007). An exception to this is waivers that are held to be against public policy. One North Carolina court (*Fortson v. McClellan*, 1998) ruled that public safety is in the public interest. Subsequently the court did not enforce a waiver designed to protect a motorcycle training school, holding it to be against public policy.

A release will not be so construed as to exempt the indemnitee from liability for his own negligence unless there is explicit language clearly indicating that such was the intent of the parties. If an agreement is ambiguous, it will be construed against the defendants, but ambiguity will not render the entire agreement unenforceable (*Bertotti v. Charlotte Motor Speedway, Inc.*, 1995).

Ski Statute. North Carolina Statute δ 99C provides that ski operators have a statutory duty of ordinary care – "Not to engage willfully or negligently in any type conduct that contributes to or causes injury to another person or his properties;" (NCGS δ 99C-2) *Thus waivers attempting to relieve ski operators of negligence are void because they cannot overcome a statute* (*Strawbridge v. Sugar Mountain Resort, Inc.*, 2004). The *Strawbridge* court ruled "the ski industry is sufficiently regulated and tied to the public interest to make exculpatory clauses improper."

Gross Negligence. Parties may not protect themselves from their own **gross negligence** by use of a waiver (*Bertotti v. Charlotte Motor Speedway, Inc.*, 1995).

Parental Waivers. In *Kelly v. United States of America* (2014), the U.S. District Court examined a case in which a 15-year-old girl was injured while running an obstacle course at a JROTC orientation session. Each parent had signed either a release or a waiver prior to the event. The court balanced the public policy of protecting minors from adverse affects of waivers versus the public policy of enforcing waivers signed by parents, thereby enabling school and community non-profit recreation to provide activities they could not otherwise provide. The court, after examining several aspects of North Carolina law as well as rulings in other states, enforced the parental waiver and granted the defendant summary judgment.

North Dakota
EXCELLENT

North Dakota courts enforce waivers that are not against public policy. Although the law does not favor waivers, the courts do not adhere to strict standards in their interpretation of waivers.

Public Policy. Whether a waiver is against public policy depends on two factors: 1) The disparity of bargaining power between the parties in terms of compulsion to sign the agreement and lack of ability to negotiate elimination of the clause; and 2) The types of services provided by the party seeking exoneration, including whether they are public or essential services (*Reed v. University of North Dakota*, 1999).

An interesting point is that North Dakota has statute **N.D.C.C. 9-08-02** which reads:

All contracts which have for their object, directly or indirectly, to exempt anyone from responsibility for ... willful injury to the person or property of another, or for violation of law, whether willful or negligent, are against the policy of the law.

In the past, Montana courts have interpreted a similar statute as prohibiting the use of liability waivers (see Montana section); however, North Dakota courts do not. The North Dakota Supreme Court interprets it as precluding parties from exonerating themselves from liability for willful acts (*Reed v. University of North Dakota*, 1999). Not only do North Dakota courts enforce waivers, they do not adhere to rigorous standards in doing so. This is evidenced by the waiver that was upheld in *Reed*:

I am entering this event at my own risk and assume all responsibility for injuries I may incur as a direct or indirect result of my participation. For myself and my heirs, I agree not to hold the participating sponsors and their directors, employees and/or agents responsible for any claims.

The law does not favor contracts exonerating parties from liability for their conduct. The courts construe contracts in light of existing statutes, which become part of and are read into the contract as if the statutory provisions were included in it --- thus a waiver exonerating "any claims" is interpreted to mean it is limited to negligent acts as a matter of law (based on **N.D.C.C. 9-08-02**) (*Reed v. University of North Dakota*, 1999). While jurisdictions in some states construe broad language as unenforceable, in North Dakota a court can interpret broad language in a release as unambiguous and enforceable. The Supreme Court construes contracts to give effect to the parties' intent, which when possible, must be ascertained by giving meaning to each provision in the contract.

Indemnity Agreements. Such agreements will not be interpreted to indemnify a party against negligence unless the construction is clearly intended (*Bridston by Bridston v. Dover Corp.*, 1984). The indemnity contract should be considered as a whole when interpreting it.

"Negligence." The court said that the omission of "magic words" such as "negligence" does not void the waiver, but stressed that use of the term would be good practice *(Bridston by Bridston v. Dover Corp., 1984)*. The Supreme Court upheld a waiver that granted relief from negligence "for any claims," clearly indicating that the use of the word "negligence" is not necessary (*Kondrad v. Bismarck Park District*, 2003).

Gross Negligence. Waivers prevent recovery from ordinary negligence only – not gross negligence. North Dakota statute, **N.D.C.C. 9-08-02,** specifies that one cannot waive willful injury.

Parental Waivers. The Supreme Court of North Dakota upheld a waiver signed by a parent of a minor participating in an after-school program. The court failed to discuss the issue (*Kondrad v. Bismarck Park District*, 2003). In a subsequent case involving a minor, the court did not enforce the waiver because it was ambiguous (*Hillerson v. Bismarck Public Schools*, 2013). The court made no indication that minor status mattered.

Ohio
EXCELLENT

The paramount public policy is that courts are not to lightly interfere with the freedom to contract. "Contract clauses, which relieve a party from its own negligence, are generally upheld in Ohio" and serve as an absolute bar to a later action (*Wheeler v. Owens Community College*, 2005).

Public Policy. Waivers that clearly and unequivocally relieve one from the results of his or her own negligence are generally not contrary to public policy, but will be strictly construed against the relying party (*Weiner v. American Cancer Society*, 2002). A participant in a recreational activity is free to contractually relieve the operator of liability for injuries caused by operator negligence. The participant must consciously choose to accept the consequences of operator negligence and that choice must be manifested by a waiver with a clear and unambiguous intent to release (*Baker v. Just for Fun Party Center*, 2009).

To be enforceable, a waiver must be expressed in clear and unequivocal terms. When a contract is unambiguous, courts may not find an intent not expressed in the clear language of the contract (*Geczi v. Lifetime fitness*, 2012). Where the language is ambiguous or too general, courts have held that the intent of the parties is a factual matter for the jury (*Bader v. Ferri, 2013*).

Waivers are generally upheld in Ohio if they are absent 1) unconscionability, 2) ambiguity, and 3) important public policy considerations (*Hall v. Woodland Lake Leisure Resort Club, Inc.*, 1998). The fundamental principle of "freedom to contract" justifies the general rule that courts will not meddle with an allocation of risk provision. But, waivers must indicate a conscious choice to accept the consequences of the other party's negligence. It must state a clear and unambiguous intent to release the party from liability for its negligence.

One reason that Ohio is classified as "Excellent" as to the likelihood of enforcement is that courts tend to enforce waivers that are not particularly strong. The Nelson Ledges Quarry Park Liability Waiver Form reproduced in Chapter 6 illustrates a waiver that was upheld by an Ohio court (*Bishop v. Nelson Ledges Quarry Park, Limited*, 2005). The waiver appeared at the top of a sign-in sheet and was enforced by the appellate court.

Ohio's approach to waivers for recreational activity is stated in *Pippin v. M.A. Hauser Ent., Inc.*, (1996).

> Express assumption of the risk occurs when a person expressly contracts with another not to sue for any future injuries caused by the negligence of that second person.... Thus, a participant in a recreational activity is free to contract with the proprietor of that activity to relieve the proprietor of liability for injury to the participant caused by the negligence of the proprietor.... In such instances, the proprietor can be held liable only if its conduct was willful or wanton.

The intention of the parties governs the interpretation of a waiver. A release that is so general that it includes within its terms claims of which the releasor was ignorant, and thus not within the contemplation of the parties, will not bar recovery.

A U.S. District Court found that a waiver purporting to protect against "all liability" for "any and all loss" did not protect against **strict liability** or **product liability** claims. In a similar case, a court stated that "The release cannot as a matter of law preclude potential product liability claims.... The plain language of the release does not preclude a player from bringing product liability claims against the manufacturers of any defective equipment" (*Curtis v. Hoosier Racing Tire Corp.*, 2004; *Mohney v. USA Hockey, Inc.*, 2001).

"Negligence." It is not necessary to expressly use the word "negligence" in the waiver if the waiver as a whole is such that the intent of the parties is clear with regard to exactly what kind of liability is being released (*Weiner v. American Cancer Society*, 2002). Nevertheless, courts suggest that the better practice would be to refer to the "negligence" of the provider (*Bishop v. Nelson Ledges Quarry Park, Limited*, 2005). In *Bader*, the court concluded that "It is difficult to construe a release 'from any and all claims' that arise 'out of any and all personal injuries' as anything but a release of liability for negligence."

Reckless Conduct. No service provider can avoid liability for reckless or willful or wanton conduct by use of a waiver (*Weiner v. American Cancer Society*, 2002). In fact, in a case involving a police officer training course waiver, the court ruled that the language "from any cause whatsoever, including negligence" was too general to be enforceable because it purports to release the defendant from any type of misconduct, whether it be negligent, wanton or willful misconduct (*Wheeler v. Owens Community College*, 2005).

Parental Waivers. The Supreme Court has ruled that parents have the authority to bind their minor children to waivers in favor of volunteers and sponsors of nonprofit sports activities where the cause of action is negligence. A minor may not disaffirm a waiver signed by the parent on his or her behalf. A parent can also waive his or her own claim (*Zivich v. Mentor Soccer Club*, 1998). Further, courts have enforced parental waivers used by commercial entities. Additionally, the equine statute **ORC 2305.321 (2)(a)** provides that a parental waiver that specifies the inherent risks listed in the statute will be enforceable.

Oklahoma
GOOD

Waivers, including those used in high-risk sports, are not against public policy and people have the freedom to contract as they see fit. Waivers must be unambiguous, made between bargaining equals, and not violate public policy or a statute (*Manning v. Brannon*, 1997; *Trumbower v. Sports Car Club of America, Inc.*, 1976).

Public Policy. In Oklahoma, the general rule is that people have the freedom to bind themselves as they see fit. The public policy of Oklahoma does not prohibit exculpatory contracts, including those used with high-risk sports. Nevertheless, waivers are not favored by law and are to be construed against the relying party (*Trumbower v. Sports Car Club of America, Inc.*, 1976).

In *Schmidt v. United States of America* (1996), the Oklahoma Supreme Court stated

> By entering into an exculpatory agreement … the promisor assumes the risks that are waived. While these exculpatory promise-based obligations are generally enforceable, they are distasteful to the law. For a validity test the exculpatory clause must pass a gauntlet of judicially-crafted hurdles: (1) their language must evidence a clear and unambiguous intent to exonerate the would-be defendant from liability for the sought-to-be-recovered damages; (2) at the time the contract (containing the clause) was executed there must have been no vast difference in bargaining power between the parties; and (3) enforcement of these clauses must never (a) be injurious to public health, public morals or confidence in administration of the law or (b) so undermine the security of individual rights vis-a-vis personal safety or private property as to violate public policy.

To meet the first requirement, the waiver must clearly and cogently a) demonstrate an intent to relieve that person from fault and b) describe the nature and extent of damages from which the party seeks to be relieved. The second requirement, equality of bargaining power, is determined a) by assessing the importance of the subject matter to the physical or economic well being of the party signing the waiver and b) by assessing the amount of free choice the signer could have exercised when seeking alternate services. The third requirement regarding public policy depends upon whether the waiver a) injures public morals, public health or confidence in the administration of the law or b) destroys the security of individuals' rights to personal safety or private property (*Manning v. Brannon*, 1997; *Burd v. KL Shangri-la Owners*, 2002; *Schmidt v. United States of America*, 1996).

An Oklahoma statute **15 O.S. 1991 @ 212.1** provides that

> Any notice given by a business entity which provides services or facilities for profit to the general public and which seeks to exempt the business entity from liability for personal injury caused by or resulting from any act of negligence on its part or on the part of its servants or employees, shall be deemed void as against public policy and wholly unenforceable....

This statute, however, has been interpreted to apply only to unilateral un-bargained-for disclaimers (such as on signs) and not to plain and unambiguous written contracts that are understood, signed, and accepted by the participant party (*Manning v. Brannon*, 1997).

Manufacturers may not contract to limit their **strict liability** for injuries resulting from defective products (*Trumbower v. Sports Car Club of America, Inc.*, 1976).

"Negligence." Waivers granted relief from negligence by use of broad or general terms, indicating that the use of the word "negligence" is not necessary.

Gross Negligence. Oklahoma statute 15 O.S. 1991 @ 212 prohibits enforcement of waivers seeking to avoid liability for willful injury. The Supreme Court deemed waivers for fraud, willful injury, or gross negligence to be unenforceable (*Schmidt v. United States of America*, 1996).

Parental Waivers. An Oklahoma federal court (predicting how the Oklahoma Supreme Court would rule) held that a parental waiver is not enforceable because of the duty to protect minor children (*Wethington v. Swainson*, 2015).

Oregon
FAIR

Although the Oregon Supreme Court has not said that waivers cannot be enforced, it has instituted significant obstacles to the enforcement of waivers. The Oregon court seems to be adapting some of the reasoning of the Connecticut and Wisconsin courts – in effect, resulting in very strict standards for the enforcement of waivers.

In a recent case (*Bagley v. Mt. Bachelor, Inc.*, 2014), the Oregon Supreme Court addressed the enforceability of "anticipatory releases" (waivers) in Oregon. The case involved a snowboarder who was injured at the resort. While both the trial court and the appellate courts found for the defendant, ruling the waiver to be enforceable, the Oregon Supreme Court decided to revisit the issue of the validity of waivers. The court stated that contract rights should not be set aside lightly; that the right to contract is part of the liberty of citizenship. Nevertheless, the court pointed out that contract rights are not absolute and must compete with the right of the public to regulate those rights in the public interest.

The court instructed that to determine if a contract is illegal, a court must determine 1) if it is against public policy and 2) whether it is unconscionable. After analysis of decisions by courts in other states, the court listed several relevant **procedural factors** as well as several relevant **substantive factors** for determining whether enforcement of a waiver would violate **public policy** or be **unconscionable**[73].

Public Policy (Unconscionability). The *Bagley* court differentiated between the concepts of procedural unconscionability and substantive unconscionability. **Procedural** refers to contract formation, focusing on oppression and surprise; **substantive** refer to the terms of the contract, focusing on whether the substantive terms contravene the public interest or public policy.

The court then named five relevant procedural factors to be considered in determining if a waiver would violate public policy or be unconscionable:

- whether the waiver was conspicuous;
- whether the waiver was unambiguous;
- whether there was a substantial disparity in the parties' bargaining power;
- whether the contract was offered on a take-it-or-leave-it basis; and
- whether the contract involved a consumer transaction.

---

[73] In its discussion, the court stated that public policy and unconscionability generally overlap.

The court continued by listing three relevant substantive factors to be considered in determining if a waiver would violate public policy or be unconscionable:

- whether enforcement of the waiver would cause a harsh or inequitable result to befall the releasing party;
- whether the releasee serves an important public interest or function; and
- whether the waiver purported to disclaim liability for more serious misconduct than ordinary negligence

The Court noted that nothing in their previous decisions suggests that any single factor takes precedence over the others or that the listed factors are exclusive. Rather, they indicate that a determination whether enforcement of an anticipatory release would violate public policy or be unconscionable must be based on the **totality of the circumstances of a particular transaction**. The analysis in that regard is guided, but not limited, by the factors that this court previously has identified; it is also informed by any other considerations that may be relevant, including societal expectations.

This list of criteria (or considerations) adds to the criteria used by previous Oregon courts for determining the enforceability of a waiver. Previous criteria have included: 1) no violation of public policy, 2) not adhesionary (where one party has an advantage in bargaining power, applicable only for essential services), 3) conspicuous, 4) called to other party's attention, 5) clear and unambiguous, and 6) the limitation of liability was bargained for (but this was never enforced).

The new criteria will have a significant effect on the validity of liability waivers.

- The criteria presume a commercial enterprise and a consumer have unequal bargaining power.
- Depending upon the interpretation, requiring negotiation for legality could abolish all waivers.
- The criteria seem to hinder waivers involving consumers.
- The criteria may prohibit any waiver that results in a harsh or inequitable ruling.
- The criteria broadens the concept of services of public interest from those such as public transportation, hospitals, and hotels, to include private recreation businesses such a ski resorts, golf courses, and health clubs.

Granted, the court does not seem to require all of the criteria to be met; however, this offers little comfort to the business owner. Uncertainty would seem to be the order of the day. "The totality of the circumstances" leaves the business owner in a precarious position and could lead to inconsistent rulings among the lower courts. This could well be the first step in the abolishing of waivers in Oregon.

In light of these Supreme Court decisions, the status of waivers is unclear. The following describes the status prior to the ruling, including statutes affecting waivers. The authors do not know how much of this case law still applies.

An agreement limiting liability is governed by the principles of contract law and will be enforced in the absence of some consideration of public policy (*Farina v. Mt. Bachelor, Inc.*, 1995) derived from 1) the nature of the subject of the agreement or 2) a determination that the contract was adhesionary (*Mann v. Wetter*, 1990). Such agreements are enforceable only if three circumstances exist: 1) the limitation of liability was bargained for, 2) the provision was called to the other party's attention, and 3) the provision is conspicuous (*Landren v. Hood River Sports Club, Inc.*, 2001).

Oregon courts have said that waivers to exempt one from liability for negligence are not favored in the state, but they are not automatically void. A waiver is governed by the principles of contract law and will be enforced if there is 1) no violation of public policy and 2) if the waiver is not adhesionary (where one party has an advantage in bargaining power). Contracts are not void as adhesionary if the plaintiff voluntarily participated in the activity and if no essential services are involved (*Silva v. Mt. Bachelor, Inc.*, 2008). Courts have also held there is nothing inherently bad about a contract provision that exempts one of the parties from liability. The parties are free to contract as they please, so long as they do not contravene the public interest.

Courts have ruled that waivers relating to sport activities (e.g., skiing, scuba diving, auto racing) are not against public policy. Since sport businesses do not provide an essential public service, any economic advantage in bargaining that a business may have over customers will not create unequal bargaining power since customers have a multitude of alternatives. A court upheld a waiver and ruled that a business had no advantage in bargaining power even though they required the waiver to be signed after the client had paid for the program since he still remained free to not continue the diving program (*Mann v. Wetter*, 1990).

It has been acknowledged that waivers between employee and employer are against public policy; however, one court decided that since the employee was only part time and this employment was not the source of his livelihood, there was no economic coercion on the part of the employer (*Finch v. Andrews*, 1993). A waiver between the employer and a full-time employee would probably be ruled unenforceable.

To be enforced, waivers must be clear and unequivocally expressed. If a waiver is ambiguous, it will be construed against the relying party. Further, the waiver must be conspicuous (*Landren v. Hood River Sports Club, Inc.*, 2001). In *Landren*, the exculpatory language was ruled inconspicuous because it was found in the middle of a paragraph on the back page of a five-page handout. The paragraph title "Liability of the Club and the Members" was in the same typeface and size as the other information within the handout.

The U.S. Court of Appeals for the Ninth Circuit ruled that a waiver referring to "negligence" was not enforceable because the term encompassed gross negligence as well as ordinary negligence. Since exculpating for gross negligence is against public policy, the court ruled the waiver to be invalid (*Farina v. Mt. Bachelor, Inc.*, 1995). In sharp contrast, the Oregon Court of Appeals, in a very similar case, disagreed with the reasoning of the U.S. court and ruled that the use of the word "negligence" was not violative of public policy in the instant case (*Harmon v. Mt. Hood Meadows, Ltd.*, 1997).

Indemnification Agreement. Oregon courts have stated that contracts of indemnity will "not be construed to cover losses to the indemnitee caused by indemnitee negligence unless such intention is expressed in clear and unequivocal terms" (*Harwood v. Planning Committee for the Senior Class of Junction City High School 1997*, 2000).

"Negligence." While Oregon does not require the use of the term "negligence" (*Steele v. Mt. Hood Meadows Oregon, LTD.*, 1999), in light of the preceding cases, it seems advisable that providers should make certain that their waivers specify that the waiver applies to claims based upon "ordinary negligence of the provider."

Gross Negligence. Waivers seeking to protect a provider from liability for gross negligence or willful and wanton acts are invalid (*Farina v. Mt. Bachelor, Inc.*, 1995).

Parental Waivers. Parental waivers are ineffective in Oregon because they may be disaffirmed by the minor (and for a reasonable time after reaching majority) (*Bagley v. Mt. Bachelor, Inc.*, 2013).

Pennsylvania
GOOD

Releases are generally held in disfavor and must be strictly construed against the relying party, however, waivers are enforceable if 1) not against public policy, 2) relates to private affairs, 3) parties have equal bargaining power, and 4) they spell out the intent with particularity (*Wang v. Whitetail Mountain Resort*, 2007).

Public Policy. In general, a waiver is valid if 1) it does not contravene any policy of the law (not of public or state interest), 2) the contract is between persons and relates to their private affairs and does not affect the rights of the public, and 3) each party is a free bargaining agent (contract is not adhesionary where one is powerless to alter and there is no alternative other than the rejection of the transaction)

(*Princeton Sportswear Corporation v. H & M Associates,* 1986). Waivers violate public policy only when they involve a matter of interest to the public or the state. Such matters of interest to the public or state include employer-employee relations, public service, public utilities, common carriers, and hospitals (*Scott v. Altoona Bicycle Club,* 2010). Further, avoidance of contract terms based on public policy grounds requires the presence of an overriding public policy – not a vague goal (cited in *Tayar v. Camelback Ski Corporation, Inc.,* 2012). According to the Supreme Court (*Chepkevich v. Hidden Valley Resort, L.P.,* 2010) the clear policy of the Commonwealth is to encourage skiing and place the risks of the sport clearly on the participant.

Even if a waiver is determined to be valid, "it will still be unenforceable unless the language of the parties is clear that a person is being relieved of liability for his own acts of negligence" (*Vinikoor v. Pedal Pennsylvania, Inc.,* 2009). The Supreme Court in *Chepkevich* stated that the intent of the parties must be spelled out with "particularity." It went on to explain that the releasing party must have been aware of and understood the terms of the release before his agreement can be deemed a *particularized* expression of intent. It gave three criteria for determining if the releasing party had such awareness: 1) the placement of the release in the document, 2) the size of the print, and 3) whether the release is highlighted in some fashion.

The *Mandell v. Ski Shawnee, Inc.* (2007) court listed four standards to be used in determining the enforceability of a valid waiver (*Mandell v. Ski Shawnee, Inc.,* 2007). They are 1) the contract language must be strictly construed, 2) the contract must state the intention of the parties with the greatest particularity, 3) the language must be construed against the party seeking immunity in cases of ambiguity, and 4) the burden of establishing the immunity is upon the party invoking protection from the waiver. In spite of these requirements, the *Wilson v. American Honda Motor Co.* (1988) court found a preprinted rental agreement to be clear and sufficiently detailed. The agreement read: "The rental agent is not responsible for accidents or injuries caused directly or indirectly in the use of the rented item."

Pennsylvania courts have enforced contracts of adhesion saying each party is free to participate or not to participate – that there is no compulsion, economic or otherwise (*Wilson*); *Valeo v. Pocono International Raceway, Inc.,* 1985). One participating in a recreational activity cannot claim an unfair bargaining position since the activity does not involve a necessity of life and there are generally other sources of the service (*Chepkevich*).

In *Lister v. Fitness International, LLC* (2014), Lister signed a waiver within a membership agreement and was subsequently attacked by four non-members. He claimed the waiver was ambiguous because it did not specifically apply to intentional injuries by club guests or to club negligence in failing to prevent those intentional acts. The court enforced the waiver pointing out that in the waiver plaintiff had agreed that use of the facilities involved risk of injury and that he had assumed full responsibility for such risk.

Unsigned ticket disclaimers. Ticket disclaimers are enforced in Pennsylvania only if the disclaimer language is clearly exculpatory and it is clear that the participant was made aware of the agreement on the ticket. The state follows the lead of Restatement 2nd of Torts in section 496B which presents two qualifications for the enforcement of unsigned disclaimers.

> In order for an express agreement assuming the risk to be effective, it must appear that the plaintiff **has given his assent** to the terms of the agreement. Particularly where the agreement is drawn by the defendant and the plaintiff's conduct with respect to it is merely that of a recipient, it must appear that **the terms were in fact brought home to him** and understood by him, before it can be found that he has accepted them.

In *Checket v. Tuthill Corporation* (2001), the court said the lift ticket was not enforceable because the lift ticket failed to 1) give advance warning that the ticket contains an exculpatory clause (e.g., a sign or verbal warning at the ticket sales counter), 2) make the disclaimer conspicuous on the ticket, and 3) properly word the disclaimer so that it clearly detailed the intent of the parties. The *Beck-Hummel* court (*Beck-Hummel v. Ski Shawnee, Inc.*) in 2006 failed to enforce a lift ticket disclaimer because the language on the ticket was not sufficiently conspicuous. The font size was so small as to be barely readable and there were no further warnings by the ski facility to put the purchaser on notice of its contents. In *Tayar v. Camelback Ski Corporation* (2008), the court did not enforce the disclaimer, noting that the lift ticket was not attached to a signed waiver, the disclaimer was in small print, and there was no evidence the plaintiff was verbally informed.

In contrast, the court in *Savarese v. Camelback Ski Corp.* (2005) stated that the clear language on the lift ticket in conjunction with the sign above the ticket window made the lift ticket a valid exculpatory agreement. The court stated that the language of the sign informed the purchaser that the purchaser was releasing the resort from liability and that by purchasing the ticket, the purchaser agreed to be bound by the disclaimer on the lift ticket. Similarly, the court in *Duffy v. Camelback Ski Corporation* (1992) enforced a forum selection clause on a lift ticket even though the type was small. The court noted two factors indicated that the plaintiff was given notice. They were 1) signs at the ticket window saying "Please Read" followed by "Acceptance of this ticket constitutes a contract" and 2) the exculpatory language on the lift ticket.

Courts do not apply these same standards to disclaimers on baseball tickets. It has long been settled that the disclaimer on a baseball ticket is sufficient to protect the club from liability for spectator injury. The court in *Romeo v. Pittsburg Associates* (2001) stated that the ticket clearly disclaimed any liability for injuries sustained from foul balls.

Commercial Transactions. The legislature has adopted a public policy regarding disclaimers of liability in commercial transactions by enacting the Uniform Commercial Code (specifically RCW 62 A. 2-316[2] and RCW 62 A. 2-179[1],[3]) which set restrictions on disclaimers and require that they be clear and conspicuous.

Whether waivers can protect providers against claims of **strict liability** relating to the sale or rental of products seems to depend upon the product. Courts (*Keystone Aeronautics Corp. v. R.J.Enstrom Corp.*, affirmed in part by *Keystone*, 499 F.2d at 148-49) have applied section 492A of the Restatement (Second) of Torts (1965) which provides

> The consumer's cause of action doesn't depend upon the validity of his contract … and it is not affected by any disclaimer or other agreement.…

One court commented that if disclaimers on the labels of products or on sales contracts were effective, then sellers would utilize such devices to nullify their responsibility (*Weiner v. Mt. Airy Lodge, Inc.*, 1989). Examining the issue in two ski bindings cases, one court (*Galisson v. Shawnee Mountain Ski Area*, 1996) determined that assumption of risk was preserved in the ski statute (42 Pa. C.S. sec. 7102) and that the phrase "as is" was a sufficiently conspicuous disclaimer to negate any implied warranties – thus allowing a waiver to overcome the statute. The other (*Jankowski v. Ski Roundtop, Inc.*, 1986) relied on the Keystone ruling and did not enforce the waiver of strict liability. The *Simeone v. Bombardier-Rotax* court (2005) stated that Pennsylvania law permits waivers between businesses of equal bargaining power, but that a form release cannot shield a defendant business from liability when a consumer is injured by a defective product.

Wrongful death claims by surviving spouses are purely derivative of the claim of the deceased party (*Brbac v. Reading Fair Co.*, 1982). In contrast, **consortium claims** are independent causes of action. However, a recent case revealed that Pennsylvania only recognizes consortium claims between spouses when the court did not allow a claim involving the injury of a child (*Chang v. Camelback Ski Slope*, 1999).

"Negligence." While some appellate courts have held that the word "negligence" must be included in the language of the waiver (*Brown v. Racquetball Centers, Inc.*, 1987), the Supreme Court (*Chepkevich*) in its reasoning appears to agree with courts that hold an exculpatory agreement can bar a negligence suit, even without the word "negligence" (*Nissley v. Candytown Motorcycle Club, Inc*, 2006; *Schillachi v. Flying Dutchman Motorcycle Club*, 1990; *Zimmer v. Mitchell and Ness*, 1978). All courts have agreed that the agreement must spell out with greatest particularity and show an unequivocally expressed intent to release a party from liability for its own negligence.

In light of the conflicting opinions by Pennsylvania courts, the safest approach would be to always include the specific mention of the "negligence" or "negligence of the provider" in any waiver to be used in that state.

Gross Negligence. Whether waivers protecting against gross negligence are enforceable is unclear; the Pennsylvania Supreme Court in 1984 declared there are no **degrees of negligence** in Pennsylvania (cited in *Scott v. Altoona Bicycle Club*, 2010). The *Scott* court held that by executing the waivers which included "negligence," plaintiff waived all claims against the club including those for recklessness and gross negligence. This indicates that when a waiver specifically mentions "negligence," gross negligence and recklessness, by implication, are included. This position was supported in *Valeo v. Pocono International Raceway* (1985) which said the language of the exculpatory clause, "...from all liability ... whether caused by the negligence of the releases or otherwise" was broad enough to exclude liability for all degrees of negligence. The Nicholson court held that waivers protect against liability for gross negligence (*Nicholson v. Mount Airy Lodge, Inc.,* 1997). In contrast, however, the Pennsylvania Supreme Court ruled in 1854 that waivers to release grossly negligent conduct are unenforceable (*Pennsylvania R.R. Co. V. McCloskey's Adm'rs*, 1854). More recently, other Pennsylvania courts have failed to enforce waivers when gross negligence or recklessness was alleged (*Galisson v. Shawnee Mountain Ski Area,* 1996; *Mandell v. Ski Shawnee,* 2007).

A ruling by the Pennsylvania Supreme Court has recently made it clear that waivers do not protect against liability for reckless conduct (*Tayar,* 2012). The court considered 1) the fact that other states are almost unanimous in prohibiting the enforcement of waivers for reckless conduct and 2) that enforcement would jeopardize the health, safety, and welfare of participants by removing any incentive for providers to adhere to minimal standards of safe conduct. The court ruled that enforcing waivers for reckless behavior violates a dominant public policy of the Commonwealth.

Parental Waivers. Only for contracts of necessity can a minor enter into a valid contract. A waiver signed by a minor is voidable and will not be upheld if challenged in court. Statute **23 Pa.C.S. 5101(a)** provides "Any individual 18 years of age or older shall have the right to enter into binding and legally enforceable contracts and the defense of minority shall not be available to such individuals." In addition, parents do not possess the authority to release the claims or potential claims of a minor child merely because of the parental relationship (*Apicella v. Valley Forge Military Academy*, 1985). To void such contracts signed by a parent on behalf of a minor, the minor must disaffirm it within a reasonable time after reaching majority (*State Farm v. Skivington,* 1996). The act of filing suit is an obvious act of disaffirmation.

In Pennsylvania, an injury to a minor gives rise to two separate causes of action – that of the minor (for pain and suffering and for the losses after minority) and that of the parent (for medical expenses and the loss of the minor's services during minority). A waiver signed by the parent on behalf of a minor will bar the parent's cause of action, but has no effect on the minor's claim (*Simmons v. Parkette Nat. Gymnastic Training Center,* 1987; *Mavreshkof v. Resorts USA, Inc.*, 2008).

In a cruise ship case, a minor was held to the forum selection clause within the passenger ticket contract. The court (*Morrow v. Norwegian Cruise Line Limited,* 2002) quoted *Leviathan v. United States* (1934), holding "[a] minor is not relieved from compliance with the lawful terms of a passage contract."

Puerto Rico[74]
GOOD

Waivers are definitely enforceable in Puerto Rico; however the courts examine them carefully for clarity and intent.

While waivers are enforceable in Puerto Rico, their enforcement is not favored. Such contracts are closely examined because they insulate one contractor from liability for future damage to the other contractor; they must be strictly interpreted against the party who relies on them to escape responsibility and, when possible, their interpretation must be contrary to the exemption from liability.

The law requires that for a waiver to be valid, 1) the signer must have had informed consent, 2) the clause must be consistent with public policy, and 3) the clause must not be an invalid adhesion contract (*Olivelli v. Sappo Corporation*, 2002). The task of the court is to determine whether the waiver is clear, conclusive, and unequivocal. Puerto Rico waiver law and federal common waiver law hold to the same basic principles: 1) whether the intent of the parties is clear and 2) whether the waiver is contrary to the law, public interest, and the public order. In other words, the court must determine if a waiver is clear, conclusive, and unequivocal (*Sylva v. Culebra Dive Shop*, 2005).

An important factor in determining the validity of a disclaimer clause is the **bargaining power** held by each of the contractors. When contractors are not equal, when one is unable to negotiate, and when one party is obliged to accept the relief from liability for negligence of the other party, the relief must be considered null.

Although the Puerto Rico Civil Code provides for freedom of contract, it also states that the contract must not be contrary to law, morals or public order (**Article 1207 of the Civil Code, 31 LPRA Section 3372**). Section 4 of the code provides the general principle of law that the right to contract is relinquished if the waiver is contrary to law, against the public interest or public order, or is detrimental to third parties. The Civil Code provides that the waiver must be clear, strict, and unambiguous. This requirement is stronger when the agreement exonerates a person for their future negligent acts.

Adhesion contracts are those in which the conditions set forth therein, are the work of one of the parties, so that the other party does not play any role in the formation of any contract. An adhesion contract is not considered invalid merely because it written by one of the parties. The primary function of a court in interpreting such contracts is to determine if the clause is ambiguous. If there is no ambiguity, the contract shall be construed according to its terms. The court must then assess the reasonableness of the agreement. The Puerto Rico Supreme Court has consistently recognized that while **adhesion contracts are allowed** in this jurisdiction, the interpretation of its provisions will be favorable to the party that did not write the contract.

"Negligence." The language exonerating one from liability for negligent acts must either make explicit reference to the negligence of the relying service provider or indicate such an intention in unequivocal terms. In *Lugo v. Health Club of America* (2013), the court pointed out that the waiver did not specify in sufficient detail that the waiver applied to negligent actions as no mention was made of negligence. The court found the waiver ambiguous and unenforceable; it reversed the summary judgment ruling and returned the case to Superior Court.

---

[74] Most of this section was drawn from *Lugo v. Health Club of America*, 2013 PR App LEXIS 1159. This case was reported in Spanish and I have relied on Google Translate in reading and interpreting it. The English translation is awkward and unclear in places—especially as it relates to the law.

Rhode Island
FAIR

While no definitive rulings on waivers relating to recreation or sport participants have been found, the Supreme Court has consistently upheld exculpatory clauses when the intent of the parties is clear and unambiguous. Such agreements are to be strictly construed against the party seeking exoneration (*Brown v. Wakefield Fitness Center, Inc.*, 1994).

Public Policy. The Supreme Court has upheld waiver and indemnity clauses that negate liability for an individual's own negligence if the clause is sufficiently specific (*Rhode Island Hospital Trust National Bank v. Dudley Service Corporation*, 1992). The agreement will not be construed to indemnify the indemnitee against losses resulting from his or her own negligent acts unless the parties' intention to hold harmless is clearly and unequivocally expressed in the contract. Contracting to relieve oneself of liability for one's own negligence is not against public policy.

Waivers must not be unconscionable, must involve parties of equal bargaining position, and not violate public policy. Such waivers are enforceable as written.

Claims by **non-signing parties** (e.g., spouses) are derivative and cannot succeed when the underlying claim fails (*Brown v. Wakefield Fitness Center, Inc.*, 1994).

In a non-sport case involving property loss at a rental storage unit, the waiver stated that the operator shall not be liable for loss or damage whether or not the loss or damage resulted from operator negligence (*Rhode Island Hospital Trust National Bank v. Dudley service Corporation*, 1992).

Parental Waivers. Based on a non-sport post-injury release case (*Julian v. Zayre Corporation*, 1978), it seems unlikely that a pre-injury waiver would be enforced.

South Carolina
GOOD

Although waivers are not favored by law and are to be strictly construed, waivers enabling sporting events and activities are in the public interest and are enforceable.

Public Policy. The South Carolina Supreme Court has held that it is in the public interest to enforce waiver agreements between event organizers and participants. It recognizes the freedom of private parties to contract as they choose; if waivers were not upheld, liability would increase and no one would be willing to sponsor sporting events (*Huckaby v. Confederate Motor Speedway, Inc.*, 1981). Statements that are overly broad will not be enforced because they are against public policy (*Fisher v. Stevens*, 2003). In *Murray v. Texas Co.* (1934) the Supreme Court addressed an indemnity provision with the wording "The agent shall ... exonerate the company and hold it harmless from all claims, suits, and liabilities of every character whatsoever and howsoever arising from the existence or use of the equipment...." The court deemed the language overbroad and unenforceable.

Notwithstanding the general acceptance of waivers, exculpatory contracts are not favored because they induce less care for the safety of patrons and are to be strictly construed against the relying party. The Supreme Court in *Huckaby v. Confederate Motor Speedway, Inc.* (1981) upheld the waiver, stating that people should be free to contract as they choose. The *Huckaby* court ruled that a voluntary waiver signed by a driver would protect the speedway from negligence claims. That court also stated that summary judgment should be granted where parties engaging in voluntary recreational activities of a hazardous nature execute a release.

"Common sense and good faith are the leading touchstones of the construction of a contract and contracts are to be so construed as to avoid an absurd result"(*Fisher v. Stevens*, 2003, p.7). In stressing the fundamental right to contract, one court stated "where a party seeks to assert an exculpatory clause and the language is unambiguous, courts should not 'override the fundamental right of freedom of contract'" (*Johnson v. Paraplane Corporation*, 1995, p.12). Consistent construction that would make the contract reasonable, fair, and just should prevail. The *Fisher* court quoted another court saying "An exculpatory agreement will be held to contravene public policy if it is so broad 'that it would absolve [the defendant] from any injury to the [plaintiff] for any reason.'"

"Negligence." The court in a paintball injury case cited a previous ruling stating that a waiver will not be enforced "in the absence of **explicit language** clearly indicating that such was the intent of the parties" (*McCune v. Myrtle Beach Indoor Shooting Range, Inc.*, 2005, p.7-8).

South Dakota
GOOD

Courts have held that recreational waivers are in the public interest and enforceable because they enable providers to offer sporting events that involve a substantial risk (*Holzer v. Dakota Speedway, Inc.*, 2000).

Public Policy. A waiver is not void as a matter of public policy. Waivers involving purely voluntary activity by the signer of the waiver and involving no relationship or activity affected by public interest are not contrary to public policy. Further, recreational waivers such as those used in automobile racing have been ruled to not violate public policy. Courts have held that waivers are in the public interest because, by providing some protection for the provider, they allow providers to offer sporting events that involve substantial risks (*Holzer v. Dakota Speedway, Inc.*, 2000). South Dakota courts follow the *Tunkl v. Regents of University of California* (1963) guidelines in determining if public interest exists (*Johnson v. Rapid City Softball Association*, 1994).

In a concurring opinion in the *Johnson* case, one judge felt that allowing waivers to free cities of liability for negligent maintenance of public athletic fields is questionable public policy. He likened the situation to the *Wagenblast* ruling in Washington (*Johnson v. Rapid City Softball Association*, 1994). This would indicate that cities and other public agencies providing recreational facilities to large numbers of participants should use caution in relying upon waivers.

Waivers are commonly used in the auto racing industry and absent "... a legislative directive, these releases have withstood attacks that they are contrary to public policy." Such releases are against public policy in only three instances: 1) Waivers attempting to protect against willful negligence or intentional torts are not valid and are against public policy. Willful and wanton misconduct was defined as "something more than ordinary negligence, but less than deliberate or intentional conduct." 2) Waivers violate public policy when they involve a matter of interest to the public at large or the state. However, to be of public interest in sport, recreation, or fitness activities would typically require a facility to be involved in providing an essential public service – which would rarely be the case. Waivers related to auto racing have very little, if any, negative impact on the general population since they deal with a fairly narrow segment of the public participating in a relatively dangerous sporting activity. 3) Waivers that are required of employees by employers may be contrary to public policy when the livelihood of the employee is at issue. Activities of public interest include employer-employee relationships, public service, public utilities, common carriers, and hospitals (*Holzer v. Dakota Speedway, Inc.*, 2000; *Lee v. Beauchene*, 1983).

To be valid, a waiver must be knowingly and voluntarily made. However, one who accepts a contract is conclusively presumed to know its contents and to assent to them in the absence of fraud, misrepresentation or other wrongful acts by another contracting party. When the issue is whether the signer was allowed time to read or was rushed in signing, the court has ruled that the waiver is enforceable unless there is evidence that the signer was denied opportunity to get out of line and read the document. Waivers involving fraud or misrepresentation would not be enforceable. Examples of such offenses are covering or folding the sheets so the waiver language is not visible above the signature space, telling the signer that the signature is for another purpose, or hiding the waiver language inconspicuously within the document. An unambiguous waiver signed, but not understood by the signer, is enforceable. Failure to comprehend the importance or meaning of the waiver is not a deterrent to enforceability. It is the duty of the signer to procure someone to explain the waiver before signing it (*Holzer v. Dakota Speedway, Inc.*, 2000).

Waivers, when used with recreational activities, are more likely to be valid and enforceable when the activity is more inherently dangerous and when they comprise a separate document rather than a part of another contract (*Holzer v. Dakota Speedway, Inc.*, 2000).

Waivers are governed by contract law. The essential elements of contracts are: 1) capacity to contract, 2) consent, 3) a lawful object, and 4) sufficient consideration (*Johnson v. Rapid City Softball Association*, 1994).

Gross Negligence. A waiver attempting to protect against liability for gross negligence, willful negligence, or intentional torts is against public policy and is unenforceable (*Holzer v. Dakota Speedway, Inc.*, 2000).

Tennessee
GOOD

Tennessee courts enforce waivers that allow one to contract away liability for one's own negligence and do not generally strictly construe exculpatory contracts against the relying party. The public policy of the state favors freedom to contract.

Public Policy. Tennessee courts have long recognized that parties may contract away their liability for negligence (*Tompkins v. Helton*, 2003). Waivers are valid in Tennessee so long as they do not extend to willful or gross negligence and do not otherwise offend the public policy of the state (*Farris v. KTM North America, Inc.*, 2006). The public policy of Tennessee favors freedom to contract against liability for negligence, except when a professional person operating in an area of public interest attempts to contract away liability for negligence. Tennessee courts follow the *Tunkl* guidelines (see the discussion in Chapter 2) in determining if public interest exists (*Floyd v. Club Systems of Tennessee, Inc.*, 1999).

It is well settled in Tennessee that a party may contract to relieve oneself of liability for negligence. An exception to this rule, however, is that a common carrier may not contract away its liability (*Moss v. Fortune*, 1960). Further, a contract is ambiguous only when it is of uncertain meaning and may fairly be understood in more ways than one. A strained construction may not be placed on the language used to find ambiguity where none exists (*Empress Health and Beauty Spa, Inc. v. Turner*, 1973).

Generally, the courts have been very lenient as to the wording of waivers. For instance, in one case, the statement "I am hiring your horse to ride today and all future rides at my own risk" was upheld by the Supreme Court (*Moss v. Fortune*, 1960). Waivers are not enforceable if the duty is a public one or in order to avoid the dictates of a statute (*Teles v. Big Rock Stables*, 2006). In the *Teles* case, the waiver protected the stables from liability for ordinary negligence, but did not release the statutory liability (Tennessee Equine Activity Statute 44-20) for injuries resulting from faulty tack.

Courts in Tennessee, unlike those in most other states, do not generally strictly construe exculpatory contracts against the relying party. Tennessee has been very consistent in upholding and enforcing exculpatory agreements in cases involving sports injuries. A 2005 court asserted that commercial white water legislation recognizes that the state has a legitimate interest in maintaining the economic viability of such operations (*Henderson v. Quest Expeditions, Inc.*).

"The cardinal rule in the construction of contracts is to ascertain the intention of the parties. If the contract is plain and unambiguous, the meaning thereof is a question of law, and it is the Court's function to interpret the contract as written according to its plain terms. In such a case, the Court must interpret the contract as written rather than according to the unexpressed intention of one of the parties. Courts cannot make contracts for parties but can only enforce the contract that the parties themselves have made. The primary objective in the construction of a contract is to discover the intention of the parties from a consideration of the whole contract" (*Tompkins v. Helton*, 2003, p.7).

Tenn. Code Ann. 47-18-305 provides requirements for valid health club agreements. It states that all agreements shall be in writing, be signed by the buyer, designate the date of signing, and contain (in boldface type of at least ten points, near the signature space) a specified right to cancel. Failure to meet these requirements rendered a waiver unenforceable (*Dunlap v. Fortress Corporation*, 2000).

An **adhesion contract** is one that is a standardized contract form offered on a "take it or leave it" basis. Its enforceability generally depends on whether the terms are beyond the expectations of an ordinary person or are oppressive or unconscionable (*Tompkins v. Helton*, 2003).

The Tennessee **wrongful death** statute provides that any cause of action of the deceased is preserved for the surviving party, but that the cause of action is dependent upon the right of the deceased (*Rogers v. Donaldson-Hermitage Chamber of Commerce*, 1990).

"Negligence." The Supreme Court deemed a waiver not containing the word "negligence" valid and enforceable.

"Gross Negligence. Waivers will not protect one from liability for gross negligence, reckless conduct, or willful negligence (*Adams v. Roark*, 1985). When gross negligence is alleged, the plaintiff must show that the defendant was negligent and acted with utter unconcern for the safety of others or acted with reckless disregard for the rights of others (*Thrasher v. Riverbend Stables, LLC*, 2009).

In a nursing home case (*McGregor v. Christian Care Center of Springfield, LLC*, 2010), the court did not enforce an **arbitration** agreement because it was deemed to be unconscionable.

Parental Waivers. A parent can sign a waiver to release their own claim in the event of an injury to an infant or incompetent, but cannot sign away the rights of the other parent or of the infant or incompetent. Additionally, a guardian may not sign away the rights of an infant or incompetent. Furthermore, an **indemnification agreement** signed by the parent or guardian so that an infant or incompetent can participate in an activity is not valid or enforceable (*Childress v. Madison County*, 1989).

Texas
GOOD

In Texas, waivers are valid and enforceable if they meet the requirements of fair notice which relate to the express negligence doctrine and conspicuousness of the waiver. A waiver operates to extinguish a cause of action as would a prior judgment between the parties and is an absolute bar to the released matter (*Dresser Indus., Inc. v. Page Petroleum, Inc.*, 1993). Further, sport-related waivers are not generally against public policy, but must be construed strictly.

Public Policy. Sport-related releases are not against public policy in Texas. A waiver must be narrowly construed, but is valid unless it is contrary to public policy. Enforcing a waiver resulting from a disadvantage in bargaining power such that the signer is practically forced to submit is against public policy (*Grewal v. Hickenbottom*, 2003).

In Texas, waivers are valid and enforceable if they meet the **fair notice requirement** (*Littlefield v. Schaefer*, 1997). The two fair notice requirements are: 1) the conspicuousness requirement and 2) the express negligence doctrine.

The **conspicuousness requirement** mandates that there must be

(1) a heading in capitals equal to or greater in size than the surrounding text, or in contrasting type, font, or color to the surrounding text of the same or lesser size; and

(2) language in the body of a record or display in larger type than the surrounding text, or in contrasting type, font, or color to the surrounding text of the same size, or set off from surrounding text of the same size by symbols or other marks that call attention to the language (*Quintana v. Crossfit Dallas, L.L.C.*, 2011 @9).

In *Littlefield*, the Texas Supreme Court rejected a waiver based on its failure to meet the conspicuousness requirement. The court felt it was not conspicuous because the print size of the heading was in four-point font with 28 characters per inch and the text was in a smaller font with 38 characters per inch.

The **express negligence doctrine** provides that to release a party from liability for its own future negligence, a waiver must express that intent in clear, unambiguous terms within the four corners of the contract. (*Quintana v. Crossfit Dallas LL*, 2011). The purpose of the doctrine is to insure that it is clear that the parties intended to exculpate one party from liability for negligence. It should be noted, however, that the fair notice doctrine is immaterial if the releaser had actual knowledge of the existence of the release provision (*Paz v. Life Time Fitness, Inc.*, 2010). One court noted that the express negligence requirement does not mandate that a waiver or indemnity clause be the best possible statement of the parties' intentions, "only that it specifically define the parties' intent" (*Rackley v. Advanced Cycling Concepts, Inc.*, 2009).

In *Jaeger v. Hartley* (2013), the waiver failed to refer to the negligence of the provider and described the risks only as "fully assume the risks involved" and "certain risks and dangers associated with the various activities, use of the facilities, and the wilderness environment...." The incident occurred when the driver of their vehicle attempted to ascend a steep slope with a jeep that had defective brakes. There was no evidence the group was warned of the risk of traversing such terrain in such a vehicle. The waiver failed to protect against negligence (because "negligence" was not mentioned in the waiver) or inherent risks (because the inherent risks were inadequately described.)

A contract of adhesion is one offered on a "take-it-or-leave-it" basis with no real opportunity to bargain. Such waivers are generally enforceable unless they are deemed unconscionable. A waiver is not considered unconscionable unless it is so one-sided as to be unreasonable under the circumstances (*Ramirez v. 24 Hour Fitness USA, Inc.*, 2013). No unconsionability exists when there is freedom of choice to contract.

The Texas Supreme Court originally adopted the express negligence doctrine for **indemnification agreements**. It provides that parties seeking to indemnify an indemnitee from the consequences of the indemnitee's own negligence must express that intent in specific terms. This doctrine applied only to indemnification agreements, and not to waivers, until the Supreme Court expanded the scope of the fair notice requirement to include releases (*Whitson v. Goodbodys, Inc.*, 1989; *Page Petroleum, Inc. v. Dresser Industries, Inc.*, 1993).

Loss of Consortium. Both a loss of consortium claim and a wrongful death claim by a non-signing spouse are derivative of the claim of the injured spouse (*Rosen v. National Hot Rod Association*, 1995; *Winkler v. Kirkwood Atrium Office Park*, 1991).

"Negligence." Many courts have held "a clause will not be construed to include an exemption for negligence unless it does so in the clearest terms, as by using the word "negligence," or language so broad and sweeping that it must be taken to have given fair notice that it includes negligence" (*Newman v. Tropical Visions, Inc.*, 1994). The *Quintana* court stated that the wording "any negligent act of [the released party]" may sufficiently meet the express negligence doctrine requirement.

The *Rackley* court of appeals, however, was quite forceful in ruling that reference to the word "negligence" was not required. It stated that the statute provides that the intent to shift the risk of one part's negligence to the other party must be specifically stated. The court pointed out that the clause in *Rackley* states that it applies to "any and all claims;" it ruled that the waiver unambiguously shows intent to release the provider from liability for negligence.

Gross Negligence. Several Texas appellate courts have ruled that pre-accident waivers of gross negligence violate Texas public policy and are not enforceable (*Texas Moto-Plex, Inc. v. Phelps*, 2006). Texas courts treat post-injury releases (as in settlements) differently from pre-injury waivers. One difference is that in order to encourage settlements, the Supreme Court has stated that while pre-accident waivers of gross negligence are against public policy, post-accident releases are not (*Sydlik v. ReeIII, Inc.*, 2006). **Reckless conduct** requires that the defendant engage in conduct he knew or should have known posed a high degee of risk of serious injury, but disregarded that risk (*Jaeger*). Such was the case in the aforementioned *Jaeger* case.

Parental Waivers. In a case in which an adult sister signed an amusement park waiver on behalf of a minor, the court ruled that such waivers, even by the parent, are unenforceable because they lack authority to waive the rights of the child to sue (*Munoz v. II Jaz Inc.*, 1993). Texas has a long-standing policy to protect the interests of its children (*Williams v. Patton*, 1991). Neither the next friend nor the parent of a minor child is authorized to agree to a judgment that "throws away" the child's substantial rights (*Lowery v. Berry*, 1954).

In *Paz v. Life Time Fitness, Inc.* (2010), the U.S. District court, predicting as to how the Texas Supreme Court would rule in a parental waiver case, held that pre-injury parental waivers are not enforceable in Texas.

Utah
GOOD

Waivers protecting providers from liability for their own negligence have long been public policy and have generally been enforced in Utah. In 2007, however, the Utah Supreme Court handed down several rulings that appear to severely limit the effectiveness of waivers in certain circumstances (e.g., waivers and indemnity agreements used by ski resorts; cases in which gross negligence is alleged).

Public Policy. Contracts to reduce the liability of one party are allowed by public policy, but must be unambiguous and will be strictly construed. The contract must be a clear and unequivocal expression of the intent to release the other from liability for future injuries (*Milne v. USA Cycling Inc.*, 2007). The federal court in *Milne* also stated that pre-injury waivers are not unlimited in power and are invalid 1) if they offend public policy, 2) for activities that fit the public interest exception, and 3) if they are unclear or ambiguous. The court noted that the Utah Supreme Court held that pre-injury releases for recreational activities are not invalid as against the public interest.

Earlier, the *Russ* court specified that three types of contractual provisions regarding liability for negligence are enforceable (*Russ v. Woodside Homes, Inc.*, 1995). They are 1) **post-injury releases** (These agreements are generally used in settlements. Interpretation is limited to the four corners of the contract when language is ambiguous.); 2) **indemnity contracts** (In the past, they have been strictly construed, but the Supreme Court in *Russ* relaxed that rule and adopted a more lenient test for enforcement.); and 3) **pre-injury exculpatory clauses** or waivers and hold harmless agreements (These agreements relieve the provider of liability for its own ordinary negligence. Waivers are binding so long as they are clear and unequivocal in expressing the parties' intent to absolve the defendant of liability.) Each of these three is enforceable if the language is clear, unambiguous, and unequivocal. The *Russ* court also stated that legal terminology must be made conspicuous to the average consumer. To assess whether a contract is ambiguous, courts look to the four corners of the agreement to determine the intentions of the parties.

The Utah Supreme Court held that "[f]or a contract to be void on the basis of public policy, there must be a showing free from doubt that the contract is against public policy" (*Penunuri v. Sundance Partners, LTD*, 2013). The court noted that "[t]o pluck a principle of public policy from the text of a statute and to ground a decision of this court on that principle is to invite judicial mischief." It went on to explain that the term "public policy" is a vague and variable quality and is very difficult to define precisely; hence, it cautioned that public policy should be utilized to void contracts only with the utmost circumspection. The court expressed that it voids waivers on the basis of public policy only when 1) the Constitution or the Legislature unequivocally expresses its view that certain contractual provisions are unenforceable as against public policy or 2) there is public policy expressed in common law or suggested by statutory text.

In 1995, the *Russ* court stated that prohibiting a business from seeking to limit its liability is not the public policy of the state. It went on to say that generally, parties not engaged in public service may bargain to relieve themselves of liability for ordinary negligence. However, in 2007 *the Supreme Court ruled that waivers and indemnity agreements intended to protect **ski resorts** are in clear violation of the Legislature's clearly articulated public policy expressed in Utah's Inherent Risks of Skiing Act* (**Utah Code Ann. 78-27-51-54 [2002 and Supp. 2007]**) *and are subsequently unenforceable* (*Rothstein v. Snowbird Corporation*). In contrast, **UCA § 78B-4-201-203 (2)(b)** allows enforcement of both adult and parental equine waivers (*Penunuri v. Sundance Partners*, LTD, 2013).

Gross Negligence. Waivers intending to protect against gross or wanton negligence or willful acts are not enforceable (*Hawkins v. Peart*, 2001). A question has arisen regarding the granting of summary judgment in cases involving gross negligence claims. In 2007, the U.S. District Court for the District of Utah ruled on a gross negligence claim in a bicycling case (*Milne v. USA Cycling, Inc.*). The Court upheld the waiver and granted summary judgment for ordinary negligence. When examining the gross negligence claim, the evidence showed that the defendant took a number of steps to protect competitors and was clearly not grossly negligent. The court granted summary judgment. Later in 2007, the Utah Supreme Court in a suit by a competitive skier refused to award summary judgment in a case alleging gross negligence (defined as the failure to observe even slight care and utter indifference to consequences) even though the facts of the case made it clear that the defendant made substantial efforts to protect participants. The court stated that *summary judgment is appropriate only when there is an applicable standard of care*, fixed by law, and where reasonable minds could reach but one conclusion as to the defendant's negligence. Again in 2008, the Supreme Court ruled against summary judgment in a gross negligence case involving a bobsled ride (*Berry v. Plaintiff v. Greater Park City Company*, 2007). *The reasoning was the same---the lack of a fixed standard of care for the conduct of the activity. Therefore, it seems that for most cases in which gross negligence is an allegation, summary judgment will not be granted and the case will have to go to trial.*

In a 2010 skiing case (*Jozewicz v. GGT Enterprises, LLC*), a federal court refused to enforce a waiver since it would have protected the defendant from liability for an **illegal act**. The bindings had been recalled by the manufacturer for safety reasons. The court held that to insulate a party for such an act is against public policy.

"Negligence." The use of the word "negligence" is not required in waivers or indemnity agreements so long as the intent is clear from examination of the entire document (*Russ v. Woodside Homes, Inc.*, 1995).

Parental Waivers. The Utah Supreme Court has made it abundantly clear that parents (absent court appointment) do not have the authority to sign away the rights of a minor (*Hawkins v. Peart*, 2001). Neither waivers signed by parents on behalf of the minor nor agreements by which parents **indemnify** the provider for loss suffered as result of the participation of the minor are valid. The exception to this is in the case of parental waivers for equine activities (**UCA § 78B-4-201-203 (2)(b).**

Vermont
Good

Waivers are disfavored and are to be construed strictly against the drafter, but are generally not against public policy and are enforceable. The Vermont Supreme Court, however, has declared that ski operator waivers do violate public policy because skiing 1) involves a large number of participants, 2) is open to the general public, and 3) the operator has control of the venue; thereby, a legitimate public interest arises. The court has indicated that waivers for recreational sports such as stock car racing, parachute jumping, scuba diving, and mountaineering are not against public policy because they do not involve large numbers and the operator cannot control the venue in which they occur.

The Vermont Supreme Court (*Dalury v. S-K-I, LTD*, 1995), when ruling on whether a ski resort waiver was against public policy, concluded that the "determination of what constitutes the public interest must be made considering the totality of the circumstances of any given case against the backdrop of current societal expectations." It went on to say "Generally, a private recreational business does not qualify as a service demanding a special duty to the public, nor are its services of a special, highly necessary or essential nature." The court, however, disagreed with this reasoning stating *"We do not accept the proposition that because ski resorts do not provide an essential public service, such agreements do not affect the public interest."* The court discussed factors it felt determined if a recreational sport business involves a legitimate public interest: 1) is the facility is open to the general public; does it allow all skill levels; and is a substantial number of the public involved (in the case of skiing, it was open to the public, open to all skill levels, and involved a thousand or more each day); and 2) is the operator in the best position to assure the safety of visitors (for instance, the ski operator controls and maintains the premises, lifts, and ski slopes).

The court said that in Vermont a business owner has a duty to keep its premises reasonably safe. It went on to say that a business invitee has a right to assume that the premises are reasonably safe; moreover, the operator, not the participants, has the expertise and opportunity to "foresee and control hazards, and to guard against the negligence of their agents and employees. They alone can properly maintain and inspect their premises, and train their employees in risk management." In a subsequent case involving a ski race open to the public (*Spencer v. Killington, LTD*, 1997), the Supreme Court again declared a ski operator waiver to be against public policy – for the same reasons as in *Dalury*. Both *Dalury* and *Spencer* make it clear that whether the race is professional or amateur is not dispositive as to the enforceability of the waiver.

In two ensuing cases, one a motorcycle test drive (*Thompson v. Hi Tech Motor Sports, Inc.*, 2008) and the other a motocross race open to only those interested members of a club with a membership of 300 (*Provoncha v. Vermont Motocross Association*, 2009), the Vermont Supreme Court determined the waivers did not violate public policy. *Thompson* differed from *Dalury* and *Spencer* in the nature of the service (test drive) and the total lack of control the provider has on a motorcycle test drive. Regarding *Provoncha*, the court stated "we have no difficulty in determining that the service provided [motocross racing] by VMA and Driver is neither of great importance to the public nor open to the public at large." The court also listed stock car racing, parachute jumping, scuba diving, and mountaineering as activities of no great public interest and not open to the public at large. In addition, it pointed out that operators in this type of activity have little or no control of the environment in which the activities occur; contrast these with the degree of control possible for activities such as trampoline parks, bowling lanes, health clubs, and golf courses.

In a zip line case (*Littlejohn v. Timberquest Park at Magic , LLC*, 2015), the U.S. District Court for the District of Vermont ruled a waiver against public policy since the business was open to the general public, participants of all skill levels were allowed, and the operator was in the best position to assure the safety of visitors. However, in *Littlejohn*, the number of clients was estimated to be about 1000 a year or about 10 visitors a day during the 100 day season – numbers that seem quite small when compared with the number of skiing participants. This reasoning seems to conflict with the "large segment of the public" utilized by the Supreme Court. The federal court seems to base its decision on the fact that the premises owner (Timberline) has the burden of maintaining safe premises and is in the best position to assure the safety of the visitors rather than basing it on the number of patrons affected. We will have to wait for more cases to see if the Supreme Court backs away from the idea that *public interest arises only when a substantial number of patrons are involved.*

Waivers are generally disfavored and are to be construed strictly against the drafter. Contractual language must be clear enough that the intent of both parties to relieve the defendant of liability is unmistakable (*Nishi v. Mt. Snow, Ltd.*, 1996). Courts have ruled that when the language is clear, parties are bound by the common meaning of their words. When interpreting contracts, courts are not required to accept every remote construction or fantastic possibility of which ingenuity is capable and elevate it to the level of an ambiguity.

The Vermont Supreme Court ruled that an **indemnification** provision should not be interpreted to allow an indemnitee to recover from his own negligence unless there is convincing evidence that such was the intent of the parties (*Southwick v. City of Rutland*, 2011). It explained that the court is reluctant to place the burden of negligent actions on one who is not at fault, particularly when there is a vast disparity in bargaining power.

"Negligence." The Vermont Supreme Courts does not require that the word "negligence" be used; it is, however, selective as to the wording that is used. In 1983 the court stated that failure to include the word "negligence" does not preclude other language from having that effect (*Douglas v. Skiing Standards, Inc.*, 1983). In the 2009 *Provoncha* case, the court upheld a waiver calling for assumption of the risks "from any cause what so ever;" however, the previous year, in *Thompson*, the court rejected a waiver attempting to protect against negligence using the following language: "… understands the operation of this vehicle may result in serious injury or even death and accepts these risks …. The undersigned waives any claim …." In addition, the court in *Sanders v. Nike, Inc.* (2004) held that the term "hold harmless" used instead of "negligence" was acceptable. However, the Supreme Court cautions that the most effective way to be certain the waiver will apply to negligent acts is to *state explicitly in the waiver that claims based in negligence are included in the release* (*Thompson v. Hi Tech Motor Sports*, 2008).

Parental Waivers. Post-injury releases of claims by minors are limited by a statute (14 V.S.A. sec. 2643) which states that the superior judge of the superior court within the county of residence must approve of and consent to a release to be executed by a parent in a settlement that does not exceed the sum of $1500. That release shall be binding on the minor and parents. Claims settled for more than $1500 require the approval of a court-appointed guardian. Parental waivers for ski resorts would be against public policy.

Virginia
POOR

The Virginia Supreme Court (*Hiett v. Lake Barcroft Community Association, Inc.*, 1992) **has ruled that waivers protecting one against liability for personal injuries due to negligence are against public policy and are unenforceable. A U.S. Circuit Court** (*Elswick v. Lonesome Pine International Raceway, Inc.*, 2001) **has ruled that *Hiett's* prohibition of waivers did not apply to agreements between race tracks and drivers.**

Public Policy. In 1992, the Virginia Supreme Court stated "to hold it was competent for one party to put the other parties to the contract at the mercy of its own misconduct ... can never be lawfully done

216

where an enlightened system of jurisprudence prevails. Public policy forbids it, and contracts against public policy are void" (*Hiett v. Lake Barcroft Community Association, Inc.*, 1992). The court further stated that releases from liability for personal injury due to future acts of negligence are prohibited, not just for common carriers, but "universally."

In a 2001 Virginia case (*Elswick v. Lonesome Pine International Raceway, Inc.*, 2001) tried in the U.S. Circuit Court of Wise County, Virginia, the court held that the public policy prohibiting the enforcement of waivers did not apply to agreements between a racetrack and a racecar driver. The court said the Supreme Court has not addressed a waiver in an industry where it is customary for the drivers to conduct their own inspection of the racetrack, nor has it addressed the validity of a waiver involving the inherently dangerous activity of racecar driving.

In a 2007 (non-sport) case (*Kocinec v. Public Storage, Inc.*, 2007) involving a storage facility, the U.S. District Court made it clear that one party can exculpate itself from liability for loss or damage to property. The waiver must 1) not contravene public policy, 2) be readily understood by a reasonable person, and 3) clearly and unequivocally release the defendant from precisely the type of activity alleged.

In *Estes Express Lines, Inc. v. Chopper Express, Inc.* (2007), an employee of Chopper was injured. The Virginia Supreme Court addressed the issue of whether an **indemnity agreement** between the two businesses would be enforceable in a *personal injury* case. The court began by saying that the law looks with favor upon the making of contracts between competent parties and that "courts are averse to holding contracts unenforceable on the ground of public policy unless their illegality is clear and certain" The court held that while a pre-injury release has as its intent to extinguish the rights of the injured party to recover for damages, the pre-injury indemnity agreement was intended to pre-determine how potential losses would be distributed and has no effect on the right of recovery of the injured party. This would allow businesses to gain some liability protection. The court ruled that the indemnity agreement is enforceable even though it is for *personal injuries*.

However, the court did not address the situation where the participant is asked to indemnify a provider for any injury caused by the negligence of the provider. To allow this would, in effect, deny the injured participant the opportunity of recovery since the victim who signed the indemnity agreement would be his or her own indemnitor. This would, in effect, give the indemnity agreement the same effect as a waiver. The court addressed this issue, at least in part, when it recognized that although allowing a party to indemnify itself for its own negligence might conceivably diminish the indemnitee's concern for safety, an indemnity provision does not guarantee reimbursement by the indemnitor. The court used the example of the indemnitor becoming insolvent and being unable to meet its obligation to reimburse. The court thought it highly unlikely that the anticipation of reimbursement for negligence would cause the business to fail to exercise ordinary care. If the court used similar reasoning in evaluating an indemnity agreement between a provider and a client, this avenue might provide added protection for providers in Virginia.

Equine Activities. One exception to the Virginia law prohibiting waivers is provided by **Chapter 62 Equine Activity Liability §3.2-6202**. The statute provides that equine professionals may use waivers for liability protection. The statute states

> … no participant or parent or guardian of a participant who has knowingly executed a waiver of his rights to sue or agrees to assume all risks specifically enumerated under this subsection may maintain an action against or recover from an equine activity sponsor or an equine professional for an injury to or the death of a participant engaged in an equine activity. The waiver shall give notice to the participant of the intrinsic dangers of equine activities. The waiver shall remain valid unless expressly revoked in writing by the participant or parent or guardian of a minor.

Parental Waivers. As with waivers for adults, parental waivers are against public policy. However, **Chapter 62 Equine Activity Liability §3.2-6202** provides for an exception allowing enforcement of parental waivers used in equine recreational activities.

Virgin Islands
GOOD

A plaintiff who expressly agrees to accept a risk of harm arising from the negligence or reckless conduct of the defendant cannot recover for such harm unless the agreement is against public policy (*Joseph v. Church of God (Holiness) Academy*, 2006).

Public Policy. In evaluating a waiver, the court must first look to the intent of the parties and make a preliminary inquiry as to whether the contract is ambiguous. Intent is determined by the "plain meaning rule" of interpretation of contracts which assumes the intent is embodied in the writing of the agreement. When words are clear and unambiguous, the intent can be discovered from the express language of the agreement (*Delponte v. Coral World Virgin Islands, Inc.*, 2006). A waiver is ambiguous if it is reasonably susceptible to two meanings. If a waiver is unambiguous, it can still be challenged on **public policy** grounds.

The *Booth* court ruled that the waiver is enforceable against the **heirs** therefore, the heirs are bound by a valid waiver (*Booth v. Bowen*, 2008).

Gross Negligence. It is unclear whether a waiver can protect when the defendant was **grossly negligent** or **reckless**. The defendant in the *Booth* case moved for summary judgment only on their negligence claim, but did not make a motion regarding the gross negligence or recklessness allegations. However, in the *Joseph* case the court clearly stated that waivers can protect providers from liability for both negligence and reckless conduct.

"Negligence." The *Delponte* court quoted another court stating that it would be difficult to draft a plainer statement than when a waiver includes the term **"negligence."** The court went on to say, however, that a waiver that encompassed "the entire cost and full liability" provided protection in spite of the absence of the specific word "negligence." In another case (*Booth v. Bowen*, 2008), the language "I further release and hold harmless … from any claim or lawsuit by me …" protected the defendant from liability.

Parental Waivers. There is no definite ruling, but statements by the *Joseph v. Church of God (Holiness) Academy* (2006) court indicate that enforcement is likely.

Washington
GOOD

Well-written waivers are enforceable if they do not violate public policy, are not inconspicuous, or are for acts that do not fall greatly below ordinary care (*Petersen v. Sorensen*, 2003). **They must be strictly construed in favor of the signer and the parties must have equal bargaining positions.**

Public Policy. Waivers are deemed against public policy when 1) public interest is involved, 2) care is greatly below standard (gross negligence, willful and wanton conduct or reckless conduct), or 3) the clause is inconspicuous (*Stokes v. Bally's Pacwest, Inc.*, 2002). Courts have also deemed that a waiver violates public policy if the signer is under the control (as in the case of medical research) of the person seeking exculpation for negligence. It is against public policy for school districts to require waivers as a condition of engaging in school-related activities such as interscholastic athletics (*Wagenblast v. Odessa School No. 105-157-166J*, 1988). Further, entities engaged in the performance of a public duty (i.e., common carriers, public utilities) cannot avoid liability by use of waivers because it is against public policy (*Broderson v. Ranier Nat. Park Co.*, 1936). In *Johnson v. Spokane to Sandpoint, LLC* (2013), a

Washington court reaffirmed that Washington courts do not favor finding adult recreational activities involve the public interest; the *Johnson* court stated that recreational activities fall outside the context of "essential service."

Washington courts often rely on the *Tunkl* factors (*Tunkl v. Regents of University of California*, 1963) for determining **public interest**. In a Court of Appeals case, the court found a waiver not to be against public policy because 1) the provider did not have "near monopoly power," 2) the contract was not an adhesion contract, 3) skiing is not a matter of public importance, and 4) the clause was not procedurally defective (*Chauvlier v. Booth Creek Ski Holdings, Inc.*, 2001). In Washington, well-written sport-related waivers (snow tubing, skiing, golf, mountain climbing, scuba diving, toboggan sliding, auto racing, ski jumping, and health club activities) are not generally held to involve public interest. In one case, the court was very explicit in deciding that a health club is not the kind of business that involves the public interest, and therefore, a waiver used by a health club is not against public policy (*Shields v. Sta Fit, Inc.*, 1995).

The issue of adhesion contracts often arises; however, adhesion contracts are usually enforceable. An adhesion contract is one that 1) is a standard form contract; 2) is submitted on a take-it-or-leave-it basis; and 3) involves parties of unequal bargaining power. The critical issue however, is the essential nature of the services being provided; when the service involves sport or recreational activities, the activity is not essential, the party has other alternatives, and the waiver is not rendered unenforceable (*DeAsis v. Young Men's Christian Association of Yakima (YMCA)*), 2014).

In a 2003 case (*Petersen v. Sorensen*), the court examined the issue of whether a waiver used by a motorcycle riding school was against public policy. The court found that motorcycle riding was neither an essential public service, nor a service of importance to the public and ruled that a waiver used by the school was enforceable.

Exculpatory clauses must be strictly construed in the light most favorable to the signer and must be clear if they are to exempt one from liability (*Petersen v. Sorensen*, 2003). The waiver protects the service provider only from those risks contemplated or assumed by the client.

The waiver must be conspicuous to the signer of the document in order to be valid. In *Kolosnitsyn v. Crystal Mountain, Inc.* (2009), the court specified that "conspicuous" means the liability language 1) is clearly displayed and 2) its meaning is clear and unambiguous. It went on to say the test is whether the language is so inconspicuous that reasonable persons could reach different conclusions as to whether the document was unwittingly signed. For example, a waiver or disclaimer located in the middle of a golf cart contract was found to be inconspicuous and against public policy (*Baker v. City of Seattle*, 1971). In *Johnson*, the court provided six factors that are helpful in determining if a waiver is conspicuous. They are: 1) is the waiver set apart or hidden among other provisions; 2) is the heading clear; 3) is the waiver set off with bold type or upper case type; 4) is the signature line below the waiver; 5) what does the language say above the signature line; and 6) is it clear the signature relates to the waiver.

Washington courts hold that an employer cannot require an employee to sign a waiver releasing the employer from liability for job-related injuries caused by employer negligence. This rule is grounded in the concept that there is a disparity of bargaining positions (*Wagenblast v. Odessa School No. 105-157-166J*, 1988).

Disclaimers. Disclaimers are sometimes used in commercial transactions. To be valid, such disclaimers must be conspicuous. (R.C.W. 62A. 2-316(2); R.C.W. 62A 2-179(1), (3))

Indemnification. Washington courts say that waivers and indemnity clauses are construed by the same principles of law (*Scott v. Pacific West Mountain Resort*, 1992). Thus "clauses which purport to exculpate an indemnitee from liability for losses flowing solely from his own acts or omissions are not favored and are to be clearly drawn and strictly construed..." (*Northwest Airlines v. Hughes Air Corporation*). Any ambiguities are settled in favor of the indemnitor.

Loss of Consortium. A loss of consortium claim by the non-signing spouse is derivative of the claim of the injured spouse (*Barber v. Cincinnati Bengals, Inc.*, 1994). Washington courts, however, recognize an independent cause of action for the loss of **parental consortium**.

"**Negligence.**" The use of the word "negligence" is not essential (*Scott v. Pacific West Mountain Resort*, 1992). The Supreme Court has stated that Washington courts should use common sense in interpreting waivers, and language such as "hold harmless ... from all claims" logically includes negligent conduct. It is still best policy, however, to use the term "negligence" in the waiver. It helps to clarify the intent of the waiver and no waiver has ever failed for being too clear.

Gross Negligence. The courts have made it abundantly clear that they will not protect a provider if the act falls to the level of gross negligence or willful and wanton misconduct (*Stokes v. Bally's Pacwest, Inc.*, 2002).

Parental Waivers. The Washington Supreme Court held that a waiver that attempts to bar a **minor** child's cause of action is invalid and against public policy (*Scott v. Pacific West Mountain Resort*, 1992). The court ruled that a parent does not have legal authority to waive a child's own right to sue a negligent party for damages. It stated that it is settled law that a parent cannot sign away the rights of the child. Washington law also prohibits post-injury settlements by parents of injured children without court approval, and says that it consequently makes little sense to conclude a parent has the authority to release the child's cause of action prior to an injury. The parent can waive his or her own right to redress for the injury to the minor.

West Virginia
FAIR

Waivers that do not violate public policy or a safety statute are generally enforceable. Waiver language must be clear and definite, must be strictly construed against the relying party, and action must be within the contemplation of the parties (*Murphy v. North American River Runners, Inc.*, 1991).

Public Policy. Generally, an exculpatory agreement is valid and not contrary to public policy if it is 1) freely and fairly made between persons of equal bargaining power and 2) where no public interest is involved. Courts also seem to stress the importance of the contract being brought home to and understood by the signer (*Barber v. Eastern Karting Company*, 1996). A waiver is unenforceable on grounds of public policy if 1) the clause exempts one charged with a duty of public service or 2) the injured party is a member of a class protected against the class to which the negligent party belongs.

The language of an agreement must be clear and definite and will be strictly construed against the relying party. The general rule is that the waiver covers only such matters as may fairly be said to have been within the contemplation of the parties (*Murphy v. North American River Runners, Inc.*, 1991).

Waivers involving inherently dangerous recreational or amusement activities are unenforceable if they involve a violation of statutory safety standards (*Barber v. Eastern Karting Company*, 1996; *Murphy v. North American River Runners, Inc.*, 1991; *Johnson v. New River Scenic Whitewater Tours, Inc.*, 2004; **W.Va.C. 20-3B-1 to 8** & **W.Va.C. 20-3A-1 to 8**). The statutes forbid waivers from shielding whitewater guides and ski operators from statutory duty of ordinary care with language such as: "All guides... shall conform to the standard of care expected of members of their profession."

An interesting case involved a waiver required of all college rugby club participants. Since other club sport participants did not have to sign a waiver, it was not upheld on the basis of a violation of equal protection (*Kyriazis v. University of West Virginia*, 1994).

"**Negligence.**" Language such as "any kind or nature whatsoever" is sufficient to waive liability for negligence. The use of "negligence" or other "magic words" is not necessary.

Gross Negligence. Waivers in West Virginia will protect one from liability for gross negligence, reckless acts, and intentional acts if this is clearly indicated within the waiver. Saying "all liability" is not sufficient language to gain such protection. One who expressly and clearly agrees to accept a risk of harm arising from negligent or reckless conduct of a provider may not recover from that harm (*Murphy v. North American River Runners, Inc.,* 1991).

Parental Waivers. Neither waivers signed by parents on behalf of a minor child nor indemnification agreements made by the parent are enforceable. However, **indemnity agreements** made by another individual or by activity sponsors are enforceable (*Johnson v. New River Scenic Whitewater Tours, Inc.,* 2004).

Wisconsin
POOR

While several sport- and recreation-related liability waivers have been enforced in the appellate courts, the Wisconsin Supreme Court has never enforced such a waiver. Three recent Supreme Court decisions have not held that all waivers are void and unenforceable, but appear to have placed such severe restrictions or requirements upon waivers as to make them impractical for mass use.

Public Policy. Over the years several sport, recreation and fitness liability waivers have been enforced by Wisconsin appellate courts. The Wisconsin Supreme Court has addressed these waivers on a number of occasions, but the authors have found no cases in which the court upheld one. In *Duszynski v. B & T Riding Academy, Inc.* (1966), the court did not rule on the waiver because of issues of facts. In *Merten v. Nathan* (1982), the court voided the waiver because of fraudulent language, but failed to address the broader question of validity of waivers in general. A year later the court (*Arnold v. Shawano Co. Agr. Socy,* 1983) rejected another waiver because the challenged action was not within the contemplation of the signer, but again failed to address the validity of waivers in general. Next, the Supreme Court in *Dobratz v. Thomson* (1991) held the waiver was not void as contrary to public policy, but failed to enforce the waiver because of ambiguity. In both *Arnold* and *Dobratz,* the courts were critical of the waivers because they did not describe conditions concerning the nature of the activity, where the event would take place, or the risk and difficulty level required.

The Supreme Court has since addressed the validity of waiver in three cases. In *Richards v. Richards* (1994), the court named three factors determining public policy and stated that a combination of the three invalidated the waiver as being against public policy. The factors were 1) the contract serves two purposes which were not clearly identified or distinguished (alert/dual purpose)[75]; 2) the agreement was extremely broad and all-inclusive (overbroad/"negligence")[76]; and 3) the contract was a standardized agreement on a printed form that offered little or no opportunity for negotiation or bargaining (opportunity to bargain). The court stated that none of these factors alone would necessarily have invalidated the waiver, but that the "combination of these factors demonstrate that adherence to the principle of freedom of contract is not heavily favored."

When ruling on a waiver in the *Yauger v. Skiing Enterprises, Inc.* (1996) two years later, the Wisconsin Supreme Court focused on two principles relevant to determining if a waiver was against public policy. They were 1) did it clearly, unambiguously, and unmistakably inform the signer of what was being waived (overbroad/"negligence")[77] and 2) did the form, when examined in its entirety, alert the

---

[75] The purposes seemed to be 1) to authorize the passenger to ride in a company truck and 2) to release the company from liability. This was not made clear in the title of the contract, which was "Passenger Authorization."

[76] The waiver attempted to excuse intentional, reckless, and negligent conduct by the company and by another entity "and by all affiliated, associated, or subsidiary companies, partnerships, individuals, or corporations, and all other persons, firms or corporations." The waiver was not limited to a specific vehicle or a specific time period. Its breadth raised questions as to its meaning and its one-sidedness.

[77] The court held that the waiver did not clearly inform the signer that he was waiving all claims against Skiing Enterprises, Inc. due to their negligence. The term "negligence" did not appear in the form and there was no language expressing the signer's

signer to the nature and significance of what was being signed (alert/dual purpose).[78] The court held that the waiver was void as against public policy under either of these two principles, thus seemingly indicating that each principle is mandatory for an enforceable waiver. The *Yauger* waiver failed, in part, because of ambiguity created by the use of the phrase "inherent risks in skiing." The court stated that when judges disagree on its definition, how could a reasonable person understand what rights he is signing away.

In the 2005 *Atkins* case (*Atkins v. Swimwest Family Fitness Center*, 2005), the Supreme Court looked at another waiver and found it unenforceable based on three factors. First, the waiver was overly broad because the provider used the term "fault" rather than "negligence" (overbroad/"negligence").[79] Second, the waiver served two purposes and required only one signature (alert/dual purpose).[80] Third, there was little or no opportunity to bargain or negotiate the terms of the contract (opportunity to bargain). Unfortunately, the court failed to say what this means or how to do it (see Opportunity to Bargain section in Chapter 2). It stated that no opportunity to bargain "presents another significant factor in the analysis of public policy," but in the next paragraph stated "All of the factors discussed lead us to conclude that the ... clause violates public policy...." Later the court reinforced this by stating "The lack of such opportunity is also contrary to public policy." The court failed to make it clear whether each of the three factors is required for enforcement (as in *Yauger*), or if enforcement is dependent upon a combination of the factors (as in *Richards*).

Two subsequent appellate court rulings have followed the Supreme Court rulings. In a post-Atkins appellate case (*Mettler v. Nellis*, 2005), the court ruled a waiver against public policy stating that the waiver was too broad and all inclusive, did not clearly inform the signer of what was being waived, and did not alert the signer to the significance of what they were signing. The ruling shed little light as to how many factors are required for the agreement to be against public policy. In *Brooten v. Hickok Rehabilitation Services* (2013), the Court of Appeals of Wisconsin addressed a health club case in which a client was injured when his weight bench collapsed. The court adhered to the *Akins* court precedent. They observed that the waiver allowed no opportunity to bargain and interpreted the waiver as being overly broad since it seemed to attempt to extend its protection beyond ordinary negligence. In addition, the court felt the waiver did not alert the signer to the significance and nature of the document; specifically, the indemnification language, the title, and the exculpatory clause were less than conspicuous.

On the other hand, two Wisconsin courts have found reason to uphold liability waivers. In a 2011 case (*Beer v. La Cross County Agricultural Society*), the court of appeals cited *Atkins* in determining waiver enforceability. *Atkins* said that first the court determines if the waiver is valid contractually (meaning the waiver is broad enough to cover the activity at issue). Second, the court is to address whether the waiver is in violation of public policy. The appellate court then relied on *Werdehoff v. General Star Indemnity Co.*(1999), a prior ruling regarding a similar case. In *Werdehoff*, the court identified five public policy factors from previous cases: 1) Does it serve two not clearly identified functions? 2) Is it extremely broad and all-inclusive? 3) Is it standardized with little or no opportunity to bargain? 4) Is it clear and unambiguous? and 5) Does the form alert the signer to the nature of the document? The *Werdehoff* court found that the document met three of the five factors and concluded that

---

intent to release the provider from its own negligence.

[78] The form did not clearly and unequivocally communicate the nature and significance of the document. The title was "Application;" it served a dual function (a season pass and a liability release); and the paragraph containing the waiver was not conspicuous, not standing out in any way.

[79] The court interpreted "fault" to include reckless or intentional acts. They stated that if Swimwest wanted release from negligent acts, it could have included the word negligence. The broadness also made it difficult to interpret what was within the contemplation of the parties.

[80] Failure to adequately notify the signer of the nature and significance of the document was indicated by the fact that the waiver served two purposes – that of a registration form and that of a liability release. The court stated that a signature space should have been provided for each of the purposes of the document. Additionally, there was nothing conspicuous about the paragraph.

the waiver did not violate public policy. The *Beer* court held that, by law, it is bound by its prior precedent and enforced the waiver.

In a 2013 case (*Hickey v. T.H.E. Insurance Company*), the plaintiff broke her leg as she was attempting to get off a chairlift at the Navarino Hills Skiing & Snowboarding Park. Hickey had signed a form that included a waiver. The agreement included an option to sign the waiver or pay an additional $15 per day and not sign the waiver. Hickey chose to sign the waiver. The trial court found the waiver was clear, the scope was communicated, and the key language was set off in bold and in a separate paragraph. The court stated that the waiver did not violate public policy. It 1) is not a take-it-or-leave-it waiver; 2) was limited to negligence – not all liability; and 3) contained clear language. The court upheld the waiver.

Wisconsin waiver authority Alexander Pendleton reminds us that Wisconsin case law clearly shows that one can never take a casual approach to drafting a waiver agreement in this state. He points out that while there are many ways by which drafters can create problems in the agreement, one certain way to make your waiver overbroad is to state that the signer is waiving "all claims" and 1) **not** go on to exclude reckless or intentional actions or 2) fail to include a severability clause.

The use of waivers might well become impractical if the Atkins decision is interpreted as declaring that the opportunity to bargain is mandatory for an enforceable waiver; however, the Hickey case may provide some guidance for waiver preparers. Reasonable minds could differ in the interpretation of the decisions and no one really knows for certain at this point exactly what the court intends. For an in-depth discussion of approaches to address this problem, refer to the Bargaining Power section in Chapter 2.

In light of these Supreme Court decisions, the status of waivers is unclear. The following describes the status prior to the ruling, including statutes affecting waivers. It is unclear as to how much of this case law still applies.

Waivers are not favored by law because they tend to allow conduct below the acceptable standard of care; however, they are not automatically void and unenforceable as contrary to public policy (*Arnold v. Shawano Co. Agr. Socy*, 1983). They are examined closely and to be construed strictly against the relying party (*Merten v. Nathan*, 1983). The court looks at the particular facts and circumstances and balances contract law with tort law (*Dobratz v. Thomson*, 1991). The *Merten* Court defined public policy as "'that principle of law under which 'freedom of contract or private dealings is restricted for the good of the community.'"

Other Wisconsin courts have found waivers unenforceable on grounds of public policy if 1) the harm is caused intentionally or recklessly; 2) there is an employer-employee relationship, a duty of public service, or membership in a protected class; 3) there is an un-bargained-for agreement with a seller of a product; 4) the incident was not within the contemplation of the signer; 5) the waiver is ambiguous; 6) there is no opportunity to read; and 7) there is no understanding of the risks (*Arnold v. Shawano Co. Agr. Socy*, 1983). Contracts are also not enforceable if there is false representation or fraud involved (*Merten v. Nathan*, 1983).

Waivers that are broad and general will bar only those claims that are within the contemplation of the parties when the contract was executed. Additionally, Wisconsin seems to give greater weight to the principles of freedom of contract, stressing that it must be a bargain freely and voluntarily made through a process of bargaining that has integrity. To determine whether the contract expresses the intent of the parties with particularity, courts consider the terms of the agreement and the circumstances under which it was entered. At a minimum, signers should have an opportunity to read and ask questions about the terms releasing liability. Faced with the argument that no one would sponsor automobile races without the protection of waivers, the Supreme Court stated that each waiver case would be decided on its merits under strict scrutiny rather than on the basis of threatened consequences (*Arnold v. Shawano Co. Agr. Socy*, 1983).

Disclaimers. A disclaimer on a lift ticket was not upheld because a meeting of the minds is necessary for a contract. The case was sent to trial (*Hackel v. Whitecap Recreations*, 1984).

Loss of Consortium. Spousal claims are independent causes of action. A waiver signed by the injured spouse has no effect on the claim by the non-signing spouse (*Arnold v. Shawano Co. Agr. Socy*, 1983; *Werdehoff v. General Star Indemnity Company*, 1999). **Wrongful death** claims, however, are derivative of a valid claim by the injured party (*Niese v. Skip Barber Racing School*, 2002).

"Negligence." Courts require that the contract clearly express the intent so that the signer knowingly agrees to excuse the relying party from negligence. The Wisconsin Supreme Court has stated that it did not intend to create a "magic words" rule requiring the use of the term "negligence," but that "it would be very helpful for such contracts to set forth in clear and express terms" that the signer is releasing others for their negligent acts" (*Dobratz v. Thomson*, 1990). Courts require that the contract clearly express the intent so that the signer knowingly agrees to excuse the relying party from negligence.

Reckless Conduct. Waivers will not protect the service provider from liability for reckless conduct or intentional acts (*Kellar v. Lloyd*, 1993).

Parental Waivers. Two Wisconsin courts have indicated that a waiver signed by the parent on behalf of a minor is enforceable (*Osborne v. Cascade Mountain, Inc.*, 2002; *Fire Insurance Exchange v. Cincinnati Insurance Company*, 2000). A caution, however, recent Supreme Court rulings have raised the bar for enforcement of any waiver.

Wyoming
GOOD

While not favored and requiring close scrutiny, waivers that release parties from liability for injury or damages resulting from negligence are valid and enforceable if not in violation of public policy (*Schutkowski v. Carey*, 1986).

Public Policy. Four factors determine if a waiver is in violation of public policy: 1) a duty to the public exists. A duty to the public exists if the nature of the business or service affects the public interest and the service performed is considered an essential service. Private recreational businesses generally perform no service that is of great importance or practical necessity for members of the public; 2) the nature of the service performed; 3) whether the contract was fairly entered into. Most recreational activities are considered nonessential services and do not possess the type of market power that would invalidate a waiver; and 4) whether the intention of the parties is expressed in clear and unambiguous language. An ambiguous release is one that is capable of being interpreted in more than one way. Private recreational businesses do not qualify as services requiring a special duty to the public nor are their services of a special, highly necessary nature (*Schutkowski v. Carey*, 1986).

The *Massengill* court (*Massengill v. S.M.A.R.T. Sports Medicine Clinic, P.C.*, 2000) adopted *Tunkl's* definition of a waiver affecting the public interest and giving rise to a public duty:

> … concerns a business of a type generally thought suitable for public regulation. The party seeking exculpation is engaged in performing a service of great importance to the public, which is often a matter of practical necessity for some members of the public. The party holds himself out as willing to perform this service for any member of the public who seeks it. As a result of the essential nature of the service, in the economic setting of the transaction, the party invoking exculpation possesses a decisive advantage of bargaining strength against any member of the public who seeks his services.

Types of businesses that generally involve a public duty include common carriers, hospitals and doctors, public utilities, innkeepers, public warehousemen, employers, and services involving extra-hazardous activities (*Massengill v. S.M.A.R.T. Sports Medicine Clinic, P.C.*, 2000).

Wyoming law states that "If the language of the contract is plain and unequivocal that language is controlling and the interpretation of the contractual provisions is for the court to make as a matter of law. The meaning of the instrument is to be deduced only from its language if the terms are plain and unambiguous" (*Massengill v. S.M.A.R.T. Sports Medicine Clinic, P.C.*, 2000, p.1135). Waivers or releases are contractual in nature and are to be interpreted using traditional contractual principles and considering the document as a whole.

The court in *Milligan v. Big Valley Corp.* (1986) points out that the fact that a contract is on a printed form and is presented on a "take it or leave it" basis does not mean it is an adhesive contract. Greatly disparate bargaining power and no opportunity for negotiation on services that cannot be obtained elsewhere must exist.

The Wyoming Constitution (**Wyo.Con., Art. 19, sec. 7**) forbids the enforcement of release agreements when an **employment** relationship exists between the parties.

The Wyoming Supreme Court has recognized the enforceability of **forum selection** and **choice of law** clauses. They are *prima facie* valid absent a demonstration by the opposing party that the clause is unreasonable or based upon fraud or unequal bargaining power (*Venard v. Jackson Hole Paragliding, LLC*, 2013). In *Venard*, Jackson Hole was a third party beneficiary to an agreement; the court held that the agreement was not enforceable because both parties did not consent to the agreement in advance.

Indemnification. The defining case regarding indemnification involved a river rafting trip in which the wife was injured (*Madsen v. Wyoming River Trips, Inc.*, 1999). The husband had signed an indemnity agreement. The *Madsen* Court indicated that indemnity agreements are disfavored and are to be strictly construed against the indemnitee, particularly when the indemnitee seeks to hold the indemnitor liable for the negligence of the indemnitee. The court ruled that the indemnity clause is unenforceable as void against public policy, indicating that the modern trend is to not enforce indemnity agreements that hold an innocent party liable for the negligence of the indemnitee.

The court further stated "general, broad, and seemingly all-inclusive language in the indemnifying agreement is not sufficient to impose liability for the indemnitee's own negligence (*Madsen v. Wyoming River Trips, Inc.*, 1999, p.7) suggesting, but not saying, that the indemnity agreement might not be enforceable because it failed to refer specifically to the "negligence of the indemnitee." The court went on to say that the Wyoming Supreme Court has deemed indemnity contracts to be enforceable in commercial contexts, but has never held such contracts enforceable in a consumer services context such as this. The court concluded by saying that such a release should advise the signer of the specific risks inherent in the activity and that it would be unjust to hold an innocent passenger in the boat liable for the negligence of the business entity.

Loss of Consortium. Claims of loss of consortium by a non-signing spouse are derivative of a valid claim by the injured party (*Massengill v. S.M.A.R.T. Sports Medicine Clinic, P.C.*, 2000).

"Negligence." The specific use of the word "negligence" is not necessary as long as the language clearly shows the intent to extinguish liability. When interpreting a contract, the primary concern is to determine the intent of the two parties. The court went on to say that under Wyoming law, "a Defendant has no duty to protect against inherent risks and the failure to do so is not negligent. It would seem, therefore, that no waiver is necessary to protect a provider against liability for injuries resulting from inherent risks ...." Regardless, best practice would call for including in the waiver language both negligence and the inherent risks (*Street v. Darwin Ranch, Inc.*, 1999, p.17).

Willful Misconduct. Waivers seeking to protect a service provider from liability for injuries resulting from **willful or wanton misconduct** are not enforceable (*Street v. Darwin Ranch, Inc.*, 1999).

Parental Waivers. In an unclear ruling, a court in an equestrian case (*Sapone v. Grand Targhee, Inc.*, 2002), addressed neither the waiver nor minor status. The waiver was apparently not upheld since the case was remanded.

Appendix A
A Comparison of Participant Forms
Intended to Limit Provider Liability[81]

Documents Based in Contract Law

Name of Agreement	Definition	Primary Function or Purpose	Effect on Liability	When Void Or Not Available
Waiver	Contract signed prior to participation releasing provider of liability for injuries due to the ordinary negligence of the provider. Can range from a clause to a multi-page document.	Lowers the standard of care for which one is liable to gross negligence.	Relieves provider of duty of ordinary care. Not liable for ordinary negligence.	Generally not valid for minors or for gross negligence, reckless, w/w or intentional acts.
Release	Synonymous with waiver in many jurisdictions. *** In other jurisdictions, it is a post-injury agreement discharging provider of liability for negligence of the provider (usually in conjunction with a settlement)	Lowers the standard of care for which one is liable to gross negligence. *** Generally to bar further legal action by agreeing on a settlement.	Relieves provider of duty of ordinary care. Not liable for ordinary negligence. *** Further liability is discharged by the settlement.	Generally not valid for minors or for gross negligence, reckless, w/w or intentional acts. *** Court approval usually required when the injured party is a minor.
Exculpatory Clause or Agreement	An exculpatory clause is the part of a document that releases a provider from liability for ordinary negligence. Exculpatory agreement is a term for a stand-alone document that is synonymous with waiver.	Lowers the standard of care for which one is liable to gross negligence.	Relieves provider of duty of ordinary care. Not liable for ordinary negligence.	Generally not valid for gross negligence, reckless, willful-wanton, or intentional acts. Also not valid with minors in many jurisdictions.
Express Assumption of Risk	Used synonymously with waiver in many jurisdictions. Contract in which the signer specifically states that *the signer agrees prior to participation that the provider owes no duty.*	Lowers the standard of care for which one is liable to gross negligence.	Relieves provider of duty of ordinary care. Not liable for ordinary negligence.	Generally not valid for gross negligence, reckless, willful-wanton, or intentional acts. Also not valid with minors in many jurisdictions.
Disclaimer	A statement in which the provider asserts that the provider is not responsible for any injury. Sometimes used synonymously with waiver, *but is a unilateral agreement and generally is not signed by participant.*	Lowers the standard of care for which one is liable to gross negligence.	Intended to relieve provider of duty of ordinary care. Not liable for ordinary negligence. Seldom enforced due to difficulty in meeting contractual requirements.	Generally not enforced due to no meeting of the minds; not valid for gross negligence, reckless, willful-wanton, or intentional acts. Also not valid with minors in many jurisdictions.
Indemnity Agreement	A contract signed prior to participation by which participant or another party agrees to reimburse the provider for any monetary loss, including attorneys fees, incurred as a result of 1) injury to the participant or 2) injury or loss caused by the participant.	Method of financial risk management often used with leases, rentals, and contracted services. Usually involves one entity indemnifying another entity.	No effect on liability. The provider can still be sued, but indemnifying party must repay provider for any loss.	When against public policy. Also, not valid in some jurisdictions 1) when provider requires indemnity from participant for provider ordinary negligence or 2) when parent indemnifies provider for loss due to minor's injury.
Covenant not to Sue	A contract signed prior to participation by which the signer agrees not to file suit against the provider for any cause of action.	Injured party is contractually prohibited from filing suit against provider. Usually ignored when in waivers.	In theory, injured party has no one to sue. Also, in settlements, effect is similar to that of the waiver except that it does not extinguish the cause of action against or release joint tortfeasors or joint obligators.	When against public policy.
Parental Waiver	Contract signed by a parent on behalf of a minor prior to participation releasing provider of liability for injuries due to the ordinary negligence of the provider.	Lowers the standard of care for which one is liable to gross negligence; to bar suit for loss suffered by parent or child from injury to minor.	Effective in protecting provider from liability for loss by parent *in most states*; also from liability for injury or loss by minor *in some states*.	When forbade by statute or courts as against public policy.

---

[81] Many legal documents aim to limit the liability of service providers. Because of the variety of documents in use, it is important that the reader understands the function of each and distinguishes among them. This figure is intended to help the reader distinguish among the various documents in terms of the definition, the purpose of the document, the legal effect of the document, and when the document is void. Twelve of the most common documents in use are included. The documents are first divided into three categories according to the field of law on which each is based – contract law, tort law, or a combination of both. This figure was adapted and expanded by the authors and Dr. Betty van der Smissen from van der Smissen, B. (1990). Legal liability and risk management for public and private entities. Anderson Publishing Co.: Cincinnati, OH.

Documents Based in Tort Law

Name of Agreement	Definition	Primary Function or Purpose	Effect on Liability	When Void Or Not Available
Agreement to Participate	Informative agreement that formalizes common law primary assumption of risk; warns of inherent risks; obtains participant acknowledgement of voluntary participation and of knowledge, understanding, & appreciation of the risks of injury; and informs of behavioral expectations.	Provides documentary evidence of 1) efforts by defendant to meet the assumption of risk requirements and 2) participant violation of behavioral expectations and responsibilities. Also good public relations device.	Strengthens the primary assumption of risk and the contributory fault defenses. If there was contributory fault, an award for provider negligence can be reduced or barred.	When assumption of risk criteria are not met or when participant responsibilities are not communicated.
Assumption of Risk Agreement	Essentially the same as an agreement to participate, but is often presented in a briefer format. Participant assumes the inherent risks of participation.	If a broad format is used, it provides documentary evidence of efforts to meet the assumption of risk requirements. Also good public relations device.	If a broad format is used, strengthens the assumption of risk defense. If there was contributory fault, an award for provider negligence can be reduced or barred.	When assumption of risk criteria not met.
Parental Permission Form	A signed statement by parent or guardian that minor can participate in the stated activity. Can be included as part of the agreement to participate. It can include a waiver or exculpatory clause.	To give permission for participation. If attached to an agreement to participate, it serves as a good public relations device.	No legal effect on liability. If the exculpatory clause is included, it gains release from the parent who relinquishes the parent's & the child's right to sue (in some states).	Always available. Exculpatory agreements signed by parent on behalf of a minor are not enforceable in many states.

Documents Based in Both Contract and Tort Law

Name of Agreement	Definition	Primary Function or Purpose	Effect on Liability	When Void Or Not Available
Informed Consent	Agreement that fully discloses 1) what the program or treatment will do to the subject, 2) the potential risks and benefits of the treatment, and 3) what results are expected. The subject releases the provider from liability for injuries resulting from the treatment risks of the treatment or program.	Allows an intelligent, informed decision regarding the treatment that the subject will undergo.	No effect on liability for ordinary negligence, but strengthens assumption of risk defense for injuries resulting from treatment risks.	When there is fraud or misrepresentation; or no full disclosure.
Participant Agreement	This is essentially a waiver, an assumption of risk agreement (or agreement to participate), and an indemnification agreement merged into one document. It stresses the sharing of information.	Lowers the standard of care for which one is liable to gross negligence and provides documentary evidence of : 1) defendant's efforts to meet the assumption of risk requirements and 2) violation of participant responsibility. Helpful in a contributory fault defense.	Relieves provider of duty of ordinary care. Not liable for ordinary negligence and strengthens the assumption of risk and the contributory fault defenses. If there is contributory fault, an award for provider ordinary negligence can be reduced or barred.	Generally not valid for gross negligence, reckless, willful-wanton, or intentional acts. Also not valid with minors in many jurisdictions. For inherent risks, when assumption of risk criteria not met or when participant responsibilities are not communicated.

Appendix B
Cruise Ship Contracts

Providers and patrons of cruise lines should be aware of three elements of a cruise ship contract. They are 1) liability waivers or disclaimers intended to protect the cruise line from liability for negligence of the cruise line or its employees; 2) choice of law clauses; 3) forum selection clauses, and 4) time limitations for legal action.

Cruise Ship Waivers and Disclaimers

Cruise line passenger contracts sometime include on the passenger ticket a waiver of liability clause or disclaimer of liability, both intended to relieve the cruise line of its liability for cruise line negligence.

A federal statute (**46 U.S.C. sec. 30509**) expressly voids any contract provision purporting to limit the liability of a ship for its negligence:

> **Sec. 30509. Provisions limiting liability for personal injury or death**
> (a) Prohibition. -
> (1) In general. - The owner, master, manager, or agent of a vessel transporting passengers between ports in the United States, or between a port in the United States and a port in a foreign country, may not include in a regulation or contract a provision limiting -
> (A) the liability of the owner, master, or agent for personal injury or death caused by the negligence or fault of the owner or the owner's employees or agents; or
> (B) the right of a claimant for personal injury or death to a trial by court of competent jurisdiction.

In addition, this statute has been upheld in numerous federal court cases in which cruise lines, like other common carriers, are held to a standard of reasonable care and their use of waivers or disclaimers is prohibited by maritime law, particularly when the health and safety of the passengers is involved (*Kornberg v. Carnival Cruise Lines, Inc.*, 1984; *Kermarec v. Compagnie Generale Transatlantique*, 1958). So it is well-settled law that cruise lines cannot shield themselves from negligence liability by including waivers or disclaimers in the passenger contract or by requiring the passenger to sign a waiver in order to participate in some activity.

Admiralty law holds that **cruise ships** also *have a non-delegable duty to transport passengers safely* to the dock while in port. In two near-identical cases, the cruise lines contracted with independent contractors to tender passengers to shore (*Samuelov v. Carnival Cruise Lines, Inc.*, 2003; *Chan v. Society Expeditions, Inc.*, 1997). A passenger was injured during transport in each case and sued the respective cruise line. Both courts declined to uphold the cruise line disclaimers because cruise ships have a duty to provide safe transportation and adequate supervision to and from the dock even though the transport was by an independent contractor.

Onboard Recreational Activities. In what was temporarily a ground-breaking case that runs counter to previous decisions regarding recreational activities on a ship, the court in *Johnson v. Royal Caribbean Cruises* (2011a) upheld a waiver signed by a ship passenger in order to use the FlowRider shipboard activity. The court reasoned that admiralty jurisdiction did not apply because the activity had an insufficient connection to traditional maritime activity. They further stated that recreational and inherently dangerous activities such as the FlowRider can hardly be considered essential functions of a common carrier and they are not related to the duty of providing safe transportation to passengers. Interestingly, less than one year later, the appellate court reversed the decision, stating that the statute **46 U.S.C. sec. 30509** clearly prohibits the use of waivers for on-board activities (*Johnson v. Royal Caribbean Cruises*, 2011b).

In a 2013 case (*In re the complaint of Royal Caribbean Cruises Ltd.*), the court stayed consistent in ruling that a waiver signed by a jet skier was not enforceable. The Jet Ski tour was owned and operated by Royal Caribbean and fell under the ambit of **Sec. 30509.**

Liability for Onboard Medical Care. It has long been held in Maritime law that the negligence of the ship's doctor could not be imputed to the cruise line. This has been based on the theory that the patient is under control of the doctor and the cruise line cannot interfere with or control the actions of the doctor – thus, the line cannot be held vicariously liable for the actions of the doctor. The doctor is generally classified as an independent contractor – not an employee; thus no cruise line liability for the negligence of the doctor. Negligence claims are often dependent upon establishing some sort of agency relationship or providing evidence that the cruise line failed to do due diligence in hiring the doctor.

Injuries on Shore Excursions. Cruise lines generally contract with local businesses to provide activities for shore excursions (e.g. zip line tours). The cruise line generally has no affiliation with the local provider other than as an independent contractor to provide the activity. In such cases, the cruise line is not responsible for the negligence of the independent contractor; it can be liable, however, if there is evidence that the cruise line was negligent in the selection of the contractor. Waivers by which the cruise line disclaims liability for injuries due to the negligence of an independent contractor are generally enforced.

If, however, the cruise line has a partnership or agency relationship with the local business and has control of how the activity is conducted, then the cruise line can be vicariously liable for injuries occurring on the excursion. Moreover, if the excursion is conducted by the cruise line (e.g., jet ski tour off the boat), the cruise line is responsible for the conduct of the activity and is liable for injuries due to negligence. Waivers required by the cruise line for excursions or activities under which the cruise line have control are not enforceable.

Non-Cruise Ship Recreational Boats. Courts have held that **recreational boats**, whose purpose is to provide recreation rather than transportation, are not subject to **46 U.S.C. sec. 30509** which prohibits limitations of liability for any vessel transporting passengers between U.S. ports or to a foreign port. Rulings have involved dive boats and "crazy boat" thrill rides (*Schultz v. Florida Keys Dive Center, Inc.*, 2000).

Choice of Law and Forum Selection Clauses

A **choice of law** clause is a passage within the passenger contract by which the passenger agrees what law will apply in any legal action. A **forum selection** clause is a passage in the contract by which the passenger agrees that any subsequent legal action taken must take place in a specified jurisdiction.

As a general rule, courts will enforce both choice-of-law and forum selection clauses agreed to by the parties in their contract (*Carnival Cruise Lines, Inc., v. Shute*, 1991; *Chapman v. Norwegian Cruise Line Ltd.*, 2001; *Hughes v. Carnival Cruise Lines*, 2003; *Harden v. American Airlines*, 1998). Each year many injured passengers from across the country in states like Montana, Iowa, and New Hampshire file suit against cruise lines only to learn that they have contractually agreed that the applicable law is admiralty law or that of the State of Florida; this is usually not too important. The problem arises when the injured passenger learns that the legal action must occur in a distant state (usually Florida). There are times when the court rules in favor of a change of forum; but these cases are few and far between.

In admiralty actions, federal law dictates that forum selection clauses are "*prima facie* valid and should be enforced unless enforcement is shown by the resisting party to be 'unreasonable' under the circumstances" (*Morales v. Royal Carribean Cruises, LTD,* 2006). The First Circuit has established a two-pronged test by which to evaluate such clauses under the "reasonable communication standard" (*Shankles v. Costa Armatori*, 1983). The court must 1) determine the facial clarity of the contract and whether the language and appearance make the provisions sufficiently obvious and understandable and 2) the opportunity of the passenger to become meaningfully informed of the terms.

To be deemed "unreasonable," the plaintiff must show:

- It is the product of fraud or overreaching;
- The party seeking to escape enforcement will "for all practical purposes be deprived of his or her day in court;"
- The chosen law is so fundamentally unfair as to deprive the plaintiff of a remedy; or
- Enforcement of the clause would contravene a strong public policy of the forum state.

Such clauses are enforceable whether or not the passenger actually reads them. Further, plaintiffs are deemed to have become aware of the clause the moment they receive the ticket. In *Irwin v. Celebrity Cruises, Inc.* (2013), the passenger bought her ticket through a cruise agent and never actually saw her ticket (contract). Plaintiff argued that the contract was not communicated to her because she did not physically have it. The law charges, however, that a passenger has constructive notice of the terms when the ticket is obtained through a travel agent; actual notice is not necessary for the terms to be reasonably communicated.

For more information on choice of law and forum selection clauses, see Chapter 5 Step 6.

Time Limitation Clauses

A **time limitation** clause is passage in the passenger contract by which the passenger agrees that a notice of a claim must be filed within a specified time period and the legal action must be initiated within a specified time period. Federal statute **46 USC sec. 30508(b)** provides for six month and one year minimum windows. To be enforceable, such clauses must be reasonably communicated to the passenger. To be reasonably communicated, the contract must direct the reader to the information (e.g., bold lettering, color, or placed in a box); the language must be understandable by a layperson; and the print size can be small, but must be easily readable.

Appendix C
List of Cases

A

Aaris v. Las Virgenes Unified Sch. District, 1998 Cal. App. LEXIS 535 (1998).
Accomazzo v. CEDU Educational Serv., Inc., 15 P.3d 1153 (ID, 2000).
Adams v. Frieden, Inc., 2002 Iowa App. LEXIS 861.
Adams v. Roark, 686 S.W.2d 73 (Tenn. 1985).
Adams v. Whitewater Mountain Resorts, 2006 Conn. Super. LEXIS 2865.
Adloo v. H.T. Brown Real Estate, Inc., 344 Md. 254, 266 (1996).
Akin v. Bally total Fitness Corporation, 2007 Tex. App. LEXIS 1218.
Alack v. Vic Tanny International of Missouri, Inc., 923 S.W.2d 330 (Mo. 1996).
Alack v. Vic Tanny International of Missouri, Inc., 1995 Mo. App. LEXIS 1473.
Alexander v Kendall Central School District, 634 N.Y.S.2d 318 (1995).
Allen v. L.A. Fitness, 2011 N.J. Super. Unpub. LEXIS 1542.
Allen v. Snow Summit, Inc., 1996 Cal. App. LEXIS 1211.
Amburgey v. Atomic Ski USA, Inc., 2007 U.S. Dist. LEXIS 92762.
American Boxing v. Young, 2005 Fla. App. LEXIS 14878.
Anderson v. Vail Corp., CO, 2010 Colo. App. LEXIS 1350.
Andrews v. Fitzgerald, 823 F.Supp. 356 (N.C., 1993).
Angelo v. USA Triathlon, 2014 U.S. Dist. LEXIS 131759.
Ansari v. Gold, 2006 Mich. App. LEXIS 388.
Apicella v. Valley Forge Military Academy, 630 F.Supp. 20 (E.D.Pa. 1985).
Applegate v. Cable Water Ski, LC, 2008 Fla. App. LEXIS 63.
Applegate-Rodeman v. JDK, 2014 Ind. App. Unpub. LEXIS 1434.
Applbaum v. Golden Acres Farm and Ranch, 2004 U. S. Dist. LEXIS 18130;
Arnold v. Shawano County Agricultural Society, 330 N.W.2d 773 (1983).
Atlantic Sounding Co., Inc. v. Townsend, 2009 U.S. App. LEXIS 18747.
Atl. Marine Const. Co. v. U.S. Dist. Court for W. Dist. Of Texas, 2013 U.S. LEXIS 8775.
Atkins v. Swimwest Family Fitness Center, 2005 Wisc. LEXIS 2.
Audley v. Melton, 1994 N.H. LEXIS 42.
Avant v. Community Hospital, 2005 Ind. App. LEXIS 720.

B

B & B Livery v. Riehl, 1998 Colo. LEXIS 451.
B & D Associates v. Russell, 2002 Conn. App. LEXIS 516.
Bacchiocchi v. Ranch Parachute Club, 273 AD2d 173 (2000).
Bader v. Ferri, 2013 Ohio App. LEXIS 3122.
Bagley v. Mt. Bachelor, Inc., 2014 Ore. LEXIS 994.
Bailey v. Palladino, 2006 N.J. Super Unpub. LEXIS 1774.
Bailey v. United States of America, 2003 U.S. Dist. LEXIS 19404.
Baker v. Just for Fun Party Center, 2009 Ohio App. LEXIS 5222.
Baker v. Stewarts' Inc., 433 N.W.2d 706 (Ia., 1988).
Baker v. City of Seattle, 484 P.2d 405 (Wash. 1971).
Ball v. Waldoch Sports, Inc., 2003 Minn. App. LEXIS 1105.
Barilotti v. Island Hotel Company Limited, 2014 2014 U.S. Dist. LEXIS 62455.
Barber v. Cincinnati Bengals, Inc., 41 F.3d 553 (1994).
Barber v. Eastern Karting Company, 1996 Md. App. LEXIS 40.
Barnes v. Birmingham International Raceway, Inc., 551 So.2d 929.
Barnes v. N.H. Karting Assoc., 128 N.H. 102, (1986).
Baschuk v. Diver's Way Scuba, Inc., 618 N.Y.S.2d 428.
Bashford v. Slater, 1959 Iowa Sup. LEXIS 419.
Beardslee v. Blomberg, 416 N.Y.S.2d 855 (1979).
Beaver v. Foamcraft, Inc., 2002 U.S. Dist. LEXIS 4651.
Beaver v. Grand Prix Karting Association, Inc., 2001 U.S. App. LEXIS 5436.
Beck-Hummel v. Ski Shawnee, Inc., 2006 Pa. Super. LEXIS 1547.
Beehner v. Cragun Corporation, 636 N.W.2d 821 (Minn., 2001).
Beer v. La Cross County Agricultural Society, 2011 Wisc. App. LEXIS 89.
Bender v. Caregivers of America, 2010 Fla. App. LEXIS 12178.
Benavidez v. The University of Texas – Pan American, 2014 Tex. App. LEXIS 11940.
Benjamin v. Gear Roller Hockey Equipment, Inc., 2000 Ariz. App. LEXIS 146.
Bennett v. U.S. Cycling Federation, 193 Cal.App.3d 1485 [1987].
Berenson v. USA Hockey, Inc., 2013 Colo. App. LEXIS 1627.
Bergin v. Wild Mountain, Inc., 2014 Minn. App. Unpub. LEXIS 212.
Bergonzine v. Maui Classic Charters, 1995 Amer. Maritime Cases 2628 (D.HI 1995).
Berlangieri v. Running Elk Corporation, 2002 N.M.App. LEXIS 39.
Berlangieri v. Running Elk Corporation, 76 P.2d 1098 (N.M., 2003).
Berry v. Plaintiff v. Greater Park City Company, 2007 Utah LEXIS 192.
Bertotti v. Charlotte Motor Speedway, Inc., 1995 U.S. Dist. LEXIS 10945.
Bhardwaj v. 24 Hour Fitness. Inc., 2002 Cal. App. LEXIS 2671.
Bien v. Fox Meadow Farms, Ltd., 574 N.E.2d 1311 (1991).
Biondi v. Motorcyle Safety Services, Inc., 2014 U.S. Dist. LEXIS 85524.
Bishop v. Nelson Ledges Quarry Park, Limited, 2005 Ohio App. LEXIS 2504.
B.J.'s Wholesale Club, Inc. v. Rosen, 2013 Md. LEXIS 897.
Blanc v. Windham Mountain, 115 Misc 2d 404 (1982).
Blau v. Mammoth Mountain Ski Area, 2001 Cal. App. LEXIS 1506.
Boateng v. Motorcycle Safety School, 2008 N.Y. App. Div. LEXIS 4167.
Boehm v. Cody Country Chamber of Commerce, 748 P.2d 704 (Wyo. 1987).
Boles v. Sun Ergoline, 2010 Colo. LEXIS 73.
Bonne v. Premier Athletics, 2006 U.S. Dist. LEXIS 77802.
Booth v. Bowen, 2008 U.S. Dist. LEXIS 1678.
Booth v. Santa Barbara Biplanes, 2008 Cal. App. LEXIS 43.
Borden v. Phillips, 752 So.2d 69 (Fla. 2000).
Bossi v. Sierra Nevada Recreation Corporation, 2004 Cal. App. Unpub. LEXIS 1992.
Bothell v. Two Point Acres, inc., 263 Ariz. Adv. Rep. 36.
Boucher v. Riner, 514 A2d 485 (Md.App., 1986).
Bowling v. Asylum Extreme, LLC, 2011 Ky. App. Unpub. LEXIS 801.
Brancati v. Bar-U-Farm, Inc., 1992 N.Y. App. Div. LEXIS 7159.

Braun v. Mount Brighton, Inc., 1989 U.S. Dist. LEXIS 17907.
Brbac v. Reading Fair Co., 1982 U.S. Dist. LEXIS 25662.
Brennan v. Ocean View Amusement Company, 194 N.E. 911 (Mass., 1935).
Bremen v. Zapata Off-Shore Co., 1972 U.S. LEXIS 114.
Bridston by Bridston v. Dover Corp., 352 N.W.2d 194 (N.D. 1984).
Broderson v. Ranier Nat. Park Co., 60 P.2d 234 (Wash. 1936).
Brookner v. New York Roadrunners Club, Inc., 2008 N.Y. App. Div. Lexis 4393.
Brooks v. Timberline Tours, Inc., 941 F.Supp. 959 (1996).
Brooks v. Timberline Tours, Inc., 1997 U.S. App. LEXIS 29862.
Broome v. Ohio Ski Slopes, Inc., 1995 Ohio App. LEXIS 5971.
Brooten v. Hickok Rehabilitation Services, LLC, 2013 Wisc. App. LEXIS 370.
Brough v. Hidden Valley, Inc., 1998 N.J. Super. LEXIS 255.
Brotherton v. Victory Sports, Inc., 2013 U.S. Dist. LEXIS 74407.
Brown v. Columbus All-Breed Training Club, 2003 Ohio App. LEXIS 1946.
Brown v. Northwoods Animal Shelter, 2011 Mich. App. LEXIS 1912.
Brown v. Racquetball Centers, Inc., 534 A.2d 842 (Pa. Super. 1987).
Brown v. Robbins, 2007 N.C. App. LEXIS 2271.
Brown v. Soh, 2004 Conn. Super. LEXIS 1517.
Brown v. Soh, 2006 Conn. LEXIS 422.
Brown v. Wakefield Fitness Center, 1994 R.I. Super. LEXIS 79.
Brozyna v. Niagara Gorge Jetboating, LTD, 2011 U.S. Dist. LEXIS 111546.
Brush v. Jiminy Peak Mountain Resort, 2009
Bryant v. Cruises, Inc., 1998 U.S. Dist. LEXIS 4372.
Buchan v. U.S. Cycling Federation, 277 Cal.Rptr. 887 [1991].
Buckeye Check Cashing, Inc. v. Cardegna, 2006 U.S. LEXIS 1814.
Bufano v. National Inline Roller Hockey Association, 2000 N.Y. App. Div. LEXIS 5107.
Burd v. KL Shangri-la Owners, 2002 Okla Civ. App. LEXIS 143.
Burke v. McKay, 2004 Neb. LEXIS 86.
Burnett v. Tofguy Productions, 2010 U.S. Dist LEXIS 112539.
Burns v. Wilderness Ventures, Inc., 2012 U.S. Dist. LEXIS 124309.
Butler v. Saville, 2014 Conn. Super. LEXIS 1584.
Byrd v. Mathews, 571 So.2d 258 (Miss. 1990).

C

Cabellero v. Willow Springs International Raceway, Inc., 2004 Cal. App. Unpub.
Cabbage Patch Settlement House v. Wheatly, 987 S.W.2d 784.
Cain v. Banka, 2005 Fla. App. LEXIS 10794.
Calarco v. YMCA of Greater Metropolitan Chicago, 501 N.E.2d 268 [Ill., 1986].
Capri v. L.A. Fitness International (2006)
Carlisle v. Carnival Corporation, 2003 Fla. App. LEXIS 12794.
Carlisle v. Ulysses Line LTD., 475 So.2d 248 (Fla., 1985).
Carnival Cruise Lines, Inc., v. Shute, 1991 U.S. LEXIS 2221.
Carpenter v. American Honda Motor Co., Inc., 2004 Cal. App. Unpub. LEXIS 10465.
Catalano v. N.W.A. Inc., 1998 Minn. Tax LEXIS 68.
Cave v. Davey Crockett Stables, 1995 Tenn. App. LEXIS 560.
Celli v. Sports Car Club of America, Inc., 105 Cal.Rptr.904 (1972).
Chadwick v. Colt Ross Outfitters, Inc., 2004 Colo. LEXIS 892.
Chan v. Society Expeditions, Inc., 123 F.3d 1287 (Cal., 1997).
Chang v. Camelback Ski Slope, 1999 Pa. D. & C. LEXIS
Chapman v. Norwegian Cruise Line Ltd., 2001 U.S. Dist. LEXIS 9360 (W.D.N.C. 2001).
Charbonnet v. Shami, 2013 Tex. App. LEXIS 7161.
Charnis v. Watersport Pro LLC, 2009 U.S. Dist. LEXIS 76022.
Chauvlier v. Booth Creek Ski Holdings, Inc., 2001 Wash. App. LEXIS 3625.
Chavez v. City of Santa Fe Springs, 2011 Cal. App. Unpub. LEXIS 9462.
Checket v. Tuthill Corp., 2001 Pa. Dist. & Cnty. Dec. LEXIS 460.
Chepkevich v. Hidden Valley Resort, 2006 Pa. Super LEXIS 3773.
Chew v. Lord, 2008 Wash. App. LEXIS 774.
Chiarizia v. Xtreme Rydz Custom Cycles, 2007 N.Y. App. Div. LEXIS 100287.
Chieco v. Paramarketing, Inc., 643 N.Y.S.2d 668 (1996).
Childress v. Madison County, 777 S.W.2d 1 (Tenn.App. 1989).
Christian v. Eagles Landing Christian Academy, 2010 Ga. App. LEXIS 284.
City of Hammond v. Plys, 2008 Ind. App. LEXIS 2593.
City of Santa Barbara v. The Superior Ct. of Santa Barbara County, 2006 Cal. App. LEXIS 84.
Clanton v. United Skates of America, 686 N.E.2d 896 (Ind., 1997).
Cobb v. Aramark Sports and Entertainment Services, LLC, 2013 U.S. Dist. LEXIS 20139.
Cohen v. Five Brooks Stable, 2008 Cal. App. LEXIS 222.
Colagiovanni v. New Haven Aquisition Corp., 2006 Conn. Super. LEXIS 3387.
Colfer v. Royal Globe Insurance Co., 1986 N.J.Super. LEXIS 1531.
Collins v. Schweitzer, 1991 U.S.Dist. LEXIS 14333.
Conkey v. Eldridge, 1999 Ohio App. LEXIS 5635.
Connolly v. The Penninsula Group, 2008 N.Y. App. Div. LEXIS 1753.
Connors v. Reel Ice, Inc. (2000 Conn. Super LEXIS 1926).
Conradt v. Four Star Promotions, Inc., 728 P.2d 617 (Wash.App. 1986).
Cook v. Crazy Boat of Key West, Inc., 2007 Fla. App. LEXIS 3303.
Cooley v. City of Carrollton, 2001 Ga. App. LEXIS 424.
Cooper v. The U.S. Ski Asso., 2000 Colo. App. LEXIS 1448 (2000).
Cooper v. Aspen Skiing Company, 2002 Colo. LEXIS (2002).
Cooper v. The Aspen Skiing Company, 48 P.3d 1229 (2003).
Coronel v. Chicago White Sox, LTD, 1992 Ill. App. LEXIS 785.
Corso v. United States Surgical Corporation, 2005 WL 1435905 (Conn. Super.).
Cortez v. Ceres Unified Sch. Dis., 2003 Cal. App. Unpub. LEXIS 2156.
Costa v. The Boston Red Sox Baseball Club, 2004 Mass. App. LEXIS 639.
Costanza v. Allstate Insurance Co., 2002 U.S. Dist. LEXIS 21991 (La.)

Couch v. Lyon, 2013 U. S. Dist. LEXIS 160770.
Coughlin v. T.M.H. International Attractions, Inc., 1995 U.S.Dist. LEXIS 12499.
Courbat v. Dahana Ranch, Inc., 2006 Haw. LEXIS 386.
Courtney v. Pacific Adventures, Inc., 1998 U.S.Dist LEXIS 6373.
Cousins Club Corp. v. Silva, 2004 Fla. App. LEXIS 4596.
Cox v. US Fitness, LLC, 2013 Ill. App. LEXIS 879.
Crace v. Kent State University, 2009 Ohio App. LEXIS 5785.
Cross v. Carnes, 724 N.E.2d 828 (Oh. App. 1998).
Cronin v. California Fitness, 2005 Ohio App. LEXIS 3056.
Cruz v. Atco Raceway, Inc., 2013 U.S. Dist. LEXIS 90414.
Cruz v. Atco Raceway, Inc., 2015 U.S. Dist. LEXIS 85524.
Cunningham v. State, 32 N.Y.S.2d 275 (1942).
Curtis v. Hoosier Racing Tire Corp., 2004 U.S.Dist. LEXIS 379.

D
Daddario v. Snow Valley, Inc., 43 Cal.Rptr.2d 726 (1995).
Dailey v. Sports World South, Inc., 2003 Minn. App. LEXIS 1223.
Dalury v. S-K-I, Ltd., 670 A.2d 795 (1995).
Danes v. Automobile Underwriters, Inc., 307 N.E.2d 902.
Dare v. Freefall Adventures, Inc., 2002 N.J.Super. LEXIS 155.
Davies v. General Tours, Inc., 2001 Conn. App. LEXIS 1999.
Davis v. 3 Bar F Rodeo, 2007 Ky. App. Unpub. LEXIS 301
Davis v. Sun Valley Education Foundation, Inc., 1997 Ida. LEXIS 82.
Dean v. McDonald, 2001 N.H. LEXIS 210.
DeAsis v. YMCA of Yakima (YMCA), 2014 Wash. App. LEXIS 2201.
Debell v. Wellbridge Club Management, Inc., 2007 N.Y. App. Div. LEXIS 5480
DeCormier v. Harley-Davidson Motor Company Group, Inc., 2014 Mo. LEXIS 215.
DeKalb v. White, 260 S.E.2d 853.
Delponte v. Coral World Virgin Islands, Inc., 2006 U.S. Dist. LEXIS 59364.
Deutsch v. Woodridge Segway, LLC, 2014 N.Y. App. Div. LEXIS 3417.
Del Bosco v. United States Ski Assn., 839 F.Supp. 1470 (1993).
Delk v. Go Vertical, Inc., 2004 U.S.Dist. LEXIS 1466.
Del Raso v. United States of America, 244 F.3d 567 (N.C.2000).
DeVeccio v. Delaware Enduro Riders, Inc (2004 Del. Super LEXIS 444.
Dieu v. McGraw, 2011 Cal. App. Unpub. LEXIS 87.
Dilallo v. Riding Safely, Inc., 687 So.2d 353 (Fla 4d 1997).
DiMaria v. Coordinated Ranches, Inc., 1988 N.Y. App. Div. LEXIS 28880.
Dinenno v. Lucky Fin Water Sports, 2011 U.S. Dist. LEXIS 17934.
Dobratz v. Thomson, 468 N.W.2d 654 (Wis. 1991).
Dobratz v. Thomson, 455 N.W.2d 639 (Wis.App. 1990).
Dodge v. Grafton Zipline Adventures, LLC, 2015 Ill. App. Unpub. LEXIS 1584.
Donahue v. Ledgends, Inc., 2014 Alas. LEXIS 153.
Donegan v. Beech Bend Raceway Pzrk, Inc., 894 F.2d 205 (Ky 1990).
Dore v. Roten, 2005 Fla. App. LEXIS 14903.
Douglas v. Skiing Standards, Inc., 459 A.2d 97 (Vt. 1983).
Douglass v. Pflueger Hawaii, Inc., 2006 Haw. LEXIS 280.
Dow-Westbrook v. Candlewood Equine Practice, 2010 Conn. App. LEXIS 78.
Downing v. United Auto Racing Association, 570 N.E.2d 828 (Ill.App. 1 Dist. 1991).
Doyle v. Bowdoin College, 403 A.2d 1206 (Me. 1979).
Doyle v. Giuliucci, 43 Cal.Rptr. 697 (Cal., 1965).
Dubret v. Holland America Line Westours, Inc., 1998 U.S. Dist LEXIS 15605.
Duchesneau v. Cornell University, 2013 U.S. Dist. LEXIS 22728.
Duchesneau v. Cornell University, 2014 U.S. App. LEXIS 4728.
Duffy v. Camelback Ski Corp, 1992 U.S.Dist. LEXIS 8988.
Dumez v. Harbor Jet Ski, Inc., 117 Misc.2d 249 (1982).
Duncan v. Ryba Company, 1999 U.S.Dist. LEXIS 12424.
Dunn v. Paducah International Raceway, 599 F.Supp.612 (Ky.1984).
Dunlap v. Fortress Corporation, 2000 Tenn. App. LEXIS 720).
Durrell v. Parachutes Are Fun, Inc., C.A. No. 85C-AU-82 (Md., 1987)

E
Eastman v. Yutzy, 2001 Mass. Super. LEXIS 157.
Easterling v. English Point Riding Stables Inc., 1994 U.S. Dist. LEXIS 270.
Eburn v. Capitol Peak Outfitters, Inc., 2012 U.S. Dist. LEXIS 106236.
Eder v. Lake Geneva Raceway, Inc., 523 N.W. 2d 429.
Egan v. Young Men's Christian Association, 2011 Cal. App. Unpub. LEXIS 3010.
Ehrenreich v. Mohawk Mountain Ski Area, 2004 Conn. Super. LEXIS 2466.
El-Halees v. Chauser, 2002 Cal. App. Unpub. LEXIS 8124 (2002).
Emerick v. Fox Raceway, 2004 Pa. D. & C. LEXIS 1241.
Empress Health and Beauty Spa, Inc. v. Turner, 503 S.W.2d 188 (1973).
Eriksson v. Nunnink, 2015 Cal. App. LEXIS 65.
Ervin v. Hosanna Ministry, Inc., 1995 Conn. Super. LEXIS 3138.
Escola v. Coca Cola Bottling Co., 1944 Cal. LEXIS 248.
Espinosa v. Arkansas Valley Adventures, LLC, 2014 U.S. Dist. LEXIS 136102.
Estate of Edwin Peters v. United States Cycling Federation, 1991 U.S.Dist. LEXIS.
Estes Express Lines, Inc. v. Chopper Express, Inc., 2007 Va. LEXIS 25.
Evans v. Pikeway, Inc., 2004 N. Y. Misc. LEXIS 2982.

F
Falkner v. John E. Fetzer, Inc., Mich. App. 317 N.W.2d 337.
Farrari v. Bob's Canoe Rental, Inc., 2014 N.Y. Misc. LEXIS 3768.
Faranso v. Cass Lake Beach Club, Inc. (1998 Mich. App. LEXIS 1697).
Faronda v. Hawaii International Boxing Club, 2001 Haw. App. LEXIS 117.
Farina v. Mt. Bachelor, Inc., 66 F.3d 233 (1995).
Farris v. KTM North America, Inc., 2006 U.S. Dist. LEXIS 1635.
Fazzinga v. Westchester Track Club, 2008 N.Y. App. Div. LEXIS 1078.
Fecke v. Board of Supervisors of LSU, 2015 La. App. LEXIS 1357.
Fedor v. Mauwehu Council, Boy Scouts of Am., 143 A.2d 466 (1958).
Fee v. Steve Snyder Enterprises, Inc., Civil Action No. 84-2323 (Kan., 1986).
Ferrari v. Grand Canyon Dories, 32 Cal.App.4th 248.
Fields v. Kirton, 2007 Fla. App. LEXIS 12241.
Filson v. Cold River Trail Rides, 1997 N.Y. App. Div. LEXIS 8524.

Finch v. Andrews, 1993 Ore. App. LEXIS 1902.
Finkler v. Toledo Ski Club, 577 N.E.2d 1114 (Ohio App. 1989).
Finley v. Club One, Inc., 2012 Cal. App. Unpub. LEXIS 2444.
Fisher v. Olde Towne Tours, 2011 Cal. App. Unpub. LEXIS 5856.
Fisher v. Rivest, 2002 Conn. Super. LEXIS 2778.
Fisher v. Stevens, 2003 S.C. App. LEXIS 109.
Fire Insurance Exchange v. Cincinnati Insurance Company, 2000 Wisc. App. LEXIS 243.
Fitzgerald v. Newark Morning Ledger Company, 267 A.2d 557 (1970).
Fleetwood Enterprises, Inc. v. Gaskamp, 280 F.3d 1069 (Tex., 2002).
Floyd v. Club Systems of Tennessee, Inc., 1999 Tenn. App. LEXIS 473.
Flood v. YWCA of Brunswick, GA, Inc., 2005 U.S. App. LEXIS 1548.
Fojtasek v. NCL (Bahamas) Ltd., 2009 U.S. Dist. LEXIS 42605.
Forrester v. Aspen Athletic Clubs, 2009 Iowa App. LEXIS 170.
Fortson v. McClellan, 1998 N.C. App. LEXIS 1436.
Frank v. Mathews, 2004 Mo. App. LEXIS 844.
Friedman v. Premier Cruise Lines, 1992 U.S.App. LEXIS 14933.
Fugaro v. Royal Caribbean Cruises, LTD., 851 F.Supp. 122 (1994).
Furlani v. Town of East Lyme, 2010 Conn. Super. LEXIS 196.

G
Gambino v. Music Television, Inc., 1996 U.S.Dist. LEXIS 10777).
Galisson v. Shawnee Mountain Ski Area, 1996 Pa.D.&C. LEXIS 182.
Gallant v. Hilton Worldwide, Inc., 2014 N.Y. Misc. LEXIS 853.
Galloway v. State of Iowa, 2010 Iowa Sup. LEXIS 109.
Gara v. Woodbridge Tavern, 568 N.W.2d 138 (Mich., 1997).
Garnett v. Strike Holdings, 2009 N.Y. App. Div. LEXIS 5457.
Garrison v. Combined Fitness Centre,559 N.E.2d 187, [Ill. 1990].
Gavin v. YMCA of Metro. Los Angeles, 2003 Cal. App. LEXIS 279.
Geczi v. Lifetime Fitness, 2012 Ohio App. LEXIS 2580.
Geo. R. Lane & Associates v. Thomasson, 156 Ga. App. 313 (1980).
Gershon v. Regency Diving Center, Inc., 2004 N.J. Super. LEXIS 143.
Ghane v. Mid-South Institute of Self Defense Shooting, Inc., 2014 Miss. LEXIS 32.
Ghionis v. Deer Valley Resort Company, Ltd., 839 F.Supp. 789 (Utah).
Gilkeson v. Five Mile Point Speedway, Inc., 1996 N.Y. App. Div. LEXIS 11275.
Gillette v. All Pro Sports, LLC, 2014 Fla. App. LEXIS 744.
Gimpel v. Host Enterprises, Inc., 1986 U.S. Dist. LEXIS 22330.
Giuffra v. Vantage Travel Service, Inc., 2015 U.S. Dist. LEXIS 70331.
Give Kids the World, Inc. v. Sanislo, 2012 Fla. App. LEXIS 17750.
Glenn v. Annunziata, 2010 N.Y. App. Div. LEXIS 3226.
Global Travel Marketing, Inc. v. Shea, 2005 Fla. LEXIS 1454.
Gomez v. Maricopa Co., 175 Ariz 469 (1993).
Gomez v. Royal Caribbean Cruise Lines, 964 F.Supp. 47 (D.P.R. 1997).
Gonzalez v. City of Coral Gables, 2004 Fla. App. LEXIS 6612.
Gonzalez v. Rusty Wallace Racing Experience, 2015 Mich. App. LEXIS 25.
Gonzalez v. University System of New Hampshire, 2005 Conn. Super. LEXIS 288.
Gorlin v. Jacobson, 2005 Cal. App. Unpub. LEXIS 10971.
Goyings v. Jack and Ruth Eckerd Foundation, 403 So.2d 1144 (1981).
Grabill v. Adams County Fair & Racing Association, 2003 Iowa Sup. LEXIS 127.
Grebing v. 24 Hour Fitness USA, Inc., 2015 Cal. App. LEXIS 153.
Greenwich Insurance Co. v. Louisville N.R.R., 1902, Ky.
Grewal v. Hickenbottom, 2003 Tex. App. LEXIS 8620.
Grigsby v. O.K. Travel, 1997 Ohio App. LEXIS 875.
Grijalva v. Bally Total Fitness Corporation, 2015 Tex. App. LEXIS 3277.
Gross v. Sweet, 49 NY2d 102 (1979).
Groves v. Firebird Raceway, Inc., 1994 U.S.Dist. LEXIS 5575.
Guerra v. Howard Beach Fitness Center, 2011 N.Y. Misc. LEXIS 3346.
Guivi v. Spectrum Club Holding Company, 2011 Cal. App. Unpub. LEXIS 3178.
Guthrie v. Hidden Valley Golf and Ski, Inc., 2013 Mo. App. LEXIS 598.

H
Hackel v. Whitecap Recreations, 357 N.W.2d 565 (1984).
Hackett v. Grand Seas Resort Owner's Association, 2012 Fla. App. LEXIS 10111.
Hague v. Summit Acres Skilled Nursing and Rehab., 2010 Ohio App. LEXIS 5400.
Haines v. St. Charles Speedway, Inc., 874 F.2d 572 (Mo., 1989).
Hall v. Bill Perry and Hidden Creek Outfitters, 2009 Wyo. LEXIS 94.
Hallman v. Dover Downs, Inc., 1986 U.S. Dist. LEXIS 377.
Hambrook v. Smith, 2015 U.S. Dist. LEXIS 70968.
Hamill v. Cheley Colorado Camps, Inc., 2011 Colo. App. LEXIS 495.
Handy-Mixon v. LA Fitness, 2007 Cal. App. Unpub. LEXIS 10037.
Hanks v. Powder Ridge Restaurant Corporation, 2005 Conn. LEXIS 500.
Hanks v. Sawtelle Rentals, Inc., 984 P.2d 122 Id. 1999).
Harden v. American Airlines, 1998 U.S. Dist. LEXIS 4325.
Hanson v. Northern J & B Enterprises, 2009 Minn. App. Unpub. LEXIS 138.
Harden v. American Airlines, 1998 U.S.Dist. LEXIS 4325.
Hardy v. St. Clair, 1999 ME 142.
Hargis v. Baize, 2005 Ky. LEXIS 834.
Harmon v. Mt. Hood Meadows, Ltd., 1997 Ore. App. LEXIS 83.
Hatch v. V.P. Fair Foundation, Inc., 1999 Mo. App. LEXIS 315.
Hawkins v. Capital Fitness, Inc., 2015 Ill. App. LEXIS 138.
Hawkins v. Peart, 2001 Utah LEXIS 177.
Hawkins v. Second KYU, Inc., 2009 Pa. Super LEXIS 1452.
Haynes v. County of Missoula, 517 P.2d 370.
Hall v. Perry, 2009 Wyo. LEXIS 94.
Hall v. Woodland Lake Leisure Resort Club, Inc., 1998 Ohio App. LEXIS 4898.
Hargis v. Baize, 2005 Ky. LEXIS 158.
Harwood v. Planning Committee for the Senior Class, 2000 U.S.Dist. LEXIS 6371.
Hazelwood v. L.A. Fitness International, 2011 Cal. App. Unpub. LEXIS 5753.
Heilig v. Touchstone Climbing, Inc., 2007 Cal. App. Unpub. LEXIs 8770.
Hellweg v. Special Events Management, 2011 Ill. App. LEXIS 725.
Hembree v. Johnson, 482 S.E.2d 407.
Henderson v. Carnival Corp., 2000 U.S. Dist. LEXIS 18821.
Henderson v. Quest Expeditions, Inc., 2005 Tenn. App. LEXIS 334.
Herren v. Sucher, 2013 Ga. App. LEXIS 873.

Mashburn v. Royal Caribbean Cruises, Ltd., 55 F.Supp.2d 1367 (S.D.Fla. 1999).
Massengill v. S.M.A.R.T. Sports Medicine Clinic, P.C., 996 P.2d 1132 (Wyo., 2000).
Maurer v. Cerkvenik-Anderson Travel, Inc.(165 Ariz.Adv.Rep. 51 (1994).
Mavreshkof v. Resorts USA, 2008 U.S. App. LEXIS 23134.
Maxwell v. Motorcycle Safety Foundation, Inc., 2013 Tenn. App. LEXIS 52.
Mayer v. Howard, 370 N.W.2d 93 (Neb. 1985).
Mays v. Valley View Ranch, Inc., 2012 Ga. App. LEXIS 674.
McBride v. Minstar, Inc., 283 N.J.Super 471 (1994).
McCarthy v. National Association for Stock Car Racing, 226 A.2d 713 (1967).
McCorkle v. Hall, 782 P.2d 574 (Wash. App. 1989).
McCurry v. School Dist. Of Valley, 1993 Neb. LEXIS 42
McClure v. Life Time Fitness, Inc., 2014 U.S. Dist. LEXIS 167483.
McCune v. Myrtle Beach Indoor Shooting Range, Inc., 2005 S.C. App. LEXIS 90.
McDermott v. Carie, 2005 Mont. LEXIS 480.
McDonald v. Whitewater Challengers, Inc., 2015 Pa. Super. LEXIS 232.
McDonough v. National Off-Road Bicycle Association, 1997 U.S.Dist. LEXIS 8036.
McDuffie v. Watkins Glen International, Inc. (1993
McFann v. Sky Warriors, Inc., 2004 Ga. App. LEXIS 857.
McGowan v. West End YMCA, 2002 Cal. App. LEXIS 2993 (2002).
McGregor v. Christian Care Center of Springfield, 2010 Tenn. App. LEXIS 309.
McGuire v. Sunday River Ski Corp., 1994 U.S.Dist. LEXIS 13061.
McMurray v. United States of America, 2012 U.S. Dist. LEXIS 176608.
McNamara v. Healthtrax Int., 2009 Conn. Super. LEXIS 2693.
Mechanic v. Princeton Ski Shop, Inc., 1992 U.S.Dist. LEXIS 19979.
Mellon v. Crunch, 2011 N.Y. Misc. LEXIS 3379.
Mero v. City Segway Tours of Washington DC, LLC, 2013 U.S. Dist. LEXIS 120304.
Messer v. Hi Country Stables Corporation, 2012 U.S. Dist. LEXIS 2675.
Merten v. Nathan, 321 N.W.2d 173 (1983).
Mettler v. Nellis, 2005 Wisc. App. LEXIS 248.
Meyer v. Naperville Manner, Inc., 1994 Ill. App. LEXIS 749.
Meyers v. Postal Fin. Co., 287 N.W.2d 614 (Minn. 1979).
Milgrim v. Backroads, Inc., 2001 U.S.Dist. LEXIS 5507.
Millan v. Brown, 2002 N.Y.App. Div. LEXIS 5937.
Miller v. Fallon County, 222 Mont. 214 (1986).
Milligan v. Big Valley Corp., 754 P.2d 1063 (Wyo. 1986).
Milne v. USA Cycling Inc., 2007 U.S. Dist LEXIS 42579.
Minnifield v. Ashcraft., 2004 Ala. Civ. App. Lexis 908.
Miranda v. Shelby Township, 2003 Mich.App. LEXIS 2690.
Missar v. Camelback Ski Resort, 1984 Pa.D.&C. LEXIS 326.
Mohler v. Kipu Ranch Adventures, LLC, 2014 U.S. Dist. LEXIS 159195.
Mizushima v. Sunset Ranch, Inc., 737 P.2d 1158 (Nev. 1987).
Moffitt v. 24 Hour Fitness Usa, Inc., 2013 U.S. Dist. LEXIS 35363.
Mohney v. USA Hockey, Inc., 1999 U.S. Dist. LEXIS 19359 .
Mohney v. USA Hockey, Inc., 2001 U.S.App. LEXIS 3584.
Mohney v. USA Hockey, Inc., 2005 U.S. App. LEXIS 14373.
Moore v. American Santic Line. Inc., 121 F.2d 767 (NY, 1941).
Moore v. Edmonds, 45 N.E.2d 190 (Ill., 1942).
Moore v. Minnesota Baseball Instructional School, 2009 Minn. App. Unpub. LEXIS 299.
Moore v. Hartley Motors, Inc., 2001 Alas. LEXIS 126.
Moore v. Minnesota Baseball Instructional School, 2009 Minn. App. Unpub. LEXIS 299.
Moore v. Waller (2007), 2007 D.C. App. LEXIS 476.
Morales v. Royal Carribean Cruises, LTD, 2006 U.S. Dist. LEXIS 7455.
Morganteen v. Cowboy Adventures, Inc., 251 Ariz. Adv. Rep. 17.
Morrison v. Northwest Nazarene University, 2012 Ida. LEXIS 82.
Morrow v. Norwegian Cruise Line Limited, 2002 U.S. Dist. LEXIS 26575.
Moser v. Ratinoff, 2003 Cal.App. LEXIS 138.
Moss v. Fortune, 340 S.W.2d 902 (1960).
Mower v. City of Realto, 2005 Cal. App. Unpub. LEXIS 11653.
Municipality of Anchorage v. Locker, 1986 Alas. LEXIS 372.
Munn v. Hotchkiss School, 2013 U.S. Dist. LEXIS 40787.
Murley v. Deep Explorers, Inc., 2003 U.S. Dist. LEXIS 14749.
Munoz v. II Jaz Inc., 1993 Tex. App. LEXIS 2550.
Murphy v. North American River Runners, Inc. 412 S.E.2d 504 [1991].
Murphy v. YMCA of Lake Wales, Inc., 2008 Fla. App. LEXIS 2035.
Murray v. Texas Co. 174 S.E.231 [1934].
Myers v. Doe, 2014 N.Y. Misc. LEXIS 4186.

N

Nesbitt v. National Muscle Car Association, 2014 Ill. App. Unpub. LEXIS 1848.
Newman v. Tropical Visions, Inc., 1994 Tex. App. LEXIS 3254.
Nicholson v. Mount Airy Lodge, Inc., 1997 U.S.Dist. LEXIS 21035.
Niedbala v. S.L. – Your Partners in Health (2002 Conn. Super. LEXIS 2835).
Niese v. Skip Barber Racing School, 2002 Wisc. App. LEXIS 190.
Nisbett v. Camelback Ski Corp. No. 2226 Civ. 1992 (Monroe Cty. Common Pleas Sept. 30, 1996).
Nishi v. Mt. Snow, Ltd., 1996 U.S. Dist. LEXIS 12638.
Nissley v. Candytown Motorcycle Club, 2006 Pa. Super. LEXIS 4472.
Nimis v. St. Paul Turners, 521 N.W.2d 54 (Mn.1994).
Northern Health Facilities v. Batz, 2014 U.S. Dist. LEXIS 8691.
Northwest Airlines v. Hughes Air Corporation, 37 Wn. App. 344.
Nutley v. Skydive the Ranch, 2009 N.Y. Misc. LEXIS 274.

O

O'Brien v. Freeman, 11 N.E.2d. 582 (Mass., 1937).
O'Connell v. Walt Disney World Co., 413 So.2d 444 (1982).
O'Connor v. The United States Fencing Association, 2003 U.S. Dist. LEXIS 7446.
Oelze v. Score Sports Venture, LLC, 2010 Ill. LEXIS 1383 (Ill., Sept. 29, 2010).
O'Keefe v. Inca Floats, 1997 U.S.Dist. LEXIS 17088.
Okura v. U.S. Cycling Federation, 231 Cal.Rptr. 429 [1986].
Olivelli v. Sappo Corporation, 2003 U.S. Dist. LEXIS 18241.
Oliver v. Tanning Bed, Inc., 2008 N.Y. App. Div. LEXIS 3147.
Ontiveros v. 24 Hour Fitness USA, Inc., 2008 Cal. App. LEXIS 2445.

Oran v. Fair Wind Sailing, 2009 U.S. Dist. LEXIS 110350.
Ormiston v. California Youth Soccer Association, 2011 Cal. App. Unpub. LEXIS 4226.
Osborne v. Cascade Mountain, Inc., 2002 Wisc. App. LEXIS 1216.
Ostrowiecki v. Aggressor Fleet, 2008 U.S. Dist. LEXIS 62713.

P

Padilla v. The Sports Club Company, 2008 Cal. App. Unpub. LEXIS 8150.
Page Petroleum, Inc. v. Dresser Ind., Inc., 36 Tex. Sup. Ct. J. 737 (1993).
Palmer v. Lakeside Wellness Center, 2011 Neb. LEXIS 62.
Paralift, Inc. v. Superior Court (1993) 23 Cal. App. 4th 748, 755.
Paredes v. Princess Cruises, Inc, 1 F.Supp.2d 87 (D.Mass. 1998).
Park-Childs v. Mrotek's, Inc., 1998 Wisc. App. LEXIS 253.
Parco v. Snow Summit, 2009 Cal. App. Unpub. LEXIS 4020.
Parveen v. Tiki Tubing, 2012 La. App. Unpub. LEXIS 115.
Passero v. DHC Hotels & Resorts, Inc., 981 F.Supp. 742.
Passero v. Killington, Ltd., 1993 U.S. Dist. LEXIS 14049.
Pastor v. Putney Student Travel, 1999 U.S. Dist. LEXIS 9194 (1999).
Patel v. ABC Unified School District, 2011 Cal. App. LEXIS 1377.
Paz v. Lifetime Fitness, 2010 U.S. Dist. LEXIS 133058.
Pazol v. Tough Mudder Incorporated, 2015 U.S. Dist. LEXIS 52784.
Pearce v. Utah Athletic Foundation, 2008 Utah LEXIS 16.
Pena v. The Roladium, 2002 Cal. App. LEXIS 1466.
Pendergrass v. Diamond Bar and Circle K Horse Rentals, 2010 Cal. App. Unpub. LEXIS 6897.
Pennsylvania R.R. Co. V. McCloskey's Adm'rs, 1854 Pa. LEXIS 145.
Penunuri v. Sundance Partners, 2001 Utah App. LEXIS 189.
Penunuri v. Sundance Partners, 2013 Utah LEXIS 62.
Perelman v. Snowbird Ski Shop, Inc., 626 N.Y.S.2d 304 (1995).
Perry v. New Jersey Sports & Exposition Authority, 2008 N.J. Super Unpub. LEXIS 591.
Perry v. Thomas, 482 U.S. 483 cited in Global Travel Marketing, Inc
(Peters v. Bally's Holiday Spa Health Clubs of Cal., 2004 Cal.App. Unpub. LEXIS 3547.
Petersen v. Sorensen, 2003 Wash. App. LEXIS 1894.
Peterson v. Flare Fittings, Inc., 2015 Fla. App. LEXIS 14990.
Petrie v. Bridgehampton Road Races Corporation, 1998 N.Y. App. Div. LEXIS 2873.
Phelps v. Firebird Raceway, Inc., 2005 Ariz. LEXIS 53.
Phillips v. Monarch Recreation Corp., 668 P.2d 982 (Co., 1983).
Pietroluongo v. Regency Diving Center, Inc., 368 N.J. Super. 237; 845 A.2d 720.
Piche v. Stockdale Holdings, LLC, 2009 U.S. Dist. LEXIS 24237.
Pineda v. Town Sports Int., 2009 N.Y. Misc. LEXIS 5082.
Pippin v. M.A. Hauser Ent., Inc., 676 N.E.2d 932, 936 (1996).
Pitasi v. The Stratton Corp., 1992 U.S.App. LEXIS 16051.
Plant v. Wilbur, 2001 Ark. LEXIS 434.
Platt v. Gateway International Motor Sports Corporation, 2004 Ill. App. LEXIS 943.
Platzer v. Mammoth Mountain Ski Area, 2002 Cal. App. LEXIS 5246.
Pollock v. Highlands Ranch Com. Asso., Inc., 2006 Colo. App. LEXIS 929.
Poole v. South Plainfield Bd. of Ed., 490 F.Supp. 948 (1980).
Porter v. Dartmouth College, 2009 U.S. Dist. LEXIS 90516.
Post v. Belmont Country Club, Inc., 2004 Mass. App. LEXIS 288.
Potrzebowski v. Redline Raceway, 2011 U.S. Dist. LEXIS 55871.
Potts v. Whitewater Mountain Resorts of Connecticut, 2001 Conn.Super. LEXIS 2433.
Powell v. American Health Fitness Center, 694 N.E.2d 757 (Ind. Ct. App. 1998).
Powell v. Trans Global Tours, Inc., 1999 Minn. App. LEXIS 591.
Poulos v. Alpine Meadows Ski Corporation, 2002 Cal. App. Unpub. LEXIS 602.
Powers v. Mukpo, 12 Mass. L. Rpter. 517 (2000).
Pride v. Southern Bell Tel. & Tel. Co., 138 S.E.2d 155 (S.C., 1964).
Princeton Sportswear Corporation v. H & M Associates, 1986 Pa. LEXIS 735.
Provoncha v. Vermont Motocross Association, Inc., 2009Vt. LEXIS 25.
Pruett v. American Motorcycle Assn., 1995 U.S.App. LEXIS 11891.
Pulford v. County of Los Angeles 2004 Cal. App. Unpub. LEXIS 8580.
Pulliam v. Pocono International, 1996 U.S. Dist. LEXIS 22792.
Putzer v. Vic Tanney-Flatbush Inc. 20 A.D.2d 821 [NY, 1964].

Q

Quirk v. Walker's Gymnastics and Dance, 2003 Mass. Super. LEXIS 210 (2003).
Quinn v. Mississippi State University, 1998 Miss. LEXIS 328.
Quintana v. Crossfit Dallas, 2011 Tex. App. LEXIS 6329.

R

Rackley v. Advanced Cycling Concepts, Inc., 2009 Tex. App. LEXIS 1888.
Rahuba v. 5 D's, Inc., 2004 Conn. Super. LEXIS 2575.
Ramirez v. 24 Hour Fitness USA, Inc., 2013 U.S. App. LEXIS 24893.
Randas v. YMCA of Metropolitan Los Angeles, 1993 Cal. App. LEXIS 729.
Raveson v. Walt Disney World, 2001 Fla. App. LEXIS 12973.
Reardon v. Windswept Farm, LLC, 2006 Conn. LEXIS 330.
Reardon v. Windswept Farm, 2005 Conn. Super LEXIS 725.
Reed v. University of North Dakota, 1999 N.D. LEXIS 27.
Reilly v. Leasure, 2010 Conn. Super. LEXIS 2704.
Reimund v. Guthrie, 2008 Cal. App. Unpub. LEXIS 1336.
Renard v. 200 Convention Center, Ltd., 728 P.2d 445 (Nev. 1986).
Reuther v. Southern Cross Club, Inc., 785 F.Supp. 1339 (Ind., 1992.
R.H. v. Los Gatos Union School District, 2014 U.S. Dist. LEXIS 47035.
Rhode Island Hospital Trust Nat'l Bank v. Dudley Service Corp., 1992 R.I. LEXIS 82.
Rice v. American Skiing Company, 2000 Me. Super. LEXIS 90.
Rice v. Harley Davidson, 2005 U.S. Dist. LEXIS 44740.
Rich v. Teebar, 2013 U.S. Dist. LEXIS 10682.
Richards v. Richards, 1994 Wisc. LEXIS 26.
Rickey v. Houston Health Club, Inc., 1992 Tex.App. LEXIS 2401.
Rigby v. Sugar's Fitness & Activity Center, 2002 Miss. App. LEXIS 9.
Rigney v. Ichabod Crane Central School District, 2009 N.Y. App. Div. LEXIS 1221.
Robinson v. Chapel Haven, 2010 Conn. Super. LEXIS 1927.
Roe v. Saint Louis University, 2012 U.S. Dist. LEXIS 183265.
Rosen v. National Hot Rod Association, 1995 Texas App. LEXIS 3225.
Rosencrans v. Dover Images, 2011 Cal App. LEXIS 177.

Rothman v. Heart Consciousness Church, 2011 Cal. App. Unpub. LEXIS 1912.
Rothstein v. Snowbird Corporation, 2007 Utah LEXIS 219.
Rogers v. Donaldson-Hermitage Chamber of Commerce, 807 S.W.2d 242 (1990).
Rogowicki v. Troser Management, Inc., 212 A.D.2d 1035 (1995).
Romeo v. The Pittsburgh Associates, 2001 Pa.Super. LEXIS 3491.
Roman v. City of Bristol, 2000 Conn. App. LEXIS 236.
Rubin v. Loon Mountain Recreation Corporation, 1985 U.S. Dist. LEXIS 14792.
Russ v. Woodside Homes, Inc., 1995 Utah App. LEXIS 110.
Rudisill v. Grand Circle Travel Inc., 1999 U.S.Dist. LEXIS 10450.
Ruppa v. American States Ins. Co., 284 N.W.2d 318 (Wis. 1979).
Russo v. The Range, Inc., 395 N.E.2d 10 (Ill., 1979).
Rutherford v. Talisker Canyons Finance Co., LLC, 2014 Utah App. LEXIS 201.

S
Saccente v. LaFlamme, 2003 Conn. Super. LEXIS 1913.
Saccente v. LaFlamme, 2002 Conn. Super. LEXIS 3630.
Salazar v. Riverdale Riding Corporation, 1999 N.Y. Misc. LEXIS 559.
Salazar v. On the Trail Rentals, Inc., 2012 U.S. App. LEXIS 25880.
Salinger v. Leatherdale, 2012 Minn. App. Unpub. LEXIS 958.
Salts v. Bridgeport Marina, Inc., 535 F.Supp. 1038 (Mo., 1982).
Samuelov v. Carnival Cruise Lines, Inc., 2003 Fla. App. LEXIS 18356.
Sanchez v. Bally's Total Fitness Corp., (1998) 68 Cal. App. 4th 62.
Sanders v. Nice, 2004 U.S. Dist. LEXIS 30757.
Sanislo v. Give Kids the World, Inc., 2015 Fla. LEXIS 214.
Santangelo v. City of New York, 66 A.D.2d 880 (1978).
Sapone v. Grand Targhee, Inc., 308 F.3d 1096 (2002).
Saude v. Red River Racquet Club, Ltd., 1989 Minn.App.LEXIS 983.
Sauter v. Perfect North Slopes, 2014 U.S. Dist. LEXIS 468.
Savarese v. Camelback Ski Corp., 417 F.Supp. 2d 663 (M.D. Pa. 2005) cited in Beck-Hummell.
Schaeffer v. Wenk, 2001 N.Y. Misc. LEXIS 415.
Schillachi v. Flying Dutchman Motorcycle Club, 1990 U.S.Dist. LEXIS 14382.
Schlombohm v. Spa Petite, Inc., 326 N.W.2d 920 (Minn., 1982).
Schlumbrecht-Muniz v. Steamboat Ski and Resort Corp., 2015 U.S. Dist. LEXIS 125899.
Schmidt v. United States of America, 1996 Okla. LEXIS 38.
Schneeloch v. Glastonbury Fitness & Wellness, Inc., 2009 Conn. Super. LEXIS 191.
Schoeps v. Whitewater Adventures LLC, 2005 U.S. App. LEXIS 13181.
Schultz v. Florida Keys Dive Center, Inc., 224 F.3d 1269 (11th Cir. 2000).
Schutkowski v. Carey, 725 P.2d 1057 (Wyo. 1986).
Schwartz v. Martin, 2011 N.Y. App. Div. LEXIS 2616.
Scoles v. Franzin, 1991 Minn. App. LEXIS 932.
Scott v. Altoona Bicycle Club, 2010 Pa. Commw. Unpub. LEXIS 513.
Scott v. Pacific West Mountain Resort, 1992 Wash. LEXIS 205.
Scrivener v. Sky's the Limit, 68 F.Supp. 2d 277 (1999).
Seibers v. Dixie Speedway, Inc., 1996 Ga. App. LEXIS 277.
Seigneur v. National Fitness Institute, Inc., 2000 Md. App. LEXIS 91.
Semeniken v. Town Sports International, 2010 N.J. Super Unpub. LEXIS 2681.
Serna v. Lafayette Nordic Village, Inc., 20 U.S. Dist. LEXIS 92669.
Sexton v. Southwestern Auto Racing Ass'n, 394 N.E.2d 49 (Ill., 1979).
Sevilla v. Estate of Lynn Maxey Wiley, 2004 Cal. App. Unpub. LEXIS 11136.
Shaner v. State System of Higher Education, No.1541 S 1989 (1998).
Shankles v. Costa Armatori, 722 F.2d 861 (1st Cir. 1983).
Sharon v. City of Newton, 437 Mass. 99 (1993).
Sharpe v. West Indian Company, 2000 U.S. Dist. LEXIS 1375.
Shawa v. City of Fairfield, 2013 Cal. App. Unpub. LEXIS 3220.
Shea v. Global Travel Marketing, Inc., 2003 Fla. App. LEXIS 12815.
Shephard v. Bear Valley Ski Company, 2005 Cal. App. LEXIS 5591.
Shepard v. Top Hat Land & Cattle Co., 560 P.2d 730, 732 (Wyo. 1997).
Shields v. Sta Fit, Inc., 903 P.2d 525 (Wash. 1995).
Shrayber v. Holiday Harbor, Inc., 2003 Cal. App. Unpub. LEXIS 5037.
Shultz v. Paradise Cruises, Ltd., 888 F.Supp. 1049 (Ha., 1994).
Silva v. Mt. Bachelor, Inc., 2008 U.S.Dist. LEXIS 55942.
Simeone v. Bombardier-Rotax, 2005 U.S. Dist. LEXIS 23544.
Simmons v. Parkette Nat. Gymnastic Training Center, 670 F.Supp. 140 (E.D.Pa. 1987).
Sipari v. Villa Olivia Country Club, 1978 Ill. App. LEXIS 3251.
Sirek v. Fairfield Snowbowl, Inc., 800 P.2d 1291 (Ariz. App. 1990).
Sisino v. Island Motocross of New York, Inc., 2007 N.Y. App. Div. LEXIS 6913.
Skotak v. Vic Tanny Inernational, 513 N.W.2d 428 (Mich. App. 1994).
Slowe v. Pike Creek Court Club, 2008 Del. Super. LEXIS 377.
Smith, Batchelder, & Rugg v. Foster, 1979 N.H. LEXIS 375.
Smith v. West Rochelle Travel Agency, Inc., 1997 N.Y. App. Div. LEXIS 3812.
Smith v. YMCA of Benton Harbor/St. Joseph, 1996 Mich. App. LEXIS 139.
Smokey, Inc. v. McCray, 396 S.E.2d 794 (Ga. App. 1990).
Smolnikar v. Royal Caribbean Cruises LTD., 2011 U.S. Dist. LEXIS 62446.
Solis v. Kirkwood Resort Company, 2001 Cal. App. LEXIS 3090.
Soucy v. Nova Guides, Inc., 2015 U.S. Dist. LEXIS 95438.
Southwick v. City of Rutland, 2011 Vt. LEXIS 51.
Sova v. Apple Vacations, 984 F.Supp. 1136 (Ohio 1997).
Spath v. Dillon Enterprises, Inc., 1999 U.S.Dist. LEXIS 22176.
Speedway SuperAmerica v. Erwin, 2008 Ky. App. LEXIS 74.
Spencer v. Killington, Ltd., 1997 Vt. LEXIS 23.
Spivey v. Challenge of Florida, Inc., 2013 Fla. App. LEXIS 16284.
Squires v. Breckenridge Outdoor Education Center, 2013 U.S. App. LEXIS 9249.
State Farm v. Skivington, 28 D.&C.4th 358 (1996).
Steele v. Mt. Hood Meadows Oregon, LTD., 1999 Ore. App. LEXIS 392.
Steinbarger v. Sahara Sam's Oasis, LLC, 2014 N.J. Super Unpub. LEXIS 2594.
Stelluti v. Casapenn Enterprises, LLC, 2009 N.J. Super. LEXIS 173.
Stephenson v. Food Bank for New York City, 2008 N.Y. Misc. LEXIS 6704.
Stevens v. Payne, 2015 N.Y. Misc. LEXIS 1298.
Stevenson v. Four Winds Travel, Inc., 462 F.2d 899 (5th Cir. 1972).
Stokes v. Balley's Pacwest, Inc., 2002 Wash. App. LEXIS 2233.
Stone v. Bridgehampton Race Circuit, 1995 N.Y. App. Div. LEXIS 7565.
Stone v. Norwegian Cruise Line, 2001 WL 877580 (E.D. Pa. 2001).

Stowers v. Clinton Central School Corporation, 2006 Ind. App. LEXIS 2151.
Strauss v. Stoneledge Farms, 256 A.D.2d 1186 (1998).
Straw v. Aquatic Adventures Management Group, 2011 U.S. Dist LEXIS 121652.
Strawbridge v. Sugar Mountain Resort, Inc., 2004 U.S. Dist. LEXIS 14561.
Street v. Darwin Ranch, Inc., 1999 U.S. Dist. LEXIS 17646.
Strickert v. Neal, 2015 U.S. Dist. LEXIS 160442.
Stuhlweissenburg v. Town of Orangetown, 1996 N.Y. App. Div. LEXIS 423.
Summers v. Slivinsky, 2001 Ohio App. LEXIS 386 (2002).
Sunny Isles Marina v. Adulami, 1998 Fla. App. LEXIS 1363.
Swartzentruber v. Wee-K Corp, 1997 Ohio App. LEXIS 159.
Sweeney v. City of Bettendorf, 2009 Iowa Supp. LEXIS 26.
Sydlik v. ReelII, Inc., 2006 Tex. App. LEXIS 4410.
Sylva v. Culebra Dive Shop, 2005 U.S. Dist. LEXIS 21478.

T
Tabrizi v. L.A. Fitness International, 2011 U.S. Dist. LEXIS 95664.
Tadmor v. NY Jiujitsu, 2012 N.Y. Misc. LEXIS 3904.
Talbert v. Lincoln Speedway, 33 D.&C. 3d 111 (Pa., 1984).
Tanker v. North Crest Equestrian Center, 1993 Ohio App. LEXIS 1173.
Tassinari v. Key West Water Tours, L.C., 2007 U.S.Dist. LEXIS 46490.
Tatman v. Space Coast Kennel Club, 2009 Fla. App. LEXIS 2537.
Tayer v. Camelback Ski Corp., 2008 Pa. Super. LEXIS 2461.
Tayar v. Camelback Ski Corporation, Inc., 2012 Pa. LEXIS 1625.
Tedesco v. Triborough Bridge and Tunnel Authority, 1998 N.Y. App. Div. LEXIS 5801.
Teles v. Big Rock Stables, 2006 U.S. Dist. LEXIS 13035.
Tepper v. City of New Rochelle School Dist., 531 N.Y.S.2d 367 (1988).
Terrill v. Stacy, 2006 Mich. App. LEXIS 522.
Texas Moto-Plex, Inc. v. Phelps, 2006 Tex. App. LEXIS 892.
Theis v. J & J Racing Promotions, 571 So.2d 92 (Fla. 1990).
Theodore v. Horenstein, 2009 Mich. App. LEXIS 1186.
Thiele v. Oakland Valley, Inc., 2010 N.Y. App. Div. LEXIS 3074.
Thompson v. Hi Tech Motor Sports, Inc., 2008 Vt. LEXIS 11.
Thompson v. Otterbein College, 1996 Ohio App. LEXIS 389.
Thoni v. Duck River Speedway, 1984 Tenn. App. LEXIS 3431.
Thorn v. Eaton, 2002 Cause No. CV 99-003025.
Thrasher v. Riverbend Stables, 2009 Tenn. App. LEXIS 50.
Tiede v. Frontier Skydivers, Inc., 2013 N.Y. App. Div. LEXIS 2877.
Tompkins v. Helton, 2003 Tenn.Ap. LEXIS 433.
Torres v. Long Island Motocross Association, Inc., 2014 N.Y. Misc. LEXIS 3168.
Troshak v. Terminix International Company, 1998 U.S. Dist LEXIS 9890.
Trumbower v. Sports Car Club of America, Inc., 428 F.Supp. 1113 (1976).
Trummer v. Niewisch, 792 N.Y.2d 596 (2005).
Trustees of Trinity College v. Ferris, 491 S.E.2d 909.
Tucker v. Albun, Inc., 1999 Del. Super. LEXIS 468.
Tunkl v. Regents of University of California, 383 P.2d 441 [1963].
Turnbough v. Ladner, 1998 Miss. App. LEXIS 1011.
Tuttle v. TRC Enterprises, Inc., 2007 N.Y.App. Div. LEXIS 2238.

U
UCF Athletics Association, Inc. v. Plancher, 2013 Fla. App. LEXIS 12805.
Umali v. Mount Snow Ltd., 2003 U.S. Dist. LEXIS 3463.
United States Auto Club, Inc., v. Smith, 1999 Ind. App. LEXIS 1831.

V
Vahedy v. Remigio, 2013 Cal. App. Unpub. LEXIS 988.
Valentine v. Leisure Sports, Inc., 2006 Cal. App. Unpub. LEXIS 3189.
Valeo v. Pocono Inernational Raceway, Inc., 500 A.2d 492 (1985).
Valdimer v. Mount Vernon Hebrew Camps, Inc., 172 N.E.2d 283 (1961).
Valley National Bank v. National Ass'n for Stockcar Auto Racing, 736 P.2d 1186.
Vanborkulo v. Keller's Motorsports, 2008 N.Y. Misc. LEXIS 10753.
Vanderbrook v. Emerald Springs Ranch, 2011 N.Y. Misc. LEXIS 4275.
Venard v. Jackson Hole Paragliding, LLC, 2013 Wyo. LEXIS 8.
Vergano v. Facility Mgmt. of Missouri, 1995 Mo. App. LEXIS 93.
ver Weire v. Styles, 2013 Ark. App. LEXIS 205.
Vine v. Bear Valley Ski Co. 2004 Cal. App. LEXIS 713.
Vines v. Birmingham Baseball Club, 450 So.2d 455 (Ala. 1984).
Vinson v. Paramount Pictures Corporation, 2013 Cal. App. Unpub. LEXIS 3380.
Viteritti v. Baseball Heaven, LLC, 2013 N.Y. Misc. LEXIS 1799.
Vokes v. Ski Ward, Inc., 2005 Mass. Super. LEXIS 346.

W
Wabash County YMCA v. Thompson, 2012 Ind. App. LEXIS 428.
Wagner v. Obert Enterprises, 384 N.W.2d 477 [Minn., 1986].
Wagner v. SFX Motor Sports, Inc., 2006 U.S. Dist. LEXIS 79099.
Wallace v. Busch Entertainment Corporation, 2011 U.S. Dist. LEXIS 91120.
Walker v. Young Life Saranac Village, 2012 U.S. Dist. LEXIS 166057.
Walton v. Fujita Tourist Enterprises Co., 1986 Minn.App. LEXIS 3890.
Walters v. YMCA, 2014 N.J. Super LEXIS 117.
Walton v. Oz Bicycle Club of Wichita, 1991 U.S.Dist. LEXIS 17655.
Waltz v. Life Time Fitness, 2010 Minn. App. Unpub. LEXIS 741.
Wagenblast v. Odessa School No. 105-157-166J, 758 P.2d 968 (Wash 1988).
Walsh v. Luedtke, 2005 Wisc. App. LEXIS 744.
Wang v. Whitetail Mountain Resort, 2007 Pa. Super. LEXIS 3050.
Ward v. Dunn, 1987 N.Y. Misc. LEXIS 2516.
Wattenbarger v. Cincinnati Reds, Inc., 33 Cal.Rptr.2d 732 (1994).
Webb v. Peak, 2002 Mass. App.Div. LEXIS 8.
Webster v. G & J Kartway, 2006 Ohio App. LEXIS 794.
Weiner v. American Cancer Society, 2002 Ohio App. LEXIS 2950.
Weiner v. Mt. Airy Lodge, Inc., 719 F.Supp. 342 (M.D.Pa. 1989).
Werdehoff v. General Star Indemnity Company, 1999 Wisc. App. LEXIS 786.
Weinrich v. Lehigh Valley Grand Prix Inc., 2015 Pa. Dist. & Cnty. Dec. LEXIS 79.

Westlye v. Look Sports, Inc., 17 Cal. App. 4th 1715.
West v. Sundown Little League of Stockton, 2002 Cal. App. LEXIS 1767 (2002).
Wethington v. Swainson, 2015 U.S. Dist. LEXIS 169145.
Wheeler v. Owens Community College, 2005 Ohio Misc. LEXIS 7.
Wheelock v. Sport Kites, Inc., 839 F.Supp. 730 (1993).
White v. Extate of Lawrence J. Neuland, 1988 U.S.Dist. LEXIS 17840.
Whitson v. Goodbodys, Inc., 1989 Tex. App. LEXIS 1940.
Wiese v. Hjersman, 2006 U.S. Dist. LEXIS 63674.
Williams v. City of Albany, 2000 N.Y. App. Div. LEXIS 4449.
Williams v. Patton 821 S.W.2d 141 (Tex. 1991).
Williams v. U.S., 660 F.Supp. 699, 703 (E.D.Ark. 1987).
Wilson v. American Honda Motor Co., Inc., 1988 U.S.Dist. LEXIS 10785.
Wilson v. American Trans Air, Inc., 874 F.2d 386.
Winkler v. Kirkwood Atrium Office Park, 816 S.W.2d 111 (Tex. App. - Houston 1991).
Winterstein v. Wilcom, 293 A.2d 821 (Md. 1972).
Wisdom Fishing Camp v. Brown, 2007 U.S. Dist. LEXIS 49896.
Winston v. Sharfstein, 2009 N.Y. App. Div. LEXIS 6250.
Wolfe v. Americheer, 2012 Ohio App. LEXIS 827.
Woodman v. Kera d/b/a Bounce Party, 2008 Mich. App. LEXIS 1708.
Woodman v. Kera, 2010 Mich. LEXIS 1125.
Wreglesworth v. Arcto, Inc., 316 Ill.App.3d 1023 (2000).
Wright v. Loon Mountain Recreation Center, 1995 N.H. LEXIS 119.
Wright v. Sony Pictures Entertainment, Inc., 2005 U.S. Dist. LEXIS 5194.
Wroblewski v. Ohiopyle Trading Post, Inc., 2013 U.S. Dist. LEXIS 119206.
Wu v. Shattuck-St. Mary's School, 2005 U.S.Dist. LEXIS 3315.
Wurzer v. Seneca Sport Parachute Club, 66 AD2d 1002 (1978).
Wycoff v. Grace Community Church, 2010 Colo. App. LEXIS 1832.

X

Xu v. Gay, 2003 Mich. App. LEXIS 1505.

Y

Yang v. Voyagaire Houseboats, Inc., 205 Minn. LEXIS 465.
Yang v. Voyagaire Houseboats, Inc., 2004
Yates v. Chicago National League Ball Club Inc., 1992 Ill. App. LEXIS 1024.
Yauger v. Skiing Enterprises, Inc., 1996 Wisc. LEXIS 111.
YMCA of Metropolitan Los Angeles v. Superior Court, 1997 Cal. App. LEXIS 392.
Young v. Carnival, 2011 U.S. Dist. LEXIS 10899.
Young v. City of Gadsden, 1985 Ala. LEXIS 3986.
Young v. Prancing Horse, Inc., 2005 N.C. App. LEXIS 1108.

Z

Zavras v. Capeway Rovers Motorcycle Club, Inc., 1997 Mass. App. LEXIS 248.

Zimmer v. Mitchell and Ness, 253 Pa. Super. 474 (1978).
Zipisch v. LA Workout, Inc., 2007 Cal. App. LEXIS 1652.
Zivich v. Mentor Soccer Club, Inc., 1997 Ohio App. LEXIS 1577.
Zivich v. Mentor Soccer Club, Inc., 1998 Ohio LEXIS 1832.
Zollman v. Myers, 797 F.Supp. 923 (Utah, 1997).

Sources

Black, H.C. (1990) 6th ed. Black's Law Dictionary. St. Paul: West Publishing Co.
Calamari, J.D. and Perillo, J.M. (1977) 2nd ed. The Law of Contracts. St. Paul: West Publishing Co.
Gregg, C.R. and Hansen-Stamp, C. "Is It Really Worth the Paper It's Written On?" Outdoor Education and recreation Law Quarterly, Vol. III Number 3, Fall 2003, pp. 4-8.
Herbert, D.L. and Herbert, W.G. 4th ed. Legal aspects of preventative rehabilitative and recreational exercise programs. Canton, Ohio: PRC Publishing, Inc.
Hroblak, K.G. Adloo v. H.T. Brown Real Estate, Inc.: "Caveat Exculpator" – An Exculpatory Clause May Not Be Effective Under Maryland's Heightened Level of Scrutiny, 27 U. Balt. L. Rev. 439, 469 (1998).
Independent Review Consulting, Inc. (2000)Post-approval requirements: informed consent. Corte Madera, CA.
Koeberle, B.E. and Herbert, D.L. (1998). Legal aspects of personal fitness training. 2nd ed. Canton, Ohio: PRC Publishing, Inc.
https://www.justia.com/trials-litigation/docs/caci/900/901.html.
Lesser, S.B. How to Draft Exculpatory Clauses That Limit or Extinguish Liability, 75 Fla. B.J. 10, 14 (Nov. 2001).
Nolan-Haley, J.M. (1999). Informed consent in mediation: A guiding principle for truly education decision making. Notre Dame L. Rev. 74, 775.
Office of Human Subjects Research (OHSR), National Institutes of Health. (2000). Guidelines for Writing Informed-consent Documents. Online, Internet.http://ohsr.od.nih.gov/info_6php3.
Olivier, S. & Olivier, A. (2001). Informed consent in sport science. Sportscience. Online, Internet. www.sportsci.org/jour/0101/so.htm.
Moss, J. "Rating releases: Our Law Review editor tears apart a release he signed recently," Law Review Quarterly: 2nd & 3rd Quarter 2006.
Personal correspondence, Charles R. Gregg, Summer, 2005.
Personal correspondence, Gary Eaton, Placentia, CA., 2008.
Restatement (Third) of Torts: Products Liability § 18 & cmt. d).
Sullivan, M. (2012). Attack of the 6.5-point typeface. Smart Money, Feb., 2012, pp. 56-62.
Williston on Contracts 9:

INDEX

Made in the USA
Columbia, SC
05 May 2019